TOTALITARIANISM

TOTALITARIANISM

The Inner History
of the Cold War

ABBOTT GLEASON

New York   Oxford
OXFORD UNIVERSITY PRESS
1995

Oxford University Press

Oxford   New York
Athens   Auckland   Bangkok   Bombay
Calcutta   Cape Town   Dar es Salaam   Delhi
Florence   Hong Kong   Istanbul   Karachi
Kuala Lumpur   Madras   Madrid   Melbourne
Mexico City   Nairobi   Paris   Singapore
Taipei   Tokyo   Toronto

and associated companies in

Berlin   Ibadan

Copyright © 1995 by Oxford University Press, Inc.

Published by Oxford University Press, Inc.,
200 Madison Avenue, New York, New York 10016

Oxford is a registered trademark of Oxford University Press

Library of Congress Cataloging-in-Publication Data
Gleason, Abbott.
Totalitarianism : the inner history of the Cold War / Abbott Gleason.
p.   cm.
Includes bibliographical references and index.
ISBN 0-19-505017-7.
1. World politics—20th century.   2. Totalitarianism.   3. Cold War.   I. Title.
D445.G54   1995   320.9'04—dc20   94-8750

1 3 5 7 9 8 6 4 2

Printed in the United States of America
on acid-free paper

Nicholas Abbott Gleason
Margaret Holliday Gleason

ACKNOWLEDGMENTS

I WOULD LIKE TO THANK my research assistants, Fran Bernstein, Deborah Cohen, Stacy Bell, Malcom Larvadain, Michelle Murphy, David Pretty, and Jessica Brooks, for their assistance and also Rob McLaughlin, whose fine seminar paper on brainwashing was of great help to me. For my chapter on Poland and Czechoslovakia, I learned much from Marek Szorc's Brown University senior honors thesis, "The Flight from Utopia: Opposition in Poland and Czechoslovakia in the 1970s," which was done under my direction.

As it has been throughout my career, the Russian Research Center of Harvard University was generous in its support of my work. Without the extraordinary resources of Widener Library, this study would have taken far longer than the decade of my time it has claimed. Claire L. Brown, the head of the Labor Collection at Harvard University's Littauer Library, found some important sources for me, in particular early editions of the *New Leader*. The staff of the Kennan Institute at the Woodrow Wilson International Center for Scholars in Washington, D.C., located some rare documents for me in the Library of Congress. I also benefited from summer support from the Center for Foreign Policy Development of Brown University in 1989 and 1990.

Sarah Gleason's substantive and editorial comments were invaluable in keeping the manuscript readable and at least moderately accessible. Blair Ruble helped me get started with social science material; Vladimir Shlapentokh, Stephen Shenfield, and Noah Rubins alerted me to some Soviet usages. Christopher Ely, Mary Gluck, Thomas Simons, and Duncan Kennedy read the entire manuscript. Their encouragement was bracing and their suggestions most helpful. Volker Berghahn tirelessly and good-humoredly answered questions about the German context and about scholars there. In addition, he gave the entire manuscript an invaluable scrutiny. William Odom questioned me closely and helpfully about a number of substantive points. Andrzej Walicki, David Joravsky, Jonathan Beecher, John Thomas, and Jerome Grieder gave me helpful criticism on draft chapters.

CONTENTS

TOTALITARIANISM

INTRODUCTION

Amongst democratic nations, each generation is a new people.
Alexis de Tocqueville

Every historical event begins with a struggle centered on naming.
Milan Kundera

TOTALITARIANISM was the great mobilizing and unifying concept of the Cold War. It described the unparalleled threat that faced the European and American democracies from a new kind of insatiably aggressive and invasive state; it provided a typology of that state, based centrally on Nazi Germany and the Soviet Union; and it channeled the anti-Nazi energy of the wartime period into the postwar struggle with the Soviet Union. Above all, it provided a plausible and frightening vision of a Manichaean, radically bifurcated world in which the leaders of the free world would have to struggle (until victory was won) or perish. The history of the Cold War cannot be well understood without taking account of this vital idea.

Perhaps I understand the evolution of the concept of totalitarianism in strongly generational terms because of the meanings it has had for me, an American growing up after World War II, whose father was a fervent member of the Cold War elite. Like many another academic, my father left the professoriat for army intelligence after the attack on Pearl Harbor and ultimately found himself in the Office of Strategic Services (OSS) in Washington. There his internationalism deepened during the struggle against Germany, and he came to believe that the worst thing that could happen on the postwar international scene would be for the United States to return to its prewar isolationism. His experience on the National Security Council under Presidents Truman and Eisenhower both reflected and strengthened his belief in a bipolar world and in the mission of the United States to preserve that world from Soviet domination.

Although my father never read much of the theoretical or speculative literature on totalitarianism, he passionately subscribed to a serviceable, workaday version of it. The Soviet Union and Nazi Germany, his genera-

3

tional tradition told him, had much in common from the standpoint of ideology and institutions and should be studied together. They were dictatorships of a new and terrible kind, violent, ideologically inspired, endlessly aggressive, and possessed of extraordinary new technological means to dominate their helpless subjects utterly. They obliterated the distinction between public and private, which even the most brutal of older dictatorships had respected. In a geopolitical sense, the Soviet threat was similar to the German threat and was its lineal successor. The great question for him and those like him between the fall of France in 1940 and his death in the mid-1970s was whether Europe would slip under the domination of one or another of those monoliths. If this happened, civilization would end and be followed by some dreadful iron age of timeless slavery. Although we never discussed the matter in great detail, I suspect the picture that was in his mind was similar to that created by George Orwell in *Nineteen Eighty-Four* and was probably much influenced by it.

The United States was thus called on, in the view of many members of his generation, to play a dramatically more important version of the role that Great Britain had traditionally played in the European state system: to keep any single power from becoming strong enough to establish hegemony over the Continent. But the stakes had grown enormously. The United States and Western Europe, with all their imperfections, were the kingdom of light, and the Soviet Union and its satellites were the kingdom of darkness. My father would never have allowed himself to view the world in terms of such a dramatic dichotomy before the rise of the totalitarian powers. Had he lived to see the presidency of Ronald Reagan, he would have rejoiced at the "Evil Empire" coinage.

If the age of Europe was already over—if Europe was no longer the center of the world—my father did not know it. He had great respect for various non-European cultures in their historical incarnation, but little interest in or regard for the postcolonial states of the postwar world. The struggle between the Soviet Union and the United States for Europe was the struggle for civilization, and the Third World was irrelevant at best, or in fact a positive hindrance.

When my time came to rebel against all of this, I eventually discovered that I was rebelling against a concept of the world to which the notion of totalitarianism was absolutely central. My initial rejection of these views, very much a generational one, began in college, took on more coherent form in the civil rights movement, continued in opposition to the Vietnam War, and petered out on the shoals of the cultural radicalism of the 1960s. In retrospect, I can see how very much of my generational experience was directed against the Manichaean worldview I had grown up with: the idea that we Americans had to—or had the right to—wear white hats, that there was really such a massive abyss between us and those who lived "under communist totalitarianism." And I have lived to witness the complex return of Cold War militancy through the agency of American and European neoconservatives—in generational terms, yet another phase, followed by the end of the Cold War.

As an adolescent and a college student, it was natural for me to question and doubt American universities and government in a way that infuriated my father. Why were these things so sacrosanct, virtually beyond criticism for him, I asked myself. In part, I now believe, the reason was the totalitarian enemy he understood us to be facing. But I did not have my father's generational understanding of that, so his reverence for institutions whose failings I very well knew invariably provoked me.

During my years in college, my roommates brought an early 1960s spirit of questioning into my life, which I embraced, sometimes eagerly and sometimes with great qualms. One of my roommates wrote as his undergraduate thesis a methodological inquiry into the origins of Nazism. Following along, I read Hannah Arendt's *The Origins of Totalitarianism*. I was disturbed and enthralled by its vision and rhetoric, but already (1958) its postwar atmosphere of Armageddon seemed anachronistic. My roommate made me aware of some of the criticisms that might be made of it. When I read Arendt's great book and discussed my friend's thesis, it was the first time I had confronted the term *totalitarianism* directly and the first time I was brought to think about the defining and explanatory power that it might have. By the time I read it, Arendt's suggestion that the rise of totalitarianism was tied to the end of the bourgeois world was difficult to accept. At Harvard College in 1958, the bourgeois world seemed far from played out.

Undoubtedly it was the experience of the civil rights movement that suggested to me most vividly that we in the United States had no right to be so high and mighty about what we represented historically. By the time the three civil rights workers had been murdered in Mississippi in the summer of 1964, my sense of exactly how the United States was different from the Soviet Union was becoming blurred. In the world of Sheriff Bull Connor and Governor George Wallace, the bombings of black churches, and the murder of the three civil rights workers, it simply became difficult as a practical matter for an idealistic young person to believe that Americans not only had a great civilization but in fact *were* civilization, which is what the totalitarian paradigm told us.

I describe this change in my point of view not to put it up for argument—as I did so very many times with my father's generation—but merely to recount, as best I can, what I felt then. The waging of the Vietnam War confirmed, for many if not most of my contemporaries, that we lived in a world where political good and evil were widely distributed, not divided into two camps. Even for the many like me who embraced no extreme political attitudes, on whom the radical 1960s left no very profound marks, the notion of our *mission civilisatrice* had eroded. The 1950s suddenly seemed very far away, except for the subversive modern culture of that time, which seemed to anticipate the loss of illusions that I was feeling by the middle of the 1960s.

At that time I thought with exasperation of my father as suspended somewhere between the worlds of John Stuart Mill and George Santayana. But I was wrong. His piety about American society that I thought so unjustified was not so antique, as I came to discover. In all of its idealism, commitment, grandiosity, self-righteousness, rigidity, evasiveness, imperial courage, and basic decency, my father's attitude was part and parcel of a generation's belief that the fate of the world was on their shoulders.

Thus I believe that the numerous radical critics in England, the United States, and Germany (where the history of the term totalitarian between 1950 and 1968 has many lines in common with what happened in the United States) who have seen the totalitarian point of view or "model" as connected to Cold War ideology are right. And no doubt the term was used to inhibit radical ideas and proposals and to tar radicals with a pro-Soviet brush, as they have often charged.

Still, with all of Stalin's caution in post-1945 Europe, I am glad his enemies on our side were ideologically well armed. And surely the metaphor of an Iron Curtain descending across Europe is a rather good one to describe what happened. If there had been only token resistance to Stalin, who can say that he would not have come father west. That the term *totalitarian* was used as weapon against the Left is far from the only thing we need to know about it.

The profound shifts in how Americans thought of themselves that became obvious between 1963 and 1975 had powerful repercussions in the more cloistered world of scholarship. There the study of Germany, the Soviet Union, and, to some degree, Spain, Italy, and even revolutionary China had been conducted under the aegis—or in the shadow—of what had been systematized by social scientists into something called the *totalitarian model*. Now much of that changed. Not only did we Americans lose our sense of ourselves as white hats during the period between the assassination of John F. Kennedy and the resignation of Richard Nixon, but the Soviet Union became harder and harder to regard strictly as a bunch of black hats.

For one thing, after 1960, the Soviet Union became much better known to foreign scholars, who spent increasingly long periods of time there. Although protracted residence and study in the Soviet Union was often an arduous, infuriating, and uncomfortable experience and occasionally even a frightening one, very few who had spent long months there could accept *in toto* the older images of totalitarianism, with their tableaux of terrorized and atomized populations. The decay of Soviet ideology, the revival of Russian nationalism, the warmth of purely private life in the Soviet Union became things experienced personally by the majority of younger American and European students interested in things Russian and Soviet. Even the shoddy goods, the shortages, and the ways that in general the society did not work seemed more like phenomena of a Third World society than the brilliant account Orwell gave of totalitarianism in *Nineteen Eighty-Four*.

It was this phase of the discussion about totalitarianism that reattracted my attention, this time from the standpoint of my interest in Russia and the Soviet Union, and led to my first efforts to write something about the concept of totalitarianism. Criticism of the "totalitarian model" has gone on apace now for almost thirty years, with its scholarly adherents gradually giving ground, until the collapse of the Soviet Union. Although the term *totalitarianism* has been widely used outside the academic community, and has wide currency today, one seldom sees it any longer used analytically in the pages of a scholarly monograph or journal. And scholars who have actually spent a good deal of time in what used to be the Soviet Union have now become the dominant academic generation in American universities, getting tenure, becoming full professors, and awarding fellowships to their junior colleagues whom they judge to be worthy (which sometimes means "like themselves"). Among these younger academics, the issue has seemd virtually closed. Many are simply not interested in the issue of whether anything is gained for a scholar by studying the Soviet Union within a totalitarian framework. Others see the term as part of the ritual dance of triumph by the conservative "winners" of the Cold War.

Some social historians of the Soviet period continue to define themselves publicly against the work of scholars who believed in totalitarianism, and for them the term retains an important, though negative, reality. We must not forget, however, that an even younger academic generation is forming, for whom the "grand failure" of Communism will be a formative experience. What they will make of these arguments about totalitarianism remains to be seen.[1]

Outside the academic community, by contrast, the term has flourished for almost two decades. Representatives of the conservative reaction against the antiwar movement of the previous decade and especially against détente with the Soviet Union in the Brezhnev era made good use of the term, principally to reassert the old sense of white-hat and black-hat worlds. For neoconservatives of the early Reagan years in particular, one of the great sins of liberals was to engage in "moral equivalency," which meant not only comparing the United States and the Soviet Union in any but a completely Manichaean way, but even suggesting that they could be compared. Heaven and hell (or the "Evil Empire," for what else could an Evil Empire be?) are not to be compared; anyone who attempts to do so is at best naive, at worst an agent of the devil himself. One is not merely better than the other; they are typologically and essentially distinct and opposed in the cosmos. In Europe as well as in the United States, conservative points of view have thrived in the most recent "generation of totalitarianism."

Michael Walzer wrote over a decade ago, when Reagan had just swept American conservatism into political power, that the neoconservatives "were right to stress the importance of the argument" that totalitarianism was a "radical break" with past tyrannies. But "the distinction they go on to draw between totalitarian and 'authoritarian' regimes plays a part in their work that the theorists of the fifties never intended: it functions very much like and often simply replaces the cold war distinction between communism and the free world."

For conservatives, Jeane Kirkpatrick's renewal of the 1950s distinction between *totalitarian* and *authoritarian* served as an important justification of the policies of the Reagan administration's first several years, when pressure was to be eased against right-wing regimes but as much pressure as possible was to be brought against the Soviet Union, particularly in the Third World. To quote Walzer again: "It was never the intention of the theorists of the fifties to celebrate authoritarianism, but perhaps the celebration is a natural step once the contrast has been drawn in this way."[2]

The neoconservatives never entirely succeeded in their efforts to revive the term, in part because the totalitarian–authoritarian debate was so caught up in the larger ideological polarization of the early 1980s. Still, the neo-conservatives did at least force academics—who had grown accustomed to the horrors of the Soviet system—to become more self-conscious about them. Jeane Kirkpatrick and her colleagues also made anti-Communism more respectable than it had been since the late 1940s. But during Reagan's second term, the extraordinary efforts at reform in the Soviet Union under the leadership of Mikhail Gorbachev and Ronald Reagan's response to them made the Manichaean beliefs of the early Reagan years seem a whole genera-tion away.

At present, however, proponents of the term have a whole new set of allies: Soviet intellectuals and academics who themselves have come to feel that no term is as suggestive of their country's experience as *totalitarianism* is. As was the case in Germany after World War II, there is an exculpatory element here. If one's country (and oneself) is in the grip of totalitarianism, then one cannot be blamed for what happened or for what one may have done, or at least not very much. But the passionate revulsion felt by many (formerly) Soviet intellectuals toward their own past will surely continue for several years at least. Whether the increasing use of the term in Russia and other formerly Soviet lands will become much more than a way of avoiding guilt and expressing anger, however, is another matter.

The Cold War has ended. No one can say for sure how the new era into which we are moving will ultimately understand the experience, its antino-mies, its values. The future of the idea of totalitarianism will be powerfully affected by how a new generation of critically minded Russian scholars and imaginative writers interprets its own past, now that they can speak and write more freely. How will these people come to regard the ideological conflicts that foreigners have been for years carrying on about them? There are rich possibilities for conflict here.

Alongside the question of totalitarianism lies another one, the question of *totality,* recently investigated by Martin Jay.[3] The idea of totality, like the idea of totalitarianism, is ultimately derived from the organic thinking of nineteenth-century Romantics. It was given classic formulation by Hegel and has become central to the whole history of Marxism, as Jay has demonstrated. There is some overlap between "totality," grasping/understanding the world as an integral whole, and "totalitarianism," making it a whole, especially in the work of philosophers who are the students of Hegel and Marx. Although the reader will notice these connections and others like them from time to time, much of this book is concerned with somewhat less theoretical political questions.

At moments I have wondered whether the question of totality and totalitarianism can be boiled down to a philosophical argument involving the right-wing followers of Hegel and the left-wing ones, especially Marx. It is easy to see how the statism that derived from conservative followers of Hegel set as a goal the absorption of the individual by the state. On a philosophical level, this project is easily seen in the philosophical system of Giovanni Gentile, discussed in Chapter 1. But it may also be that the Left Hegelianism of Marx and others pushed humanity in the same direction. As Andrzej Walicki noted in 1983, Marx was quite willing to sacrifice the human beings of his present day for the better ones that the revolution would create. In addition, he

> saw no positive value in privacy; his ideal of the total subordination of the private sphere to the public sphere, of extending the scope of political decisions to all spheres of life and thus abolishing the autonomous existence of economy, deserves to be classified as a kind of democratic totalitarianism.[4]

Most people on the Left have been highly resistant, until recently at least, to any suggestion that the classification of the Soviet Union as totalitarian is more than a conservative canard. The deeper reason for this is that to do so calls into question whether or not Marx's philosophy, the predominant idiom of the Left in the twentieth century, was really liberating. That idea is under heavy siege now in the Western world.

I believe that the earlier phases of the life of the term *totalitarianism* may also be usefully approached in terms of *generations* (pun intended). The term came into existence in Fascist Italy and was rapidly picked up in Germany along with its slightly less influential cousins, *total mobilization* and *total war*. Between 1925 and 1935, the argument about "the total state" or "the totalitarian state" (the two were largely synonomous at the time) was basically an argument about the nature of Fascism. It was between Fascists/Nazis and their opponents and also among them, for they had their own disagreements. The philosopher Giovanni Gentile, operating in the highly abstract vocabulary of conservative Hegelianism, produced a brilliant and premonitory justification of the totalitarian state that seems amazingly like Hannah Arendt's and George Orwell's demonic visions of the later 1940s, only with the value signs inverted.

Some Nazi ideologues, like Alfred Rosenberg, however, believed that idolatry of "the total state" directed attention away from the German *Volk* and from issues of race, as well as from the dynamism of the Nazi movement. So after the early 1930s, the Nazis largely eschewed the term. In both Italy and Germany there were arguments about dynamic movements versus all-encompassing statism, arguments later echoed in Soviet experience. This too is a leitmotiv of my study of totalitarianism.

Also by the early 1930s, opponents of Fascism were using the term more and more often. Between 1935 and 1945, my father's generation adapted the term to their missionary internationalism, not merely to describe the institutions of certain states, but also to suggest the coming of a terrible new challenge to civilization. Before that could happen, of course, the Soviet Union had to be describable as totalitarian, as it began to be during the 1930s. The coming of World War II, followed by the Cold War, confirmed the unprecedented challenge of the totalitarian states and (for most of the writers concerned with them) their radical newness.

If one analyzes the evolution of totalitarianism in generational terms, there are intellectual consequences. Certain questions are naturally posed; others recede. For one thing, no two generations' understanding of the term has been quite the same, and the underlying arguments about totalitarianism in the seventy years of its existence have been constantly changing. There is, nevertheless, a core of meaning to the term *totalitarian* that was discovered early on and has never been completely lost: the idea of a radically intrusive state run by people who do not merely control their citizens from the outside, preventing them from challenging the elite or doing things that it does not like, but also attempt to reach into the most intimate regions of their lives. These totalitarian elites ceaselessly tried to make their subjects into beings who would be constitutionally incapable of challenging the rule of the state and those who control it. This element—the state's remaking of its citizens and their whole world—has remained central to the term's meaning until this day.

That said, however, the differences in meaning over time and place have been considerable. To arrive at those meanings is not simply a matter of defining a word. In order to see what the term means, one must examine the context in which it is defined. Who uses it? Against whom? When someone is called *totalitarian,* what is the meaning of the disagreement, and what are the stakes? If, as I have suggested, it has many generational meanings, how do the generational battles that have surrounded it differ? *Totalitarian* had shifting ideological meanings in the 1930s and during World War II. With Germany defeated, the term became a rallying cry for resistance to Soviet expansionism. But it soon became clear that the term had considerable utility in a more directly ideological realm. Many German conservatives felt guilty about their record of semicollaboration with Hitler, or insufficiently zealous resistance to his rule (sometimes justified as a "bulwark" against Bolshevism" or whatever), and were anxious to suggest that Nazism was an aberration of the Left rather than the Right. (The Left, of course, has been correspondingly anxious to link Hitler as closely as possible with German "capitalism" and has been notably reluctant to regard Nazism as more than a late, brutal phase of capitalism, or the real face of the bourgeoisie with the parliamentary mask torn off, etc.)

A global term linking Nazism to Stalinism or Communism was ideal from the point of view of such conservatives. It helped divert attention from their lack of anti-Nazi zeal; it made a more active resistance to Hitler seem to have been virtually impossible for ordinary people at least; it emphasized Nazism's popular, modern, and revolutionary elements. Perhaps not least, it could be used to attack the Left. Thoroughly socialist solutions to domestic problems were made politically far more difficult when socialism (or even liberalism) were at least related to totalitarianism. In the United States as well, general acceptance of the term surely hindered the Left; one did not have to be a McCarthyite to suggest that one or another liberal organization might "mean well" but "did not understand totalitarianism." Friedrich Hayek's linking of any serious social or economic planning to totalitarianism in *The Road to Serfdom* not only helped conservatives combat what soon became known as the "Old Left" in the United States, but also helped launch a revival of neoclassical economics that has culminated in work of such contemporaries as Milton Friedman.

Most recently, Jeane Kirkpatrick, in particular, made the term an effective ideological weapon against the Left of the late 1970s: the Left that gave us détente and suggested that we could deal with the Soviet Union because "it is a state like any other state" rather than something typologically distinct.[5] Because in the ideological arena the Carter administration had been merely in favor of human rights and "democracy" and against "dictatorship," the conservatives of the earlier 1980s found it vital to make distinctions between right-wing "authoritarian" dictatorships that might be reformed and left-wing "totalitarian" dictatorships that could not be. With the former, they wished to try private diplomacy. Against the latter, they wished to define their very existence, to reinvoke the early messianism of the Cold War.

But the context in which Kirkpatrick employed the term is important. The messianism of the late Carter and early Reagan years had a more narrowly and explicitly political purpose, and so it lacked the capacity to create a consensus comparable to the one that emerged in the late 1940s. This time Americans were not "discovering" the totalitarian menace; it was being revived as part of a general challenge to the fading world of the New Deal and the "Great Society." There was no broadly orienting dimension to the reemployment of the term or element of intellectual discovery, as there had been earlier. The 1950s belief in totalitarianism was less narrowly partisan, less clever. It was less frequently invoked to zap one's political enemies. It compelled belief in a far wider segment of the electorate.

To point to the self-consciously political nature of the term's use during the Reagan administration, however, is not to discredit the term. It has always contained a series of political arguments within it, some winding down, others heating up. From the very beginning of its career, *totalitarian*—and *total* before it—have been both normative and descriptive.[6] No term that is so passionately intended by its proponents to describe and to damn (or, at times, praise) can avoid leaving a trail of violent arguments behind it; indeed, without those arguments it could not exist.

To relate totalitarianism to Rousseau specifically and the Enlightenment generally, for example, as such scholars as J. L. Talmon have done, is to make a very political judgment. To ground "Stalinism" and Nazism in the more encompassing word *totalitarianism* is another such judgment. I have tried to lay bare the judgments and to elucidate the arguments as fully and as fairly as possible. None of the points of view discussed in these pages is devoid of merit; none is entirely unassailable.

I want to stress that I do not want the term *argument* to be understood merely as the clash of conflicting definitions (best left to lexicographers, political scientists, and philosophers). Since the term *totalitarian* came into existence in 1923, it has helped focus public debate in Germany, England, France, and the United States on the most central political issues of the century: the nature of freedom, justice, and revolution. Especially in Germany and the United States, the quarrels over the meaning of totalitarianism have reflected deep political disagreements for the past forty-five years. This book will not just discuss the argument about analytical concepts, but also try to discern the underlying issues expressed in the debate over the nature and meaning of totalitarianism.

ONE

Fascist Origins

The era of tyrannies dates from August 1914, that is, from the time when the belligerent nations turned to a system which can be defined as follows:

(a) In the economic sphere, greatly extended state control of all means of production, distribution and exchange;—and, at the same time, an appeal by the government to the leaders of the workers' organizations to help them in implementing this state control—hence syndicalism and corporatism along with *étatisme*.

(b) In the intellectual sphere, state control of thought, in two forms: one negative, through the suppression of all opinion deemed unfavorable to the national interest; the other positive, through what we shall call the organization of enthusiasm.

Elie Halévy

The division between politics and life was basic to liberalism.

George Mosse

I N THE SPRING OF 1923, Benito Mussolini proposed changing the existing election laws in Italy. These changes, realized later in the year, were the first substantial alterations in the Italian constitution, broadly understood, and thus they were a milestone in the development of Fascism's conquest of Italy. The ostensible purpose of the changes in existing law was to eliminate coalition governments, widely regarded as a scourge of Italian political life, by making the party with the most votes a really big winner. The actual purpose was to make impossible any parliamentary opposition to Fascism. The law of 1923 stipulated that the political party that "obtained the largest number of votes in the whole country—if at least 25 percent of the total votes cast—should receive two-thirds of all the seats in the Chamber of Deputies."[1] The true importance of this scheme, wrote the British historian of Fascism Adrian Lyttleton, was not so much in the technical provisions of the premium, but in its moral effect. It discouraged all shades of opposition, and more especially attempts by the allies of Fascism to assert their independence. Before the introduction of the measure, *La Stampa* commented that "the fundamental question of principle now is not and cannot be that of the electoral system, but that of the very existence of Parliament and of parliamentary government."[2]

Giovanni Amendola, a forty-two-year-old journalist and politician, prominent in the opposition to Mussolini until he was beaten to death by Fascist goons four years later, led the resistance—halfhearted and irresolute—to the new electoral law. To those who maintained that it was prudent to accept Mussolini's electoral "reform" in order to stave off a more frontal assault on the constitution, Amendola pointed out that the new electoral law was itself a drastic change: "the first *legal* alteration of the fundamental features of the representative state."[3]

On May 12, 1923, Amendola referred in *Il Mondo* to the Fascist refusal to allow the opposition to prepare and present its list for the election as a "totalitarian system" (*sistema totalitaria*), as opposed to the "majoritarian" and "minoritarian" systems previously prevailing. The German historian Jens Petersen writes that "this, so far as one can tell, was the first time that the word 'totalitarian' turned up, and it seems meaningful that it is used in a quasi-technical sense to designate a breach of election procedure."[4] On June 23, Amendola used the term again in his polemic against the Fascist election law, sarcastically denying in the newspaper *Il Mondo* the Fascist claim that Cavour was "the sacred founder of the fascist election reform and the totalitarian system."[5]

By the time Amendola used the term on the anniversary of the March on Rome a few months later, it had developed a meaning so much broader that it could seem to characterize Fascism as a whole, by comparing it with a religion:

> Actually, the most salient characteristic of the fascist movement . . . remains its "totalitarian" spirit. This spirit will not allow any new day to dawn that has not rendered the fascist salute, just as it does not allow the present era to know a conscience that has not bowed the knee and confessed: "I believe." This remarkable "war of religion," which has been raging for over a year in Italy . . . denies you the right to possess a conscience—of your own, not one imposed by others—and burdens the future with a mortgage heavy as lead.[6]

The term seems to have spread among anti-Fascist journalists during the second half of 1923. The "totalitarian spirit" about which the journalists wrote was one that sought a monopoly on power, as opposed to the pluralist orientation of liberalism. Petersen cites instances from *Il Secolo*, *La Critica politica*, and *Rivoluzione liberale*. In the last of these, Dom Luigi Sturzo, the leader of the Catholic People's Party, complained about the "new fascist conception of a Party state," which was bent on the "totalitarian alteration of every ethical, cultural, political and religious power." He clearly intended to emphasize that those possessed by the "totalitarian spirit" were activists.

The new pope, Pius XI, was not sympathetic to Sturzo's resistance, however, and forced him out of his position as head of the Popolari in 1923. From his London exile, Sturzo published one of the earliest "warnings to the West" about what was happening in Italy:

> The pressure of State centralization and of a party monopoly combined to undermine all public bodies, so as to create a general situation favourable to the dominion of the Fascist minority which, after having captured the Government, by the successful *coup* of October, strove to capture the country.
>
> This tendency is called *totalitaria*. The theory is that Fascism, now National Fascism, is everything, the rest of the country nothing. The former has all the rights derived from power and strength, the latter only the obligations of obedience; the former is the Nation, the latter the Anti-Nation; the former is *la Patria,* the latter *l'Anti-Patria.*[7]

By early in 1924 the usage was becoming general, if strikingly inconsistent, among the anti-Fascist opposition. A particularly interesting case is presented by the noted Communist intellectual Antonio Gramsci, whose commitment to understanding the totality of social relations "organically" often led him to use the term positively, the only positive usage on the Italian Left that I have been able to find.[8]

During that year, the term *totalitarian* became much more prominent in the debates about the nature of Fascism and its likely future development. Writing on January 2 in *La Rivoluzione liberale* under the pseudonym "Prometeo Filodemo" (Prometheus Peoplelover), the young socialist Lelio Basso described the full extent of Fascist autocracy, concluding: "All the organs of the state, the crown, Parliament, the law . . . the armed forces . . . are becoming instruments of a single party that makes itself the interpreter of the people's will, of undifferentiated totalitarianism!"[9] The sense of authoritarian intrusiveness that the term already conveyed was becoming more clearly linked to the dictatorship of the single party. By April 1928, we find Filippo Turati, the "grand old man" of Italian socialism, prophesying a "worldwide conflict between fascistic totalitarianism and liberal democracy."[10]

By the spring of 1925, the Fascists themselves had become interested in the term, perhaps in part because of another, related cluster of meanings that it had been acquiring on the lips of the opposition: its "wild radicalism" and "possessed will," in the words of Amendola.[11] "Wildness" and "ferocity" were qualities that apparently attached themselves to the term *totalitarian* in a primary way only in 1925.

Just a week after Amendola's June 15 speech to the National Union's First

Party Congress, Mussolini spoke at the Fourth Congress of the Partito Nazionale Fascista, where he said (without direct reference to Amendola's usage):

> We want the Italians to make a choice. . . . We have conducted the struggle in so open an arena that there can now be only a clear For or Against. And furthermore: we will pursue what has been called our fierce totalitarian will [*la nostra feroce volonta totalitaria*]. We want to make the nation fascist, so that tomorrow Italians and Fascists . . . will be the same thing.[12]

Several things are striking about Mussolini's usage. He uses the term to suggest that the totalitarians are determined "totally" to transform Italy in a way hitherto unknown in the annals of nations. But is is not merely the totality of the transformation that he wants to express, but also a kind of dynamic style—spirit, Mussolini surely would have claimed—that also is new.

Totalitarian, then, suggested during the first two years or so of its existence a fiery spirit and a commitment to a total transformation of society, partly through a kind of religious monism and partly through the ultimately healthful ordeal of violence—very much in the spirit of *squadrismo.* In this period, Fascism was preeminently a movement, only beginning to come to grips with the challenges entailed in learning to govern. It was clearly committed to violence and coercion as necessary and even desirable ways to humiliate and ultimately destroy decadent Italian liberal culture.

Increasingly after 1925, however, *totalitarian* came to be used less to indicate ferocity or voluntarism than the intent of the state to absorb every sphere of human life into itself.[13] This meaning of the word was the result of the growing influence of traditional nationalists on Mussolini personally and of a pervasive nationalist emphasis on state power, rather than on the unpredictable and violent dynamism of the Fascist Party and "movement."

The articulation of the new meaning of *totalitarianism* was closely connected to the intellectual influence of the philosopher Giovanni Gentile.[14] His education in the Hegelian tradition, with a strong stress on "organic thinking," lent the term, in the late 1920s, a different emphasis than it had had before 1925, in harmony with the increasing statist influence on Fascist politics.

In Gentile's thinking, we can see how the intellectual universe of Hegel could become "modernized" to suggest the term *totalitarian* in later meanings with which we are familiar. In his academic career and in his wartime commentary on public affairs, Gentile had always called himself a liberal, opposed alike to socialism and clericalism, to the Reds and the Blacks. But his liberalism centered on the conservative state building of Cavour and had little tolerance for the ideological reformism of the eighteenth century.

The experience of the war enhanced Gentile's already pronounced statist tendencies as well as his admiration for soldiers and military styles, so alien to the Italian inertia, sentimentality, and lack of focus. According to one student of his thought, "Gentile wanted to see the attitude of the good soldier carried over into civil life." He believed that only a continuation of the wartime spirit of self-sacrifice and self-discipline, to the point of being willing to "die at one's post," would ensure what Italy needed by way of postwar reconstruction.[15]

Thoroughly impatient with the immediate postwar government's policy of drift and increasingly antagonistic toward the permissive liberal politics of such old-line politicians as Giovanni Giolitti, Gentile drew nearer in his thinking to the ideas of the Italian nationalists between 1919 and 1922. When Gentile was recruited into the Fascist Party in May 1923, he still claimed to be a liberal who, like Mussolini, was for a strong state, conceived "as an ethical reality" because it provided the necessary conditions for the existence and development of the human individual.

When Gentile first began to use the term *totalitarian* in March 1925, he used it both to suggest the religious character of Fascism and to assert that the "totalitarian," Fascist spirit would renew Italian society by *penetrating every area of human life*.[16] In fact, the two senses of the term are close, for what Gentile seems to have meant by the religious character of Fascism was that it made a total demand on every individual, as did a religion in its most militant, crusading phase. But it was Gentile's statism that increasingly shaped the meaning of the term *totalitarian* in Italy after 1925, as Fascism entered its state-building phase.

Gentile's long-standing Hegelianism led him to criticize wholeheartedly any effort to consider the human individual without reference to a larger totality; he was strongly against opposing individual self-fulfillment to the claims of the state. Gentile's philosophical point of view, which he dauntingly called the "method of absolute immanence," led him to regard the state, which he understood as "Objective Spirit," as immanent in the human individual, by which he meant to identify the individual's moral conscience in all its concreteness directly with the state. He also believed in the obverse—that is, understanding the state as the independent and freely expressed will of the national community. It may be, in fact, that "the logic of Gentile's rationale requires (irrespective of qualifications) that the *individual,* the *people,* the *party,* the *nation,* and the *state* be, in some sense, substitution instances of each other."[17]

Gentile denied liberty any conceptual basis of its own. As early as 1916, he spoke of the "identity of the individual and the state, a seamless identification predicated on Hegelian 'universalism' that absorbed the 'elements' of society into the 'totality' of the state."[18] This identification distinguished his statism from the run of Italian political nationalists, for whom the claims of the individual may have been less compelling than those of the state but were at least given a tacit reality and independence.

Gentile set great store by education, whose function was to achieve the complete formation of the spirit and its full existence within each citizen. It was consequently necessary to ensure that the inner conscience of each citizen became identical with the sovereign will of the state. The practical object of education, therefore, was "the good citizen," who, as Harris put it, "hears the voice of 'the State' within him."[19] Gentile, in theory, did not identify "the government" in an empirical sense with the state in the transcendental sense defined by his philosophy, nor did he identify "the sovereign will of the State" with an actual decision by a monarch or a dictator. But at the very least, we can say that when he moved from the university lecture hall to the political world of Italy in the 1920s, crucial distinctions were frequently overlooked.[20] In the words of Adrian Lyttleton, "the way was thus open to the total identification of the citizen with the purposes of the State,"[21] producing what the philosopher Benedetto Croce, then in the process of breaking with Gentile, termed "governmental morality." In practice, citizens who failed to work wholeheartedly for the ends defined for them by "the state" were outside the boundaries of the moral life and had to be dealt with harshly. Antonio Gramsci's Marxist usage was not altogether dissimilar. Gramsci, too, made no ultimate distinction between a dictatorially imposed "collective will" and one "spontaneously" accepted by the masses.[22]

Neither the family nor "civil society"—both important spheres of human activity in Hegel's thought—had any substantial reality in Gentile's. The individual's noblest purposes were, by definition, those of the state; education consisted of making the individual understand that fact; and there was no sphere outside the state in which any individual could find refuge. So total was Gentile's identification of the power of the State with the will of the individual that he regarded the enemy of the state as a criminal not merely because he had broken its laws, but because by doing so he had "betrayed his status as a free and moral being."[23]

Gentile's attitude toward coercion did not help matters. Although he often referred to *squadrismo* as if it were a juvenile and faintly regrettable phase of Fascism, he forthrightly admired the spontaneity, directness, and lack of calculation characteristic of World War I front fighters, as well as their willingness to die for the nation and state, which he considered the supreme realization of the individual moral personality. Even more ominous was the way that Gentile talked about how coercion had to be part of the state's power, denying in the process any real distinction between physical and moral force, between "the sermon and the blackjack."[24] It would eventually be necessary, he believed, for the state to proceed beyond compulsion, to the point where the law, "immanent in compulsion should become the conscious will of the person subjected to it."[25] In other words, it would be necessary to employ coercion until the individual had internalized what the state demands. We are not too far, at this point, from what George Orwell later described as learning to love Big Brother.

Finally, Gentile's elitism, at first glance so stodgy and aristocratically conservative, looked with approval on the spectacle of the manipulation of the masses by crude slogans. . . . One had to distinguish between the simple slogans for the masses "which practically and immediately distinguish friends from enemies," create myths, arouse blind, total support, and put into motion the forces of will and feeling, and the true ideals of Fascism. The masses were mere instruments animated by the "thought" of "a few guiding spirits."[26]

After 1925, Gentile's statism dominated the discussions of the nature of Fascism. The term *totalitarian* was often used, though seldom with precision or a generally understood definition. In "The Doctrine of Fascism," published in the *Enciclopedia italiana* in 1932 under Mussolini's name, Gentile wrote that

> the fascist conception of the State is all-embracing; outside of it no human or spiritual values can exist, much less have value. Thus understood, fascism is totalitarian, and the fascist state—a synthesis and a unit inclusive of all values—interprets, develops and potentiates the whole life of a people.[27]

Gentile's highly abstract, philosophical discussions of the totalitarian state seem prophetic when read today. It was extraordinary how he envisioned a new kind of activist state that would try to make an end of civil society and even the family, employing the traditional means of coercion, the mystification and social myths made famous by Georges Sorel, and the most invasive methods that the twentieth century could perfect. Gentile deserves to be called the first philosopher of totalitarianism.

The term, then, originated in the militant hatred for Italian liberalism and admiration for a warrior culture that animated Gentile and most other early Fascists. It first appealed to Mussolini in part because of his previous experience with the maximalist rhetoric of socialism and perhaps also because of its early emphasis on will.[28] The term appears also to have suggested to Mussolini his personal dictatorship.[29] Its extremist ring was attractive, and it sounded "modern," supporting Fascist claims to have created new state and social forms appropriate to the present and breaking decisively with the decadent, liberal past. But it still was only one term among many.

Totalitarianism probably already had greater significance to the opposition, who also used it to suggest something violently and frighteningly new. To liberals and socialists, it rapidly came to convey that sense of a historically unprecedented regimentation and loss of liberty, possibly on a worldwide basis, that has continued to our own time.

Despite the term's blurred meanings in this early Italian context, the striking diversity in usage between the dynamism, voluntarism, and ferocity of "totalitarian" action, as it was often described before 1925, and the devouring statism of Gentile directs our attention to one of the major conflicts within Italian Fascism between the mid-1920s and the mid-1930s: how to reconcile the violent social and political movement deriving from the front-fighter mentality with the authoritarian state structure that the more traditional conservatives were attempting to impose. As earlier noted, the evolution from a dynamic meaning of *totalitarian* to a statist one was connected with the eclipse of the Fascist Party after 1925 and its replacement by a more static governmental authoritarianism. This conflict had its analogues in both Nazi Germany and the Soviet Union, places where the term *totalitarian* would be of greater political and philosophical importance than in Italy. There, too, the achievement of state power by "radical" regimes was partially dependent on a culture of violence, spontaneity, and extremism, which became markedly less useful when the radical party had to govern under more or less normal conditions. But both the violence and the statism of these movements were central to the dramatic revolt against "liberal decadence" that swept over Europe after World War I.

IN GERMANY, like Italy, the destruction of a decadent liberalism was the issue as National Socialism was gaining power. Between 1929 and 1933, there was a vigorous discussion on the Right about a "national revolution" to replace the Weimar Republic with a much stronger state that could represent Germany more forcefully in the world. Almost immediately after Hitler's accession to power, it became clear that the National Socialist state would be an extremely activist one. From the Reichstag fire through the *Gleichschaltung* and beyond, 1933 was a year of violence and upheaval in Germany, created either directly or indirectly by those who controlled that state, Hitler above all. The ambition of the Nazi leadership to control spheres of life that had hitherto remained private quickly became apparent. Most of the quarrelsome rightist intellectuals who had been arguing about what the national revolution should be accepted the one they had, with varying degrees of enthusiasm.

By this time, the term *total* had already been in use for a number of years. Among those who had done the most to acclimatize it in Germany was the rightist political philosopher and subsequent Nazi collaborator Carl Schmitt.[30] Schmitt was one of the most talented of those German intellectuals who experienced the 1920s as a crisis of liberalism and the liberal state. The terms *total* and *totalitarian* offered him, like many others, the possibility of addressing the current crisis of liberalism and expressing their longing for a more authoritarian political world. Although Schmitt applied the term to Germany while taking specific note of its Italian origins, there were several important differences between the old field of battle in Italy and the new one in Germany. In Italy, the term had been used to discuss a social reality that was changing, to be sure, but in which the "totalitarians" were already in power. In the initial phase of its usage, the term described primarily their political ambitions and behavior in an almost quotidian way. In Germany, the term had, from the start, a more abstract and analytical quality, but also constituted a prediction. Schmitt, like other rightist intellectuals in the discussion, was not charting the activities of totalitarians already in power, but was analyzing the collapse of liberalism in Europe as a whole, with special reference to Germany and its future.

Unlike other intellectual leaders on the Right, Schmitt was neither *völkisch*-racist minded nor directly representative of the "front-fighter" mentality. His background was western German Catholic authoritarianism of a quite ordinary sort, and his training was in law. He was the most original of those many Germans concerned with "order" in the chaotic world of the 1920s. He developed a vision of the political world akin to that of such political philosophers as Hobbes, Bodin, and Machiavelli, rooted in a dichotomy of friend and enemy that existed prior to any kind of constraining law. The Catholic thinkers that Schmitt most admired were the most resolutely pessimistic and reactionary theoreticians of the European counterrevolution: De Maistre, Bonald, and Donoso Cortés.

At bottom, Schmitt believed that the state existed to oppose the enemies of the national community and to ensure order at home. Modern men and women had embarked on a fruitless crusade to escape inevitable political conflict by expanding the power of the state and its representative aspirations. He thus directed his fire against parliamentarianism, demonstrating brilliantly not only that the Weimar constitution ensured a "weak" state in the international arena, but also that much of its representative character was purely formal; it did not even do the things that it claimed as its justification. Debate and discussion did not define voting, which was now entirely along party lines. To use one of the several dichotomies he popularized, it had legality but not legitimacy. For the latter, a much stronger state with a "positive content" was necessary.

Elaborating on his first important statement about the "total state," his version of the *stato totalitario*, Schmitt introduced a distinction quite foreign to the term's previous Italian usage.[31] His description of the evolution of the modern state system began with the powerful, "executive" state of the old regime, whose principal function was not to create behavioral norms through positive law, but to create an effective arena in which such norms could come into existence and function. He contrasted the *ancien régime* state dialectically with its successor, the minimal "liberal" state of the nineteenth century, ending in the present with the destruction of liberalism through the fusion of state and society. As they lost their distinct outlines and blended into a single swollen, amorphous entity, either a "quantitatively total state" or a "qualitatively total state" might be produced.

In the case of Schmitt's "quantitatively total state," society triumphed over the state, with the result that the state's executive authority, the dynamism of the political factor, was lost. The social welfare demanded by the masses absorbed all the state's energies, producing a hugh and permanent welfare bureaucracy, amounting, Schmitt claimed, to a "totality of weakness." At the same time, the organized political and social interests that dominated the welfare state indoctrinated the masses with a powerful, all-encompassing ideology, obviously the Marxism of the Social Democratic and Communist parties and trade unions. The Weimar Republic represented this sort of ideologized and flaccid mass democracy in which "authority" had been replaced by "majority" and parties, together with mass welfare organizations, and had permanently triumphed over the state's authority. Society had defeated the state and organized itself as a replacement.

Schmitt's clearly disliked this sort of welfare state because he feared that it would greatly diminish the importance of ideological nationalism in organizing society. Schmitt's almost horrified evocation of the triumph of welfare administration over the national state even recalls Karl Marx's celebrated meditations about how the rule over individuals would ultimately be replaced by the administration of things. Schmitt exactly reversed Marx, regarding that development with horror.

A state, though, could become "qualitatively total," like Fascist Italy, in which case it would triumph over society. Such a result entailed a powerful renewal of the state's executive authority (and here Schmitt cited the examples of both Italy and the Soviet Union), leading to the end of that pluralism and the concentration on alleviating the masses' material needs that had so weakened the liberal state in its decadence. State and society would again, as in the nineteenth century, be understood as opposites, with primacy clearly belonging to the state.

Schmitt, in terms not unlike Gentile's, asserted that there was nothing undemocratic about the reassertion of a strong state, since democracy was simply the identity of the ruler and the ruled. Schmitt combined this old Aristotelian point of view with a version of Rousseau, noting, in George Schwab's words, that citizens agree

> even to those laws which were enacted against their will, because law is the *volonté generale* . . . and the general will is in accord with true freedom . . . there is nothing incompatible between democracy and dictatorship, because the essence of democracy is identity, and not necessarily liberty. In Schmitt's construction the antithesis of dictatorship is discussion and not democracy.[32]

As opposed to the state, governed by the minority, the people are simultaneously omnipotent, since they have the ultimate say about the state's survival, and impotent, since they cannot initiate political process but only respond to the government's posing of the question. Practically speaking, this is plebiscitarian democracy at best.

A good many philosophers, politicians, and jurists in early 1930s Germany were in favor of a more authoritarian state. But Schmitt went further: Everything that had been the province of society—the upbringing and education of citizens, the nation's industrial life—would now have to serve the purposes of the "qualitatively total" state. And those purposes, for

Schmitt, were at bottom conflictual, for the ultimate purpose of the state is war. This dichotomy between the two kinds of total state recalls Elie Halévy's 1936 observation that

> the Conservative parties call for the almost unlimited strengthening of the state with the almost unlimited reduction of its economic functions. The socialist parties call for the unlimited extension of the functions of the state and, at the same time, for the unlimited weakening of its authority. The compromise solution is "national socialism."[33]

Modern economic life, according to Schmitt, drives this process forward. No sooner has the "quantitatively total" state been victorious in its struggle with the political forces of the old regime than it faces a new and more deadly challenge. Its materialistic self-absorption, its loss of national consciousness and élan mean that it cannot match the focused economic power and dynamism that the concentrated modern economies give the "qualitatively total" state. It must either plunge the nation into disaster or give away to its "qualitatively total" rival and successor.

Schmitt's version of the "total state" differs from the Italian variants in several ways. The split between "quantitatively" and "qualitatively" total robs the term of some of what was arresting about Gentile's version or even about the earlier Italian rhetoric. The "quantitatively" total is really just a version of the modern welfare state. The "qualitatively" total state is closely akin to a ferocious but rather traditional kind of authoritarianism. Neither seems to embody the combination of ferocity and militant invasiveness, on the one hand, with the vision of the total absorption of all social and cultural life, on the other, that was characteristic of the Italian version as sketched out by Gentile. One is tempted to ascribe this difference to Schmitt's juridical academic background, which may have suggested to him a less radical version of the future than Gentile's philosophical training did to him.

When Schmitt describes the "qualitatively total" state, he mentions an "eminent representative of the German front soldier, Ernst Jünger, to whom he admiringly ascribes a formula describing the "astonishing development" of the state "taking over all spheres." The formula is that of "total mobilization."[34]

Jünger was a far different figure from Schmitt: not an academic, but a writer of bizarre and brilliant gifts; not an authoritarian jurist, but an active man of obvious physical and existential courage; a man torn between anarchism and extreme authoritarianism; an aesthete and a nihilist who aspired to be a prophet. Above all, in the early stages of his career, Jünger spoke as the most powerful representative of the front-fighter mentality. His diary of World War I, *The Storm of Steel,* was the most intransigent statement of those who held that the bourgeois world had been destroyed in all but name by the holocaust of 1914 to 1918 and that a whole new world had to be created by those who had the courage to obliterate the past.[35] "We ourselves were the war," he liked to proclaim.[36] Out of his terrible wartime experiences he developed a vision of a totally militarized warrior society that would make an end of the bourgeois Europe still organized by civilians.

During the 1920s, Jünger began to develop a vision of this new civilization that would replace the decadent liberal world. At the heart of this new civilization was a figure Jünger called "the Worker" (der Arbeiter). This "worker" was a more emblematic and stranger figure than the Marxist "worker," but also a type rather than an individual, totally representative of the new civilization, created by it and also its creator.[37] The ends for which the worker would achieve power and the means by which he would achieve it were identical but not entirely knowable in advance. Freedom consisted in understanding the necessity of the new order and being willing to discover it.

Like Schmitt, Jünger saw war and industrialism as having destroyed the past and producing the future. The figure of "the worker" embodied the fusion of the two into a "totality," weapons and tools being merely variants of the same thing. Industrial life and military life demanded the same relentless organization, mechanization, and will.

Jünger's vision was developed as a nationalist alternative to Marxism. For all the differences between Jünger and the Bolshevik leadership, the student of the Soviet Union is irresistibly reminded of Trotsky and his call for the "militarization of labor" in early 1920s Russia.[38] Both men believed that they were living in an age of revolutionary transition. As Jünger did, Trotsky regarded violence and warfare as the fundamental means through which the new historical era was replacing the old one, whose potency and authority were in irrevocable decline.[39] The new world order, Jünger believed, would not be a "gift from the heavens," nor would it be a "product of utopian reason," but would be achieved through "a chain of wars and civil wars," a kind of non-Marxist version of Trotsky's "permanent revolution."[40]

These violent struggles not only propelled the historical process toward the desired goal, both men believed, but also would give birth to a new type of human being, imbued with the brutal heroism necessary for the struggle ahead.[41] One may perhaps also discern similarities to the warrior Maoism of the Chinese Cultural Revolution, as well as to Georges Sorel's notion of a technological elite that will change the world, not to mention the general celebration of action and dynamism in the manifestos of Italian Fascism.[42] Most immediately, however, Jünger's emphasis on violence presaged the advent of Adolf Hitler.

From early in his life, Jünger had thought of himself as a disciple of Friedrich Nietzsche. His vision of "the worker" and his world as transcending the bourgeois order, as well as his specific hostility to the meek, the clerkly, the peaceful, the mercantile, and the individual, was certainly in the spirit of Nietzsche as Jünger understood him. "The Arbeiter is to be recognized as the direct successor of the reasonable–virtuous individual."[43] He was also clearly connected to Nietzsche's idea of the Übermensch. But this was a Nietzschean spirit violently refashioned by the militarism of World War I.

It was in *Total Mobilization* (1930) that Jünger first sketched out his views of what would replace decadent liberal civilization.[44] He introduced the phrase by noting that war was more and more coming to depend on the most total employment of all the resources of the state, which at bottom meant that the most developed industry most effectively and single-mindedly focused on military power and its effective employment. Hence, war becomes a "gigantic work process" (and, conversely, work becomes more like war).[45]

World War I, Jünger continued, had demonstrated what was to come. In Germany, Generals Hindenburg and Ludendorff had clearly seen how victory could have been achieved only by a "total" effort of the entire society. Not merely was the "militarization" of the "total" society and economy essential; so were the militarization and mobilization of the deepest impulses of the human individual. Furthermore, Jünger observed, the wars of the future will be wars of entire societies; the power and range of modern weapons dictate that. And total war demands total mobilization. Historically speaking, the wars of the kings and queens were followed by the wars of the bourgeoisie, to be followed in turn by the wars of the workers. In the postwar period, we have seen these tendencies first, he pointed out, in Soviet Russia, then in Italy, and now in our own country. Developments in American industry have helped show us the way, but the Soviet Five-Year-Plan is of even greater importance. Jünger's writing had the effect of imbuing the term *total* with connotations of a universal, collectivist industrial order on a planetary scale, even though it was generally used to modify the single word *state*. The term *totalitarian* still bears some of that connotation today.

Jünger's vision of the "total" future, created and dominated by the enigmatic figure of the soldier-worker, had a considerable impact on "national revolutionaries" and revolutionary conservatives all over Germany, many of whom, like the National Bolshevik Ernst Niekisch, learned to use the word *total* in this thrilling, frightening, and premonitory way.[46] From this audience of apocalyptically minded and vaguely politicized intellectuals, the word spread in an even less precise way to the larger German public.

But however influential Jünger's vision was on broader segments of German society, in the short run it was Schmitt's rather traditionalist idea of the totalitarian as an extreme version of traditional authoritarianism that had greater influence on the debate about the "total state" in the final days of the Weimar Republic and in the first few months of National Socialist Germany. Franz Neumann believed that this was because before 1934,

> the political theorists and lawyers of the previous era had retained their positions of prominence in the matter of formulating ideology. These men looked upon the National Socialist revolution as a new edition of the imperial system, with its basis in the authority of the bureaucracy and the army. Now that it was back in the hands of reliable leaders, the German state would again embody the highest values.[47]

At all events, the leaders of National Socialism used the term less and less after Hitler's accession to power, while conservative professors and jurists continued to discuss the dissolution of Weimar and the future—obviously a dramatically more authoritarian one—in a vocabulary in which the word *total* frequently appeared. In intellectual terms, the period was marked by a feverish debate among the numerous enemies of the Weimar Republic who now saw that it was about to be replaced by some far more authoritarian kind of government. Some were seized merely by spasms of prediction. Others hoped by means of their writings to influence the course of events or to ingratiate themselves with one or another of the more or less conservative groups: monarchists, racist or *völkisch* thinkers, National Bolsheviks, the semipermanent adolescents of the German youth movement, or circles closer to the Nazis themselves.[48]

In this chaotic intellectual arena, one of the most characteristic and often cited formulations regarding the new kind of government that would replace the hopeless Weimar Republic was Ernst Forsthoff's *Der totale Staat* (*The Total State*).[49] Writing in the year of the Nazis' accession to power, Forsthoff made clear his debt to Schmitt from the first page of his short book. Political life in Germany, he asserted, is dominated by relations of friend and enemy, "we" and "they," and the total state is the antithesis of the liberal state. The anti-Semitism of his book suggests romantic-*völkisch* thinking, but the point of view is more fundamentally that of a traditional authoritarian. There is a decided tendency toward violent rhetoric (the *Liquidierung* of the bourgeois past is demanded) and a militant, almost lip-smacking optimism about the Nazi future appropriate to a young scholar getting on with his career in 1933. Forsthoff repeatedly expressed his contempt for liberal parliamentarianism and especially bureaucracy and demanded a drastically more authoritarian state in the hands of a new elite and led by a great man in the mold of Bismarck. Authority should be personal, not abstract.

In his repeated claim that the most important aspect of nineteenth-century society, historically considered, was its constitution out of romantic "communities" (*Gemeinschaften*), Forsthoff was clearly indebted to sociologists like Ferdinand Tönnies, but only the elites that "grow out of" the popular soil could be permitted to rule. For the rest, organization into a corporate state, along vaguely Italian lines, in order to facilitate the smooth functioning of German industry, was all that could be envisaged.

Forsthoff mentioned Jünger's *Der Arbeiter* admiringly, but his own vision was of a community of workers organized by profession. They were to be imbued with traditional German nationalism, together with a deferential understanding of their equally traditional place in the world.

Forsthoff's version of the total state, even more than Schmitt's, was at bottom a reworking of the *ancien régime*. Rather than defining the interests of the ruler and ruled as identical, Forsthoff regarded the lower orders as unqualified to rule themselves, much as any conservative aristocrat of the nineteenth century would have done; indeed, he saw the new state's fundamental mission as the undoing of the French Revolution.[50] Germany needed an autocratic government based on an elite, even though that elite could not, under Hitler, be one of birth but had to be forged and proven in what would be a long, hard struggle to realize the Nazi program. Forsthoff believed that the new society would be hierarchical, from Hitler on down, as even the *ancien régime* had not been.[51]

Der totale Staat was a highly theoretical work by a rather traditional conservative, trying to discern what was going to happen and to influence events in the direction of a highly authoritarian dictatorship. And yet there is an extravagance about Forsthoff's rhetoric that points to the future development of the "total state." As Martin Jänicke has pointed out, his hostility to individualism was extreme by previous standards, as was the vehemence of his nationalism. Germans could live only for the nation, Forsthoff concluded, and he looked forward to the "abolition of the private character of the individual life."[52]

Adolf Hitler was by no means a traditionalist like Forsthoff, however psychologically extreme the latter may have been, and he consistently subordinated the German state to the Nazi movement.[53] Nevertheless, he used the term several times in his speeches during the summer of 1933.[54] In November 1933, Josef Goebbels could refer to the mission of the "total state" in language almost identical to Forsthoff's, and even to a general "totalitarian standpoint" (with reference to Italy), but he was soon corrected by Alfred Rosenberg.[55] In an article published in the *Völkische Beobachter* on January 1, 1934, entitled "Total State?" Rosenberg urged all National Socialists to drop the phrase. What should be emphasized, he urged, was "not the so-called totality of the state, but rather the totality of the National Socialist movement."[56] Again the dichotomy between dynamic movement and devouring state that we saw in Italy!

The Italian comparison had been, on the whole, popular with most prominent National Socialists in the years before 1933. As late as January 1933, Carl Schmitt made the comparison quite explicitly, writing in an article entitled "The Further Development of the Total State" that Germany needed a version of the Italian *stato totalitario,* which—tolerating no internal dissent of any kind—would abolish the ideological totalism of the welfare state and its all-powerful party organizations, take the modern means of communications into its hands, and restore state power.[57]

But conservative statism would not triumph so easily in Germany as in Italy. A number of Nazi jurists were soon inspired to join the discussion, to the effect that the *Führer* was creating not a "fascist state" but a "German state." German racialism was mentioned specifically as differentiating Germany from Italy. As a German scholar shrewdly observed, the term *total state* had come in Germany to have the connotation of a type; it implied a specific comparison with Italy and perhaps even the Soviet Union.[58] It is hard to say how significant this terminological dispute was to Hitler himself. He used the term on only a very few occasions after 1933, once when he wished to express the close relationship between his regime and Mussolini's.

———

IN SUM, all those in Italy and Germany who wrote of the "total" or "totalitarian" state saw it as the antithesis of the liberal state. There was increasing agreement in both countries, all along the political spectrum, that the liberal state, parliamentarism, and pluralism were in deep trouble. The "total" or "totalitarian" state was one of several ways of describing the strong state that authoritarians believed had to emerge to succeed liberal decadence. All these Germans and Italians believed that the *stato totalitario* was a historical novelty and the product of a crisis of liberalism and parliamentarianism.

But the vision of Germans and Italians of what totalitarian or total meant before 1935 was fragmentary and unclear. The meanings of *totalitario* before Gentile took up the term had a dynamic element, with components of *will* and *action* that the German variant normally lacked. Then, too, despite the fact that the Italian dictatorship was never as "total" as the German one soon became, Gentile's Hegelianism made possible a more theoretically extreme vision of state power over the individual than anything to be found in Germany, with the possible exception of Jünger's vision of "total mobilization." Fortunately for the Italians, however, their government was unable to realize Gentile's vision.

In Germany, though, Carl Schmitt and those influenced by him produced a notion of the "total state" that was theoretically less radical than the Italian version, despite the subsequent extremism of German practice. But unlike the Italians, they were not groping for a new vocabulary to describe *praxis,* but were adopting the Italian term to describe incipient German reality. In 1933, Forsthoff and Schmitt in particular began to suggest how the new state would monopolize every sphere of private life and utilize all existing means of communication to control the citizenry. The Nazi hostility to the terms *total* and *totalitarian,* however, prevented any serious, long-term discussion of the possibilities of this new kind of state.

Carl Schmitt used the term *total state* as late as 1937, but he was already a marginal figure in the Third Reich.[59] A year before his death in 1937, General Erich Ludendorff, now just another disinherited rightist, published a book entitled *Der totale Krieg (Totalitarian war)*, but his usage was neither original nor influential.[60] It was among the émigré opposition to Germany and Italy that those discussions were to continue, albeit in a very different spirit, and new meanings were to emerge. And those meanings were developed largely in England and the United States, two cultures that as yet were almost entirely unaware of the total and totalitarian.

Ideological critics on the Left have often stated that the term *totalitarian* is chiefly useful to conservatives who wish to suggest, falsely, that the Soviet Union and Fascist states were significantly alike. We should point out that from early on, the example of the Soviet Union was of considerable interest to those who employed the term, in both Italy and Germany. Among the very first to use the term in Germany were right-wing radicals like Jünger and Niekisch, who indeed were interested in comparing both the experience of Fascist Italy and that of the Soviet Union with their own. They did regard Italy and the Soviet Union as significantly alike, but they hardly put forward this analogy in disapproval. Rather, they found it fascinating and enticing. Jünger, for example, wrote:

> Today the similarity between left and right becomes obvious and even the dream of freedom withers away in the iron grasp of necessity. This is a grandiose and horrid drama—these movements of ever more uniform masses caught in the mesh of the times. Forms of compulsion are at work here that are stronger than torture: they are so strong that men greet them with fervor. Behind each exit marked with the sign of happiness lurks pain and death. It is necessary to enter this arena well-armed.[61]

A second aspect of the definitional wars in both countries reflected the conflict between proponents of a dictatorship that was dynamic and movement oriented and one that was static, authoritarian, and statist in a traditional, if extreme, way. In Italy, the term continued to be used by Fascists until the regime ended, but it changed in its meanings from the dynamic and descriptive evocations of will and "spirit" before 1925 to the extreme statism of Gentile.

In Germany, Schmitt and his followers adopted the term to describe their increasingly ferocious authoritarianism. In his vision of a totally mobilized world, Jünger shared Gentile's radicalism, but his vision of "totality" was more a Nietzschean vision of a new world in which traditional notions of good and evil had been transformed by economic and social forces than the lesson plan of a Hegelian educator.

Those who understood National Socialism as a dynamic movement never accepted the term at all, because it neglected crucial elements of the Nazi *Weltanschauung*, like racism, and because its statist meaning had previously won out in Italy. To call Germany a total or a totalitarian state was to group it with other states—Italy and perhaps even the Soviet Union—and the Nazi leadership was unwilling to do that.

In various conservative and extreme right circles in Spain, there was considerable talk about the *estado totalitario*,[62] beginning late in 1933 with the foundation of the Falange Española. José Antonio Primo de Rivera, its moving spirit, spoke and wrote frequently of the totalitarian state,[63] and his phraseology contained references to corporatism Italian style, but his program remained nationalist and Catholic in quite an old-fashioned way. When Franco came to power, he used a good deal of Falangist rhetoric, especially during the first five years of his regime. In the spring of 1938, he proclaimed in an interview that his state structure would "follow that of the totalitarian regimes, such as Italy and Germany . . . but with distinctly national characteristics. It will be a suit tailored to Spanish measurements."[64] There is little to suggest, however, that Franco's use of the term was ever more than what he deemed suitable rhetoric.

It would be a mistake to see the debate in Italy and Germany over the total and totalitarian as more significant than it was. However deep their adherence to certain ideas and points of view, Fascist ideologues were opportunistic in their rhetoric. The intellectual confusion was dense in Germany between 1929 and 1934, with a bewildering variety of nationalist, racist, authoritarian, and antibourgeois groups maneuvering for position in a changing world. Almost all of them wanted to heap a few shovelfuls of earth on the coffin of republican, democratic, and socialist government. The interest of the leaders of National Socialism in the new terminology was less than it had been in Italy. Had it not been for the later prominence of the term among opponents of Nazism and Fascism, it would be today largely of interest to scholars. But that, of course, has emphatically not been the case. We must now turn to the first and central phase of the term's internationalization and rise to world prominence.

TWO

A New Kind of State

Italy, Germany, and the
Soviet Union in the 1930s

I N LOOKING to see how people began to see Stalinism and even Bolshevism as "like" Fascism in the 1930s, one is brought face to face with
the French ideologue of syndicalism, Georges Sorel.[1] Although Sorel did
not speak of totalitarianism, many of the elements that commentators began
to see as "alike" in the Soviet Union, Italy, and subsequently Germany were
aspects of the twentieth-century radicalism about which Sorel had spoken.

First, there was the remarkable stress on violence. Both Fascism and
Bolshevism emphasized (in slightly different ways) will and, despite the
roots of Stalinism in Marxism, saw the primacy of politics over economics in
postrevolutionary economic development and state building. Both movements combined voluntarism with elitism. The role of public myth was
central to both. Myths, according to Sorel, provided the driving force behind all great accomplishments in human history; they were "not descriptions of things but expressions of the will."[2] Syndicalist and Sorelian elements played a significant role in Fascism.[3] That they were strikingly similar
to aspects of Leninism is revealed in the comparisons that began to be made
in the mid-1930s, more and more frequently with reference to the word
totalitarian.[4]

The antiliberalism of all three movements was central. Fascism, Nazism,
and Bolshevism all employed what a prominent student of Fascism calls a
"totalitarian vocabulary of combat."[5] In both their official and their unofficial rhetoric, Soviet Communists and German and Italian Fascists expressed
their hatred of the soft and cowardly bourgeoisie. (In the next moment,
however, the Bolsheviks in their public utterances might call the bourgeoisie
violent, ravening, crazed with hatred for the Revolution, etc.)

Connected to what seems Sorelian is also the emphasis of both movements on mobilization. The use of inspiring folklore, contemporary worker
heroes and legends, and political initiatives decided on by the leadership was

31

often accompanied by mobilization campaigns. The best Soviet example is the Stakhanovite campaign of the late 1930s.[6]

But it was, above all, the strong state, the dictatorship, and the role of the dictator that caught people's attention, that convinced them that these new regimes had something important in common. On occasion, Mussolini was quite willing to admit it himself. He told the Communists in the Chamber of Deputies on December 1, 1921, that

> I recognize that between us and the communists there are no political affinities but there are intellectual affinities. We, like you, consider necessary a centralized and unitary state which imposes an iron discipline on all individuals, with this difference, that you arrive at this conclusion via the concept of class, and we arrive there via the concept of nation.[7]

Palmiro Togliatti, the Italian Communist leader, noted in a circumspect way in a 1935 speech that the dictatorship of a "new" party was common to both Communism and Fascism.[8] According to a prominent scholar of Fascism, "while the . . . Fascists were formulating the rationale for a mass-mobilizing, developmental, authoritarian, hierarchical and statist program, the Bolsheviks were forced to assume similar postures by the course of events."[9]

The context for the spread of the term *totalitarian* to the English-speaking world in the mid-1930s was the growing interest in the study of comparative dictatorship by commentators largely liberal or socialist in their political sympathies.

The consciousness that World War I marked a dramatic break with the past was less developed in England and the United States before the mid-1930s than in Italy or Germany.[10] In retrospect, it is clear that American and British public opinions were remarkably slow to see how dramatically the world had changed and that Hitler and Mussolini were not traditional European statesmen. Still, by the mid-1930s, journalists, academics, and even politicians were making that discovery. Some of them found the term *totalitarian* a handy way to distinguish between "old" dictatorships, such as that of tsarist Russia, and "new" ones with a far greater dynamism and ruthlessness.

As we have seen, even those on the political right who employed the term *totalitarian* in a positive sense in Italy and Germany of the 1920s and 1930s had often mentioned the Soviet Union in the same breath.[11] Even among those who, like Ernst Jünger, were most opposed to Communism, there was a sense that the Soviet dictatorship grew out of the same soil as did the dictatorships that they were supporting or hoped to support in the future. In the 1930s and early 1940s, this "proximity" of the Soviet Union to previous notions of the "totalitarian state" became more widely accepted.[12] Ultimately, it was only in Marxist circles on the extreme Left that the totalitarian state continued to mean only Germany, or Germany and Italy.[13] The key event in this change was the violent and radical transformation that Hitler rapidly undertook after his accession to power.

The term *totalitarian* appeared several times in the English-language press between 1926 and 1934, usually in discussions of Italian politics by scholars, journalists, or émigré activists.[14] Usually the sense in which it was used could be traced back fairly easily to Italian or German usage. Often it turned out that the connection had been made through émigrés, but occasionally it would be clear that some scholar or journalist had actually read Gentile or Carl Schmitt. Sometimes the Soviet Union would also be cited as an instance of a "totalitarian state."

As early as the fall of 1929, an article in the *Times* had even defined *totalitarian* as meaning "unitary," including the Communist state as well as Fascist ones as "unitary" in such a sense.[15] George Sabine, a well-known academic chronicler of political theory, wrote about a totalitarian state in much the same sense in 1934.[16] Nevertheless, the term was not well known in England or the United States before 1935.

After Hitler came to power, it did not take long for a new set of émigrés to find themselves resident, for some indefinite period, in the English-speaking world, just as Gaetano Salvemini and other Italians had earlier. The fugitives from Germany brought with them a vocabulary that included frequent references to the totalitarian power that had taken over their country. These new arrivals were intensely oriented to the German experience. Their sense of what the category of the totalitarian meant was quite various, but reflected their German-centeredness and their generally left political orientation. Italy was something secondary or tertiary in their attempts to analyze what had happened in Europe. They tended to have begun with the belief, widely held in Marxist circles and influential everywhere on the Left, that Fascism originated in the crisis of capitalism, brought on by overproduction, the struggle for raw materials and/or markets, and the rise of organized worker militancy. A bourgeois fear of the proletarian revolution and Communism was central to all these theories. Nazism and Soviet Communism appeared in these theories as the most extreme opposites.

A particularly self-confident and uncompromising version of this theory had been promulgated by the Comintern in Moscow in 1928, in a form generally referred to as *Social Fascism*. The Comintern accepted the general notion of the capitalist crisis, but added to it other propositions, to the effect that since Fascism was the harbinger of the capitalist crisis that would lead to the revolution, it was in some sense actually to be welcomed. In terms of its "class content," it was no worse than liberalism or social democracy, since all were "essentially" bourgeois and hostile to the revolution. The worse things got, the better it was, since the sharpening of class contradictions meant that the proletarian revolution was approaching. This line was not changed until the Seventh Congress of the Comintern in 1935.

Some of the most interesting men and women who began immediately after Hitler's accession to power to arrive in English and American exile were part of that aggregation of innovative Marxists subsequently known as the Frankfurt School (as members of the Institut für Sozialforschung were described after 1950). Upon their arrival in the United States, they gravitated to hospitable institutions, usually academic ones, in and around New York: Columbia University, Union Theological Seminary, New York University. The institute's generous endowment, combined with housing from Columbia University, enabled these radical scholars to reconstitute their institutional base as the Institute of Social Research (a literal translation from the German), in a remote affiliation with Columbia.[17]

Herbert Marcuse, who remained for the time being at the institute's Geneva office, produced the first work by a member of the Frankfurt School that used the term *totalitarian*. Despite its philosophical interest, his essay, "The Struggle Against Liberalism in the Totalitarian View of the State," derived from the Marxist critiques of Fascism that had been in vogue for almost a decade, which helps account for the thin and abstract quality of his analysis.[18]

Another aspect of Marcuse's attempt to define the essence of the new "total-authoritarian state" (he used this term, apparently synonomously, with "totalitarian state") was his passionate hostility toward the extreme *Realpolitik* of Carl Schmitt and his desire to expose it. Marcuse also wanted to take account of the *völkisch* nationalism that was so much a part of Nazism, so he began his account with the creation of what he called "heroic *völkisch* realism" in reaction to the dessicated and decadent political and social theory of early-twentieth-century liberalism.

Although Marcuse believed that the crisis of liberalism was at bottom a crisis of the capitalist economic system, as a radical Hegelian student of Heidegger, he was less concerned with economics than were more orthodox Marxist interpreters. Marcuse saw the current crisis as an Armageddon between the most developed manifestation of Enlightenment rationalism (Marxist collectivism) and the systematic irrationalism of Nazism, based on racism and static mystifications of "life" and "nature" (blood and soil, nation, "totality," life as beyond all intellectual systems, etc.).

There was no returning to the liberal world. What was progressive in liberalism had been taken over by Marxist collectivism, while the threat from the Left had caused bourgeois liberal society, irrevocably in decline, to adopt the brutal measures of Fascism against it.[19] "It is liberalism," Marcuse intoned, "that 'produces' the total-authoritarian state out of itself, as its own consummation at a more advanced stage of development."[20] Nazism was even, in a small way, progressive, for it shattered the decadent privatism of the late bourgeois world and "consciously politiciz[ed] the concept of existence."[21]

In his essay, Marcuse made no suggestion that the Soviet Union had anything to with the rise of the "totalitarian" state, although it was, of course, the most tangible manifestation of the crisis of liberalism in Europe. Two years later, when Marcuse turned to a brief study of influential antiliberal thinkers of the twentieth century, he observed that Lenin's notion of the revolutionary avant-garde, as well as the *Führerelite* of Fascism, could be connected to Sorel's elitist point of view.[22]

In Marcuse's later thought—most significantly in *Soviet Marxism* and *One-Dimensional Man*—he extended his notion of "totalitarianism" to include all technologically advanced industrial society.[23] According to Harold Bleich,

> The individual human subject [in all such societies] is overwhelmed by the reified relationships that originate in technology and that constitute the form as well as the content of advanced industrial society. The predominance of the technological structure of societies is so prevalent that it . . . all but obliterates conceptualizations and potential realizations of human reality that may transcend the parameters of totalitarian culture.[24]

Totalitarianism became a culture devoid of subversive or alternative possibilities, rather than an intrusive dictatorship, and in this reading, the Western capitalist world became more thoroughly totalitarian than even the Communist world.

Other Marxists connected with the Institute for Social Research also wrote or spoke about the "totalitarian state." In his ambitious study of Nazism, *Behemoth,* Franz Neumann took note of the rich literature describing and analyzing the totalitarian state that appeared in German in the early 1930s. He himself did not provide any precise definition of what the totalitarian state was, beyond noting its extreme centralization, its function as an "order of domination," and, in the German case, its extreme racialism. From a strictly ideological point of view, Neumann noted that the "totalitarian" phase of Nazism was strictly confined to the first two years of Nazi rule, encompassing the *Gleichschaltung* and the purge of Röhm and the "radicals" of the Sturmabteilung (S.A., storm troops). The term ceased to be used by the Nazi elite after that period because Hitler had neither the need nor the desire to emphasize in Germany the conservative statism of the Italian Fascist type. Rather, the dynamic racism of the "movement state" was at the heart of Hitler's vision.[25]

Neumann used the term *totalitarian* throughout *Behemoth* to describe the all-powerful state that he believed to be one of the two central elements of Fascism. The other was monopoly capitalism. Like Marcuse, Neumann regarded Nazism as in large part a development out of political liberalism and late capitaism, rather than primarily an attack on them. As a Marxist, he regarded Hegelian statism as "progressive," even it its German development, and regarded capitalism, rather than anticapitalist racism and romanticism, as more crucial to the rise of Hitler. His sense of totalitarianism was derived from Ernst Forsthoff's and especially Carl Schmitt's usages. He never discussed the Soviet Union as "totalitarian," although he did take note of such usage in the German literature.[26]

Dialectic of Enlightenment, by Max Horkheimer and Theodor Adorno, was a quite different sort of book from Neumann's prolix, heavily documented orthodox Marxism. In an even deeper and more passionate way, however, Horkheimer and Adorno saw the totalitarian as growing out of the heart of bourgeois liberalism. Beginning in a deep and indefinite past, they suggested the crafty Ulysses as an ancient prototype of the cunning, manipulative *Homo economicus;* they pointed to Bacon's emphasis on the domination of nature and continued with the Cartesian mathematization of the universe and "cogito, ergo sum," ending their introduction with the proclamation: "Enlightenment is totalitarian."[27]

Above all, Horkheimer and Adorno wanted to puncture bourgeois illusions about their complicity in the most horrific events of the time. They were deeply frustrated by the ability of the bourgeois world to make unimaginable any world other than the existing one, by creating a hegemonic mass culture. Essentially this was what they, like Marcuse, found to be "totalitarian."

It was above all in the eighteenth-century Enlightenment that Horkheimer and Adorno found the identity of reason and domination. Reason, as invoked by the ascendant middle class, ceased to have any substance and became a mere process harnessed to the new elite's drive for economic domination. As the power of intellectual systematization grew, the previous integration of human beings into nature through mythology was lost. The goal of the bourgeoisie was the transformation of the world into industry, of qualities into functions, of the apprehension of the world into pure formalism. Administration gradually came to shape every area of modern life. The ultimate issue of the instrumental Reason of the Enlightenment was totalitarianism. Their radical book was a deeply felt protest against the secularization process that Max Weber called the "disenchantment of the world." It owed a good deal to Nietzsche's jeremiads against modern culture, and it suggested the future cultural criticism of Jürgen Habermas and Michel Foucault.[28]

Not everyone in the wave of radical immigration from Hitler's Germany took the view that the totalitarian state was either a Nazi or a Nazi/Fascist state. Among the earliest arrivals from Germany was the theologian Paul Tillich, who had enjoyed cordial relations with charter members of the Frankfurt School like Adorno and Horkheimer. A few months after he arrived in New York in the autumn of 1933, Tillich wrote an article entitled "The Totalitarian State and the Claims of the Church," which was published in the New School's journal, *Social Research,* inaugurated in 1934.[29]

Tillich also regarded the Nazi achievement of power as resulting from the crisis of "late capitalism." The economic dynamism of capitalism had brought about a worldwide mutual interdependence that combined in an unstable way with an increased competition for steadily diminishing resources. Tillich regarded the only adequate solution to these interconnected problems as a "radical amalgamation of the interconnected parts" of the world, by which he seems to have meant something between a world revolution in the Marxist sense and a more pacific world federalism.

Tillich, however, could no longer share the optimism about the coming of world revolutionary deliverance that had prevailed until recently in Marxist and progressive circles. Progressive solutions having failed (or at least being everywhere in the world on the defensive), a virulent and destructive competitiveness had come to dominate instead. This, in turn, was forcing the "disintegration" of the two main groups of late bourgeois society, the proletariat and the bourgeoisie itself (a clear reference to the stock market crash of 1929 and its aftermath).

The chain of events, continued Tillich, that led up to the present crisis, had begun with World War I (by implication the result of capitalist competition for diminishing resources and markets), followed by the economic crisis of the postwar period. This, together with the concurrent rise of "revolutionary secularism" (Marxist states and movements), had made "reintegration the central problem of late capitalism."[30] But so far the human response to the crisis had been dramatically inadequate, for the only port that had been found in this storm was the national state.

These circumstances explain why increasing numbers of people were willing to accept the drastic curtailment of individual and group liberties in the name of the whole nations' well-being. Such attitudes led to the emergence of the totalitarian state, for "only authoritarian concentration of all forces and the ejection [*sic*] of all resisting tendencies provide a guaranty for the effectiveness of a militant nationalism."[31]

Then came the surprise: "Even where a communist world organization of economy and politics has been aimed at, the first and at present the only form of realization is the national state, as evidenced by the Russian example."[32] Coming from the German world as he did, Tillich believed that a theory explicitly glorifying "totalitarian" unity was an essential part of the totalitarian state. Consequently, he found that only Germany in all of Europe had realized the totalitarian state in both theory and practice. But even though the Soviet Union's Marxist justification was couched in the language of the Enlightenment, "in Russia the totalitarian state has been more effectively realized than even in Germany."

What did Tillich mean by calling Germany and the Soviet Union totalitarian? (He found Italy only ambiguously so.) Essentially, that all economic, political, cultural, and educational life had been taken over by a state subject to no effective restrictions, constitutional or otherwise. The individual no longer had rights of any kind. Nothing was said explicitly about dictatorships or single-party systems.

In the Soviet Union, the justification for doing this was different from that in Nazi Germany (the rationale in the Soviet Union being the exclusion of bourgeois capitalism and the development of "communist enlightenment"), but the resulting state was of much the same type.

In Germany, Italy, and the Soviet Union, it had become clear that the development of a full-fledged totalitarian state required mythic underpinnings. In Italy and Germany, the myth was national, with a strongly racial elaboration in Germany, a Roman-imperial one in Italy. The myth underlying the Soviet totalitarian state was social justice. Tillich concluded his gloomy survey with an analysis of the situation of the churches under the totalitarian state.

———

IT WAS not merely among émigrés that Hitler's rise to power and the upheavals that followed in Germany sounded an alarm. In neither England nor the United States was the intellectual and political response to Hitler particularly vigorous or astute, although not everyone was oblivious to the crisis of democratic institutions that Europe was undergoing. In England, the church historian Christopher Dawson, then teaching at University College, Exeter, diagnosed the new totalitarian state as a threat to religion at almost the same time as Tillich did. "The modern state," he wrote in *Criterion* in October 1934,

> is daily extending its control over a wider area of social life and is taking over functions that were formerly regarded as the province of independent social units such as the family and the church, or as a sphere for the voluntary activities of private individuals. It is not merely that the state is becoming more centralized, but that society and culture are becoming *politicized*.

And statesmen were increasingly unwilling to accept their limited traditional role. Now, according to Dawson, the statesman "may even be expected to transform the whole structure of society and refashion the cultural traditions of the people."[33]

Not surprisingly for a Catholic historian, Dawson's analysis showed no trace of Marxist thinking. Instead he connected the rise of totalitarianism to a more general increase in the authority and reach of the modern state, which made possible "universal compulsory education" and "universal military service." What was special about the totalitarian states was that their dictatorship was that of a "hierarchical party" that resembled "a religious or military order more than a political party of the old type" and thus made them inevitable rivals of the church.[34]

A survey of American political writing made in 1934 reveals an increasing interest in the comparative study of dictatorial regimes among both academics and the lay public.[35] *Dictatorship in the Modern World*, edited by Guy Stanton Ford of the University of Minnesota, for example, is a collection of essays by well-known academics and publicists that appeared in 1935 and in a second edition in 1939.

In the first edition, only Max Lerner, a radical student of Charles Beard and Thorstein Veblen, referred to certain modern dictatorships as being "totalitarian." His use of the term clearly derives from Italy. Lerner asserted that *totalitarian* means "corporate," involving "the organization of the economic groups that compete for the distribution of the national income into government-supervised associations or 'corporations,' with the government holding the balance of power. All open conflict in the form of strikes and lockouts is banned and the labor movement is nationalized." This, he noted, is a *stato forte,* except in the economic sphere, for all it does there is to regularize and stablize capitalism.[36]

Lerner's analysis was clearly, like Tillich's, indebted to Marxist analyses regarding support for Fascism and Nazism as deriving from inflation and middle-class fears of proletarianization, both of which stemmed ultimately from the same crisis of late capitalism that had produced the stock market crash of 1929.[37] Although Lerner used the term to describe only Nazism and (implicitly) Fascism, the Soviet Union in fact appeared as the third of the great "modern" dictatorships described in Lerner's essay, sharing with Germany and Italy a one-party state, a "far-flung local party organization," and purges. Not only were all three states led by a dictator, but little dictators were in charge of local party organizations.[38] It is not hard to see how the word *totalitarian* could be used to sum up this comparison rather than standing for one aspect of it. But Lerner, like many other leftist intellectuals in the 1930s, refused to take this step.

Hans Kohn's essay in the same volume did not clearly indicate why regimes so different from the dictatorships of the past appeared after World War I. But he treated the Soviet Union, Germany, and Italy as the three great exemplars, observing that the Soviet dictatorship differed from the others in its commitment to what would later be called "modernization" and in its relationship to the French Revolution. But otherwise he developed a typology of the three as characterized by a dictatorship, a one-party state, total control of the media and the economy, and an utterly pliant citizenry.[39] Kohn did not use the term *totalitarian* in the original, but in the version rewritten for a collection of his own essays, he used it in a sense clearly derived from Jünger and Schmitt, whose work he knew.[40]

Not all these early essays were entirely geared to what was happening abroad. Beginning about 1934, with the publication of Thomas Lengyel's *The New Deal in Europe,* a literature developed that pointed out similarities in especially the economic policies of Italy, Germany, and the Soviet Union and compared them with those of the New Deal in the United States. On occasion, inquiring academics and journalists wondered whether the United States and other Western powers might be on the verge of developing some brand of totalitarianism.[41] But although it was often suggested, especially by American opponents of the New Deal, that Roosevelt's economic policies had aspects in common with those of the three powers most often labeled totalitarian, the word itself was far from commonly used.

During the same or a slightly extended period, one can trace a kind of "radicalization" of influential American academics, beginning with the Nazis' accession to power. In the early 1930s, many of them found it more or less plausible that Fascism was, as the Marxists believed, crucially rooted in a capitalist crisis. Their belief in the capitalist crisis often endured throughout the decade, but by 1937 or 1938, few of them believed that Fascism could be solely explained by a declining capitalism, and many academics came to regard the similarities between Nazism and Stalinism as more striking than their differences.

Calvin Hoover of Duke University is an excellent example of such an academic. He had been teaching comparative economic systems at Duke since the 1920s and in 1929 visited the Soviet Union for the first time and set about learning Russian.[42] When he participated in the Yale conference on the economies of Bolshevism, Fascism, and capitalism in 1931, he did so as a budding specialist on the Soviet economy and the author of a newly published book, *The Economic Life of Soviet Russia*. At that time he showed no particular interest in comparing the Soviet economy or political structure with that of Fascist Italy.[43]

Late in 1932, convinced that Hitler would come to power, Hoover arranged to spend some months in Germany, and he subsequently described the Nazi takeover in a vivid, disturbing book that had some influence in American academia.[44] In February 1933, after witnessing Hitler's accession to power, Hoover took a trip to the Soviet Union, the locus of his old academic specialty. "In Russia," he wrote a few months later,

> there was famine, an increased terror and the failure to realize the economic expectations of the spring of 1930. [I] had returned to Germany with the feeling that if the National Socialist régime was the alternative to Bolshevism, much could be forgiven it. If a curtailment of individual liberty under a dictatorship were the price which had to be paid to avoid the unlimited terror which held sway in Russia, then the price seemed worth paying. The writer was astonished to discover upon his return that the conditions of terror in Russia were rapidly being duplicated in Germany.[45]

Having described the arrests and terror of the winter and spring of 1933, he concluded his account of Germany with a direct comparison of the Nazi regime with those of the Soviet Union and Italy, in terms of the ability of a monocratic regime—governed by a single party and willing to use terror without stint—to stay in power indefinitely.

Hoover continued to mull over the similarities among the regimes and, beginning in the spring of 1934, wrote a series of articles for the *Virginia Quarterly Review* that were later revised and published, with two additional essays, in a single volume. In the preface, which he completed in the early summer of 1937, he concluded:

> When I wrote *Germany Enters the Third Reich*, I was conscious that the conclusions to which I came were far different than they would have been had I not already made the study involved in writing *The Economic Life of Soviet Russia*. As I noted at the time, I was tremendously struck by certain psychological similarities between the National Socialist and the Soviet regimes, just as was everyone else who possessed an intimate

acquaintance with both. I found, too, that the naive ideas which I had had of National Socialism as simply the creature of reactionary capitalists were quite untenable.

For a time I thought of the National Socialists as a type of National Bolsheviki. Eventually I realized that if I had written the two books in reverse order I might just as well have thought of the Soviet Communists as a kind of National Socialists. I began to understand that there was developing in both Germany and Russia a new form of social organization which differed in important respects as it manifested itself in one country after another, but which had as its core the principle of totalitarianism.[46]

Hoover argued in his first essay, which appeared in the spring of 1934, that a new age of "Caesarism," which he identified with the rise of totalitarian states, had arrived in Europe. The devastation of World War I had led to political and economic chaos, which in turn produced an extreme loss of confidence by the masses of people in their governments. The ensuing crisis of parliamentarism, liberalism, and individualism produced three totalitarian governments and would likely produce more. In arguing for the typological similarity among Italy, Germany, and the Soviet Union, Hoover mentioned political institutions (dictator, single party, control of the economy), psychological similarities (ruthlessness, fanatical hostility to liberalism, individualism), the cult of force, and the urge toward expansionism.

As a general war in Europe became increasingly probable, the sense that the inner structure of the totalitarian states disposed them to expansion became a more prominent aspect of the analysis of journalists and especially of academics like Hoover. Hoover's sense of what German expansion would mean for Europe, how England and France must fail to halt it, and how Germany and the Soviet Union would likely interact on the way to a war that he judged to be inevitable makes his articles among the most prescient written at that time.[47] Like a few other journalists in the 1930s, he believed that totalitarianism might be threatening to the Western democracies if it tempted them to jettison their traditions of civil liberties in order to oppose such a powerful enemy more effectively.

A better-known journalistic effort linking the Soviet Union and Nazi Germany (Fascist Italy was mentioned only at the end) was produced by a close friend of Hoover, William Henry Chamberlin, author of a brilliant and durable history of the Russian Revolution. Chamberlin, who was becoming more conservative in the mid-1930s, published an essay comparing Germany and the Soviet Union in the *Atlantic Monthly* in the fall of 1935.[48]

Chamberlin's analysis was not very different from Hoover's, although he was more historically oriented and was interested in such questions as whether the masses in the two countries were actually devoted to their remarkable leaders, as they were always represented to be. But in addition to mentioning the similarities with respect to state institutions and repressive techniques, Chamberlin pointed to a number of striking cultural similarities.

He reported how ordinary Russians and Germans seemed to have much the same fear of foreigners, often combined with a willingness to speak with them when nobody was around. He was also struck by a similar emphasis on youth among the Nazis and Communists and on youth culture and youth organizations. He laid more stress than Hoover had on the growth of labor and concentration camps in both Germany and the Soviet Union.

Both Chamberlin and Hoover underscored the similarity in purge techniques. Both saw a similarity between the fate of the Jews and the fate of the kulaks (although it was impossible to discern as early as 1934 or 1935 the enormity of what was to happen to the Jews later on). Chamberlin was already struck by the growth of subversive political jokes in both Germany and the Soviet Union, a similarity that proponents of the totalitarian typology often suggested was characteristic of a political culture in which not only was dissent not permitted, but the regime insisted on the public profession of loyalty.

Chamberlin took note in passing of the democratic and international bases of Soviet ideology, but he spent more time describing its eclipse under Stalin. Like Hoover, Chamberlin clearly expected the two regimes to converge even further. After describing Stalin's attack on wage egalitarianism and similar measures, Chamberlin guessed that

> while Bolshevism is thus rapidly shedding its international revolutionary skin and evolving into something that might reasonably be called Red Fascism,[49] it is conceivable, although not certain, that Germany will go through a reverse process. Hitler's socialism of economic necessity, backed up by a dictatorial state, may in time become a nationalist socialism of definite policy.[50]

Chamberlin clearly regarded Nazi Germany as far more dangerous and dynamic than the Soviet Union, but believed the Soviet Union nevertheless to have been guilty of greater cruelty and violence up to that time. "The establishment of one-party dictatorships," he concluded, "which rule without benefit of parliamentarism and civil liberties and attempt to knock the heads of labor and capital together, is a worldwide trend."

Like Hoover, Chamberlin saw the undeniable differences between Germany and Soviet Russia as resulting from differences in history and national character. The parallels, he felt, "are often attributable to the common element of revolutionary fanaticism, which almost instinctively generates the method of governing by a mixture of red-hot propaganda and merciless repression."

It was not only academics like Hoover and academic journalists like Chamberlin who argued between 1934 and 1939 for a notion of the totalitarian state that encompassed both Germany and the Soviet Union. So did many American newspapers and popular journals. In 1977, the American historian Thomas R. Maddux surveyed a substantial number of newspapers and periodicals of differing political persuasions and discovered how important the events of this period were in suggesting to Americans a Soviet–German comparison.[51]

Hitler's so-called Blood Purge of the S.A. in 1934, in which between 150 and 200 victims were liquidated, ended the "movement" phase of National Socialism. It was frequently compared with Stalin's purges of the leadership, which began a short time later. As Maddux noted, "The *Baltimore Sun,* for example, pointed to the absence of a trial, legal counsel and due process in both situations, and the *Kansas City Star* believed that the purges revealed 'again the real basis of power in every dictatorship, whether Communist or Fascist.' "[52] Comparatively few of these newspaper and journal accounts set out a rigorous or systematic comparison, and comparatively few used the term *totalitarian,* although its usage definitely increased between 1937 and 1940.

Still, it is clear that the notion that Nazism and Bolshevism were opposites, more frequently noted in American public opinion before 1934, was substantially modified over the next half-dozen years.[53] If a relatively sophisticated and apocalyptic idea of the "new age of caesarism," the "era of tyrannies," of the "age of totalitarian states" was making headway among elite readers, a more casual comparison of two similar "dictatorships" was becoming coin of the realm in the mass press and in a wide variety of periodicals.[54]

In 1935, the Communist International abandoned its suicidal policy of branding Social Democrats and liberals "Social Fascists" and set out to create what quickly became known as the "Popular Front" against Fascism. This welcome, if belated, policy shift heartened the Left, in English-speaking countries as elsewhere. Among other things, it encouraged those large numbers on the Left whose instinct was to resist strongly any attempt to analyze the Soviet Union along with Italy and Germany. So whereas much of academia and the press on the whole gravitated increasingly toward the totalitarian usage, the political Left resisted for a longer time and then entered a period of split and mutual recrimination in the late 1930s.

But even some radicals, even Marxists, began to use the term in the early and mid-1930s. Some were Russian Mensheviks, now in Parisian exile; others were older socialist intellectuals like the Austrian Marxist theorist Otto Bauer. As a student of the term among the Russian Menshevik émigrés pointed out, however, even those who used the term did so loosely, reluctantly, with quotation marks around it, or with complex qualifications.[55]

Among those most strongly identified with the American Left who embraced the "totalitarian" usage was the philosopher John Dewey. Dewey was drawn to an intimate and serious consideration of similarities and differences between Germany and the Soviet Union by his inquiry into the charges against Trotsky made in the purge trials in Moscow over many months in 1937. Following his committee's vindication of Trotsky, Dewey and his associates were subjected to a sustained campaign of vilification by Communists and fellow travelers all over the world. The day after the innocent verdict, Dewey broadcast his conclusions on CBS radio. In a news release distributed at the same time, he wrote:

The revolutionary methods used in Russia are held up to us as a model [for solving American problems]. If the consequences of those methods have been not even a dictatorship of the proletariat, but a dictatorship of a small group over the whole country, workers included, and if it maintains itself in power by suppression of all individual liberties of thought, speech and press, if it suppresses all political opposition to itself and its tactics as a crime against the Workers' State, the conditions in the Soviet Union strikingly illustrated in the Moscow trials and recent blood purges certainly concern Americans who believe in democratic methods. *A country that uses all the methods of Fascism to suppress opposition can hardly be held up to us as a democracy as a model [sic] to follow against Fascism.*

Next time anybody says to you that we have to choose between Fascism and Communism, ask him what is the difference between the Hitlerite Gestapo and the Stalinite G.P.U. so that a democracy should have to choose between one or the other.[56]

Dewey laid great stress on totalitarianism in his popular *Freedom and Culture,* written in 1939 and published in October, less than two months after the signing of the Nazi-Soviet Pact.[57] Indeed, there is little doubt that Dewey's growing concern about this new kind of state lay behind *Freedom and Culture* and its clarion call of support for democracy. It formed the centerpiece of "I Believe," a popular essay he wrote the same year, and informed much of his occasional journalism over the next several years. Dewey thus came to see the world as confronted by a stark conflict between democracy and militant totalitarianism, a point of view whose messianic power would soon be revealed to the world.[58]

Between 1934 and 1936, the journal *Partisan Review* had been the organ of the Communist John Reed clubs. After the editors broke with the Communist Party in 1936, the reconstituted journal began again in 1937, and the term *totalitarianism* remained into the 1950s an integral part of its anti-Stalinist rhetoric. According to its initial editorial statement,

Formerly associated with the Communist Party, PARTISAN REVIEW strove from the first against its drive to equate the interests of literature with those of factional politics. Our reappearance on an independent basis signifies our conviction that the totalitarian trend is inherent in that movement and that it can no longer be combatted from within.[59]

In the following issues, following William Phillips, Philip Rahv, and particularly Sidney Hook placed the evolution of the Soviet Union into a totalitarian state at the center of their analysis of the world situation.

In 1938, Leon Trotsky—at this point the real guru of the *Partisan Review*'s journalists—elaborated on the brief reference that he had made in *The Revolution Betrayed* to the Soviet Union as totalitarian, lamenting the fate of "revolutionary" art in "the East" and claiming:

The October Revolution gave a magnificent impetus to all types of Soviet art, [but] the bureaucratic reaction, on the contrary, has stifled artistic creation with a totalitarian hand. Nothing surprising here! Art is
basically a function of the nerves and demands complete sincerity. Even
the art of the court of absolute monarchies was based on idealization but
not on falsification. The official art of the Soviet Union—and there is no
other over there—resembles totalitarian justice, that is to say, it is based
on lies and deceit. The goal of justice, as of art, is to exalt the "leader," to
fabricate an heroic myth. Human history has never seen anything to
equal this in scope and impudence.[60]

In the same issue, Victor Serge, also intellectually close to Trotsky, described
how in the "decadence of Bolshevism," the Marxism of the bureaucratic
caste that was currently running the Soviet Union had become "totalitarian,
despotic, amoral and opportunist. It ends up in the strangest and most
revolting negations of itself." The young critic Dwight Macdonald analyzed
Soviet films in similar, Trotskyist terms. "In a totalitarian state", he wrote,
"art functions as an opiate, not a stimulant—or irritant."[61]

The young intellectuals who wrote for *Partisan Review* still thought of
themselves as revolutionaries, however deep their detestation of Stalinism,
with most of them Trotskyists.[62] Although they enthusiastically accepted the
term *totalitarianism,* many of them, like Dwight Macdonald, still clung to
elements of the well-established Marxist explanation of the rise of Fascism
(now often described as totalitarianism). They did not, as yet, accept the
opposition of totalitarian states to "the democracies," usual in more moderate circles.[63]

THE *Partisan Review* crowd regarded the intellectuals who clung to less
revolutionary views on social questions and a more favorable view of the
Soviet Union as both timidly bourgeois and potentially totalitarian, a position not far from that toward which George Orwell was evolving in England. Macdonald soon described them as "totalitarian liberals." Most of the
Partisan Review group also resisted the tendency of the Popular Front intellectuals to support a war against Fascism. In the summer of 1939, Philip
Rahv wrote an editorial entitled "Twilight of the Thirties" in which he
decried the hysteria with which many "bourgeois" anti-Fascist writers had
embraced the cause of a "new war to save democracy." He remarked acer-
bically that "as the tide of patriotism and democratic eloquence rises, one
observes an ebb of creative energy and a rapid decline of standards in all
spheres of the intellect and of the imagination."[64]

The argument on the Left came to a head in the spring of 1939, with the
formation of the Committee for Cultural Freedom. Several hundred intellectuals, ranging from the moderate Left to the moderate Right, signed a

manifesto that began: "The tide of totalitarianism is rising throughout the world . . . the totalitarian idea is already enthroned in Germany, Italy, Russia, Japan and Spain."[65] Signers included liberal historians like Philip Mosely and Merle Curti, philosophers like Dewey, journalists like Eugene Lyons, the black poet Countee Cullen, and the socialist leader Norman Thomas.

Of the *Partisan Review* intellectuals, Sidney Hook was the only one to sign the Committee for Cultural Freedom's manifesto. The others founded their own group, the League for Cultural Freedom and Socialism, which produced a manifesto of its own, based on a year-old surrealist–Marxist manifesto of the artists André Breton and Diego Rivera. According to the authors, during the "present period of the death agony of capitalism, democratic as well as fascist," when "every progressive tendency in art is described by fascism as 'degenerate' " and "every free creation is called 'fascist' by the Stalinists," independent revolutionary writers and artists must gather their forces for the struggle against reactionary persecution. Their aims must be "the independence of art—for the revolution; the revolution—for the complete liberation of art!"[66]

In the same issue of the *Nation* in which the Committee for Cultural Freedom's manifesto appeared, Freda Kirchwey, the editor, replied for what was still probably a leftist majority that either felt the manifesto weakened the Popular Front against Fascism or still believed the Soviet Union to be a progressive force in the world. Her language was conciliatory, but she made it clear that she felt the signers paid insufficient attention to what the Communists were doing to oppose Fascism.[67] A few months later, four hundred leftists attacked the Committee for Cultural Freedom for "encourag[ing] the fantastic falsehood that the U.S.S.R. and the totalitarian states are basically alike."[68]

It is not difficult to understand the Left's, even the moderate Left's, reluctance to understand the Soviet Union as a totalitarian state like Germany or even Italy. Whatever the excesses of Stalinism—and neither the British nor the American Left was on the whole eager to confront them—men and women who had staked their intellectual and moral faith on the necessity or desirability of revolutionary change had enormous difficulty in believing that the Russian Revolution had gone so badly wrong as to produce a regime that was typologically akin to Fascism. To believe any such thing was to lose what remained of one's faith in revolutions and revolutionary politics as they had existed since 1917. All one could do was to become a Trotskyist, like Philip Rahv and Dwight Macdonald, or move into uncharted terrain.

There was also a disagreement over the value of liberalism, broadly, even amorphously, understood to include parliamentary politics, private property, and individualism. Liberals like Dewey and Hook and large numbers of journalists and ordinary American citizens had come to regard these institutions and values as the great enemies of totalitarianism—and it was becoming an "ism" in its usage precisely in these years.

But a radical Hegelian like Herbert Marcuse or a more orthodox Marxist like Franz Neumann was almost as hostile to these institutions of "bourgeois democracy" as was Gentile, Forsthoff, or Carl Schmitt. So were the young Trotskyists at the *Partisan Review*. To the Marxist Left, sham democratic values distracted the masses from their mission to create a truly just society. These disagreements were passionate.

To the Frankfurt School, however violently Fascist totalitarianism excoriated liberalism, and vice versa, totalitarianism was liberalism's natural heir in a situation of crisis. Not liberalism, as Hook or Dewey might argue, or "democracy," but "revolutionary collectivism" was the polar opposite of totalitarianism for most Marxist radicals.

The Soviet Union had been regarded for years as the progressive opponent of both liberalism and the German variant of totalitarianism. The resistance on the Left to serious consideration that the hope of the civilized world lay in the resuscitation of "bourgeois democracy" and the center of the political spectrum was enormous. Some, like Dwight Macdonald, did not feel they had to make that choice until the 1950s (1952, to be exact).[69] But an event lay just ahead that persuaded many to make such a painful and drastic break with their most cherished beliefs.

By the summer of 1939, the comparisons in newspapers and larger circulation journals were also becoming more systematic, or at least more sweeping. Stressing that both Germany and the Soviet Union were hostile to democracy, individualism, and capitalism, the *Christian Science Monitor* concluded that "Communism and Fascism are essentially alike, for each means the exaltation of force, the suppression of liberties, a regimentation and discipline by one will which brooks no opposition and which subordinates the individual to the demands of the State."[70]

With the signing of the Nazi-Soviet Pact in August 1939, all but a few far-left activists either accepted the new terminology or ceased to oppose it actively. Even the Russian Mensheviks in exile had never expected that Stalin could do such a thing. For some, "life did not seem worth living after they had heard the news."[71] Such veterans of the German Marxist ideological wars as Rudolf Hilferding explicitly recognized the Soviet Union as totalitarian.[72] The Soviet Union, wrote this eminent Marxist economic theoretician, "represents a *totalitarian state economy,* i.e. a system to which the economies of Germany and Italy are drawing closer and closer."[73]

Max Eastman wrote to the *New Republic* in October that it and other journals, such as the *Nation,* should admit "We were wrong. YOU CANNOT SERVE DEMOCRACY AND TOTALITARIANISM." In reply, the *New Republic* asserted, a bit uneasily, that "the editors . . . have never said or believed that totalitarianism and democracy are compatible. We have repeatedly criticized the lack of civil and political liberties in Soviet Russia."[74] Editor Freda Kirchwey was in fact finally moving toward the view that the Soviet Union was becoming more like Nazi Germany. Eastman elaborated his views in a book, *Stalin's Russia and the Crisis of Socialism,* which was published in the first few weeks of 1940.

The quarrel rocked the American Civil Liberties Union, which in early 1940 passed a resolution drafted by its *eminence grise,* Roger Baldwin, stating that supporters of "totalitarian dictatorships" could not serve on the ACLU board.[75] After considerable controversy, the board voted (by a margin of ten to nine) to expel longtime labor activist and Communist Party member Elizabeth Gurley Flynn, on the grounds that she was an "apologizer" for totalitarianism, not a true defender of civil liberties.[76] In the midst of a long and heated exchange, Flynn asserted that "the stigma of being totalitarian has been placed upon me. Therefore it becomes necessary for me to demonstrate that the Soviet Union . . . is not a totalitarian state." But what she actually attempted to demonstrate was that American Communists like herself had been determined and passionate advocates of civil liberties in the United States.[77]

In the mass media, too, most of those who had maintained before the signing of the pact that distinctions between Germany and the Soviet Union were important also changed their tune for the time being. Papers like the *Hartford Courant* and the *Cleveland Plain Dealer* had thought of the Soviet Union and Nazi Germany as being ideologically very different. But Maddux demonstrated how, after the pact was signed, "the Soviet Union very quickly demolished the press's last distinctions when it participated in the dissolution of Poland, reestablished a dominant position in the Baltic states and invaded Finland."[78] The term *totalitarianism* was widely used in the fall and winter of 1939; so were "red Fascism" and "brown Communism."[79] The term was sufficiently established in the academic community that the first of what were to be countless symposia on the totalitarian state could take place in November 1939, under the auspices of the American Philosophical Society.[80]

Religious groups also continued the tradition, earlier pioneered by Paul Tillich, in proclaiming the threat to organized religion represented by totalitarianism.[81] Reinhold Niebuhr appended the term to his hostility toward "rationalist utopianism"; his essays and speeches in 1939 and 1940 were sprinkled with references to totalitarianism.[82]

American Catholics were divided.[83] Catholic dislike of the Soviet Union ran very deep, except on the far Left. Even those in favor of intervention felt that if the United States were allied with the Soviet Union, the war could not be described as "against totalitarianism." After June 22, 1941, almost all organized Catholics opposed fighting the war in an alliance with "atheistic Russia."[84]

It was easier for Protestants. By May 7, 1939, the antithesis of Christian and totalitarian values had reached the cover of the *New York Times Magazine.* In an article entitled "The Titanic Twofold Challenge," John Alexander MacKay, president of the Princeton Theological Seminary, declared that "religion and democracy are linked today as never before." Viewing the present as a time of challenge fundamentally religious in nature, MacKay argued that both religion and democracy were under siege by a "new mystic power . . . to which the ugly word 'totalitarian' has been given" and that the entire "Hebrew–Christian religious tradition . . . where Christ sits in the lap of Moses" hangs in the balance. An ominous cover illustration depicted two titanic figures poised for battle, one bearing a bludgeon and the other holding the shield of "religion and democracy." Beneath it a caption read: "The totalitarian church-state, presenting a species of man-god, presumes to offer a substitute for both religion and democracy."

As with other segments of the population, religious groups used the term even more frequently after the Nazi-Soviet Pact and the invasion of Poland on September 17. Jews were particularly active. In December, for example, a rally organized by the American Jewish Congress and the Jewish Labor Committee in support of the victims of Nazi and Soviet aggression drew a crowd of twenty thousand to Madison Square Garden; the gathering was addressed by "prominent Christian and Jewish speakers," including Herbert Hoover, Mayor Fiorello La Guardia, and William Green, president of the American Federation of Labor. According to newspaper reports, the largely Jewish crowd cheered "every reference to President Roosevelt's neutrality program, booed every mention of Hitler and Stalin . . . [and] applauded statements that the real issue was the defense of democracy against totalitarianism."[85]

On April 1, 1940, a thousand delegates of the Young People's League of the United Synagogues of America publicly demonstrated their commitment to democracy by adopting a resolution opposing "any form of totalitarianism, be it fascism, communism or nazism."[86] In the same month, the Methodist and Presbyterian churches also joined the Roman Catholic and Jewish leaderships in officially denouncing totalitarianism.[87]

It is striking that even though some American Catholics were active in the publicistic war against totalitarianism, the Vatican itself remained discreetly silent on the subject. Nearly all American Catholic commentary about totalitarianism was obliged to dilate on the antitotalitarian "implications" of the pontiff's public statements rather than to quote him directly. During the war, the pope was willing to denounce Communism but not totalitarianism. Then, after the war was over, the papacy suddenly discovered the term.[88]

———

IN SUMMING UP, it is clear that what happened between 1932 and 1939 was not merely a shift in American (and, to a lesser degree, British and French) perceptions of the Soviet Union, Italy, and Germany, although that was part of it. The violent Nazi *Gleichschaltung* and the Stalinist onslaught on the kulaks, not to speak of the purges in both countries, played an important role in forcing unwelcome new valuations on many in the English-speaking world. Conservative politicians, in particular, fought against the idea that Nazi Germany was determined to impose a new order on them and their world. Radicals, especially intellectuals, fought against the idea that there could be commonalities among Germany, Italy, and the Soviet Union. But both ideas gained in plausibility.

In 1937, it was far easier to believe that there was a "new kind of state" that could be called totalitarian than it had been even a few years previously. With the signing of the Nazi-Soviet Pact in 1939, all doubts were swept away for most Americans. It was largely on the fringes of the Marxist Left that the idea persisted that whatever one might think of the Soviet Union under Stalin, its rootedness in Enlightenment traditions of liberation separated it typologically from Fascism and Nazism. This was a highly unfashionable viewpoint in 1940, but it would reemerge more than once in postwar Europe and America.

THREE

Wartime in the English-Speaking World

IN THE YEARS 1940 and 1941, with a general sense of crisis hanging over the Western world, the terms *totalitarian* and *totalitarianism* became familiar to millions of Americans. They were coin of the realm in the popular press, among the readers of highbrow periodicals, and to the more middlebrow readers of the *Saturday Review of Literature*. Summed up the writer of *Time*'s "Year in Books," 1941

> was a year so political that there was scarcely a book, no matter how literary, which was not also a political document. For 1941 was above all the year when men were trying to readjust themselves in books to two years of political shocks, from Munich to Dunkirk, which challenged every value by which men had thinkingly or unthinkingly lived. The greatest challenge of all was the triumphant emergence of a new human type, totalitarian man—superbly armed, deliberately destructive and dominant—at the very heart of what had been Europe's cultural sanctuaries.[1]

For the first time, this new terminology was used seriously in a presidential election. American officials had used the term for several years to characterize Latin American dictatorships, like that in Paraguay, as totalitarian. After 1938, Joseph Grew, then serving as the American ambassador in Tokyo, had been afraid that Japan was becoming "totalitarian" as it moved toward close ties with Italy and Germany.[2] But the term had never been as important in the political arena as in the election of 1940. Both Republicans and Democrats used the term trivially and irresponsibly, as both tried to convince the American public that Hitler would benefit from an election victory of the other party.

A strong liberal like Governor Herbert Lehman of New York said that "nothing that could happen in the United States could give Hitler, Mussolini, Stalin and Japan more satisfaction than the defeat of . . . Franklin D. Roosevelt." Vice President Henry Wallace, who subsequently learned something about innuendo and slander himself, alleged that Nazi agents were under orders to help Wendel Willkie win. "The friends of the totalitarian powers," he proclaimed, "have decided that the stupidity and lack of leadership of the Republican candidate qualify him as their candidate."[3]

The Republicans were no more scrupulous. In July 1940, for example, former President Herbert Hoover published an inflammatory article in the *American Mercury,* in which he drew direct analogies between the developments—economic, political, and psychological—that had preceded the establishment of totalitarian regimes in Germany and other countries with the situation of the United States under the New Deal. He even referred to Roosevelt and the New Deal brain trust as "totalitarian liberals," a different usage of this opprobrious phrase from Dwight Macdonald's several years earlier.[4] As used by Hoover, it seems to be roughly synonymous with *socialistic,* not at all the same thing, for example, as Carl Schmitt's definition of *totalitarian.*[5] To Hoover, a New Deal liberal was an incipient totalitarian. Hoover repeated the message in a June 25 speech at the Republican National Convention in Philadelphia.[6]

Republican Wendell Wilkie, who was running in part against the New Deal's hostility to business, threatened the voters that if "you return this Administration to office, you will be serving under an American totalitarian government before the long third term is up".[7] Even Norman Thomas got into the act. Speaking at the closing session of the June conference of the League for Industrial Democracy, Thomas predicted the rise of "fascism here" should Roosevelt drag the United States into the war. Reportedly arguing that it was "fantastic" to believe that this racist and violent country could resist the development of totalitarianism in time of war, Thomas recommended that the nation address itself instead to the "conquest of poverty" at home.[8]

For Americans linked by ancestry to nations currently under Fascist rule, public denunciations of totalitarianism provided an opportunity to demonstrate their loyalty to the United States. This was highly desirable for German and especially Italian Americans, many of whom had been rather favorably disposed toward Mussolini and his regime. On June 17, 1940, Mayor Fiorello La Guardia of New York led a group of six hundred Italian-American businessmen in voicing the opposition of Americans "of Italian blood" to the "cruel philosophies of the totalitarian states."[9]

Willkie's formulation of the issue may have been election year extremism, but quite a few Americans could still see some parallels between the New Deal and the totalitarian experiments in Europe, and more feared the future consequences of competing with "totalitarians," whether in Britain, France, or the United States. Back in 1936, Lawrence Dennis had been one of the very few Americans ever to advocate the necessity of Western democracies "becoming totalitarian"; they must do so in order to survive.[10] The early days of the war, however, saw apprehensive revivals of that sort of thinking.

"England and France condemn totalitarian government," wrote one reluctant totalitarian to the *New York Times*, "but yet they must adopt it in order to cope with Germany."[11]

Dennis himself returned to the fray in 1940 with a book entitled *The Dynamics of War and Revolution*, in which he began with the German ideologue Oswald Spengler's assertion that capitalism and democracy were bound to give away to some form of "Caesarism." The latter term, according to Dennis,

> means both "socialism"—that is, military totalitarianism resting on a dynamic faith and a will to action—and "internationalism"—that is, the end of national sovereignty in favor of a world state or a small number of world empires. Both are necessary for the survival of Western civilization in the age of its fulfillment and decline.[12]

In an article in the *New York Times Magazine*, the editor of the *Economist* observed gloomily that the war economies of Britain and France had become nearly as "disciplined" as that of Germany. His definition of the totalitarian state was typical of the popular usage of the times: "By etymology, [it is] . . . merely one in which the government runs everything. [But] by popular usage [it is] . . . one in which the government not merely runs everything, but runs everything for the objectionable ends of aggression and conquest." Optimistically, however, he concluded that the European democracies had not yet succumbed to the "totalitarian trend." Despite their "outward forms of government," the "inward spirit that inspires them" was still democratic, and thus the "economic totalitarianism" of wartime Britain was only a temporary condition.[13]

The rapidity and completeness of the German victory over France encouraged the idea that the war was between democracy and totalitarianism and increased the tendency for the opponents of totalitarian regimes to endow them with powers of a positively mythic kind. The belief that "democracy, being old, familiar homestuff . . . naturally cannot compete with the totalitarian glamour girls" was sufficiently widespread that the editors of the *New York Times* felt that they had to address the question: "If ardent and idealistic American youth really had its eyes opened to the fatal glamour of the new totalitarian creeds, red or white," observed an editorial on May 7, 1941, "why should it be necessary for democracy to provide them with a 'new' faith? What is the matter with the old democratic faith from which so many young people have been lured by the come-hither in Hitler's and Stalin's eye?"[14]

American isolationists were often among the most disposed to "come to terms" with the totalitarians. Before 1940, continuing their opposition to what they regarded as Roosevelt's domestic high-handedness, they often argued that the real danger of "totalitarianism" came from within the United States. Senator Arthur Vandenberg, still a strong opponent of war, wrote in a letter to a friend that we cannot regiment America (and how!) through another war and ever get individual liberty and freedom of action back again. We shall be ourselves a *totalitarian state*, to all intents and purposes, within ten minutes after we enter this war as a protest *against* totalitarian states. And we shall remain one forever.[15]

Both Charles Lindbergh and his wife, Anne Morrow Lindbergh, were against a "hopeless crusade to save democracy."[16] Colonel Robert McCormick's *Chicago Tribune* took the view that the European democracies were being "compelled to accept totalitarian methods to wage total war, and the US would do likewise if she intervened."[17] After the German invasion of the Soviet Union in June 1941, isolationists argued futilely that the United States should not go to war with one totalitarian regime in alliance with another.[18]

On the interventionist side, use of the term was more significant. As Thomas E. Lifka has pointed out, groups like the Committee to Defend America and the Fight for Freedom Group "stressed the inherently dynamic, revolutionary foreign policy of the totalitarian state." Men like Will Clayton, Dean Acheson, Robert Sherwood, and James Bryant Conant all brought their understanding of "totalitarian" dynamics to the foreign policy of the Truman administration after the war.[19]

Roosevelt himself began to use the term with increasing frequency from the fall of 1940 but did so for only about a year, and it is not easy to say how influential his usage was. Lifka speculated that "under his tutelage, the American people were taught to accept the characterization of their international adversaries as totalitarian states, with all that that definition implied." Roosevelt's usage was probably influential with respect to public opinion in general and certainly with the young internationalists of 1940.[20]

The great events of 1941, especially Germany's June 22 attack on the Soviet Union, stopped a great deal of this talk of totalitarianism, although privately a strong residue of belief in Soviet totalitarianism remained in many circles. When Great Britain and then the United States became allies of the Soviet Union, the term that had increasingly seemed to many Americans to sum up the embodiment of evil in the modern world became both ambiguous and embarrassing. The absolute confrontation of "totalitarian dictators" with "democracies" was shattered. Almost overnight, use of the term greatly diminished, although it never disappeared entirely. Furthermore, it was now often employed to refer to only Nazism and Fascism and occasionally, in ways that were ambiguous about the referent, as a forbidding development in the modern world or the dramatic opposite of democracy.

Religious groups and conservatives continued to use the term on occasion, but so did socialists like Norman Thomas and David Dubinsky. On the whole, the user was likely to be someone who did not mind offending the United States' ally, the Soviet Union, or someone who was eager to do so. The young Trotskyists of the *Partisan Review,* for example, hardly used the term in 1941 and 1942, and when it did appear, it was used much less analytically than in the late 1930s.[21]

There were more people on the right, of course, who did not mind offending the Soviet Union. One was the conservative (but not reactionary) Catholic historian Carlton J. H. Hayes. Author of an influential study of Europe on the eve of the twentieth century,[22] Hayes, the Seth Low Professor of History at Columbia, had used the term in the 1930s in his essay to the American Philosophical Society's important 1939 symposium.[23] Honored at a luncheon on the eve of his April 1942 departure for Madrid as American ambassador, he compared the current "threat to the thing we call the historical civilization of the West" with the Muslim invasions of the seventh century: "The rise of this thoroughly pagan totalitarianism, playing with absolutely false and pseudo-scientific notions such as race purity, is an absolutely new threat in this terrible war."[24]

Spain was occasionally still described as totalitarian by both Spaniards and foreigners,[25] but another American Catholic academic present did not agree, finding Spain's "spiritual vitality" so strong that totalitarianism would never take root there.[26] Hayes himself actually did believe that Spain was totalitarian, although he never said so publicly, and he subsequently reported that he tried privately to persuade Franco to "give up totalitarianiam."[27] Significantly, Franco did change his mind in 1942 about referring to Spain as "totalitarian". In a December speech he announced, with reference to the prospects for Europe after the war: "Then, whatever projects there may exist now, the historic destiny of our era will be settled, either according to the barbarous formula of bolshevist totalitarianism, or according to the spiritual, patriotic formula Spain offers us, or according to any other formula of the fascist nations."[28] During this period, Franco still supported the Axis, but his support was growing more cautious, which may account for his shift to a more Western definition of totalitarianism.

In early August 1942, a group of American Protestant leaders, including John R. Mott and Reinhold Niebuhr, met to take a position on the war. Eighty-seven of them signed the congress's concluding statement, which stated in part:

> We do not fail to remember that we are united with our foes by a common humanity and by our common need for divine grace. [But] as Christians we cannot remain silent. . . . At issue are our Christian concept of man's destiny, and our opportunity, for years to come, to work toward a larger earthly fulfilment of that destiny. . . . Totalitarian aggression must be halted or there will be no peace and order in the world.[29]

In 1941 a book was published that had a significant effect on future discussions about totalitarianism, although the term was actually used only once. That book was Arthur Koestler's *Darkness at Noon,* a fictional study of the Soviet purge trials and the motives of the "Old Bolsheviks" for confessing to absurd, fantastic, and internally contradictory charges of which they were innocent. The vehicle is the arrest of Rubashov—an Old Bolshevik whose character, looks, and beliefs owe something to both Trotsky and Bukharin—by Stalin's government and his gradual capitulation to those who interrogate him. The primary reason Rubashov gives in is that he comes to recognize that he has relinquished the possibility of being right "against the Party" and that only by doing what the Party needs can he render a final service to the cause in which he still believes. His principal tormentor, who is given the expressive name of Gletkin, is represented as a new kind of Stalinist man, but one who might well be understood to have a close analogue in Germany. *Darkness at Noon* was published in England in December 1940, and the first American edition appeared in May 1941.

Time magazine's critic, assessing the books published in 1941, noted with disappointment that even the best books did not adequately interpret the terrible events of the year. He found, however, that in *Darkness at Noon,* "novelist Koestler came closest to doing it," particularly in the scene in which the "nameless, faceless, voiceless Tsarist," when asked why he had smuggled tobacco to Rubashov from his neighboring cell, "taps back [in code, over the metal pipes connecting the cells] his reason to the totalitarian who once thought he was the hope of the world: 'Decency—something your kind will never understand.' "[30]

The comparison between Nazism and Stalinism hovers in the background, but is not a central feature of the novel. When Rubashov is being awakened by the Soviet police at the very beginning of the novel, he loses track of where he is and imagines, for a moment, that he is being arrested by the Gestapo, but the comparison is not explicitly developed. It is with additional shock, therefore, that the reader arrives at the murder of Rubashov on the last page:

> But whose colour-print portrait was hanging over his bed and looking at him? Was it No. 1 [Stalin] or was it the other—he with the ironic smile or he with the glassy gaze? A shapeless figure bent over him, he smelt the fresh leather of the revolver belt; but what insignia did the figure wear on the sleeves and shoulder straps of its uniform—and in whose name did it raise the dark pistol barrel?[31]

Koestler thus reserved the most direct statement of his own position for the end. From the standpoint of *Darkness at Noon* as a novel, one may question the tactic, but as a political tract it is effective.

———

Darkness at Noon was widely read at the time of its publication, and at the end of the war and the beginning of the Cold War it enjoyed a renewed spate of popularity. One should, however, note a small irony. So effective was the statement of the Communist position that the book could be read in strongly leftist circles such as existed in postwar France in such a way as to encourage conversion to that point of view.[32]

Darkness at Noon was not the only important book on totalitarianism to appear in 1941. Academics were beginning to get into the act with more ambitious publications. Significantly, the three authors of the first important academic studies all were refugees from Germany. We discussed Franz Neumann's *Behemoth* in Chapter 2. In 1941, an émigré jurist named Ernst Fraenkel published a study of the Nazi German governing apparatus entitled *The Dual State*.[33] Evoking a well-established theme in the analysis of totalitarianism, Fraenkel labeled National Socialist Germany a "dual state" to elucidate the contradiction, or paradox, that the government of Germany seemed to be divided into two parts. One was a relentless whirlwind of totalitarian activity that spared nothing in its path. Fraenkel called the sum of these agencies "the prerogative state." At the same time, however, many of Germany's traditional administrative and legal institutions continued to function as they had, but without hindering the operations of the "prerogative state." Fraenkel named the sum of these organizations "the normative state," and he analyzed their interaction under his title rubric of "dual state."

Sigmund Neumann's *Permanent Revolution* was far and away the best study yet of the Nazi dictatorship, with a good Italian comparison and somewhat less of a Russian one.[34] Fraenkel's *The Dual State* probably had less impact in the English-speaking world than did either *Behemoth* or *Permanent Revolution*. Fraenkel's restatement of the conflict between the dynamic and the statist in totalitarianism, however, had a profound effect on postwar studies of National Socialism by German scholars.

James Burnham's *The Managerial Revolution*[35] was far from an academic study,[36] but its impact on intellectuals was comparable in the short run with that of *Darkness at Noon*. Burnham considered socialism and capitalism to be far from the only alternative forms of government that the world might anticipate. Indeed, he argued, capitalist society was declining, but it would not be replaced by socialism, but by an essentially new kind of planned, centralized society controlled by "managers."

Burnham's version of the crisis of capitalism was drawn from his previous radical experience and contained little that was new. But he contended that the Russian experience showed that the elimination of private property was not necessarily a step toward socialism. Moreover, the continuing decline in the numbers and power of the working class, the presence of large-scale unemployment in its ranks, and the growth of new technologies would doom any political movement based on it. Marxist parties had not been able or willing to introduce socialism in the past and would be unable to do so in the future.

The new ruling class, Burnham predicted, would be the managers, whose bureaucracies would increasingly control the means of production. Dominant ideologies would reflect this change. Instead of the liberationist ideologies of socialism or those of capitalism emphasizing individualism and natural rights, the managers would stress the power of the state, self-sacrifice, and discipline. They would increasingly fuse the political and economic orders of society, and as this happened, the managerial society would move toward totalitarianism. It was these irresistible economic and political pressures that accounted for how Germany and Russia had become so alike; indeed, the recent history of the United States revealed the same tendencies, although they were far less advanced.

Burnham's sense of the future was full of foreboding, but ideas not unlike his about the meaning of *totalitarianism* could be expressed in much less negative terms. In England, in particular, the term was occasionally used on both the Left and the Right less as a pejorative than to express the idea that in the future human society would have to be far better and far *more* organized than previously. In a popular tract published in 1941, the geneticist and scientific popularizer C. H. Waddington defined *totalitarianism* in complexly positive terms:

> These two results of technical development—large-scale organisation, and intrusion into the privacy of the individual—are, when they are given a political form, the hallmarks of what are usually called totalitarian systems. The meaning of this term is also coloured by our feelings about the countries in which such political regimes have been set up—hatred for the Nazi and Fascist systems, and usually at least scepticism about the Russian. But the objectionable features of these states are not inevitable accompaniments of totalitarian systems, as one can see from the fact that the three differ among themselves. Totalitarianism, on the other hand, does seem to be inevitable; the whole trend of recent history is towards it. One cannot dismiss the Nazis, Fascists and Communists for being, in their different ways, totalitarian; fairly soon we shall all be so, in some way or other. The Totalitarians of today have taken, with the wrong foot foremost, a step which we shall all have to take to-morrow.[37]

Waddington clearly thought that liberal civilization had come to an end: Indeed, it had "suffered a stroke in 1914 and been moribund ever since."[38] English totalitarianism would be national in character, differing markedly from that prevailing in Germany and even from Soviet Communism, presumably because English people were different from Russians, and so the way they planned and executed their plan would be different, too. In England, Waddington wondered, would it be "possible, for instance, to combine totalitarianism with freedom of thought, or with initiative in execution"? The most important question, he implied, was "how can the most able men be picked out for authority?"[39] They would be people like himself, in other words, who understood the scientific character of the modern world, who were not sentimental, and who knew how to plan.

George Orwell's view in 1941 of the likelihood of a totalitarian future was not too different from Waddington's, although for Waddington's insufferable complacency Orwell substituted a deep pessimism not unlike Burnham's. He was in fact fascinated by *The Managerial Revolution* and Burnham's later work, which he reviewed and discussed extensively.[40] The notion, so frighteningly expressed in *Nineteen Eighty-Four,* of a permanent struggle between superstates for world dominion came from *The Managerial Revolution.* The mythical treatise by Emanuel Goldstein, "The Theory and Practice of Oligarchical Collectivism," also was drawn from Burnham's work.[41]

In "Literature and Totalitarianism," a talk delivered on the BBC, Orwell told his audience that

> we live in an age in which the autonomous individual is ceasing to exist— or perhaps one ought to say, in which the individual is ceasing to have the illusion of being autonomous. . . . When one mentions totalitarianism one thinks immediately of Germany, Russia, Italy, but I think that one must face the risk that this phenomenon is going to be world-wide.[42]

Orwell now saw both socialism and capitalism moving toward increased state control, plausibly toward totalitarianism.[43]

Orwell's pessimism lightened somewhat over the next year or two, as England withstood the Nazi challenge and the tide of the war began to turn, but he still looked to the future with gloom and apprehension, seeing it as likely to be totalitarian in a somewhat broader sense than he had earlier employed. He wrote in a letter dated May 18, 1944:

> You ask whether totalitarianism, leader worship, etc are really on the upgrade and instance the fact that they are not apparently growing in this country and the USA. . . . All the national movements everywhere, even those that originate in resistance to German domination, seem to take nondemocratic forms, to group themselves round some superhuman fuehrer (Hitler, Stalin, Salazar, Franco, Gandhi, De Valera are all varying examples) and to adopt the theory that the end justifies the means. Everywhere the world movement seems to be in the direction of centralised economies which can be made to "work" in an economic sense but which are not democratically organised and which tend to establish a caste system. With this go the horrors of emotional nationalism and a tendency to disbelieve in the existence of objective truth because all the facts have to fit in with the words of some infallible fuehrer. Already history has in a sense ceased to exist, i.e. there is no such thing as a history of our own times which could be universally accepted. . . . Hitler can say that the Jews started the war and if he survives that will become official history.[44]

Orwell's preoccupation with totalitarianism did not diminish as the war moved toward its close. By his own account, the idea for what was to become *Nineteen Eighty-Four* came to him in 1943, and the sense of a world divided into spheres of influence perpetually at war with one another occurred to him as he was reading the news about the Teheran Conference.[45]

In the article on Arthur Koestler, published in 1946 but written two years earlier, Orwell revealed how interested he had become in the Soviet purges and the ways in which confessions were extracted from prisoners. These questions were also central, of course, to *Darkness at Noon*. Through Koestler's novel as well as historical–political literature on the Soviet Union under Stalin, such as the Trotskyist Boris Souvarine's *Nightmare in the U.S.S.R*, Orwell came to regard habitual lying and even the total destruction of objective truth as integral to "Stalinist totalitarianism."[46]

By the summer of 1946, Orwell was able to write that "every line of serious work that I have written since 1936 has been written, directly or indirectly, *against* totalitarianism and *for* democratic Socialism as I understood it."[47] He was also preoccupied with the idea that despite the infection of the British Left with "totalitarian ideas" (a combination of rationalism, sadism, elitism, and power worship), normal English people had no understanding of totalitarianism:

> There has been nothing [in England] resembling, for instance, *Fonta-mara* or *Darkness at Noon*, because there is almost no English writer to whom it has happened to see totalitarianism from the inside. . . . England is lacking . . . in what one might call concentration-camp literature. The special world created by secret-police forces, censorship of opinion, torture and frame-up trials, is of course, known about and to some extent disapproved of, but it has made very little emotional impact. . . . To understand such things one has to be able to imagine oneself as the victim, and for an Englishman to write *Darkness at Noon* would be as unlikely an accident as for a slave-trader to write *Uncle Tom's Cabin*.[48]

Orwell determined, somewhere around 1943 or 1944, to give the English-speaking world his own version of "concentration-camp literature."[49]

Until the end of the war, it does not appear that any significant American observer was so preoccupied with the problem of totalitarianism as was Orwell in England. We should note, however, that Dwight Macdonald, writing in *Partisan Review* and later in his own journal, *Politics,* shared many of Orwell's apprehensions and continued to use the vocabulary of totalitarianism. No doubt this is part of the reason that Orwell wrote the *Partisan Review*'s "Letter from London" for much of the war.

Macdonald, for example, took violent exception to the patriotic upsurge that affected some American intellectuals at the beginning of the war, particularly as it led two of the best known, Archibald MacLeish, the Librarian of Congress, and the literary historian Van Wyck Brooks, to criticize many modern writers for their pessimism and alienation from the society that now needed so badly to be defended against Fascism. Both men made the suggestion that these highbrow moderns had undermined Western morale and abetted the triumph of Fascism.

Brooks in fact made the remarkable suggestion in a letter to *Time* that local committees be constituted in American towns to collect "objects made in Germany" that would then be burned publicly. It is also true, as Macdonald angrily pointed out, that the dichotomies that Brooks alleged in his criticisms of modern writers (optimism versus pessimism, the intellect versus "life," the destructive versus the constructive) were very close to the same categories used against modernist literature in Nazi Germany and Stalinist Russia. On these grounds he felt he could claim that "Van Wyck Brooks has become, doubtless with the best intentions, our leading mouthpiece for totalitarian cultural values."

In his conclusion to the piece, considering both Brooks and MacLeish, Macdonald remarked with Orwellian pessimism that "the recent growth of this tendency over here is an ominous sign of the drift towards totalitarianism."[50] Despite the accuracy of some of Macdonald's individual points, his belief in an incipient American totalitarianism seemed excessive even to his colleagues on the *Partisan Review*.[51]

The funeral of the radical Italian-American publicist Carlo Tresca on January 16, 1943, provided an occasion for a more moderate segment of the American Left to use the term *totalitarian,* albeit in highly general terms. Socialist leader Norman Thomas, having described Tresca's murder as an "assassination,"[52] concluded that Americans should oppose any "totalitarian doctrine" that made use of "political murder."[53]

Throughout the wartime and postwar periods, Thomas used the term *totalitarian* simply to point to the similarity of the Communists and Fascists, although at the outset of the war, he had argued that if the United States became engaged, it would likely evolve into some kind of "monopoly state capitalism with a totalitarian military state," and he had joined the America First Committee.[54] In 1944 he noted privately that "Stalin . . . rather than Hitler has pioneered the techniques of a cruel and amoral totalitarianism."[55]

IN THE SUMMER OF 1945, with jubilation over the Allied victory in Europe giving way to concern over Soviet maneuvers in occupied Germany and Eastern Europe, the concept of totalitarianism became markedly more popular again in the United States, and the trend accelerated throughout 1946 with the deterioration of Soviet–American relations. By 1947, it may be said to have entered into its golden age with the proclamation of the Truman Doctrine, in which the term played an essential role in linking America's former Soviet allies with Nazi Germany. Perhaps the climax of this period came in the fall of 1950 when the McCarran Internal Security Act barred "totalitarians"—meaning Communists—from entering the United States. During these five years, the idea that the United States had to meet the totalitarian challenge came to hold undisputed sway as the key to America's future and had its most direct influence on American political thought and foreign policy.

The totalitarian enemy seemed, at first glance, to transcend traditional distinctions between Right and left, as it certainly had in the 1930s. During the war, many of those who employed it did so in contexts that suggested that only Nazism or Fascism was being discussed. Its reinvigoration in 1945 served to channel powerful anti-German sentiments into the growing anti-

Communist movement and at the same time helped ease the formation of new international alliances.

But soon the term began to seem more exclusively directed against the extreme Left. The Germans were being de-totalitarianized, and the Russians had ripped off their mask of wartime collaboration with the democracies and were now the totalitarians. The term helped to make sense of the postwar world. With totalitarianism as the enemy, it became easier to understand how formerly deadly enemies of the United States could so quickly become friends, and vice versa.

It was above all among the literary newspapers and journals of the intellectuals that the terms *totalitarian* and *totalitarianism* had remained alive during World War II and especially toward its end. What kept this terminology vital was the continuing argument over the nature of the Soviet Union: Flawed or not, did it remain the hope of the Left, or had it so dishonored traditional socialist aspirations that it might be compared with the National Socialists in Germany or at least with the Italian Fascists?

No periodical pressed the latter case with anything like the single-minded zeal of the *New Leader,* a labor-oriented weekly newspaper (later a journal) run by the Social Democratic Federation. Among those who wrote about the Soviet Union and Eastern Europe for the *New Leader* were Soviet émigrés, often of a Menshevik orientation, like Boris Nicolaevskii and David J. Dallin, one of the few first-rate scholars then writing about Russia. The Trotskyist Victor Serge and anarchists Max Nomad and Paul Goodman also contributed.[56] The anti-Soviet fervor of the Mensheviks and Trotskyists hardly requires explanation. Nicolaevskii, Dallin, and Serge in particular had participated in the passionate debates of the 1930s about how to characterize the social essence of the Soviet regime, and they were well acquainted with the concept of totalitarianism.[57]

There were also anti-Soviet labor activists and journalists of various ideological persuasions, like Abba Lerner, Max Eastman, William Henry Chamberlin, John Chamberlain, and Eugene Lyons. And among the most important figures animating the *New Leader*'s passionate criticism of the Soviet Union were John Dewey and especially Sidney Hook, both of whose particular hostility to the Soviet Union dated back to the Dewey Commission's efforts to vindicate Trotsky in 1937 and the ensuing attacks on them by Stalinists. Future neoconservatives who became important figures later, like Melvin Lasky and Irving Kristol, launched their careers writing for the *New Leader,* as well as the *Partisan Review.*

The anti-Communism of some of these men[58] later moved them entirely into the conservative camp; some remained on the Left; and some are hard to classify. But they consistently fought against the efforts of American Communists to dominate the labor movement in the United States and, beginning in 1945, against Soviet expansionism in Eastern Europe. Their purpose, in which they ultimately were successful, was to drive the Communist activists out of the labor movement altogether and the political Communists to the fringes of American political life.

The term *totalitarian* was a godsend for the *New Leader* writers. It linked the lack of political democracy in the Soviet Union with its lack of labor democracy and both with Soviet expanionism. It also tied the American domestic fight against Communists in the labor movement to the great international struggles of the late 1940s.

The *New Leader* writers employed the term sporadically throughout the war,[59] but by the beginning of 1945 the attack on Soviet totalitarianism dominated virtually every issue of the paper.[60] It influenced even their advertising and efforts to expand circulation. Any reader who persuaded a friend to subscribe, for instance, received a free copy of Arthur Koestler's *Darkness at Noon*.[61]

All postwar struggles involving Communist parties were interpreted by the *New Leader* staff as part of the inevitable worldwide struggle against totalitarianism, from Hollywood to Beijing. The *New Leader* was violently opposed to Tito, for instance.[62] As the civil war in China began to heat up, the journal demanded that the Chinese Communists not be allowed to impose a "totalitarian dictatorship" on China.[63] When, under Pietro Nenni's leadership, the Italian Socialists began to cooperate with the Italian Communists, the *New Leader* was outraged, heaping bitter reproaches on even such of its heroes as the anti-Stalinist novelist Ignacio Silone.[64]

In part because of its émigré writers, the *New Leader* undoubtedly knew the Soviet Union and Eastern Europe better than did the more accommodationist journalists writing for the *Nation* and the *New Republic,* and its understanding of the Soviet takeover in Eastern Europe was far more accurate than that of any other American journal.[65] And yet its linking of Soviet expansion in Eastern Europe with Communists in the American government has in retrospect seemed alarmist and obsessive, and some of its writers engaged in excessively sweeping characterizations of individuals and organizations in the United States as totalitarian. The *New Leader*'s repeated demands that individuals with Communist pasts or associations be fired were often not sufficiently discriminating.[66] And it tended to idealize those who were strong enemies of Communism, downplaying the corruption of Chiang Kai-shek and the collaborationism of the partisan leader Draža Mihajlovic in Yugoslavia, seeing them only as anti-Communist.[67] Finally, the journal's passionate hostility to all forms of Communism, both at home and abroad, eventually led it to support the nihilistic crusading of Senator Joseph McCarthy.

Already in March 1945, the anti-Communist journalist Eugene Lyons, former editor of the *American Mercury* and author of *The Red Decade,* wrote a provocative piece that foreshadowed the intellectual world of the Truman Doctrine, which did not come into existence for another two years. Taking issue with Wendell Wilkie's claim that we live in "one world," Lyons proclaimed that the slogan "*two* worlds" is closer to the dominant facts of our day. . . . Though mankind is for the most part unconscious of the fact, it is suspended between two worlds, two systems of life and thought, two faiths. . . . The two worlds have geographical addresses. Now that Fascism in Italy and Germany is being destroyed, the Center of totalitarian dynamics is in Russia. The democratic forces are for the most part in Britain, America and the fringes of Europe still beyond the grasp of Moscow.

Lyons closed his essay by claiming that humanity must choose between "freedom" and "submission" to totalitarianism.[68]

While liberals remained split over whether the Soviet Union was totalitarian, it was natural for the more conservative part of the American political spectrum to use for its own political purposes the growing hostility to the Soviet Union in the United States. It was plausible to do so by linking the terms *totalitarian* and *totalitarianism* as closely as possible with *socialism* and even *liberalism*. This vision of totalitarianism as an extreme form of socialism and/or liberalism had begun in the United States with the debates about whether the New Deal was socialistic and whether President Roosevelt aimed to become an American dictator, analogous to the European totalitarians. As we mentioned, in the 1940 presidential campaign, former President Herbert Hoover claimed that "totalitarian" meant "socialistic" and that the situation in the United States during the New Deal was quite like that of Weimar Germany before the advent of Hitler.[69]

Hoover, however, was avowedly partisan and, after his political defeat, to some extent discredited. But this was emphatically not the case with Friedrich Hayek, an Austrian émigré economist in his mid-forties who had been teaching at the University of London since before the outbreak of the war. Hayek's book, *The Road to Serfdom,* first published in September 1944, not only put the term *totalitarianism* back on the front burner, but did so with a subtle new emphasis: less on overt violence and invasiveness and more on the slippery slope that allegedly led from almost all forms and degrees of economic planning to totalitarianism.[70] Hayek's contribution to the British and American understanding of totalitarianism was original in its virtually total emphasis on the economic bases of both democratic freedom and totalitarian servitude.

Unlike Hoover's, Hayek's tone was not accusatory; he made it clear that socialists and liberals were not "like" totalitarians, although they did pave the way for them. Socialism in its real—that is, its "totalitarian" sense—he thought, could be realized only by means that were repugnant to Western socialists.

Thus Hayek's book was ideally suited to make the debate over totalitarianism a more integral part of arguments between conservative Republicans and liberal Democrats in the postwar United States, although it was not initially intended for that purpose. Now it could be contended that liberals and "planners" not only were wrong on economic issues, but also had paved the way for the Nazis and the Communists and might have a similar effect in the United States.[71] Conservatives saw how such arguments served to contain New Deal reformism and might help roll it back.

Despite the mildness of its tone, *The Road to Serfdom* was extreme in many of its assertions and in its Manichaean distinction between the market and planning. Among the controversial points made in *The Road to Serfdom* was the assertion that all collectivism was totalitarian,[72] that totalitarianism was not a reaction against Socialism and Communism but a continuation of them,[73] and that planning was incompatible with the rule of law.[74] A passionate devotee of classical English liberalism, Hayek went well back into history in search of where Europe had gone wrong. The idealist philosopher J. G. Fichte and the state Socialists K. J. Rodbertus and Ferdinand Lassalle were among the German villains, whose statist and nationalist ideas began, in the second half of the nineteenth century, to lessen the influence of healthy English philosophies in Europe.

Not all of Hayek's villains were German. August Comte, the founder of positivism, was a "nineteenth-century totalitarian."[75] Nor did Hayek make his seemingly total hostility to planning more intelligible by announcing, midway through the book, that there was also a good kind of planning that facilitated rather than inhibited competition. Economists like Alvin Hansen of Harvard made this difficult distinction the object of much criticism and even mild ridicule.[76]

The book was obviously timely. It was a sensation in the United States and to a lesser extent in England. Henry Hazlitt in the *New York Times* called it "one of the most important books of our generation,"[77] and Hansen more circumspectly described it as "perhaps the most discussed non-fiction work since the war began."[78] It made the front page of both the *New York Times* and the *New York Herald Tribune* book reviews on Sunday, September 24, 1944. There was an extended discussion in *Fortune,* and a condensed version ran in the April 1945 issue of *Reader's Digest;* the Book-of-the-Month club distributed the condensation at a very low price. (It is not surprising that a book with a point of view so attractive to conservatives was heavily promoted by big-time American publishers.) The year after *The Road to Serfdom* was published, Hayek traveled to the United States on a lecture trip and was widely interviewed by the press.[79]

Hayek was soon enmeshed in partisan politics. Social scientists and believers in planning, such as Charles Merriam and Louis Wirth, attacked him on the radio. But senior American business moguls like Albert J. Nock defended him.[80] In June 1945, Hayek debated Harold Laski in a two-part series entitled "Tomorrow's World: Is It Going Left?" Needless to say, Laski believed the leftward movement was "irresistible." His views were very much those of a prewar radical, for whom the wartime experience had changed little:

I think it is quite certain that during the next half-century we shall be engaging in the hard task of reshaping the foundations of our civilization. We shall have to make up our minds about the urgent issue of whether the immense productive capacity which science has placed at our disposal is to be operated through a system which gives abounding wealth to a few and condemns in every community the overwhelming majority to live on a standard which denies tham adequacy both in material comfort and spiritual welfare or whether it is to be operated through a system which, like that so dramatically emerging in the Soviet Union, operates through planned production for community consumption.[81]

One can hardly imagine views in greater contrast with those of Hayek, who the following week offered a summary of his book's arguments. Whereas for Laski, Soviet planning was still a model for Europe, Hayek believed that Communism had been discredited. As he put it, "political extremism is dead, at least in Britain." Nevertheless, in their "complete muddle and intellectual confusion," the so-called progressive socialist parties in Western Europe continue "to drift toward that totalitarian socialism which, at the same time, they are beginning to dread."[82]

The appearance of Hayek's book was of immense help to American conservatives in setting the political agenda of postwar intellectual debates. Harold Laski suddenly appeared even to some liberals as a slightly embarrassing figure from a bygone era. The Cold War liberalism of the late 1940s was far less sanguine about what could be achieved through planning than the radical liberalism of the 1930s had been. One must credit Hayek's book with a major role in that change, especially his linking of totalitarianism with planning.

Hayek's influence, furthermore, extended beyond day-to-day politics and economics. It was partly through his "interest and support" that Karl Popper's *The Open Society and Its Enemies* was published a few years later.[83] Popper's book, years in the making, was an attack on "closed societies" and especially on three major philosophers whose influence he deplored: Plato, Hegel, and Marx. Popper and Hayek alike detested utopianism, disbelieved in historical laws, and distrusted predictions of the future, particularly any that had a whiff of historical necessity. References to totalitarianism abounded in the book; Popper even asserted that "what we call nowadays totalitarianism belongs to a tradition which is just as old or just as young as our civilization itself."[84] Popper's doughty style won him admirers, but his influence on philosophy was nothing like as deep or long lasting as Hayek's was on economics.

On November 19, 1945, President Truman offered a comprehensive medical-insurance program to Americans of all ages. He was immediately attacked by Dr. Morris Fishbein, editor of the *American Medical Association Journal,* in rhetoric that owed much to Hayek:

The movement for placing of American medicine under the control of the Federal Government through a system of federal compulsory sickness insurance is the first step toward a regimentation of utilities, of industries, of finance, and eventually of labor itself. This is the kind of regimentation that led to totalitarianism in Germany and the downfall of that nation.[85]

In American politics, the onset of the Cold War was already leading to political polarization on domestic issues, and Secretary of Commerce Henry Wallace was one of the first to take the heat. His proposed "economic bill of rights," which would guarantee full employment, housing, and medical care, was viewed by some as a well-intentioned but dangerous step along the way to a planned economy. The allegedly protototalitarian implications of the Wallace plan were explained in a letter to the editor of the *New York Times* from Arthur A. Ballantine, a lawyer and former Undersecretary of the Treasury. Acknowledging his debt to Hayek, Ballantine argued that economic planning was "the polite name for totalitarianism."[86]

As these debates were percolating in the spring and summer of 1945, the venerable British Fabian scholar of European and American government, Herman Finer, was working furiously at a counterblast, which was published in November as *The Road to Reaction*. Finer, a colleague of Harold Laski at the London School of Economics, did not emulate Hayek's courtesy and instead adopted a highly polemical and personal tone. "Friedrich A. Hayek's *The Road to Serfdom*," he began, "constitutes the most sinister offensive against democracy to emerge from a democratic country for many decades."[87] His short book was not merely a reply to Hayek's arguments, but an all-out attack on unregulated capitalism, beginning with a lengthy broadside against business for producing the worldwide depression of the 1930s. Now that Hitler was defeated, he wrote, the great conflict in the world was

> whether or not the kind of social and economic progress made, especially since 1933 in the United States and since 1906 in Great Britain—that is, the remedying of the shocking deficiencies of private, economic enterprise, and the positive contribution of the state to the raising of the standard of living by its economic initiative—shall continue and be increased.[88]

In many respects, Finer's book was also a hymn to the welfare state, to the fusion of liberalism and socialism that linked the constituencies of the New Deal in the United States and the mainstream of the Labour Party in England. But its principal theme, that the great struggle in the world was between the reactionary advocates of unregulated capitalism and the humane proponents of the welfare state, was already an anachronism.

A more discriminating criticism of Hayek's notion of totalitarianism was recently made by the Polish sociologist and historian Andrzej Walicki.[89] Walicki believes that Hayek's definition missed the essence of totalitarianism because it took insufficient account of the centrality of freedom of conscience and expression. Rather, the essence of totalitarianism is its determination to enforce conformity, and in an activist sense. Without that determination to reshape the human psyche, the worst that one can arrive at is a kind of oppressive bureaucratic collectivism.

By the end of 1944, many American government officials concerned with Soviet activities were steadily finding analogies with Germany. By the spring of 1945, Averell Harriman, the American ambassador to Moscow, was telling Washington that "the Soviet program in Eastern Europe is the establishment of totalitarianism, ending personal liberty and democracy as we know . . . it."[90] From the Potsdam Conference on, American officials responsible for dealing with Soviet policy toward Eastern Europe were increasingly willing to characterize, in confidential documents, the Soviet Union as totalitarian.[91]

Ordinary Americans wavered. The rhetoric of totalitarianism was returning from its wartime hiatus, but at first it was largely confined to the pages of ideologically committed journals and books. Most Americans hated to give up the idea that the United States and its Western allies would be able to cooperate with the Soviet Union after the war was over.

The year 1946 brought a sharp deterioration in Soviet–American relations.[92] Soviet forces were reluctant to leave either Iran or Manchuria, and the ensuing crises fostered the view that the Soviet Union was proving that totalitarian states would expand until and unless they were confronted. "Getting along with Russia" would be very difficult.

In February, Stalin made a speech in Moscow that stressed the incompatibility of capitalism and Communism and blamed capitalist instability for the outbreak of World War II. A week later came the so-called Gouzenko case, a senstational incidence of espionage in Canada in which, on information provided by a Soviet cipher clerk in the Ottawa embassy, twenty-two people were arrested for stealing nuclear secrets for the Russians. Leads derived from the case ultimately led to the arrests of Klaus Fuchs in England and the Rosenbergs in the United States.[93] A few days after that came George Kennan's famous "Long Telegram," analyzing "the sources of Soviet conduct" as internally driven and providing the intellectual rationale for a major change in American policy toward the Soviet Union, although the public did not become aware of it until an abbreviated version was published the following year in *Foreign Affairs*.[94]

The split on the American Left over the Soviet Union continued to become clearer and sharper. It was between those who identified with what they described as a Rooseveltian point of view and were in favor of "accommodating" the Soviet Union's "legitimate" security needs and those who were moving toward the point of view that the Soviet Union was insatiably expansionist, a menace to world peace, even *the* menace to world peace.

A telling episode occurred in February 1946. The fairness of the elections taking place in Eastern Europe was a subject of passionate interest among liberals and radicals. Ted Weeks of the *Atlantic Monthly* had asked Raymond Leslie Buell to cover the Polish elections for the magazine. When Buell wrote that the elections were fraudulent, Weeks rejected his piece on grounds that it was not "objective" and substituted one by Anna Louise Strong, a deeply committed Communist impervious to any other point of view. Weeks was savagely attacked in open letters to the *New Leader* by Buell and William Henry Chamberlin, later joined by the anti-Communist novelist James T. Farrell.[95]

Then, on March 5, Winston Churchill made his "Iron Curtain" speech at Fulton, Missouri. Almost immediately, the metaphor made its way into mainstream American political discourse. Churchill's speech pushed further into crisis the policy of compromise toward the Soviet Union associated with Secretary of State James F. Byrnes.

Churchill used the term *totalitarianism* twice in his speech.[96] The first time was to observe that "the fear of [nuclear weapons] might have been used by them [some Communist or neo-Fascist state] to enforce totalitarian systems upon the free and democratic world, with consequences appalling to the human imagination."[97] He also spoke of the small Communist parties of Eastern Europe seeking to establish "totalitarian" control.[98]

Not only did Churchill call Communism "totalitarian," but his references to the Soviet Union in the speech also implied clear analogies to Nazi Germany and shattered the convention, still basically intact in official communications in the West, of referring to future collaboration between the West and the Soviet Union, even while criticizing aspects of Soviet policy.

Although Truman went to Fulton to introduce Churchill, he did not rush to identify himself with the new usage (and, by implication, policy), which split the American political spectrum right down the middle.[99] Over the spring and summer, however, his political position continued to erode, with American policy toward the Soviet Union one of the important issues. Even Truman's firing of Henry Wallace from his cabinet seemed an inept concession under pressure, rather than a decisive move toward a new and tougher policy toward the Soviet Union. By September, fear of the Soviet Union's aggressive intent had joined with labor problems as the first concern of the American electorate, and it became clearer and clearer that the Republicans were going to use both of them.

The Republicans took the gloves off in the 1946 congressional election campaign and defined the fundamental issue as a fight between Communism (often tied to radicals in the American labor movement) and Americanism. They did extremely well, taking control of both houses of Congress for the first time since 1928.[100]

Just as the Republicans, especially those on the more extreme Right, began to suggest that there was a slippery slope from liberalism to totalitarianism, the Democrats were concerned with upholding the proposition that liberalism was the great enemy of totalitarianism—historically the more accurate proposition. In May 1946, for example, Assistant Secretary of State

Spruille Braden delivered an address at Clark University, "bristling with criticism of totalitarian ideologies, both of the right and left,"[101] the substance of which was a lengthy definition and defense of "true liberalism."

Although *totalitarianism* had been part of the American partisan political vocabulary since the late 1930s, Roosevelt used the word infrequently and usually to refer only to Germany and Italy. The case was different with Truman, however, whose private use of the term dates back at least to the spring of 1945.[102] Publicly, Truman began to use the term about a year later, at first to refer specifically to Nazi Germany or very generally. The Democratic theme of the opposition between liberalism and totalitarianism, for instance, was the subject of a letter written by Truman and read at the second annual dinner of the Liberal Party (a bastion of anti-Communism), held in New York on June 5, 1946. According to the president's letter,

> Never before did our country and all mankind have such great need for democracy. Never before was there such an urgent need for the open mindedness and constructively critical spirit of true liberalism as there is today. There are still many vestiges and expressions of totalitarianism to be overcome. Here is the first test and the greatest task of all genuine liberals.[103]

The meaning here is ambiguous. If pressed, the president might have claimed that "vestiges . . . of totalitarianism" referred to Nazi survivals or other right-wing governments. Another of the evening's speakers, the journalist and former Soviet sympathizer Louis Fischer, was much more forthright. He was recorded by the *New York Times* as having observed that "the threat of the totalitarian Axis powers to destroy democracy had been ended, but more and more persons were convinced that democracy is again threatened by totalitarianism in the shape of Soviet Russia and her foreign Communist agencies."[104]

It is interesting that one may discern a Soviet parallel to the increasing American recourse to the term *totalitarianism*. Noting what appeared to be a hardening of British and American policy in the summer of 1946, a Soviet official on the Central Committee staff in charge of agitation and propaganda made a speech accusing Britain and the United States of pursuing fascist policies:

> [Fedor Nesterovich] Oleshchuko's thesis is that notwithstanding the victorious conclusion of the war the struggle [of the Soviet Union] against Fascism is continuing. He states that "Fascism is a manifestation of capitalist society in its imperialistic phase." . . . Fascism is supported by "reactionary" forces in capitalistic countries. Both the United States and Great Britain are supporting Fascism in the hope of using it to fight democracy and the Soviet Union. . . . Fascism can only be defeated by striking heavy blows against the reaction which nourishes it and uses it as a weapon.[105]

This was an attempt to assert the Marxist countermyth to totalitarianism: the idea of the integral connection between capitalism in its decline and Fascism. But the audience in the West prepared to accept the "Fascism" of Churchill and Byrnes, never very large, had dwindled in recent months.

By 1946, the stage was set for the Cold War. Intellectual polarization soon achieved its apogee. The term *totalitarianism*, having become part of the political vocabulary of many Americans by the outbreak of the war, was about to become a central part of the Western vocabulary that defined the world as divided between two irreconcilable antagonists.

FOUR

The Cold War

THE YEAR 1947 began with the split on the American Left over the Soviet Union continuing to deepen and become more embittered. Those most suspicious of the Soviet Union and Stalin were increasingly ready to characterize the Soviet Union publicly as a totalitarian state. As they witnessed the Soviet takeover of Eastern Europe, they linked its expansionism to its autocratic, centralized, internal structure and its relentless invasiveness. This was a viewpoint that had often been publicly expressed in the late 1930s, but that between 1941 and 1946 had been largely confined to the pages of the *New Leader* (and, to some extent, the *Partisan Review*) and (right after 1945) to scattered conservatives taking their cue from Hayek.

In the *Partisan Review,* anti-Communist liberals and radicals battered Soviet totalitarianism in a series entitled "The Future of Socialism," which ran from January to August. The editors, Sidney Hook, William Phillips, and Philip Rahv, wrote that the workers had failed to realize their historical mission of liberation, succumbing to Communism and Fascism in Russia and Germany, respectively, while remaining aloof from genuine socialism in the capitalist West. "As a result," they concluded, "the Left has fallen into a state of intellectual disorientation and political impotence."[1]

The split between the Popular Front Left and the emerging Cold War Left took on organizational form around the turn of the year, when those who favored what they called accommodating Soviet interests, led by Henry Wallace, founded the Progressive Citizens of America (PCA). A few days later, the anti-Communists organized themselves as the Americans for Democratic Action. The ADA, which included such strongly anti-Communist liberals as Reinhold Niebuhr and Arthur Schlesinger, Jr., "quickly indicated its vital interest in opposing the activities of what its leaders called the 'totalitarian left' both at home and abroad."[2]

Indeed, the whole point of the ADA might be summed up in the assertion that totalitarianism existed and had to be fought. Chester Bowles clearly expressed what was later described as "the new spirit of cold-war liberalism" in an opening address that fiercely condemned both Communist totalitarianism and Republican reaction.[3] The new, more conservative Congress that convened in January heard a great deal of antitotalitarian rhetoric, including a fiery speech by Senator Everett Dirksen explicitly reviving the idea that Soviet Communism was merely "red Fascism."[4]

In late January, Henry Wallace traveled to England, where he projected himself into an ongoing political controversy, aligning himself and his followers with left-wing critics of the British Labour government's foreign policy, which, like that of the United States, was becoming increasingly anti-Soviet. The *New Leader* immediately sent a cable to the British foreign minister, Ernest Bevin, signed by what was alleged to be a group of American liberals. It stated that Wallace's support in the United States consisted of Communists, fellow travelers, and "totalitarian liberals."[5] The letter was signed by several prominent Americans, of whom many, like A. A. Berle, were indubitably liberals; others, like Henry Luce, Republican Congressman Walter Judd of Minnesota, and the Roman Catholic bishop of New York had less impressive liberal credentials.[6]

Totalitarian pressure became dramatically more visible during the winter of 1947, at least if one was viewing the world from Washington. The crises in the Middle East caused by the withdrawal of British forces from Greece and Turkey gave rise to renewed fears in Washington that totalitarianism was on the march. In response, the president announced his Truman Doctrine on March 12 before a joint session of Congress.[7] This dramatic shift in policy committed the United States to help "democracies" all over the world "maintain their free institutions and their national integrity against aggressive movements that seek to impose on them totalitarian regimes."[8] Truman made no direct reference to the Soviet Union, subsuming it under "totalitarianism."[9] Foreshadowing the theme that evolved into the Marshall Plan, the president maintained that "the seeds of totalitarian regimes are nurtured by misery and want. They spread and grow in the soil of poverty and strife. They reach their full growth when the hope of a people for a better life has died. We must keep that hope alive."[10]

The rather Wilsonian connection between economic misery and repressive political regimes had already been made in the relative obscurity of the *State Department Bulletin* some two years earlier by Edward Stettinius, who discerned a vital connection "between American economic prosperity, world economic prosperity, and anti-totalitarian political ideals":

> Economic distress, widespread and enduring, is a menace to the preservation of political freedom. We who have been through the ghastly events of the last decade cannot be blind to the danger that men who suffer and lose hope will trade their freedom for totalitarian promises. Totalitarianism thrives on suffering, for hungry men are desperate men, and desperate men are sensitive to the appeals of demagogs.
>
> No country can safely ignore the decline of liberty and the emergence of totalitarian government in a neighboring country. Bitter experience

has taught us that totalitarianism is too often associated with sudden and armed aggression. . . . Wisdom in international relations demands that we strive to organize the world for prosperity.[11]

This position had been frequently represented in the intervening period by public officials like Will Clayton, concerned with the impact of the postwar economic situation on European political stability. It was now fervently taken up by the president himself.

Truman's rhetoric conferred the ultimate legitimacy on the term *totalitarianism* in the American political lexicon, as well as making the struggle against it the order of the day. Truman had now defined the current phase of the antitotalitarian movement and put himself at the head of it. Had he not done so, the term might well have become the property of conservative critics of his administration, for the totalitarian idea—that the Communists were the successors of the Nazis and closely connected to them—was the most powerful political idea of the late 1940s. The internationalist wing of the Republican Party, preeminently Senator Arthur Vandenberg, insisted on this sweeping rhetoric as the price of their bipartisan cooperation.[12] Somewhat paradoxically, Vandenberg's determination that Truman be compelled to take a far-reaching anti-Communist position began almost immediately to help Truman regain some momentum against Republican criticism that Democrats were what was later called "soft on Communism."

The profound change in policy represented by an open declaration that the Soviet Union was now the principal enemy of the United States called for new ways of understanding Soviet ambitions. Many of the most serious students of the Soviet Union, such as George F. Kennan, preferred to rely on themes and continuities in Russian history to provide an analytical framework, but increasingly the general notion of the Soviet Union as the surviving totalitarian state in the postwar world and the dark power of the planet took hold of the administration and much of the public.[13] Even in the case of Kennan, it must be conceded that his extremely grim view of the Soviet Union was not obviously antithetical to the idea that it was totalitarian. John Lewis Gaddis recently took note of the prominence of rhetoric about totalitarianism in this period and its connection with Kennan:

> The "long telegram" had the great influence that it did because it provided a way to fuse concerns about totalitarianism and communism in dealing with the Soviet Union. It portrayed that state as one in which an autocratic tradition had become incorporated within an ideological compulsion to treat the outside world as hostile. The conclusion was clear: No actions that the United States or its allies could take would alleviate Stalin's suspicions; the best that one could do was to look to one's own defenses.[14]

Truman's bold stroke climaxed changes in the American attitude toward the Soviet Union that had been building for many months and for which the passionately anti-Communist journalists of the *New Leader* had argued. The dramatic change also helped the unpopular president and his strife-ridden party to recover from their recent domestic troubles, especially from the Republican sweep of the congressional elections. In the words of Felix Belair, the Washington correspondent of the *New York Times,* "having been repudiated in the Congressional elections as leader of the party of supposed Communist sympathies, Mr. Truman would now lead the peoples of the world in the fight against Communist-inspired totalitarianism." Belair was not accusing Truman of having become a crusader in Europe for domestic political reasons, but he could not help noticing that "unless all signs are misleading, he has stolen a lot of Republican thunder."[15]

According to Belair, the initial foreign reaction to the president's message was extremely positive, and his low prestige abroad began to improve at once:

> To what extent Mr. Truman's popularity at home will be affected by his leadership of the anti-totalitarian movement will depend, among other things, on how well the policy succeeds and into what corollary issues it may lead. Nevertheless, . . . it is difficult to see how the President and the Democratic Party can fail to benefit from the leadership assumed by Mr. Truman this week. The issue [of totalitarianism] is fundamental and world-wide. Moreover, it seems unlikely to be subordinated to any domestic problem between now and the 1948 conventions. If anything, it promises to assume even larger proportions.

Belair concluded with a prophetic discussion of how much "selling" the president's new policy would require. The idea that the United States faced an implacable totalitarian enemy would be helpful in that great project and, indeed, was highlighted partially with that in mind. Belair saw the moment as a turning point in Truman's presidency in both foreign and domestic terms.[16]

The language of the Truman Doctrine had an immediate and striking influence on public discourse about totalitarianism. Public officials close to the president were the first, not surprisingly, to affect his aggressive new tone. One of the most interesting of these was Spruille Braden. Braden had been ambassador to Argentina from April to September 1945, but his "open opposition" to Juan Perón's regime resulted in his being recalled and made Assistant Secretary of State for Inter-American Affairs.

Braden was a believer in the universal challenge of totalitarianism to American interests. This had been an aspect of his strong opposition to Perón in Argentina, where he had discerned connections between the Perónist government and local Communists, as well as Nazis.[17]

In the spring of 1947, Braden continued to preach against totalitarianism, now in its Soviet form. In an address to the American Institute of Mining and Metallurgical Engineers on March 19, he boldly declared that "only when totalitarianism of every color has been exterminated may civilization

resume its upward march."[18] Echoing another term that had become prominent in the late 1930s, Braden went on to declare that

> the greatest barriers to man's progress . . . are those raised by the red and
> black Fascists. Call them Communists, Nazis, or by any other name, all
> are of the same totalitarian stripe and all are dangerous.
>
> Make no mistake, the black Fascists are still a threat to our way of life.
> Their insidious maneuvers, like those of the red Fascists or Communists,
> are a major peril to the fundamental freedoms of workers and employers
> alike, and can only be destroyed by the strong light of truth.[19]

On the following day, Braden's colleague, Assistant Secretary of State for
Public Affairs William Benton, charged the Soviets with waging "psychological warfare" against the United States by means of its "propaganda line"
of state-controlled newspapers, magazines, and radio broadcasts. "Free people could not carry on the kind of psychological warfare waged by totalitarian states even if they wanted to," Benton said, "but they can and should use
all the media of modern communication to cover the world with truth—as
Secretary of State George C. Marshall put it."[20]

The president himself returned to the attack several times. On May 13, for
example, his informal remarks to the Association of Radio News Analysts
contained the assertion that "there isn't any difference in totalitarian
states . . . Nazi, Communist or Franco, or anything else—they are all
alike."[21] The language of the Truman administration was now indistinguishable from that of the *New Leader*.

On the same day he announced the Truman Doctrine, the president
promulgated Executive Order 9835.13. This "loyalty order" was considered
by the opposition on the Left to be the domestic equivalent of the Truman
Doctrine. It

> called for the investigation of all employees of the executive branch, not
> just those in sensitive positions; it provided for a master index on all
> persons ever investigated for loyalty since 1939, and it directed the attor-
> ney general to compile a list of all subversive groups and organizations.
> Further, the order established procedures for loyalty hearings which did
> not permit confrontation or cross-examination of witnesses nor disclo-
> sure to the accused of the sources of the evidence against him.[22]

The individuals, groups, and organizations against which the order was
directed were exhaustively defined as "totalitarian, fascist, communist or
subversive."[23] ADA liberals like Arthur Schlesinger understood the necessity of excluding those who adhered to "totalitarian political philosophies," but condemned the actual procedures as "shocking" and "inexcus-
ably defective."[24]

The Marshall Plan developed not only out of the Truman Doctrine, but
also out of the administration's growing sense of the misery of Europe in the
spring of 1947.[25] In an important speech before the Delta Council in Cleve-

land, Mississippi, on May 8, Undersecretary of State Dean Acheson suggested the sort of European recovery program now being contemplated by the administration. Such a program, he suggested, was

> merely common sense and sound practice. It is in keeping with the policy announced by President Truman in his special message to Congress. . . . Free peoples who are seeking to preserve their independence and democratic institutions and human freedoms against totalitarian pressures, either internal or external, will receive top priority for American reconstruction aid."[26]

After a slow start, the new administration policy found surprisingly ready, if not uniformly enthusiastic, acceptance by the center of the American political spectrum. The globalism of Truman Doctrine and its emphasis on military aid to regimes that might be politically unsavory were least popular, especially with the Wallaceite left wing of the Democratic Party and the isolationist Republican Right. The Marshall Plan generated much more general enthusiasm, although by the election of 1948, Wallace and the PCA had come to oppose that, too.

The Truman Doctrine, the Marshall Plan, and the aggressive anti-totalitarian rhetoric that accompanied them did indeed produce a striking change in Truman's popularity. According to the Gallup Poll, in January 1947, only 35 percent of Americans thought that Truman was handling his job well; by February, his approval rating stood at 48 percent; and by the latter part of the year, it had reached 60 percent.[27]

Much of the Old Left was unhappy, however. On March 14, Max Lerner wrote bitterly in *PM* that Truman did not seem to mind totalitarianism in (Nationalist) China or Portugal; it was only Soviet totalitarianism to which he objected. Henry Wallace repeatedly made the same point in the *New Republic,* and this argument would be heard over and over again on the Left for the next thirty years: By implication, the term *totalitarianism* was a way to distinguish between right-wing dictatorships that for reasons of convenience the United States should support and left-wing ones that were dangerous to American interests.[28]

Many American liberals agonized over whether to align themselves with the new Americans for Democratic Action, which supported the administration, or to stay with Wallace and the PCA in supporting a policy of greater accommodation toward the Soviet Union. It is not too much to say that the rhetoric of totalitarianism played the central role in swaying the uncommitted toward the administration's position: "Elmer Davis [radio commentator and former head of Office of War Information] expressed the equivocal attitude which many of them [the ADA leaders] felt. The Greek government was hopelessly reactionary,[29] he told his radio listeners, but . . . America, he had decided, could not avoid the responsibility of blocking totalitarian expansion."[30]

The hostility of the ADA toward Henry Wallace came to a climax during the election campaign of 1948, in which he was constantly linked to "totalitarianism." "In view of these grave consequences to the country and the world," ran the concluding report to the ADA convention in February 1948, "this convention appeals to liberals to reject the candidacy of Henry Wallace, recognizing that any success his movement may have will inevitably produce the worst reaction at home and the success of totalitarianism abroad."[31]

In 1948, too, Arthur Schlesinger, Jr., began his *Vital Center,* one of the manifestos of the Cold War Left, published the following year. The idea of totalitarianism is arguably the central concept in the book, although it is dealt with as an entity in only one chapter. Citing Thoreau, Kierkegaard, Dostoevsky, and Erich Fromm, Schlesinger evoked the loneliness and angst of the twentieth century, in terms that soon became the staple of college humanities courses. The influence of Erich Fromm's analysis of Nazism in *Escape from Freedom* was particularly striking:

> The totalitarian state, which has risen in specific response to this fear of freedom, is an invention of the twentieth century. It differs essentially from old-style dictatorship, which may be bloody and tyrannical but yet leaves intact most of the structure of society. Totalitarianism, on the contrary, pulverizes the social stucture, grinding all independent groups and diverse loyalities into a single amorphous mass. The sway of the totalitarian state is unlimited. This very fact is a source of its profound psychological appeal. On an economic level, it seeks to supply the answer to the incoherence and apparent uncontrollability of industrial society. On the political and psychological level, it holds out hope of allaying the gnawing anxieties; it offers institutional outlets for the impulses of sadism and masochism . . . against totalitarian certitude, free society can only offer modern man devoured by alienation and fallability.[32]

The *New Leader* was enthusiastic. According to Gus Tyler, although democracy lacked the "dynamic of the simple totalitarian appeal," we must realize that "freedom and security are not realizable by some single great act of Utopian creation but are to be found in the mature, measured, eternal struggle of men toward social and personal aims."[33] The hostility toward any revolutionary point of view could hardly be more explicit.

Among the most dramatic arenas of confrontation during the early years of the Cold War were international cultural events—celebrations of youth, literature, peace, cultural freedom. The Soviet side tried to promote peace and solidarity with Soviet policies, and the United States in particular celebrated the freedom to write and read without interference from the totalitarian state. One of the earliest of the many confrontations came on October 27, 1947. Melvin J. Lasky, then a bearded twenty-seven-year-old correspondent for the *New Leader* and the *Partisan Review,* created an uproar at the Russian-sponsored German Writers Congress in Berlin with "a slashing attack on totalitarianism's effects on freedom of culture." *Times* reporter Jack Raymond described how Lasky contrasted the democratic liberties enjoyed in the United States and the slavery of writers to party cultures in the totalitarian lands. Suddenly, the crowd realized that he was talking about the Soviet Union.

Anna Seghers, gray-haired German author of the novel "Seventh Cross" . . . left her seat in the front row and rushed out of the theatre auditorium to get Col. Alexander Dymschitz, editor of the Russian Army's Taegliche Rundschau. Other Communists gathered in groups for consultation. Meanwhile Mr. Lasky . . . related how during the war the publication of books such as Trotsky's biography of Stalin has been withheld because Washington officials felt that they might injure the unity of purpose of the Allies. Other books, he said, describing the Russian system of concentration camps and forced labor were also withheld. Happily, he continued, they were only detained and since have been published.

By this time the protests became heard and some of the Communists tried to shout Mr. Lasky down. Immediately there was an overpowering demand from the others that the American be heard just as the Russians has been the day before. . . . "The sympathies of American writers are allied with the German writers who suffered under Hitler and the Spanish writers under Franco," declared Mr. Lasky, "and no less with writers of the Soviet Union, because they, too, know how difficult it is to work behind a censor when behind the censor stands the police."

This last bit proved almost too much for the Communists and they set up frantic shouts. But the other Germans won out and Mr. Lasky concluded, after which he was congratulated by many in the audience.[34]

The Cold War continued to deepen in 1948 and 1949, with struggles between anti-Communists and those who would support or tolerate Communism in the American labor movement.[35] With the Communist coup of February 1948 in Czechoslovakia, belief in a Communist "blueprint" or "master plan" for world conquest grew.[36] The *New Leader* inveighed passionately against the "Slanskys [Slansky, a Czech Communist leader] all over the world" who were the "product and at the same time the motor of the Stalinization of the Third International. They represent the backbone of the totalitarian apparatus." One staffer prayed that "the Western world, properly organized under American leadership, will be strong enough not only to check, but to roll back the tide of totalitarian aggression which has as its ultimate objective the destruction of the mind and soul of western man."[37] Albion Ross, the *New York Times* correspondent in Prague, featured the term in virtually every story he sent out.[38] On February 24, the *Times* editorialized: "In 1938 Mr. Benes resigned as President and fled the country rather than turn it over to German totalitarianism. Now his country faces a similar threat of absorption by totalitarianism of the Russian variety."[39]

In 1948, the fear that totalitarianism would come farther west was very great. There was special anxiety about the Italian elections in mid-April. The

New York Times Magazine did a story entitled "Pattern for a Totalitarian State" on whether Italy "would choose eastern 'democracy,' " as exhibited in Yugoslavia.[40] Domestically, the Hiss and Rosenberg trials became the focal point for the passionate struggle over whether Communist spies were a genuine threat to national security, and those in the Truman administration who favored much greater American military preparedness began to gain the upper hand. If a totalitarian state were inevitably expansionist, as seemed clearly the case, a much larger military establishment would be necessary to "contain" it.[41]

Soon a more analytical (but still rhetorical) definition of totalitarianism began to emerge from Truman administration organizations, foreshadowing the efforts of political scientists and model builders in the 1950s and 1960s. On May 27, 1948, in the context of an article on the National Security Resources Board's newest anti-Communist program, board chairman Arthur M. Hill listed fifteen points of similarity between Communism and the "Nazi-Fascist" systems:

Abolition of the right to freedom of speech, press, assembly and religious worship.

Elimination of all political parties other than the ruling party.

Subordination of all economic and social life to the strict control of the single-party bureaucracy.

Suppression of individual initiative, and liquidation of free enterprise.

Destruction of all independent trade-unionism, and the creation of labor organizations completely servile to the totalitarian state.

Establishment of concentration camps, and use of slave labor on a vast scale.

Utter disregard for an independent judicial system, and creation of courts completely subject to the control of centralized political authority.

Glorification of a single leader, who is all-powerful and subject neither to criticism nor removal through the ballot.

Utilization of a special form of social demagogy—for example, incitement of race or class against class—elimination of all opposition and concentration of power into the hands of the ruling dictatorship.

Subordination of all economic and social life and the everyday needs of the population to the requirements of an expanding military machine seeking world conquest.

Reduction of parliamentary bodies to a rubber-stamp status, automatically approving all decisions of the one-party dictatorship.

Establishment of a system of nationwide espionage and secret police to which the entire population is subject.

Severance of social, cultural and economic contact between the people of the totalitarian states and those of other countries, through a rigorous press and radio censorship, travel and other personal restrictions.

Open disregard for the rights of other nations and the sanctity of treaties.

The maintenance and encouragement of fifth columns abroad.[42]

Someone interested in what in the future be called the totalitarian model might find this list of fifteen points somewhat sprawling. The subordination of "society" to the state and its organs, for example, could be more concisely described. Hill's fifteen points also embraced practices common to a variety of regimes, such as spying and disregard for the sanctity of treaties. Later models put greater emphasis on the necessity for such a regime to have an ideology to mobilize the masses; Hill merely mentioned "a special form of social demagogy." But his fifteen points stand out as one of the first efforts to list the salient characteristics of a totalitarian society.

The Truman administration continued its usage of the word *totalitarianism* into 1949 and 1950 in much the same way as it had since 1947. Administration spokesmen routinely used the rhetoric of totalitarianism in pressing the case for the North Atlantic Treaty Organization (NATO), which was signed into life on April 4, 1949. As Thomas E. Lifka wrote, "the argument that in the Soviet Union of 1949, the NATO allies faced a totalitarian menace similar in all ways to Hitler in 1939–1941 was by far the most common argument heard in support of the treaty."[43] On July 20, the *New York Times* reported that the president, in urging ratification of the North Atlantic Treaty as well as adequate appropriation for the Economic Recovery Program before the Senate, treated his audience to a

> non-partisan and almost philosophic discussion of the principles and motives of American foreign policy in a world menaced by totalitarian dictatorships. . . . In making this appeal, Mr. Truman put these measures within the framework of the conflict that dominates our age—the conflict between two concepts of world order. . . .
>
> This conflict, Mr. Truman declares, does not need to lead to war. On the contrary, he is confident that in the long run the principles of democracy will have a greater appeal to men's minds and hearts than the totalitarian principle of force.[44]

On July 21, 1949, the NATO treaty was ratified by the Senate.

———

IT IS HARD to overestimate the importance of the rhetoric of totalitarianism and the Nazi-Soviet comparison in the foreign policy of the Truman administration. By leaning hard on the terminology, by "putting himself at the head of the anti-totalitarian party," Truman was able to save his presidency and ensure that the Cold War would be waged under Democratic auspices. Senator Robert Taft on the Right and Wallace on the Left were routed; the Old Left was history. George Kennan objected to what he thought of as the militarization of his containment policy, but his was, as it was so often, a lonely voice. The creation of NATO and the rearmament of West Germany followed from the idea that the Soviet Union was an insatiable, expansionist, "totalitarian power."

The Korean War, as we shall see, revived the term, which had become a somewhat routinized and less frequent term of abuse by the middle of 1950. A few days after the North Korean invasion of South Korea had begun, Truman

> hotly denounced totalitarian movements . . . only a few hours after his historic pronouncement that the United States would resist the spread of communism in the Pacific area. Totalitarianism, he said, has "made a mockery of the forms of justice" in the countries "under the sway of tyranny" . . . their judges are prosecutors; their prosecutors are hangmen; their defense attorneys are puppets. . . .
>
> In those areas under their control, these totalitarian movements have swept away all restraints on their own power. They have subjected their own people to all the evils of tyranny, to kidnapping, torture, slavery, murder, without hope of redress or remedy.[45]

Despite the fascination with the vocabulary of totalitarianism among officials of the administration, it was intellectuals and writers who most lastingly established the term. And no book was of greater importance in establishing the idea of totalitarianism (and in giving it a visual dimension) than George Orwell's *Nineteen Eighty-Four*.

By the spring of 1946, George Orwell had begun the actual writing of his book. Two or three months earlier, he had produced a brief essay, "The Prevention of Literature," which shows how the themes of the novel were becoming more explicit in his mind.[46] He wrote of the stress on the machine-made quality of literature under totalitarianism, the loss of a sense of "absolute truth" or the existence of "facts," the necessity of changing one's opinions drastically on a moment's notice when the political line of the regime changed, and the necessity of maintaining two contradictory ideas simultaneously, which he described in *Nineteen Eighty-Four* as "doublethink." Orwell published the essay in the small-circulation radical journal *Polemic,* distinguished for its anti-Communism.

At about the same time (January 1946), Orwell had gotten hold of what was then still a rather little known book: the dystopian novel *We,* written in the 1920s by Evgenii Zamyatin, a Soviet novelist who soon thereafter received Stalin's permission to emigrate. Orwell's deep interest in *We* was obvious from the review of it he wrote for the British Labour newspaper, *Tribune*.

We influenced *Nineteen Eighty-Four* in numerous ways. It is obvious, for instance, that the torture/betrayal scene in *We* made a considerable impression on Orwell and no doubt played a role in Julia's and Winston Smith's mutual betrayal in *Nineteen Eighty-Four*. Summing up in his review, Orwell wrote: "It is this intuitive grasp of the irrational side of totalitarianism— human sacrifice, cruelty as an end in itself, the worship of a Leader who is credited with divine attributes—that makes Zamyatin's book superior to Huxley's [*Brave New World*]."[47]

Thoughts about totalitarianism were also evident in Orwell's much praised and much attacked essay "Politics and the English Language":

> Consider, for instance, some comfortable English professor defending Russian totalitarianism. He cannot say outright, "I believe in killing off your opponents when you can get good results by doing so." Probably, therefore, he will say something like this: "While freely conceding that the Soviet regime exhibits certain features which the humanitarian may be inclined to deplore, we must, I think, agree that a certain curtailment of the right to political opposition is an inevitable concomitant of transitional periods, and the rigors which the Russian people have been called upon to undergo have been amply justified in the sphere of concrete achievment." The inflated style is itself a kind of euphemism.[48]

Nineteen Eighty-Four was published simultaneously in the United States and the United Kingdom in June 1949. It has been constantly in print since its publication, translated into virtually every European and Asian language and must be one of the most widely read books in the history of the world.

The novel's enduring popularity would probably have surprised some of its earliest reviewers. Although *Nineteen Eighty-Four* was widely acclaimed as the most compelling novel of the year, many critics suspected that its appeal was very much to the present moment. Mark Schorer, for instance, reviewing it in the *New York Times,* described it as a work of "kinetic art," by which he meant

> that its greatness is only immediate, its power for us alone, now, in this generation, this decade, this year, that it is doomed to be the pawn of time. Nevertheless it is probable that no other work of this generation has made us desire freedom more earnestly or loathe tyranny with such fullness.[49]

It was precisely the novel's alleged timeliness in 1949 that provoked doubts about its durability. According to William Soskin in the *Saturday Review of Literature,* Orwell's novel

> escorts us so quietly, so directly and so dramatically from our own day to the fate which may be ours in the future, that the experience is a blood-

chilling one. . . . It is because he creates the totalitarian future in terms of passion and human feeling close to our own that his book has immense stature.[50]

James Hilton in the *New York Herald Tribune Book Review* was more succinct: "It is as timely as the label on a poison bottle."[51]

There is no question that Orwell aimed to provide a set of novelistic images, "pictures" of what life in a totalitarian society might be like, and he succeeded superbly. As a twelve-year-old, my efforts to understand the Cold War and what it was like in the Soviet world (and would be like everywhere if the Russians "won") began with Orwell's images of a totalitarian world; they were always the jumping-off place for my imagination and, it appeared, for those of many of my contemporaries as well. The bleak gray tableau of the Ministry of Truth blended in my mind with the equally gray photographs of men and women confined to barbed wire–enclosed camps that I saw on the streetcar, urging the American public to support Radio Free Europe.

As is well known, many conservative reviewers from that day to this have used *Nineteen Eighty-Four* to launch an attack not only on totalitarianism, but also on all forms of socialism. This upset Orwell, and a few months before the end of his life he wrote to Francis A. Henson of the United Auto Workers that

> my recent novel is NOT intended as an attack on socialism or on the British Labour Party (of which I am a supporter) but as a show-up of the perversions to which a centralised economy is liable and which have already been partly realised in Communism and Fascism. I do not believe that the kind of society I described necessarily *will* arrive, but I believe (allowing of course for the fact that the book is a satire) that something resembling it *could* arrive. I believe also that totalitarian ideas have taken root in the minds of intellectuals everywhere, and I have tried to draw these ideas out to their logical consequences. The scene of the book is laid in Britain in order to emphasise that the English-speaking races are not innately better than anyone else and that totalitarianism, *if not fought against,* could triumph anywhere.[52]

Despite this disclaimer, undoubtedly sincere, there is no question that *Nineteen Eighty-Four,* like so much other work produced by liberal or socialist antitotalitarians, benefited political conservatives as well as others. The John Birch Society used to sell the book, and its main office in Washington, D.C., at one time used 1 9 8 4 as the final digits of its telephone number.

The Marxist historian Isaac Deutscher was, in places, both unfair and inaccurate in "The Mysticism of Cruelty," his influential attack on Orwell, but he was surely right when he wrote in 1955:

> Few novels written in this generation have obtained a popularity as great as that of George Orwell's *1984.* Few, if any, have made a similar impact

on politics. The title of Orwell's book is a political by-word. The terms coined by him—"Newspeak," "Oldspeak," "Mutability of the Past," "Big Brother," "Ministry of Truth," "Thought Police," "Crimethink," "Doublethink," "Hate-Week," etc.—have entered the political vocabulary. Television and the cinema have familiarized many millions of viewers on both sides of the Atlantic with the menacing face of Big Brother and the nightmare of a supposedly communist Oceania. . . . As in no other book or document, the convulsive fear of communism, which has swept the West since the end of the Second World War, has been reflected and focused in *1984*.[53]

The argument over Orwell's larger meaning in the Cold War era and the struggle for his mantle and legacy have been a major argument of our times. Here we may merely emphasize, with William Lee Miller, what an important "part of the general postwar atmostphere" Orwell provided with *Nineteen Eighty-Four*.[54]

In the political, as opposed to the literary, realm, totalitarianism had already become routinized and more obviously sloganistic by the end of 1949. The idea of totalitarianism had played its most important journalistic role in linking Soviet Communism with Nazi Germany and, to a lesser extent, Fascist Italy. It had served to persuade, sometimes to bully, moderates and leftists into believing that Communism was a very bad thing at a time when Communism had enjoyed considerable acceptability in American intellectual circles.

But as Nazism and Italian Fascism receded into the past, the day-to-day political struggle against Communism had less need for the typology of totalitarianism. The events of the early Cold War had sufficiently alarmed Americans (and, to a much lesser extent, the British) about the Soviet Union that "Communism" could now stand by itself as something obviously evil, rather than as a radical political theory. Almost all of what had been intended by the term *totalitarian* seemed now clearly implied by the word *Communist*. So although the term continued to be used in American political discourse, for a time it no longer had the rhetorical novelty or shock value of the early postwar period, especially when applied strictly to the Soviet Union.[55] In addition, by 1949 the sense of an immediate Soviet threat to Western Europe had lessened, and there was even a certain amount of talk about how the United States and its allies were winning the Cold War, or at least its first round.

These changes are clearly visible in the reception of two influential anti-Soviet documents of the early 1950s: Whittaker Chambers's autobiography, *Witness,* and Igor Gouzenko's "novel," *Fall of a Titan*. The publication of the former in May 1952 was no small event. Over the weekend of May 24/25, readers of the *New York Times Book Review,* the *Saturday Review, Time, Newsweek,* and the *New York Herald Tribune* were assaulted by ten full-length articles about *Witness,* by such writers as John Dos Passos, Richard Nixon,

Irving Howe, and Arthur Schlesinger, Jr. The *Saturday Evening Post* paid $75,000 for the serial rights to *Witness,* which it excerpted for eight weeks. It was a Book-of-the-Month Club selection and among the ten best-selling books of 1952.[56] Nevertheless, the word *totalitarian* was rather rarely used, perhaps because *Witness* defined the antinomies of the book so clearly and specifically as "Communism" and "Christianity."[57]

A number of hostile reviewers, however, all of them on the Left, suggested that Chambers's own view of the world, utterly and crudely dualistic, self-confidently and rigidly moralistic, was akin to the totalitarian. This was the opinion of John Strachey.[58]

Elmer Davis took the same view, which he ascribed to the growing category of "communists and ex-sympathizers" who "continually abuse the patience of the vast majority which had sense enough never to be communists or sympathizers at all." Like Strachey, Davis believed that despite the 180-degree turn in their political opinions, the former Communists had clung to their belief in their own superiority and in the absolute rightness of what they currently believed. "They used to tell us that black was white, and damn us for doubting them. Now they admit that it is black; but then and now they insist that there is no such thing as gray." Davis described this mental attitude as "the mark of the *anima naturaliter totalitariana*." These ex-Communists, he argued, are totalitarian in their aptitude for self-deception, in their mission to convince the rest of the world of the rightness of their claim, and, most perniciously, in the "melancholy satisfaction" they derive "from the conviction that they are on the losing side." One can see here how the term was becoming domesticated, routine by the early 1950s. "One grows bored," Davis concluded.[59]

Many liberal journalists were also calling Senator Joseph McCarthy's activities "totalitarian." Marya Mannes, for example, decribed the Army–McCarthy hearings in the following terms:

> When you come right down to it, slowly, reluctantly, but inevitably, the real horror of these hearings has been in this: that the pattern of the protagonist was totalitarian. Senator Potter got closer to it than anyone when he said, "We have all been through a brainwashing here." For here were all the dread, familiar methods: the relentless, interminable breaking down of the witness; the repeated statements of unverified fact; the assumption of guilt without proof; the deliberate evasion of the basic issues; the constant diversionary moves to obscure them. Here were the totalitarian clichés, the inversions of communist labels: "Pentagon Politicians," "Fifth Amendment Communists," "Leftist Press."[60]

To many liberals there seemed a peculiar, even lip-smacking, appropriateness in pinning the "totalitarian" label on the senator from Wisconsin, but whatever the horrors of the McCarthy period and what the senator wrought, the term seems inappropriate.[61]

Igor Gouzenko's *Fall of a Titan,* a badly written, wooden novel of 629 pages, based loosely on the Canadian government's report on the "Gouzenko case," was the midsummer choice of the Book-of-the-Month Club in 1954. Although there was virtually no pretense that the book had any literary merit, the author's own past lent an aura of plausibility to the events he described. "When we are reading," wrote Ben Ray Redman in the *Saturday Review of Literature,* "we are constantly aware that the fiction which is passing under our eyes is solidly grounded in fact." He went on to hail the book as "an authoritative revelation of the human elements that animate the totalitarian power that has declared war on the non-Communist world."[62] The movie rights went for $100,000, a fairly large sum in those days.

By 1950, the term *totalitarianism* had become coin of the realm for official government publications. The struggle against "Communist totalitarian dictatorship," which "threatens to engulf and destroy all of the free peoples of the world," was the explicit justification for the passage of the Internal Security Act of 1950 (otherwise known as the McCarran Act), over a presidential veto, on September 22/23.[63] Furthermore, the text of the act itself was laced with references to "totalitarian dictatorship" and "Communist totalitarian dictatorship," especially in the preliminary Section 2, "Necessity for Legislation." There, a "worldwide Communist movement" was alleged, which through "treachery, deceit, infiltration into other groups, espionage, sabotage, terrorism and any other means deemed necessary" was attempting to realize such a "totalitarian dictatorship."

A few lines later, the system of government known as a "totalitarian dictatorship" was defined as having "a single political party, organized on a dictatorial basis, and by substantial identity between such a party and its policies and the government and governmental policies of the country in which it exists." The prose is not crystalline, but the meaning is discernible. In this and the following section, "Definitions", Soviet messianism is repetitively defined as the drive to set up other "totalitarian dictatorships" subordinate to the Soviet Union, and the definition of what constitutes a "totalitarian dictatorship" is repeated in slightly different language. Subsequently in the text, it is forbidden by law "knowingly to combine, conspire, or agree with any other person to perform any act which would substantially contribute to the establishment within the United States of a 'totalitarian dictatorship.' " Communists and anarchists and especially "totalitarians" are among the aliens specifically excluded from entering the United States.[64]

The *New York Times* account stressed how unwelcome the McCarran Act was to the State Department, which

is now squirming under the necessity of having to enforce a law it regards as highly difficult to administer as well as one that . . . complicates and even endangers the Government's relations with certain friendly powers [e.g., Argentina, Spain, and Yugoslavia].

The State Department will be required first of all . . . to devise a political spectrum of the governments of the world for the purpose of deciding what governments are totalitarian and what are not.

"To make the rules workable," one authority said, "we may have to broaden our concept of democracy and narrow our concept of totalitarianism." Under a dictionary definition of totalitarian, officials of several governments with whom the State Department hopes to keep on friendly terms would be barred from the United States, some in the Federal service argued.[65]

The term *totalitarianism,* earlier prized by politicians for its linking of Communism with Fascism, was to prove an embarrassment when it became embodied in legislative politics. Was Argentina under Perón "totalitarian"? Nobody could say for sure.[66] When improved relations with Franco Spain seemed desirable, the term *totalitarianism* had unpleasant associations; far better to stress anti-Communism.[67]

The breakup of the Communist monolith provided additional complexities. What did Yugoslavia's achievement of independence from Soviet "totalitarianism" say about the term's validity? What if the United States supported one "totalitarian state" (Yugoslavia) against another (the Soviet Union)?[68] Such difficulties had been scarcely imaginable a few short years ago, when the Truman Doctrine had been proclaimed. But they would not go away in the years ahead.

The routinization of the term *totalitarian* changed rather abruptly at the outbreak of the Korean War, when the Korean and Chinese emphasis on reeducation created a new sense of the weakness and vulnerability of the individual under a totalitarian government and a new sense of the ways in which totalitarian intrusiveness could exploit that weakness. A perception developed, however, that Chinese totalitarianism was especially terrible for its non-Western, "oriental" qualities. At almost the same time, historians and political scientists began to try to give this useful term greater precision, by both exploring its causes and antecedents and attempting to define it more rigorously.

FIVE

Brainwashing

Communist China as a Totalitarian State

Two principles must be observed. The first is, "punish the past to warn the future" and the second, "save men by curing their ills."

Mao Zedong

O N JUNE 25, 1950, the Congress for Cultural Freedom was constituted in Berlin to provide further organization and inspiration for the anti-Communist Left in Europe and the United States. It was a well-organized gathering of the Cold War Left, with a scattering of friends who were sliding farther to the Right. The principal organizer was Melvin Lasky, who had electrified anti-Communist intellectuals with his dramatic public opposition to the Communist organizers of the Berlin writers' conference some two and a half years earlier. Lasky, Sidney Hook, and others had been steaming for months over the way that Western Communists and Soviet sympathizers had again been using culture and creative people to build support for the Soviet side in the Cold War, through correspondence and meetings. Hook finally hit on the idea of reviving the organization that he had helped found to oppose Soviet influence in the cultural wars of the late 1930s.[1] Hook's Committee for Cultural Freedom would for a time become the American affiliate of the congress.[2]

The American intelligence community knew a good thing when it saw one. According to a recent, thorough investigation, the CIA funded the initial meeting in Berlin and within three years, through Lasky, was supporting the congress itself.[3] This was one of the most dramatic instances of a recurrent conflict for writers and intellectuals of the anti-Communist Left. The government, including the intelligence community, was often eager to work with them, but such an alliance could easily compromise their independence and make them appear the mirror image of the coerced and kept intellectuals on the Soviet side.

The explicit purpose of the congress's founders was to combat the idea that morally serious writers could be neutral in the Cold War. James Burnham,[4] Sidney Hook, and Arthur Koestler were the most extreme in their depiction of their own commitment to the West and their demand that others make the same. Soviet "totalitarianism" and American "materialism" (the basis for so much anti-American feeling, then and later) were not equivalent. This point of view was later revived by American neoconservatives in the late 1970s and 1980s to combat what they regarded as the creeping "equivalency" brought by the radical 1960s.

Present at the congress were many veterans of the struggle waged by the *Partisan Review* and the *New Leader,* along with such European anti-Communist stalwarts as Ernst Reuter, the socialist mayor of West Berlin; Franz Borkenau; David Rousset, a Frenchman who led the effort to publicize the Soviet labor camps; the English historian Hugh Trevor-Roper; the German philosopher Karl Jaspers; and many others.[5] The English seemed reluctant junior partners of the Americans (and even the Germans!); Hugh Trevor-Roper sniffed at the passionate anti-Communism of Koestler, Hook, and Borkenau and helped defeat their resolution excluding totalitarian sympathizers "from the Republic of the Spirit."[6]

From the standpoint of the rhetoric of totalitarianism, the congress provided no novelties, but some of the passion with which it denounced totalitarianism derived from North Korea's invasion of the south on the day that the congress convened. Rumors were rife that the Russians might "march in Germany," and many participants feared for their lives.[7]

The outbreak of the Korean War at approximately the same time as the rise of McCarthyism in the United States revitalized the use of the term *totalitarianism* and in particular the idea that it was more than a longer word for Soviet Communism. Vital to this new, post-1950 situation, of course, was the consolidation of the Chinese Revolution and the additional sense it provided of an increasingly dangerous and divided world.

At the outbreak of the Cold War in 1947, both the State Department and the American military tended toward the view that the Chinese Communists were both totalitarians and agents of the Soviet Union. As John Gaddis has pointed out, "the Joint Chiefs found it difficult to accept the view that significant differences could exist between the Chinese communists and the Russians."[8]

According to Admiral Charles M. Cooke, commander of U.S. naval forces in the western Pacific, the situation in mid-1947 should have been compared "to that of the 1930s, when Japanese aggression, beginning in Manchuria, eventually led to American involvement in a major war. 'Now once more political and ideological totalitarianism is on the march,' he declared, 'energized by the conviction of providential appointment to save the world.' "[9] By 1948, the American ambassador to China, John Leighton Stuart, regularly referred to the Communist Chinese as "totalitarian."[10]

But the fortunes of Nationalist China steadily declined through 1947 and 1948, and the exasperation of the State Department grew with the corruption and incompetence of the Chiang regime. It was therefore not surprising that discussion increased as to whether—and how—the Communist Chinese might be detached from the Soviet Union, a discussion connected with the growing realization that the Yugoslav breach with Moscow was real and serious. But after Mao Zedong made his famous statement that

> the Communists would "lean to one side" in favor of the Soviet Union, Acheson apprehensively instructed Ambassador-at-Large Philip Jessup on July 18, 1949, "to make absolutely certain that we are neglecting no opportunity that would be within our capabilities to achieve the purpose of halting the spread of totalitarian Communism in Asia."[11]

The appearance of the "China White Paper" in August provided fuel for further debate about the reasons for the Communist victory and increased the volume and frequency of the administration's antitotalitarian rhetoric.[12]

In the eighteen months between the final victory of the Chinese Communists and the outbreak of the Korean War, the Truman administration and its new secretary of state groped for a China policy.[13] The conservative China Lobby and its allied "China bloc" in Congress were passionate adherents of the Nationalists. They were sure that Mao would be totally subservient to Stalin, but the ability of this formless coalition to threaten the executive branch and its policies was not great before the outbreak of the Korean War and the rise of Senator McCarthy.

Most Americans were suspicious of Chiang Kai-shek and not interested in becoming actively involved in the struggle in China. Still, Republicans and conservatives were clearly disposed to criticize Roosevelt's and Truman's China policy. Vandenberg had made it known that his bipartisanship did not extend to East Asia (then known as the "Far East"). With the benefit of hindsight, one can see that the Republican battle cry that the Democrats "lost China" was not far off. For many China hands and journalists, however, the talk continued to be of Chinese Titoism and the likelihood of a "Sino-Soviet split."[14]

"The Sino-Soviet alliance of February 1950 reinforced the monolithic view of communism and sharpened and extended the cleavage set forth in the Truman Doctrine between the free and the totalitarian worlds."[15] At the same time, McCarthy had begun his drumfire of accusations that the China specialists who had advised the administration since the mid-1940s—Owen Lattimore, John Stewart Service, John Patton Davies—were either Communists or the dupes of Communists.[16]

American public opinion lagged behind. Foster Rhea Dulles, among many others, was struck by how remote China seemed to most Americans. The Truman administration repeatedly asserted that public attitudes toward Communist China were "vague and uncertain" (although hostile) and clearly hoped that the public would continue to accept the guidance of experts. Even so, the Truman Doctrine had clearly been effective in linking all Communism to Moscow. According to a Gallup Poll, five out of six Americans believed in mid-December 1949 that the Chinese revolutionaries "take their orders from Moscow."[17]

Among the policymakers and the activist minority with definite views, the conflicting currents swirled initially around the issue of diplomatic recognition, which was still unresolved at the time of the North Korean invasion, although those in favor were increasing their numbers and influence. The invasion changed all that. The other important issue was whether the United States should prevent Communist China from invading Taiwan and finishing off the Nationalists. Again, the outbreak of war changed American policy; the Seventh Fleet was immediately ordered into the Straits of Formosa to prevent an invasion from the mainland.

On July 9, 1950, a mere four days after United Nations ground forces commenced military action against the North Koreans, an American army officer of the Twenty-fourth Infantry Division "made a nine-hundred word broadcast in the enemy's behalf over the Seoul radio."[18] From then on, as described by a China-watching journalist,

> the free world began to hear strange reports from the Communist-operated prisoner of war camps in North Korea. Broadcasts were heard in voices recognized as those of normal young men of the American, British and other UN forces. The voices belonged to these men, but the language did not. Procommunist publications everywhere began to carry purported confessions and grotesquely worded statements said to have been signed by these soldiers in support of whatever propaganda appeal international communism was making at the moment.[19]

What was happening? An answer quickly emerged, which was taken up by interested journalists and then scholars: The soldiers were being subjected to invasive techniques of thought control that collectively came to be called brainwashing.[20]

The term was introduced to the English-language public by Edward Hunter in his 1951 book *Brainwashing in Red China*.[21] Hunter believed that the word was a translation from the Chinese *hsi-nao* (literally a "cleansing of the brain" or "mind"); he wrote that he had encountered the term repeatedly when interviewing Europeans who had been trapped in China in 1949. Eleutherius Winance, a French Roman Catholic missionary in China, was subjected to three years of "brainwashing" until his release in 1952. He claimed that the original term was *hsio-hsi,* which he translated as "to receive teaching and to put it into practice."[22]

Whatever its origins, the English term *brainwashing* quickly achieved notoriety because of its connection with the experience of Western prisoners of war in Korea and was increasingly broadly applied:

> The term became so popular and sounded so terrifying that people really thought that something very odd and frightening was going on and the

word was applied indiscriminately to the process of political indoctrination carried out by the Chinese on civilians, to Eastern European methods, and to those used by the Russians during, and presumably since, the purges of the 1930s.[23]

It was not long before the word began to lose its cultural specificity: Jokes about parents brainwashing their children began to be heard, and the reverse as well.[24] By 1961, Brian Inglis, in the British journal *Spectator,* could write seriously of the peculiar behavioral codes of the English public school and the brainwashing that perpetuated them.[25]

As the term became somewhat better understood in the United States and Europe, it lost some of the terror it originally inspired and became, in certain contexts, almost banal. It was clearly a form of indoctrination, a much less enigmatic and scary term, a particular form of twentieth-century thought control that, although in some ways specifically Chinese, could be plausibly related to broader Communist practice. It thus reinforced a key tenet of the theory of totalitarianism: the notion that one, perhaps the, central goal of the totalitarians was the holistic reshaping of the individual to conform with the ideology and practice of the totalitarian state. In the overheated atmosphere of the McCarthy period, the radicalism of Chinese practice rekindled people's horrified memories of the coerced confessions of the Soviet 1930s and of fictionalized accounts like Orwell's in *Nineteen Eighty-Four.*

Even so, the precise experiences that early became known as brainwashing were not well understood for several years. Most prisoners of war had been repatriated by the fall of 1953, and many of them offered explanatory accounts, but contradictory reports continuned to circulate. According to one rather sophisticated investigator, "the articles themselves were often conflicting: some mentioned the overpowering effects of physical torture;[26] others doggedly successful resistance to it; some stressed widespread American treachery, and others widespread American heroism."[27] Communist techniques of interrogation and indoctrination were mentioned in all this material, but no clear picture of what brainwashing really was emerged.

Over time, the question of Chinese indoctrination became less radical. Psychologists and sociologists pointed to certain similarities that it had not only with other forms of political indoctrination, but also with the imposition of values more generally, in particular with Western advertising. It became clear that people who had been brainwashed were not likely to be permanently changed, especially after they had spent some time in their former milieu.[28]

In more recent years, a view of brainwashing has emerged that treats it "as an extreme example of traditional conversion similar to Paul's experience"[29] and, more recently, comparable to "programming" and "deprogramming." By that time, however, the connection with totalitarianism or "totalism," as Robert J. Lifton and other influential scholars called the psychological dimension of "totalitarianism," had long since had its impact.[30]

A few years earlier, during the late 1940s when the term *totalitarianism* had reached its apogee of acceptance in the United States, the emphasis had fallen on those aspects of the term's meaning most directly associated with Western perceptions of the Soviet Union: its apparent dynamic expansionism, its dictatorial political system, its intolerance of any sort of pluralism, its ready resort to violence.

The renewal of the term in the 1950s restored greater significance to one of its central meanings: the Hegelian stress on "totality." The kind of extreme and sophisticated state-sponsored indoctrination encountered by the American POWs suggested—in a way that would have been readily recognizable to Giovanni Gentile—that the Chinese Communists were prepared for almost any quantity and quality of coercion in order to make the ideas of an individual mirror those of the Party and state, *become* them.

That these revelations came just after the revolutionary Chinese government had come to power was of further importance. The Chinese Communists were doing these things to their own people. In the global struggle now entering a new stage, they were equally willing to do them to Europeans and Americans. Brainwashing was, among other things, merely an export version of evolving Chinese domestic practice, and it was shocking to Americans that some of their boys had not been able to resist "totalitarian" pressures.[31] Hitherto, the victims of these techniques had been almost entirely Germans, Russians, Chinese, and East Europeans, and so it had been possible to fantasize that Americans would do much better. Their capitulation to their Chinese captors was thus an ominous sign.

It is important to understand that the Korean War in general and the experiences of American prisoners in North Korean and Chinese camps in particular were the first direct experience of ordinary Americans with the demonic world of totalitarianism. The struggle with the Soviet Union had actually been quite remote and abstract for them, productive of fantasy rather than anything approximating the actual experience of war. Many Western prisoners died on forced marches or were shot by the North Koreans before they even got to the Chinese-run camps.[32]

The Chinese commitment to achieve totality[33] implied, as Hannah Arendt wrote, that law and ethics are one and that success entailed the ability "to organize the infinite plurality and differentiation of human beings as if all of humanity were just one individual."[34] The domination of totality must be universal; "it must embrace the whole of life and society. It must determine all realms of individual and social existence."[35]

The Korean War experience also reinforced the idea that totalitarians were fanatic believers in an ideology comparable to a religion. "Totalitarianism," wrote Else Frenkel-Brunswik at the end of the war, "seems to create the illusion that merely embracing its ideology confers a kind of magical participation in the source of all power and thus provides absolute salvation and protection."[36] Perhaps most important of all, as Gentile had understood long ago and Orwell had recently reaffirmed, totalitarianism had to be accepted in the sense of being willed by all and internalized by all. "Totalitarianism is never content to rule by external means," observed Hannah Arendt. "Thanks to its peculiar ideology and the role assigned to it . . . totalitarianism has discovered a means of dominating and terrorizing human beings from within."[37]

"The Russian Communist contribution to thought reform is immediately apparent in much of the content and many of the forms of the process," Robert J. Lifton noted,

> the allegedly scientific Marxist-Leninist doctrine; the stress upon criticism, self-criticism, and confession as features of the ideological struggle; the organizational techniques of "democratic centralism"; the combination of utopian imagery and iron discipline; the demands for purity of belief and absolute obedience; and the practice of informing upon others in the service of the Party.[38]

In particular, the stress on coercion to achieve some kind of total unity between the views of the Party and those of recalcitrant individuals was certainly a common feature of the Stalinist forced confessions of the 1930s and the Chinese ones after 1949. "Chinese communist thought reform," psychologist Edgar Schein pointed out, "is a dramatic instance of the totalitarian passion for unanimity, both in the intensity with which it has been pursued and the wide range of participation which it has demanded."[39]

But there were also differences between Chinese and Russian practice. The Stalinist government in the 1930s aimed to extract confessions in order to "destroy their authors and remove them from society."[40] Perhaps more important, the ritual of confession criminalized, indeed demonized, dissent or opposition. Not only are the Party, its ideology, and tactics proved always to have been right, but it was demonstrated that an individual could be right only through the Party, for history provided no other way.

The sort of Chinese indoctrination that was called brainwashing, on the contrary, was generally an attempt "to cure the disease and save the man."[41] Lifton labeled the Chinese efforts "purist totalism," a real effort at conversion. There was, of course, ample emphasis on the importance of education and "correctness" in Confucian thought. There was also a tradition of self-cultivation that contained a self-critical component; this tradition clearly influenced such important Communist documents as Liu Shaoqui's "How to Be a Good Communist."[42] "In evolving their programs," wrote Lifton, the Chinese "have on a pragmatic, trial-and-error basis called forth their long-standing cultural emphasis and skill in the conduct and manipulation of personal relationships—combining these with their Marxist imports in what is probably the totalitarian expression of a national genius."[43] Lifton reported that Chinese indoctrinators often quoted a speech of Mao Zedong that seemed to capture both what was traditional and what was strikingly modern about Chinese Communist practice:

[O]ur object in exposing errors and criticizing shortcomings is like that of a doctor in curing a disease. The entire purpose is to save the person, not cure him to death. If a man has appendicitis, the doctor performs an operation and the man is saved. If a person who commits an error, no matter how great, does not bring his disease to an incurable state by concealing it and persisting in his error, and in addition if he is genuinely and honestly willing to be cured, willing to make corrections, we will welcome him so that his disease may be cured and he can become a good comrade. It is certainly not possible to solve the problem by one flurry of blows for the sake of a moment's satisfaction. We cannot adopt a brash attitude toward diseases of thought and politics, but must have an attitude of saving men by curing their diseases. This is the correct and effective method.[44]

The historian Benjamin Schwartz linked thought reform to what he regarded as Mao's tendency toward a "populist" interpretation of the path to socialism, as opposed to a strictly Marxist class interpretation. The key idea was that the entire people, even the "national bourgeoisie," rather than just the proletariat, could be "educated" to an acceptance of socialism. As Schwartz put it, "the whole 'people' can build socialism precisely because the whole people can be spiritually transformed by proper educational (and therapeutic) methods,"[45] which is close to Maurice Meisner's injunction to us to remember that for Mao, "history was determined by conscious human activity" rather than a more "orthodox" Marxist stress on the workings of historical laws. For Mao, "the most important factors in the making of history were how men thought and their willingness to engage in revolutionary action."[46]

Perhaps the best-known Chinese technique of persuasion was called "the Lenient Policy" in the West; it was well described by a British chaplain after his release from captivity.[47] The usual lecturer to the prisoners, a Commander Ding, greeted them with the reminder that they had been liberated. He told them that the Lenient Policy had not been invented for the Korean War, but was a policy "deeply rooted in our People's Army from the beginning." He knew, he said, that the Western soldiers believed in the Geneva Convention and the Red Cross, but they were "instruments of bourgeois idealism . . . impracticable to carry out . . . [and] used by the imperialists and capitalists to cover their evil plans." The Lenient Policy was sufficient for all the prisoners' real needs, as they would come to understand.

Since the prisoners had come to Korea as the "dupes of the Wall Street big shots" to fight their dirty war "for blood-soaked profits," it would be perfectly just for them to be killed as enemies of the peace-loving peoples of the world. But we, said Commander Ding, are going to "extend leniency toward you and help you."

The commander then told his captives that they were divided into four types of men: "righteous, progressive men who are self-consciously learning the truth . . . we shall shake their hands." Then there were the "semi-righteous men who are uncertain" and the "men who are easily influenced by the bad men," who "believe all the slanderous things" and "close their minds against the truth." Finally, there were the "bad men," the "real enemies of the people, the hired tools of the Wall Street warmongers, the absolute reactionaries." This last category might be treated very roughly indeed, with beatings, deprivation of food and water, torture, or long spells in solitary confinement.[48] To the British chaplain who heard this talk over and over again, it seemed to be "a kind of political system of salvation, parallel with the Christian one," a chance for the prisoner to learn the truth, be converted, and join the ranks of "the people."[49] Lifton agreed, calling thought reform "an agonizing drama of death and rebirth."[50] Sometimes whole camps were organized on the basis of whether the prisoners there were "reactionaries" (in those camps, little indoctrination was attempted) or "progressive."

Four basic types of meeting were designed to create this conversion: First was the "accusation meeting" or "grievance-telling meeting." Second was the "study meeting," in which the prisoners had to "correspond their subjective thoughts to objective facts," such as Marxist-Leninist theory or party directives. After that came the "thought-revealing meeting," at which everyone had to talk and expose his mental processes and at the end the leader would "provide the correct interpretation." Often the leader would specifically call for people's "bad thoughts" so that they could be criticized. A fourth, important type of meeting was the "criticism and self-criticism meeting," fundamentally concerned with the creation and group criticism of autobiographies. Criticism focused on a subtle blend of political correctness and good moral principles in such a way that the two came to seem synonomous.[51] Less important to the POWs than to the Chinese were the meetings in support of a "campaign," for example, "resist America—aid Korea."[52]

Much of the interrogation of the POWs, especially at the beginning, was conducted in solitary situations by a guard, an interrogator, and perhaps a translator. Often after the grueling interrogation was finished, the prisoner would be subjected to additional long hours of "help" from specially designated fellow prisoners back in his cell.[53] At the same time, news from the outside world—mail from home, newspapers, magazines, books—would be kept from him or cleverly manipulated.[54] The Chinese aimed, to the greatest degree possible, to replace the prisoner's "internal milieu" with their own, external milieu. People lost their bearings, lost track of who they were, and became willing not only to say but to *be* what their captors wished. The Lenient Policy may have been maximally effective when it was preceded by or interspersed with weeks or months of harsh interrogation accompanied by beatings and deprivations.[55]

In addition to the meetings, which were sometimes merely lectures, the "students" were required to fill out questionnaires and take examinations, answering such questions as "Why does the Soviet Union head the World Peace Camp?" or "Who is the unjust aggressor in Korea?"[56] If a "student" did not cooperate, not only he but his entire group could be made to suffer.[57] Autobiographical reports were often demanded and might be extensive. Some men wrote up to five hundred pages "about their lives, their family, their friends and their relationship with the Army."[58] Some valuable information of an indirect sort was undoubtedly gained by this method, which was also designed to fabricate a sense of guilt, a quality not native to Chinese elite culture.[59]

Almost certainly the Chinese believed that their indoctrination could produce conversion; this was the primary reason for the process. According to Albert Biderman, a social scientist who studied the POW experience for the U.S. Army: "[P]olitical indoctrination itself appears in large measure to have been an ultimate objective of the communists rather than one instrumental to a more remote purpose. Communism is a proselytizing movement and proselytizes assiduously whomever, wherever and however it can."[60]

In this connection the confession was important, and if the prisoner seemed insincere, his interrogators would often work on him, sometimes for months. Lifton plausibly remarked that "confession is as much a part of re-education as re-education is of confession. The officials demanded that their accusations become the prisoner's *self*-accusations . . . they required that he present himself in the evil image they had constructed for him."[61] The Presidential Advisory Committee on POWs declared in its report that the "political" schools in North Korea had been indoctrination facilities, being "part of a mass program to spread Marxian ideology and gain converts for international communism. The progressives were called upon to deliver lectures, write pamphlets and make propaganda broadcasts. Progressive leaders were sent among reactionary groups to harangue the men."[62]

The second and more instrumental purpose served by brainwashing was simply the isolation and control of the prisoners in the camp, preventing them from creating any sort of mutual solidarity. Every effort was made to keep prisoners from interacting in any but a wholly public sphere. It was difficult and dangerous to risk sharing subversive thoughts with other prisoners. To students of totalitarianism, this seemed a simple effort to replicate the larger "totalitarian" society among the prisoners. Lifton found the Chinese Communist prison "probably the most thoroughly controlled and manipulated group environment that has ever existed."[63]

Finally, the testimony of the prisoners against their own government was useful to the Chinese and the North Koreans in their struggle to get their version of events accepted, especially by the non-Western world. General William Dean observed in his account of his imprisonment that

these people were much more anxious to have me say what they wanted me to say than to extract any really new or useful information.[64] Pressure on me was greatest to agree to perfectly obvious falsities: that the U.S. was an aggressor; that we had exploited the people of South Korea or wished to do so.[65]

The fact is, of course, that the Chinese were able to gain some good propaganda mileage. They were able, for instance, to publish two books containing the "candid confessions of American POWs who professed to having been converted," and including such statements as "we should never have poked our noses in here. We had our own Civil War in the States and would have resented any other country interfering."[66]

Probably the most significant progaganda coup during the Korean War was the "germ-warfare campaign." Typhus had apparently been well controlled in Korea during the period of Japanese rule but, it has been argued, crossed the Yalu River with the Chinese People's Volunteer Army in 1951.[67] A small epidemic ensued, and on May 8, 1951, the North Korean foreign minister, Pak Hen Yen, alleged that the United States had deliberately spread smallpox germs in the country, and a Chinese spokeswoman soon echoed the charges.[68] Almost a year later, on February 2, 1952, Jacob Malik, the Soviet ambassador to the United Nations, accused the UN of using "toxic gases" spread by bullets.[69] On February 18, 1952, the charge was picked up and amplified by Radio Moscow. The United States was accused "of having poisoned wells in North Korea, of having spread typhus and smallpox viruses, and even of having sent lepers into the country."[70] Three days later, an even larger "worldwide" campaign began.[71] The Chinese, led by Chou En-lai, and the North Koreans added the air-drop of germ-carrying insects, snails, and disease-ridden rats into the country.[72] "The germ warfare thing was pretty big," recollected Morris Wills, one of the "turncoats" who originally decided to stay in China.[73]

On March 17, Secretary of State Dean Acheson stated "categorically and unequivocally" that the charges were entirely false. In a few days, the *New York Times* undertook to investigate them. On April 3, several scientists reported their findings. C. H. Curan, Chief Curator of Insects and Spiders at the American Museum of Natural History, reported that "pictures billed in the Chinese captions as deadly bugs dropped by the U.S. invaders, were distorted photographs of harmless insects, incapable of carrying disease." The bacteriologist René Dubos testified that "microscope pictures of bacteria—the Chinese said they were meningitis and gangrene germs let loose by the U.S.—were either fakes, photographs of utterly innocuous bacteria or meaningless blotches."[74]

Finally, in the first week of May 1952, two U.S. Air Force pilots, Lieutenants John Quinn and K. L. Enoch, who had been under interrogation since mid-January, broke and signed a confession of germ-warfare activity, given a "literary form and style" by Wilfred Burchett, an Australian Communist journalist reporting for *Ce soir* in North Korea. (He also did the screenplay for a major propaganda film exploiting the two men.) Eventually, thirty-eight U.S. Air Force POWs signed the confession extracted from Quinn and Enoch.[75] They were subject to a much more severe regime than "normal" POWs, far more like the interrogation of the "Old Bolsheviks" under Stalin than the Lenient Policy.[76]

Opinions differ on how effective the germ-warfare campaign actually was. Biderman described it as unsuccessful,[77] but others have disagreed. The

Soviet Union and the entire East bloc worked hard to publicize the charges; the Hungarian Red Cross, among scores of others, asked the UN to move against "the American Imperialists."[78] Exhibitions of bacteria and other alleged evidence were held in Communist capitals and were credited by a surprisingly large number of Western leftists, including Hewlett Johnson, the "Red Dean" of Canterbury.[79] Eventually, an "International Scientific Commission," which included a distinguished historian of Chinese medicine, Joseph Needham, found the charges against the United States to be accurate.[80]

A recent historian of the Korean War cited a State Department intelligence report asserting that the bacteriological-warfare campaign "represented the greatest single effort [up to that time] ever undertaken by the communists to discredit the United States."[81] A Yale professor guessed that "no less than half the world's political leaders and intellectuals believe this charge and consider the United States an outlaw power, capable of dread and stealthy attacks on civilians."[82]

The Communist press in France "whipped up a demonstration against the new NATO commander, General Matthew Ridgway, who was denounced as a 'microbe killer,' " and protest demonstrations in France, Holland, Belgium, Italy, and West Germany soon followed.[83] In Teheran, "communist youths shouting 'germ warfare' touched off a major riot that left twelve dead and two hundred and fifty wounded."[84] The American Communist Party joined the chorus.[85]

The experience of American prisoners of war in Korea profoundly affected the Americans at home. Some 10,000 Americans had been taken prisoner or had been under Communist control at least briefly. Almost 3,000 seem to have been killed almost immediately or ended in the missing-in-action category.[86] Of the 7,190 who remained, approximately one-third (2,730) died in Communist hands. Of the approximately 4,400 who survived, 192 were found "chargeable with serious offenses against comrades of the United States." Twenty-one refused repatriation, and another 40 or so "remained convinced communists."[87]

A much higher number of Americans had engaged in activities regarded as collaborationist to some degree, from writing propaganda for the enemy or informing, to such innocuous activities as broadcasting Christmas greetings home and allowing the enemy to appear in a "good" light.[88]

One careful student of the problem believed that "ten percent of the Army prisoners of war in Korea informed on fellow prisoners at least once during their internment."[89] Eventually, fourteen Americans were court-martialed, of whom eleven were convicted and three acquitted. All further action was dropped, at least partially because of a wave of public sympathy for, as Congressman William Wampler, a Republican from Virginia, put it, "mere country boys victimized by a shrewd propaganda in technique."[90]

A British historian recently wrote that

the shock of the discovery of the prisoners' plight placed Chinese conduct in a new, infinitely more disturbing light. Mao Tse Tung's China acquired a new, far more frightening and disturbing aspect. From this, arguably, its image in the West never recovered. Long after the Korean War receded into memory, the fear of "the Manchurian candidate" remained.[91]

An important indicator of how seriously this new manifestation of the totalitarian menace was considered in the aftermath of Korea is provided by the time and effort put into studying what happened to the POWs, trying to ascertain why their resistance had not been better (both British and Turkish troops resisted the Chinese far better than the Americans had) and how their treatment at the hands of such captors might better be resisted in the future.

A total of just under 4,500 prisoners were studied exhaustively. By far the largest group was repatriated in August and September 1953, under what was called Operation Big Switch. Army intelligence devised a seventy-seven-page battery of questions for each returnee and required a biographical statement as well. In addition, as the former prisoners made the return journey to the United States across the Pacific, well-drilled psychiatric teams interviewed each one for at least an hour and provided group therapy as well.

After these data had been received, Communist publications were analyzed, and radio broadcasts were monitored to try to ascertain whether the returnees had collaborated, how, and to what degree. Millions of pages of extensively cross-referenced files, accounts, explanations, accusations, and denials were produced. The returned Korean POWs became, for a time, one of the most extensively studied groups in United States history. The army was interested in whether individuals should be tried for treason, but the deeper rationale was to understand how Chinese totalitarianism worked—in particular, how it worked on Americans.[92]

Accounts by POWs themselves began with repatriation, but public interest and concern were evident from the early summer of 1955 and lasted for more than a year. Mass-circulation periodicals like the *Saturday Evening Post* and *Life* featured lengthy accounts by POWs who had confessed to germ-warfare charges, about how they had been tortured and brainwashed.[93] An air force colonel broke down at a news conference and claimed that he had been subjected to "persuasion that civilized people simply do not know about" in efforts to make him confess to spy charges.[94]

Editorials such as "Out of Bondage" were common in major newspapers, as were nervously supportive statements such as "it is recognized that the POW may be subjected to an extreme coercion beyond his ability to resist."[95] A *New York Times Magazine* piece revealed differences between the U.S. Army and U.S. Air Force with respect to what standard of resistance prisoners should be held (the army was tougher) and called American policy "shaken and divided."[96]

Captain Theodore Harris told a Senate subcommittee a tale of horrifying and diverse tortures (interspersed with episodes of "leniency") by which the Chinese had tried to induce him to confess to biological-warfare charges.[97] He also expressed a view that others, including the government, would endorse: that he knew absolutely nothing about Communism and would have been better able to withstand the pressure if he had.

Not all the accounts justified why their authors had confessed. Air Force Major David MacGehee told a lurid tale in *Collier's* about the various treatments to which he had been exposed in his almost three years in captivity— everything from the Lenient Policy to brutal beatings, solitary confinement, mock executions, and the tearing off of his fingernails and toenails. He lost some 122 pounds before he was thrown into a camp for incorrigibles[98] and ultimately repatriated, but he refused to confess to anything.[99]

In May 1955, the secretary of defense created the Defense Department Advisory Committee on Prisoners of War to study the whole POW question and recommend a policy.[100] After taking testimony from a variety of experts, on August 18 the committee published the results under the title *POW: The Fight Continues After the Battle.*[101] The overall experience of American GIs in Korea was reviewed, as was the history of prisoners of war, with a heavy emphasis on the recent, Communist phase. The committee sensibly concluded that the American prisoners would have been much better off if they had known more about their own society, as well as about Communist doctrine, as their ignorance of both had placed them more directly at the mercy of their interrogators and indoctrinators.[102]

Albert Biderman recalled that he

> heard a group of education officials place the blame for the "fiasco in Korea" at the door of McCarthyism in the United States. The schools were intimidated so that they could not teach "about communism," the educators contended, hence the prisoners were completely open to being taken in by the communists.[103]

Certainly it was not easy to teach about Marxism or Communism in American schools in the 1950s, and McCarthyism played a role in that. But McCarthy was a virtual unknown until a few months before the outbreak of the Korean War, so he surely cannot be saddled with the entire blame for American ignorance of Marxism.

A new, clarified, and simplified code of conduct for American soldiers also was issued.[104] It stressed the need to maintain leadership, to "keep faith" with one's fellow POWs and remain true to one's beliefs, not to inform or in any other way assist the enemy, not to attempt to escape, and so on. It concluded with the resounding declaration that "I will never forget that I am an American fighting man, responsible for my actions and dedicated to the principles which made my country free. I will trust in my God and in the United States of America."[105] To combat totalitarianism, it appeared, a nation must in some ways imitate it, indoctrinating its citizens in the image of a wholesome "American" totality.[106]

The *New York Times* was confident that the promulgation of the new code would end the national debate about brainwashing, but the issue continued to claim a good deal of public attention for several years longer. In the short run, some politicians and academics found it unrealistic to suggest that the mere promulgation of such a code would do much good.[107] They also questioned the newest government plan: opening a "torture school" in Nevada to prepare servicemen for what they might encounter in future wars with the Communist enemy.[108] In a few months, however, the British military was going through much the same process of self-questioning and debate.[109]

The whole "brainwashing episode," for which the overwhelming majority of Americans was quite unprepared, made a powerful impression on public opinion, suggesting to people in variously sophisticated ways that totalitarianism was at bottom the effort of a conspiratorial elite to achieve total control of the human individual. The popular idea of what the totalitarian menace fundamentally was shifted during the mid- and latter 1950s from institutions to the enslavement of the helpless individual psyche. It may be that this shift did not result solely from Chinese actions. David Riesman's *The Lonely Crowd,* Vance Packard's *The Hidden Persuaders,* and many other books were suggesting to Americans that hidden forces were attempting to control them, for their own sinister purposes. The individual was isolated and under siege. It is difficult to measure the extent of such fears or their boundaries, but they were very much part of the 1950s in the United States.

More analytical and professional students of China were clearly affected by the popular and governmental furor over brainwashing. Throughout the 1950s, journalists and scholars across the political spectrum, from liberal academics like John Fairbank of Harvard to conservatives sympathetic to the China lobby, used the language of totalitarianism to describe the political system and the system and the society of mainland China. With the Korean War as a backdrop for the first stage, and with Senator Joseph McCarthy pursuing liberal China experts for their earlier words about the Communists being merely "agrarian reformers," use of the totalitarian paradigm was convenient in multiple ways. "The totalitarian-China paradigm," Steven W. Mosher later wrote,

> was shared by correspondent and reader, layman and scholar, and even by those who had originally supported the Chinese Communists. To paraphrase [Harold] Isaacs, it became clear to even sympathetic Americans that "Chinese Communism" was not a significant modification of generic communism, at least in those areas which made it serve so well the purposes of bureaucratic totalitarianism.[110]

The earlier hopes that Mao might turn out to be a Chinese Tito and that there might in the future be a Sino-Soviet split now seemed wishful thinking, if not evidence that the writer might be "naive" or "soft on communism." "If there is anything recent arrivals from the mainland can agree on," wrote Henry R. Lieberman in the *New York Times*, "it is the fact that the communists have been able to establish an unusually tight control over China in an amazingly short time. The methods of the Chinese communists are totalitarian; their distant objective is Chinese collectivization."[111]

Walt Whitman Rostow was one of the first scholars to write about the new China using the category "totalitarian" extensively, although not systematically. Rostow told his readers that learning about Chinese totalitarianism would confirm what we already knew from studying the Soviet Union:

> The principal outlines of the pattern of the impact of Communist totalitarianism on human society are widely known to be about the same everywhere; and the Chinese Communists run generally true to form. . . . The phenomenon we confront [is that] a unified, confident, ambitious group of men deeply committed to the use of totalitarian techniques has mastered mainland China.[112]

The highly conservative Richard L. Walker reported that "refugees who streamed from China in late 1950 and during 1951 revealed that far more coercion had been applied during the seemingly welcome flush of the victory period than outside observers had realized, but in 1951 the totalitarian terror in China was manifest to everyone."

More cautious and academically respected scholars (and also those with greater sympathy for the Left) came to use the term *totalitarian* as well. "China's past and the Western example are both rich store houses," reflected John Fairbank, "but the selections made from them [by the Communists] add up to a totalitarianism which is something quite new in China's experience."[113] Benjamin Schwartz saw Mao's "overall vision" as that of a "totalitarian society by consent, so to speak," but he emphasized that "the authority of the state . . . remains supreme and the basic concept is still fundamentally totalitarian."[114] Arthur Wright struck an even more orthodox note in observing that "with modern techniques and instruments of coercion at its command, the Communist regime is seeking to impose a system that surpasses in its totality anything that China has experienced in the past."[115] And according to Roderick McFarquhar, then on the staff of the London *Daily Telegraph* and later a sinologist at Harvard,

> at no point in the development of Chinese Communist totalitarianism—past or present (and the author is tempted to add, future)—have economic factors been (or will they be) decisive. What has been decisive so far has been the Chinese leaders' partiality, primarily for political reasons, to the Stalinist form of totalitarianism.[116]

In addition to these well-modulated voices were some academics who were considerably more strident. Jost Meerlo, an instructor in psychiatry at Columbia, published a sensational attack on the Chinese brainwashers that he entitled *The Rape of the Mind*. He coined a new term, *menticide*, to describe what they had done, referring often to "the robotization of man" and the "womb state" in the modern world of "Totalitaria."[117]

In many cases, popular literature suggested the same thing. Pat Frank's 1951 novel *Hold Back the Night* portrayed the Korean War as a continuation of the World War II struggle against totalitarians who would enslave the world. The novel assumes that the victory over Japan and Germany was an incomplete one, that the Americans were continuing, in Korea, the long struggle against the forces of totalitarianism. According to one of his soldiers, a World War II veteran, "For us, for our generation, it might as well go on forever. But our generation has the duty. If we win, our children are going to live."[118] In *Hold Back the Night*, the North Koreans and Chinese are also mere surrogates for the Russians.

In LeSelle Gilman's *The Red Gate*, the Chinese Revolution has been sold out to the Russians. An old Chinese revolutionary denounces "the Comintern agents who try to dictate our policy" to his American prisoners:

I speak plainly of our Russian brothers and their spiritual allies. Surely you have seen them! You can't miss them if you step outside into the street. There seem to me more of them now than of my own people—at least in government offices and in every influential corner. I am speaking of Slavic scum lusting for power, arrogant chauvinists, gabbling of conquest. They slyly urge us to join their plans, and they divide us and rule. Under them there is no hope.[119]

Although American relations with Communist China remained in a deep freeze until well into the next decade, the excitement about brainwashing and the fear of Chinese totalitarianism gradually subsided after 1957. Americans did not want war with China and accordingly began, almost imperceptibly, to learn to live with the Communist leadership.

Books and articles on brainwashing continued to appear, but they became more analytical and in most cases more dispassionate. Eugene Kinkead's 1957 *New Yorker* article was dispassionate enough, but was subsequently criticized for uncritical acceptance of the assertions and statistics of various "experts," especially those of the U.S. Army.[120] A respected psychiatrist, Edgar H. Schein, who had been interested in brainwashing throughout the decade, synthesized eight years worth of research and published *Coercive Persuasion* in 1961.[121] Both Schein and Kinkead continued to use the term *totalitarianism*.

Another psychiatrist, Robert J. Lifton of Yale, also published his research in the same year. *Thought Reform and the Psychology of Totalism* was, if not the best book on the subject, certainly distinguished by its imagination and rigor and by the author's intellectual range, erudition, and attention to context. Unlike most Western students of brainwashing, Lifton interviewed both Chinese and a variety of Westerners: Germans, Italians, and French as well as Americans, priests and doctors as well as military personnel. He focused not merely on coercion; for him, "it was the combination of *external force or coercion* with an appeal to *inner enthusiasm through evangelistic exhortation* which gave thought reform its emotional scope and power."[122]

Later he wrote about "a cult of enthusiasm . . . [that] seems to have entered China from the outside, carried in on the ideological wings of Western nationalism, international Communism, and displaced Judeo-Christian demands for ecstatic repentance and histrionic remorse."[123] In Chinese "totalism," what was most "illiberal" in the Communist and Confucian traditions flowed together and combined.

Lifton's case studies of the ordeals of individual prisoners were sensitive, sober, and circumstantial—and therefore all the more devastating in their impact. His rendering of the prisoners' experiences tended powerfully to reinforce the conclusion that grew out of the American encounter with Chinese indoctrination in the 1950s: that the drive of totalitarians to control the individual was more a psychological than a political or an economic one.

This point was reinforced by Lifton's later book, *Revolutionary Immortality,*[124] in which he started from the premise that the evolution of Communist systems elsewhere, especially in the Soviet Union, "posed a severe threat to the totalistic vision of absolute subjugation of self to regime upon which the overall claim to revolutionary immortality had been built. . . . The very fruits of liberalization became, for Mao and certain other Chinese leaders, death-tainted threats to the immortal revolutionary vision."[125] The ensuing Cultural Revolution was at bottom a struggle to reassert a "confident relationship to history."[126] The principal means of doing so was what Lifton called "psychism," and extraordinary emphasis on revolutionary will and heroism, to overcome human limitation and the tyranny of technology. Proclaiming ideological purity and the necessity of force, Mao sought to reconcile his vision of a golden age of Communist purity in the past with a present and future of ceaseless revolutionary change.

The work of the Belgian art historian Pierre Ryckmans, who wrote under the name Simon Leys, is very different, but as translated into English had a considerable impact on American intellectuals' view of China in the latter 1970s and beyond. Ryckmans showed none of the cautious high seriousness common to even critical Western assessments of Communist China. Quoting frequently from well-known works of Orwell (*Nineteen Eighty-Four,* "Politics and the English Language"), Ryckmans straightforwardly and without apology referred to China under Mao as totalitarian.[127] Instead of struggling conscientiously and painfully to discover how Mao could have launched the Cultural Revolution, as Lifton had done, he dismissed it as "the magical hysteria of the Mao cult."[128]

Perhaps because of his erudition, his passion for the art of China, and his Belgian nationality, Ryckmans's use of totalitarianism as a fundamental approach to understanding China did not stir up a hornet's nest in the English-speaking world. In 1978, he returned to the fray with an essay castigating "old China hands," "Maoist adolescents," "timid sinologists," and others for refusing to describe China as totalitarian. Analyzing China without using the word, Ryckmans maintained, was like describing the Sahara without using the word *sand*. Associating himself with the Polish philosopher Leszek Kolakowski's definition of totalitarianism, Ryckmans described it as

> a political system where all social ties have been entirely replaced by state-imposed organization and where, consequently, all groups and all individuals are supposed to act only for goals which both are the goals of the state and were defined as such by the state. . . . [Such a system would] consist in the utter destruction of civil society, whereas the state and its organizational instruments are the only form of social life; all kinds of human activity—economic, intellectual, cultural—are allowed and ordered (the distinction between what is allowed and what is ordered tending to disappear) only to the extent of being at the service of state goals (again, as defined by the state). Every individual (including the rulers themselves) is considered the property of the state.[129]

We should point out here two innovations in the use of the term, both of which emerged in the 1970s: the stress on the *aspiration* of the state to totalitarianism, rather than its achievement, and the introduction of the term *civil society* as a shorthand indicator of what totalitarianism destroyed. We shall return to both of these themes.

But perhaps to the exasperation of Ryckmans, students of China have never cared as deeply about the idea of totalitarianism as a scholarly paradigm. They used it in the 1950s, but largely as an easy way of suggesting a Soviet comparison. Regardless of their political mood, sinologists have always cared more about studying China itself than they have about cross-cultural comparison, let alone ideal types.

The same cannot be said of the academic students of Germany and especially the Soviet Union, and it is to the rise and fall of their paradigmatic "totalitarian model" that we must turn, following an examination of the first Western attempts to ascertain how totalitarianism came into existence historically.

SIX

Searching for the Origins
of Totalitarianism

SOMETIME IN 1945, Hannah Arendt began to write the book that six years later was published as *The Origins of Totalitarianism*. Behind her decision to pull a number of her long-standing interests into a major study lay in part her increasing realization of the scale of the death camps and the radicality of Nazi intentions.[1] It is actually not easy to say when she began to "write" the book, since its themes were mostly those with which she had been occupied since the early 1930s. Much of her work on anti-Semitism and imperialism had been completed before 1946; her analysis of the nation-state really originated in the 1930s, as did the expression of her critical attitude toward the historical leaders (*notables*) of the Jewish community, beginning with the eighteenth-century court Jews. Her study of Proust and the post–World War I minority treaties, which dated back to her final, harried days in France at the very end of the 1930s, also found their way into the book.

Most of those who had earlier sought to understand the origins of totalitarianism had stressed that it was a twentieth-century evil, but Arendt thought of her book as a "frontal assault" on Europe's nineteenth century, the "bourgeois century," during which she believed the most fateful developments had taken place.[2] She experimented with various titles, most of them reflecting her preoccupation with racism, anti-Semitism, and especially imperialism. On occasion she called the book "A History of Totalitarianism," but in fact the theme of totalitarianism did not become central until the book was almost finished.

She did not set out to write any ordinary work of history. Rather, her aim was "to find out the main elements of Nazism, to trace them back and to discover the underlying real political problems . . . not to give answers but rather to prepare the ground."[3] At the outset, at least, Nazi Germany was the outcome that had to be explained. Apparently it was not until well into 1947 that it became clear to her that a study of the Russian experience would have to form a central part of the third section of her book.[4]

By 1948, Arendt had come to believe it was the systematic reliance on terror, institutionalized in the concentration camp, that linked Russia and Germany and made them both totalitarian: "All other differences between the institutions of democracy and totalitarian countries [she believed] can be shown to be secondary and side issues."[5] This being her definition, it was natural that she refused to consider Fascist Italy to be totalitarian, also pointing to the survival under Mussolini of the monarchy, the church, the army, and the economic elite in a fashion quite different from the situation in Nazi Germany or the Soviet Union.[6]

The manuscript of *The Origins* was completed in 1949, although the preface was not finished until shortly after the outbreak of the Korean War. The book appeared in 1951, just as brainwashing was becoming an important issue for the general public. Arendt focused the attention of scholars and intellectuals on totalitarianism in a profoundly historical way that was quite new.[7] No book available in English attempted to analyze the long-term fault lines in European history that had produced totalitarianism, despite the vague consensus that it was tied up with the development of nationalism, technology, and perhaps racism.[8]

Nor was Arendt's primary context the Cold War, as it was for most of the subsequent scholarly literature on totalitarianism. Instead, she participated in considerably broader debates—about the rise of "mass society," the loneliness of crowds, anomie, and the fanaticism of the marginalized. Students of contemporary society, who had learned from José Ortega y Gasset and more recently Talcott Parsons and David Riesman (whose *Lonely Crowd* was finished at roughly the same time),[9] were often struck by the way that Arendt related totalitarianism to mass society and to modernity itself.[10] It was at least theoretically easier to incorporate the Soviet Union into this kind of analysis relatively late in the day.

Arendt's friends and associates tended not to be university professors and certainly not card-carrying cold warriors.[11] Her university education had led her deep into the study of the phenomenology of Husserl and Heidegger, whom she had known, Heidegger extremely well. In the United States, apart from her base among German-speaking émigrés, her friends tended to be such writers and "New York intellectuals" as the poet Randall Jarrell and the critics Alfred Kazin and Dwight Macdonald, the last of whom was passionately interested both in mass society and culture and totalitarianism.

For Arendt, the rise of totalitarianism was preeminently the story of breakdown: of the nation-state, the class system, the political parties. The roots of this breakdown were in the nineteenth century; it was largely accomplished in the twentieth; and its most terrifying fruits were the totalitarian regimes of Germany and the Soviet Union.

The development in the nineteenth century of what Arendt referred to, rather obscurely, as the "mob," prefigured the creation of the "modern masses," although the two were quite distinct.[12] The former were déclassé individuals, "both rootless and ruthless and particularly available for criminal activity."[13] The masses, by contrast, were much larger numbers of people, produced overwhelmingly by World War I, who "do not have common interests to bind them together nor any kind of common 'consent' which, according to Cicero, constitutes *inter-est,* that which is between men, ranging all the way from material to spiritual to other matters."[14] The intellectual historian Philip Rieff interpreted her view as meaning that "man emancipated from his particularity becomes not human but demonic."[15] Without a concrete world of interests, such people find it easy to identify with nebulous entities such as race.

The lack of common interests among modern "mass men" and their related lack of the capacity to "act together in pursuit of a common concern," maintained Arendt, contributed to mass loneliness and isolation, its social analogue. And "isolation may be the beginning of terror; it certainly is its most fertile ground; it always is its result."[16] Arendt thus approached totalitarianism through its existential underpinnings, rather than as a traditional political philosopher might have. And as Margaret Canovan shrewdly observed, Arendt "differs [from other analysts] in placing much less emphasis on the influence of ideas, and much more on the establishment of *practices* that were not totalitarian themselves, but that totalitarians could draw on."[17]

The unrestrained working of the capitalist system before World War I led to what Arendt regarded (as Lenin and Rosa Luxemburg also did, but in different ways) as the breakdown of the nation-state, with its commitment to a real politics and to the rule of law, in favor of a world of total economic competition. But how such a development, if it really took place, led to totalitarianism is not at all clear. Arendt repeatedly counterposd the bourgeois, whom she despised, to the "citizen," whom she revered as the person concerned with public affairs "as the affairs of all."[18] The citizen lives in the nation, whose viability was destroyed by the "emancipation" of the bourgeoisie from its constraints. But as an astute observer noted,

> [Arendt's] basic paradigm of the nation-state is post-revolutionary France; what is by no means clear, however, is what other states would count as nation-states in her sense. She writes about the downfall of the nation-state in terms that might give one the impression that Europe had consisted of such states until the coming of imperialism. When one considers, however, that most of Europe, and particularly the German and Austro-Hungarian parts of it, with which she is most concerned, had belonged to states that could not possibly be thought of as national, it is difficult to tell what she is talking about.[19]

Similarly, traditional social classes "lost their specific class interests by involving themselves in the bourgeoisie's capitalistic ventures—expansion for expansion's sake, profit for profit's sake, power for power's sake"—and eventually "the classes crumbled."[20] The nineteenth-century "mob" was the by-product of capitalism, the underworld of the bourgeois class, and paro-

died its "emancipation" from the moral law, its readiness to sacrifice everything for power. The stage for totalitarianism was set.

But of course, not all parts of this decayed world produced totalitarian
leaders or states. Nineteenth-century imperialism, in connection with racism, helped form the ideological roots of totalitarianism, which played an
important role in the emergence of these horrible regimes.[21] In making this
assertion, Arendt relied on literary sources, such as Joseph Conrad's novel,
Heart of Darkness, rather than on evidence that could be more readily as-
sessed by scholars.[22] In so doing, she wanted to elucidate

> the experience of uprooted Europeans finding themselves at the other
> side of the world among strange, and, in Africa, primitive peoples. There
> they realized that their conventional ideas of what it is reasonable or sane
> to do *were* conventional and that there are no limits other than conven-
> tion to what it is possible to do.[23]

Arendt here meant to link the ease with which whites killed Africans, seeming to lack stable institutions and to be close to the natural world, with the
way that the victims of Nazism were later stripped of their citizenship and
killed.

Pan-Germanism and Pan-Slavism, Arendt believed, provided the ideological roots of the two real totalitarianisms of the twentieth century. These
"tribal nationalisms," for which people were either "ours" or "not-ours,"
flourished "when superfluous capital and superfluous people were put in the
service of national expansion."[24] Arendt believed that the type of person
who in England went out to Africa on imperialist ventures stayed home in
the Russian- and German-speaking worlds and joined one of the pan movements.[25] The ultimate horror was achieved when leaders from the mob or
the déclassé masses without real, concrete class interest mobilized their followers on the basis of extravagant, totalitarian ideologies.

Although she described events in the nineteenth century that she regarded as fateful, Arendt did not really make clear how such terrible and
extraordinary things had happened. Out of her interest in Nietzsche, perhaps, came her belief that the totalitarian elites found it necessary to change
human nature and in this way to make the world over into something with
an insane and total consistency, to "eliminate every competing nontotalitarian reality."[26] They refused existing reality and set about to remake the
world "*with an absolute lack of restraint.*"[27] They could be safe only when men
and women had lost what was distinctively human about them and had been
reduced to being merely a part of the natural world, "deprived of freedom
and individuality."[28]

Because totalitarianism aspired thus to change human nature, through
the terror and coercion of the concentration camp, it could not rest, Arendt
believed, until it had achieved this goal worldwide. Unquestionably this
belief, which she so powerfully expressed, contributed in the 1950s to the
demonization not only of Germany but also of the Soviet Union, as did her

evocation of a vague but theological notion of the "radical evil" allegedly displayed by totalitarian regimes (but first manifested by the European bourgeoisie in the nineteenth century).[29]

Observers quickly noted that Arendt knew far more about Germany than about the Soviet Union and that there was an imbalance in the book: In many passages, the discussion of the Soviet Union appeared to have been mechanically made similar to that of Germany, as if it had been later inserted for symmetry's sake.[30] For example, Pan-Slavism was not a real parallel of Pan-Germanism, and the nineteenth-century Russian intelligentsia was not Pan-Slavic "with only a few exceptions," as Arendt asserted.[31] "We are suddenly confronted with Soviet communism as the totalitarian equivalent of Nazism," wrote H. Stuart Hughes in the *Nation*, "without any adequate account of how it got to be that way."[32]

A complexly related difficulty lay in the enormous stress on the history of anti-Semitism, which although fascinating, was idiosyncratic and far more relevant to German history than to Russian. Arendt's historical criticism of the leadership of European Jewry, beginning with the court Jews of the eighteenth and early nineteenth century, derived from her earlier work and achieved its own explosive conclusion with the publication of her *Eichmann in Jerusalem* a few years later. In addition, although she brilliantly and idiosyncratically chronicled anti-Semitism, she essentially left economic issues untouched.[33]

Arendt's book was generally received with enthusiasm. Phrases like "densely imaginative," "truly serious," and "seminal" abounded. Yet there was an undercurrent of unease and even incomprehension in many of the reviews, even the most enthusiastic. The long chains of linked ideas that yet did not seem to claim any ordinary causality bewildered some reviewers. What in fact was the connection between the court Jews of the eighteenth century and Stalin's totalitarianism? The sociologist David Riesman, in a characteristic review, praised the book extravagantly, but at the same time noted that it "skates daringly over documentary gaps." He found the connection between the British bureaucracy in nineteenth-century South Africa and twentieth-century totalitarianism "slim indeed," but he also found the book unduly deterministic.[34] It is striking how often it inspired reviewers to write long and highly subjective essays on the character of the times, rather than any serious analysis of the text.

Philip Rieff believed *The Origins of Totalitarianism* to be "covert theology," something comparable to Oswald Spengler's *Decline of the West*, not history, but "a vast spiritualization of history." He hailed it admiringly but perhaps a bit ironically as introducing a new vocabulary and set of concepts that would keep the intelligentsia occupied with creative discussion for some time to come.[35] A later commentator, despite her admiration for Arendt as a political philosopher, wrote that "her whole technique [in *The Origins of Totalitarianism*] is a social scientist's nightmare."[36]

The émigré political philosopher Eric Voegelin spoke for others, both in the United States and especially in the German-speaking world, who believed that Arendt was not theologian enough. Voegelin, like other religiously minded thinkers, rooted totalitarianism ultimately in secularism. He agreed with Arendt that the effort to change human nature was the essential aspect of totalitarianism. But he believed it to be finally a secularized version of the Christian idea of redemption, distorted by medieval immanentist heresy and Enlightenment ideas of social transformation.[37]

Arendt herself recognized that her indictment was oriented to the Nazi outcome of its pan-European roots; something different was required to explain totalitarianism in the Soviet Union. So she undertook a project, for which she received a Guggenheim Fellowship, to investigate the roots of totalitarianism in Marx's philosophical and economic doctrines. She never concluded it, but her investigations of Marx as simultaneously the inheritor of the Western philosophical tradition and a rebel against it led her to what many scholars regard as her masterpiece, *The Human Condition*.[38]

There is a particular risk in trying to sum up such an incomplete project, but one may at least note some of the factors that Arendt believed involved Marx's doctrines with the rise of totalitarianism. At no time did she blame Marx for "causing" totalitarianism, but she did find elements in his thought that suggested aspects of modernity connected to the growth of totalitarianism. Perhaps most basically, she faulted Marx for the necessitarian dimension of his thought, specifically for submerging human freedom in a "collective life process."[39] At the same time, Marx suggested that if one understood historical necessity properly and acted according to its dictates, "everything was possible." It was this combination that created a doctrine that could be employed by totalitarians. Both capitalism and socialism in the late nineteenth and early twentieth centuries subordinated human beings to a worldwide and uncontrollable process of production and consumption that could not be resisted. Marx's socialism suggested that history would end with human beings experiencing life "as a single entity with a collective 'species life.' "[40] Human beings would then be reduced to "a conformist herd of laborers" with only material preoccupations. Other concerns that Arendt had about Marxism were Marx's devaluation of law and government, his "emancipation of thought from experience," and the determinism of his system, which tried to persuade people that even though they had no power of independent action, the future was utopian, predictable, and impossible to resist.[41]

A few months after *The Origins of Totalitarianism* was published, there appeared, with far less fanfare, another history book that would significantly shape the long-term debate over how totalitarianism happened. *The Origins of Totalitarian Democracy*[42] was the work of Jacob Talmon, a then obscure Israeli professor, trained partially in England. He, too, was setting out to explain the horrifying events of his time, but his intellectual focus was not initially on Nazi Germany but on Soviet politics and ideology, which he believed were derived from the Enlightenment. What turned out to be his lifelong project originated, he later explained, in an undergraduate seminar on the Jacobin terrorist dictatorship in France that he took as the Moscow trials were reaching a climax in 1938. It was there that he first apprehended the Jacobin–Bolshevik connection.[43]

Jacob Talmon was a passionate devotee of Alexis de Tocqueville, and he regarded his own effort to understand the revolutionary messianisms of the mid-twentieth century as an extension of Tocqueville's quest to explicate the threat of "democratic despotism" as it had appeared in the post–French Revolutionary world.[44] In *The Ancien Régime and the French Revolution,* Tocqueville wrote that

> no previous political upheaval, however violent, had aroused such pas-
> sionate enthusiasm, for the ideal the French Revolution set before it was
> not merely a change in the French social system but nothing short of a
> regeneration of the whole human race. It created an atmosphere of mis-
> sionary fervour and, indeed, assumed all the aspects of a religious re-
> vival. . . . It would perhaps be truer to say that it developed into a species
> of religion, if a singularly imperfect one. . . . Nevertheless, this strange
> religion has, like Islam, overrun the whole world with its apostles, mili-
> tants and martyrs.[45]

Clearly Talmon saw a similar phenomenon coming to maturity in his own time, an even more dreadful maturity than Tocqueville had imagined.

Central to Talmon's investigations was the division between totalitarian-ism of the Right and of the Left. Totalitarianism of the Right, about which he said very little in his first volume, took as its starting point "the collective entity, the State, the nation or the race," as opposed to the individual. And although both may use coercion, he observed, totalitarians of the Left "pro-claim . . . the essential goodness and perfectibility of human nature," and their opposite numbers on the Right declare "man to be weak and corrupt." The term *democracy* may therefore be used of totalitarians of the Left, but not of the Right.[46]

In beginning his project, which resulted in three very large volumes, Talmon asserted that "totalitarian democracy has its roots in the common stock of eighteenth-century ideas."[47] The Enlightenment, he believed, had produced two distinct kinds of democratic thinking. There was a liberal one that assumed politics to be a matter of trial and error and political systems as "pragmatic contrivances of human ingenuity and spontaneity." There was also a "totalitarian democratic school . . . based upon the assumption of a sole and exclusive truth in politics." Talmon called this school "political messianism, in the sense that it postulates a preordained, harmonious and perfect scheme of things to which men are irresistibly driven, and at which they are bound to arrive."[48] To Talmon, this political messianism, moving from the ideas of the *philosophes* through Jacobin and Babouvist politics to twentieth-century radicalism, was the driving force behind the creation of Soviet Communism and provided the principal support for the Russian Revolution among intellectuals. It has some similarity to Hannah Arendt's conviction that totalitarian elites were driven to remake the world no matter what the cost.

Anticipating that he might be criticized for asserting the influence of messianism before it had even developed intellectual and political content, Talmon rather defiantly proclaimed that

> he was concerned with a state of mind, a way of feeling, a disposition, a pattern of mental, emotional and behavioristic elements, best compared to the set of attitudes engendered by a religion. Whatever may be said about the significance of the economic or other factors in the shaping of beliefs, it can hardly be denied that the all-embracing attitudes of this kind, once crystallized, are the real substance of history.[49]

The first section of Talmon's book is devoted to a discussion of the ideas and to some considerable extent the temperament of certain *philosophes;* Talmon laid great stress on their social maladjustment and found several of them "paranoiac."[50] The suggestion was unmistakable that bad ideas might derive in part from the experience of people who were misfits, an idea more commonly held in less academic circles than those frequented by Talmon. He spent some time discussing *philosophes* like Helvétius, Holbach, Morelly, and Mably, but he concentrated on the ideas and biography of Jean-Jacques Rousseau.

In his discussion of Rousseau, Talmon emphasized the "general will." In Rousseau's scheme of things, this concept expressed the sovereignty and the will of the political community but could yet be distinguished from the "will of all," which was merely the sum of the individual wills of the members. The general will existed "whether willed or not willed by anybody. To become a reality it must be willed by the people. If the people does not will it, it must be made to will it, for the general will is latent in the people's will."[51] In other words, there was a difference between what most people in a polity might appear to want and what a legislator, embodying or claiming to embody the general will, might tell them they *must* want. People could be forced to be free. For Talmon, this situation, as put into political practice by the Jacobins, was the prototype of later developments in which Lenin, for example, might formulate what the proletariat must want, regardless of any voting that might (or might not) take place. In the final two sections of the book, Talmon discussed how the Jacobins, Robespierre in particular, and the followers of Babeuf made Rousseau's key ideas the basis of their policies.

The Origins of Totalitarian Democracy did not have anything like the public impact of Arendt's *The Origins of Totalitarianism*. It did not speak directly about the present, nor did it deal with such exciting topics as racism and imperialism. The New York intellectuals hardly noticed it at all,[52] but the reviewers were respectful. Crane Brinton of Harvard University wrote (somewhat undiscriminatingly) in the *New York Times* how he had seen

> all the essentials of the Marxist-Leninism-Stalinism [*sic!*] appear back in 1796: class struggle, role of the enlightened vanguard or elite, ambivalent

attitude of contempt for and ultimate trust in the masses, a chosen people of the revolution that need to be protected from foreign corruption by an iron curtain, dictatorship of the proletariat, withering away of the state and all the rest.[53]

Within a few years, however, Talmon's view of Rousseau as an important precursor of totalitarianism did penetrate academia. F. C. Greene of the University of Edinburgh, in a new study of Rousseau, argued that Rousseau had "conceived the formula for a process of judicial murder which with various refinements was destined to form the basis of the twentieth-century totalitarian State." His reviewer, in repeating this sweeping statement, mentioned Talmon respectfully.[54] John W. Chapman, a professor at Smith College, whose Ph.D. was from Columbia, published an entire monograph on the question of whether Rousseau was totalitarian. Although Chapman conceded parts of Talmon's argument, he maintained that Talmon was in error when he claimed that Rousseau's legislator was a "charismatic leader through whom the general will may be expressed. Expression of the general will requires both group effort and individual integrity and is based on a process of dynamic interaction."[55]

By the time Talmon was well into the second volume of his monumental trilogy, *Political Messianism: The Romantic Phase,*[56] it was also clear that he had blended his Tocquevillian critique of democratic despotism with a practical anti-ideological conservatism akin to that of Edmund Burke. In a revealing essay written for *Commentary*[57] Talmon criticized "reason alone" as a guide to political action because it led to "utopian blueprints." Human beings need, he argued, to take account of habit, tradition, and prejudice. He was nostalgic for lost religious faith and especially for original sin, in which he seemed not to believe, but whose disappearance had made the rise of utopian thinking possible, "since it encouraged appetites that could never be satisfied."

"Men had been taught that they had a right to happiness forthwith," he wrote disapprovingly, "and a series of great technological discoveries seemed [by the mid-nineteenth century] to have created instruments to ease man's toil and to satisfy his needs, while industrial organization and division of labor appeared to foreshadow a high degree of social cohesion." But the industrial revolution initially produced social misery instead, and the resulting disappointment led to the creation of a revolutionary movement. The intellectuals who composed it were, according to Talmon, "utterly restless"; they were fodder for demagogues and dictators; and they soon had resort to "totalitarian coercion." For the revolutionary movements of Europe, with few exceptions, had taken over Rousseau's "utopian blueprints" and were not content with piecemeal progress. As ideologues rooted in "totalitarian democracy," they could not realize that "reason" never commands universal assent. Therefore, "if you expect unanimity, there is ultimately no escape from dictatorship. The individual must either be forced to agree, or his agreement must be engineered by some kind of fake plebiscite, or he must be treated as an outlaw, or traitor, or counter-revolutionary subversive, or whatever you will."[58] In conclusion, Talmon reemphasized his distinction between modern revolution, which meant "a sustained and violent effort to make all things new," and the sort of piece-meal reform that he could accept.[59]

Talmon's second volume, *Political Messianism: The Romantic Phase,* appeared in 1960. In it, he continued the story of the march of totalitarian democracy through Saint-Simon and his disciples, through Fourier to Marx; he now employed the term *political messianism* as providing even greater breadth than *totalitarian democracy* but amounting to the same thing.[60] But the most important development in *Political Messianism* was that in the course of writing it, Talmon concluded that he could integrate the totalitarianism of the Right, Fascist Italy and especially Nazi Germany, with the totalitarianism of the Left, which he had originally set out to study. The bridge was provided by nationalism.

After 1848, according to Talmon, the original totalitarian democratic idea—blocked in Western Europe by material progress and the lessening of class antagonisms—"wandered eastwards," following the pattern of previous religious movements, which were not accepted in the land of their begetters but achieved dominion over vast continents elsewhere.[61] Nationalism, wrote Talmon, replaced "the promise of universal regeneration by the pledge of happiness or greatness to the tribe." What Talmon called "bastard messianism" made "nationalist fury and social resentment converge upon the same target, the Jews, who were held to embody both . . . a national enemy and a cosmopolitan exploiter." And under the Nazis, "the mysterious uniqueness of the Nordic race took the place of the Absolute of Political Messianism—the rational pattern at the end of the days."[62]

Following the publication of *Political Messianism,* Talmon received more criticism than previously, and his reviewers, whether they were historians, political scientists, or philosophers, were more often concerned with his method and less impressed with the vistas he displayed to his readers. It may be the case that because the guiding principle of his work was so straightforward and insistent, the actual working out of the story became less interesting to readers.[63] And by 1960, academic criticism of the whole idea of totalitarianism was beginning to develop.

The young philosopher Charles Taylor wrote rather critically in England's *New Statesman and Nation* that Talmon did not treat the socialist diagnoses of social ills as "actual," but merely as a psychological response to the "inevitable stresses of the Open Society." He extensively discussed the industrial revolution and the enormous dislocations it caused, but merely as background.[64]

In the same year, a well-established British historian of France, Alfred Cobban, published a general interpretation of Enlightenment thought in which he criticized Talmon in a not dissimilar way:

[T]he game of chasing origins can easily lead to very peculiar conclusions, as Voltaire indicated when he wrote that all children have parents but not all possible parents have children. Tracing a line of descent backwards is bound to produce positive results, and then by a simple process of reversion we can create the illusion of a necessary catena of cause and effect. Thus one could trace a train of influence leading from Stalin back through Lenin, Marx, Hegel, Kant, Rousseau, Locke and Hooker to Aquinas. Each link in the chain is valid, yet it must be confessed that, though there are common features and affinities in the ideas of Aquinas and Stalin, the whole has distinctly less value than the parts.[65]

Several years later, Peter Gay entered the fray in a book arguing that the dominant strain of the Enlightenment was quite different from what Talmon had described: It was pragmatic, open, empirical. In his preface, Gay decried what he called "the fallacy of 'spurious persistence'—the fallacy of treating ideas as independent, unchanging entities."[66] He went on to criticize Talmon by name for his choice of sources and his use of them: "[F]ar from 'speaking for the eighteenth century' or even for the Enlightenment, his proto-totalitarians are exceptional men in exceptional moods."[67] Gay concluded his argument with Talmon by asserting that the latter

> takes the unrepresentative man as representative of a movement, and unrepresentative quotations out of context as representative of a man's ideas. Even worse than that, [he] plays games with the subtlest of problems to which the intellectual historian must devote his best efforts: the problem of influence. Rousseau influenced the widest variety of political thinkers, and by no means all of them were extremists: reactionary counterrevolutionaries, virulent terrorists, moderate democrats, moderate aristocrats can all be shown to have read Rousseau with approval. And it is equally easy to show representatives of all these groups who read him with loathing.[68]

Richard Hunt, in his subsequent study of the political ideas of Marx and Engels, was principally concerned with showing that they could not be linked in any simple way with totalitarian democracy. He accepted Talmon's category as valid for extreme Jacobins, but he also complained that in Talmon's work,

> one is either a totalitarian or not, and the merest hint of millennial aspirations or self-righteous certainty brings down the damning epithet. But surely, even in the Christian tradition one recognizes infinite shadings of chiliastic longing, ranging from the blandest nod toward the Second Coming doctrine to the most concrete, immediate and fanatical expectations. May not the same be said of the socialist tradition? And it cannot be simply the conviction of one's own rightness (which nearly everyone shares), but the willingness to tolerate differing ideas that separates the fanatic from the non-fanatic . . . even in extreme cases, if impa-

tient chiliasm and bigoted self-righteousness suffice to define the totalitarian mentality, then we have had totalitarians throughout the ages, and the word becomes nothing more than a synonym for fanatic.[69]

The philosopher Bernard Yack welcomed, he wrote, "recent studies that turn away from the search for intellectual 'ancestors' of fascism and totalitarianism in the writings of philosophers 'from Plato to Fichte' and concentrate instead on the more immediate intellectual environment out of which these movements grew." Talmon's work, according to Yack, has provided "only suggestive analogies," which Talmon simply assumes

> provide sufficient evidence of a fundamental continuity in the expression of social discontent. . . . Like far too many historians who suspect unexpected continuities over traditionally recognized historical dividing lines, Talmon proceeds as if the discovery of similarities between phenomena on either side of the division is, in itself, a demonstration of structural continuity.[70]

By the end of the 1970s, Talmon's historical derivation of totalitarian democracy, which had never had a wide currency among intellectuals, had ceased to be of great interest to the run of scholars actively working in French or Enlightenment history. Such appeal as it retained was largely to scholars concerned directly with the problem of totalitarianism, especially those in the United States and Western Europe inclining toward a conservative point of view.[71] Talmon's final volume, *The Myth of the Nation and the Vision of Revolution*, was published in 1980. One reviewer acknowledged that the book was a compendium of fascinating material, but concluded that "the all-encompassing synthesis he was reaching for has eluded his grasp."[72] And yet the germ of Talmon's huge project, the fear of being "forced to be free" by coercive authority, is still around, as is the idea that from the Jacobins to the Bolsheviks, the creation of utopia by force has been a central strand— now usually regarded as a deplorable one—of modern left-wing thinking.

To the historian Karl Dietrich Bracher, writing in the early 1980s, it was obvious that the totalitarian party was "a complete embodiment and realization of the popular will, of the *volonté générale*."[73] Charles Taylor, who as a young reviewer had criticized Talmon's passionately idealist method, wrote in 1992 that

> self-determining freedom has been an idea of immense power in our political life. In Rousseau's work it takes political form, in the notion of a social contract state founded on a general will, which precisely because it is the form of our common freedom can brook no opposition in the name of freedom. This idea has been one of the intellectual sources of modern totalitarianism, starting, one might argue, with the Jacobins. And although Kant reinterpreted this notion of freedom in purely moral terms, as autonomy, it returns to the political sphere with a vengeance with Hegel and Marx.[74]

More closely connected to the Cold War's main lines of development than the work of either Arendt or Talmon was the series of books published largely by political scientists, but also by sociologists, anthropologists, and historians, that provided an academic analysis of the Soviet Union as totalitarian. These scholars were at first largely unaware of Talmon's work.[75] They sometimes cited Arendt, but almost invariably those sections of her book dealing with the direct comparison of Nazi Germany and the Soviet Union. They seldom discussed the historical sections at all, and dealing with "origins" was anything but the strong point of their work.

SEVEN

"Totalitarianism" Among
the Sovietologists

IN ORDER that a more focused analysis of the contemporary Soviet Union as totalitarian could develop, the idea of totalitarianism had to be expressed in a more concise but also a more comprehensive way; in the early 1950s, its usage was overwhelmingly journalistic and imprecise. The process of definition soon led to its refinement into a "syndrome," and a "model" soon followed.

The appropriation and development of the idea of totalitarianism by the American scholarly community was intimately connected to the development of Soviet studies or Russian studies after 1945.[1] Substantially aided by various branches of the government and by such foundations as Ford, Carnegie, and Rockefeller, major centers of Soviet area studies were established at Columbia, Harvard, the University of California at Berkeley, the University of Washington, and (slightly later) Indiana University, to name only the first generation.

The Cold War was a major spur to investment in Soviet studies by both foundations and such government agencies as the U.S. Air Force, whose Human Resources Research Institute sponsored the Project on the Soviet Social System at Harvard.[2] There was open and at least some secret collaboration among foundations, universities, the Central Intelligence Agency, the Federal Bureau of Investigation, and the State Department to develop Soviet studies and keep it free of pro-Soviet personnel.[3] It was in this generally harmonious, if occasionally uneasy, atmosphere that American scholars began to study Soviet totalitarianism in the late 1940s and early 1950s.

It was thus quite natural that the concept should have made an easy transition from politics and journalism into the increasingly well-organized and well-supported world of Soviet studies. Although the McCarthyite Right was no doubt threatening (and there was also J. Edgar Hoover, interested in who was interested in Russia), most of the academics drawn into the study of Russia and the Soviet Union after 1945 were of the same mind and part of the same intellectual world as official Washington. Many were émigrés, and many had worked in Washington during World War II. They were as eager to contain Communism as were Dean Acheson, George Kennan, and the intellectuals who wrote for the *New Leader*. Political pressure to achieve conformity was rarely necessary in that age of consensus.[4] Fellow-traveling scholars of the older generation, like Frederick L. Schumann, then at Williams College, were regarded by the new generation as beyond the pale.

The Russian Research Center was established at Harvard University on February 1, 1948, with grant support from the Carnegie Corporation; the anthropologist Clyde Kluckhohn was its first director. Among his early recruits was a young sociologist from the University of Chicago named Barrington Moore, Jr. Moore was already working on a study of Soviet politics that was published in the summer of 1950.[5] But Moore did not use the term *totalitarianism,* nor did his emphasis on the role of ideas in social change have much to do with the future direction of analyses based on the view that the Soviet Union was totalitarian. Moore called it "authoritarian" and showed no awareness that to do so might be controversial.

The situation soon changed, however, and by 1953, important books were appearing that utilized the concept in the political and intellectual context of the Cold War. Merle Fainsod's *How Russia Is Ruled* (1953), which retained its dominant position as the basic college and graduate school text on Soviet politics for a long generation, was the most important. Fainsod had taught in Harvard's Government Department since the 1930s and was a founder of Soviet studies in the American university world. "The aim of this book," he began, "is to analyze the physiology, as well as the anatomy, of Soviet totalitarianism and to communicate a sense of the living political process in which Soviet rulers and subjects are enmeshed."[6]

Fainsod did not define what he meant by totalitarianism, but the comparison with Italy and Germany was explicit.[7] His account of the Soviet system was thorough, nuanced, careful, and vastly more knowledgeable than anything previously published. Although Fainsod regarded the ideology of Marxism-Leninism as important, he did not spend a great deal of time analyzing its role in the system. And despite his emphasis on terror as "the linchpin of modern totalitarianism," he did not stress the sheer *invasiveness* of the Soviet system as had Orwell or even Arendt, nor did he deal extensively with Soviet propaganda. The result was that his picture of the Soviet system suggested that Soviet totalitarianism was an extreme form of authoritarianism rather than a system bent on eliminating even the theoretical possibility of its subjects' developing other views of reality. The dictatorship, the Party, the instruments of administrative control, the training of youth, the military—it was these on which Fainsod laid the greatest emphasis.[8]

As was often the case with earlier generations of political scientists, there was a strong historical element in Fainsod's study. The chapters were organized chronologically, and the main body of the book was preceded by a historical introduction. Here at the outset, Fainsod provided a highly condensed history of late imperial Russia in which he came close to asserting that "Communism [is] Tsarism turned upside down" or that tsarist maximalism created Bolshevism. The imperial regime could not or would not relieve the poverty and backwardness of the peasant masses; political polarization was extreme; the middle class and the political center were weak; and there was a clear separation of the passive society from the sporadically activist state. By the end of the imperial regime, a small Russian proletariat, dominated by an even smaller Marxist intelligentsia dominated by Lenin and a few like-minded associates, was the highly authoritarian and elitist political force that the tsarist government had created, very much in its own image. The organizational and tactical premises of Bolshevism (indistinguishable from Leninism) led to totalitarianism.[9] "Toward this larger end," Fainsod concluded,

> Bolshevik doctrine, organization and tactics were all directed. The period before 1917 was a proving ground in which doctrine was elaborated, organization tempered, and tactics tested. In this crucible the strategy of 1917 was developed, and Bolshevism as a system of governance took form. . . . Out of the totalitarian embryo would come totalitarianism full-blown.[10]

The strongly Russian origins of "Communist totalitarianism" in Fainsod's account passed virtually unnoticed in the 1950s, but in retrospect the drastic scholarly disagreement about the "origins of totalitarianism" among these early historical accounts should be noted. Talmon stressed the political messianism that grew out of the Enlightenment and the French Revolution. Arendt stressed the racism and imperialism of the post–French Revolutionary European world. Fainsod stressed that old standby for Russian historians: Russian backwardness, which at the end of his life Leon Trotsky had also believed had made Russia totalitarian. But if Russian backwardness had made Russia become totalitarian, did some form of "German backwardness" play the same role there? There was almost no common ground here.

At almost exactly the same time that Fainsod was finishing his book, another professor from Harvard's Government Department, Carl J. Friedrich, organized a conference on totalitarianism with the sponsorship and support of the American Academy of Arts and Sciences.[11] The list of invited participants was various, in academic field, generation, and nationality. There were pioneers of the term, such as Waldemar Gurian, who had emigrated from Germany in 1937 as was now teaching, late in his career, at Notre Dame; George Kennan came from Washington; there were young historians and political scientists, like Fainsod and Adam Ulam, who were much involved with the new Soviet studies; there were psychologists like Erik Erikson,[12] Else Frenkel-Brunswik,[13] and David Riesman; and there were former radicals like Bertram Wolfe, who was now evolving into a conservative liberal historian.

The first paper was by George Kennan. Entitled rather grandly "Totalitarianism and Freedom," it was a useful attempt to discern what in the experience of two such diverse European societies as Russia and Germany—which Kennan suggested were the only real "totalitarian states"—could have led to such unpleasantly similar results. Disclaiming any fixed opinions on the causes of totalitarianism, Kennan discerned several factors at the level of "hunch," about which he spoke briefly: (1) the large size of the two nations; (2) the impact of World War I, which enormously strained the systems of both nations, overthrew the monarchy, and "decisively disrupt[ed]" the power of the aristocracy; (3) the late survival of feudal institutions and a "relatively shallow, brief and imperfect development of bourgeois-democratic institutions" in both countries; (4) the strong development of romantic nationalism in the nineteenth century; and, finally, (5) the fact that both Russia and Germany were "great military landpowers" long characterized by "a relatively high degree of centralization and bureaucratization."[14] For all his brevity, Kennan's five generalizations, with a few amplifying remarks, arguably provided his hearers with a more sound preliminary guide to the subject than did Hannah Arendt's and Jacob Talmon's massive works, for all the brilliance of the one and the tenacity of the other.

Carl J. Friedrich's paper was important because it was his first effort to state succinctly what Nazi Germany, Fascist Italy, and the Soviet Union had in common, despite their ideological and other differences. He also insisted that largely because of the technological means available to twentieth-century dictatorships, totalitarian society was "historically unique and *sui generis.*" He disagreed with several others on the program who treated totalitarianism merely as an extreme form of autocracy analogous to earlier ones. Friedrich's five points were

1. An official ideology, consisting of an official body of doctrine covering all vital aspects of man's existence, to which everyone living in that society is supposed to adhere at least passively; this ideology is characteristically focused in terms of chiliastic claims as to the "perfect" final society of mankind.[15]

2. A single mass party consisting of a relatively small percentage of the total population (up to 10 percent) of men and women passionately and unquestioningly dedicated to the ideology and prepared to assist in every way in promoting its general acceptance, such party being organized in strictly hierarchical, oligarchical manner, usually under a single leader and typically either superior to or completely commingled with the bureaucratic governmental organization.

3. A technologically conditioned near-complete monopoly of control (in the hands of the party and its subservient cadres, such as the bureaucracy and the armed forces) of all means of effective armed combat.

4. A similarly technologically conditioned near-complete monopoly of control (in the same hands) of all means of effective mass communication, such as the press, radio, motion pictures, and so on.

5. A system of terroristic police control, depending for its effectiveness on points 3 and 4 and characteristically directed not only against demonstrable "enemies" of the regime, but against arbitrarily selected classes of the population . . . and systematically exploiting scientific psychology.[16]

Friedrich was already suggesting that the whole of these points was more than the sum of the parts. In discussion, he asked the group rhetorically whether one could define totalitarianism other than through a "set of inter-connected traits—a syndrome rather than a motif." He also criticized those scholars who had failed to distinguish totalitarian from authoritarian systems, believing this terminological issue to be "of fundamental importance" and insisting on a distinction that would become more important with time:

Totalitarianism is precisely the opposite of authoritarianism, for it involves the elimination of all stable authority. Those psychologists who have concentrated on the "authoritarian" personality and have linked "conformity" with "authority" must have missed this point. . . . I believe that it is important to realize that every society must be "authoritarian" in some degree, every society must contain "authoritarian" personalities. . . . But totalitarian societies attempt to shatter all traditional types of authority and to replace them with a new kind of social control. In a very real sense, in a totalitarian society true authority is altogether destroyed.[17]

Following the conference, Friedrich continued to work on the problem of totalitarianism. Recognizing how heavily his research would have to deal with the Soviet Union, Friedrich recruited Zbigniew Brzezinski, a young Soviet specialist also from Harvard's Government Department, as a collaborator. *Totalitarian Dictatorship and Autocracy* (1956), the fruit of their labors, was for a time the most influential and "authoritative" treatment of totalitarianism ever written.[18]

In *Totalitarian Dictatorship*, Friedrich and Brzezinski insisted on the modernity of totalitarianism, giving it a "preliminary characterization as . . . an autocracy based on modern technology and mass legitimation." "In this sense," they argued, "totalitarian dictatorship is the adaptation of autocracy to twentieth-century industrial society."[19] Friedrich and Brzezinski also expanded the "syndrome, or pattern of interrelated traits" from five to six by adding the necessity of "a centrally directed economy."[20]

The essence of their book was a careful analysis of Nazi and Soviet politics (and, to some degree, economics) in terms of their six points. They freely conceded many differences between the two—more than their subsequent critics often seem to have realized—but saw them as essentially alike.

In the same year, Brzezinski's own first book appeared: *The Permanent Purge: Politics in Soviet Totalitarianism.* Brzezinski did not use the six-point syndrome directly, but his account did indicate that he had a subtly more radical sense of totalitarian power than Fainsod had evinced. Brzezinski emphasized the total mobilization by the state of all resources, the "pulverization" of all opposition, the threat to the idea of man as a moral being, and the pervasiveness of terror. He emphatically supported Friedrich's condemnation of those who did not sharply distinguish between "authoritarian" and "totalitarian" governments.[21]

Between the early 1950s and the 1960s, references to the Soviet Union as a totalitarian state were numerous in the burgeoning literature of Russian and Soviet studies. Barrington Moore, for example, who had not mentioned totalitarianism in his first book, *Soviet Politics,* did so with gusto in his much admired *Terror and Progress USSR.*[22]

There was really no rival interpretation in the 1950s American academic community. The radical historian Isaac Deutscher, drawn to Trotskyism, produced a study of Stalin that concluded, in a phrase that scandalized the dominant cold warriors, that Stalin "drove barbarism out of Russia by barbarous means."[23] Deutscher did not use the term *modernization,* but he really differentiated Stalin from Hitler on those grounds. Deutscher's account of Stalin contained some elements of the later conception of a "developmental dictatorship," as used, for example, by the noted student of Italian Fascism, A. James Gregor.[24] But Stalin's "modernization" of Russia turned out to be much less notable than his application of barbarous means.

The concept of totalitarianism also became a staple of college textbooks and sometimes even of books for secondary-school students.[25] Robert Palmer's *History of the Modern World,* for example, was between the early 1950s and some point in the 1970s one of the most popular and influential textbooks in the United States for students at elite colleges and universities. In the first edition, published in 1950, Palmer described how "solidarity [in the Russian Revolution] was purchased at the price of totalitarianism"; he discussed both National Socialist Germany and Fascist Italy as "totalitarian states"; and he included a lengthy exposition of the historical roots of totalitarianism. We should note that Palmer's account was published at least a year before Hannah Arendt's *The Origins of Totalitarianism* and five years before Friedrich and Brzezinski's *Totalitarian Dictatorship and Autocracy.*[26] Influential textbook history was telling college freshmen about totalitarianism even before the monographs of the specialists had reached the more advanced.

The concept also spread to other fields of academic specialization. "Totalitarian art," for example, became an important rubric for studying the art of Nazi Germany and the Soviet Union together (and sometimes the art of Fascist Italy as well). In Werner Haftmann's influential *Painting in the Twen-*

tieth Century, we find a section entitled "The Assault of Totalitarianism," in which we read that

> totalitarianism is the concept which subsumes three such seemingly differ-
> ent movements as the Leninist-Stalinist stage of Bolshevism, Mussolini's
> Fascism, and Hitler's National Socialism. The clearest and most striking
> expression of the inner affinity of these three movements, all of which
> were directed against human freedom, is that they all produced identical
> conceptions of art and the same brand of official art.[27]

Although Italy did so least effectively and violently, all three states demanded that art take sides, glorify the leader, serve the state, and dramatize
its ideology. This being so, the main thing in totalitarian art was its content,
its form serving only to make that content accessible to the largest possible
number of people.[28]

In Russia, a pinch of nationalism was added, and the result was called
socialist realism, sharply distinguished from the bourgeois formalism of ex-
perimental modernism. Its function was, according to Haftmann, "to show
the bright side of socialist construction."[29] Haftmann went on to describe
how in Germany "degenerate art" (*entartete Kunst*) was ruthlessly and violently eliminated and how Germany's racially pure totalitarian art was presented to the public in the "monstrous" House of German Art. Totalitarian
art in Germany differed from Soviet socialist realism "only in the uniforms";
it was a "glib, mendacious, stereotype realism."[30] Haftmann concluded that
neither Nazi Germany nor Stalinist Russia ever produced a single artist or
work of art of any value whatsoever.

The most respected 1950s synthesis on how Soviet society functioned,
How the Soviet System Works, by Raymond A. Bauer, Alex Inkeles, and Clyde
Kluckhohn, gave a general definition of the totalitarian society, "in which
those who hold political power attempt to coördinate for the attainment of
their goals all the material and human resources of their society, extending
even to the private feelings and sentiments of the populace."[31] The three
authors wanted to understand the Soviet social system by elucidating as fully
as possible its "operating characteristics"—which were aspects of the totalitarian syndrome or model, taken rather broadly.

Many of these early Harvard studies made good use of the interviews
conducted by the Harvard Project on the Soviet Social System.[32] This material, most of which came from refugee interviews, helped mitigate the tendency of the totalitarian "syndrome" to deal with the Soviet scene from an
abstract, centralizing, and top–down perspective.

It did not take too long for dissatisfaction with the totalitarian model to
manifest itself; initially, this dissatisfaction had little to do with political
controversy and a good deal to do with the growing influence of the social
sciences on various academic disciplines, particularly political science. In
1960, Robert Tucker of Princeton's Politics Department read a paper at the

American Political Science Association in which he called for "a more effective theoretical apparatus" to keep empirical studies of the Soviet Union
fresh and vital.[33]

Tucker was the first to express a feeling that was almost certainly more
broadly shared: that study of the Soviet Union was taking place in too isolated an arena. He contended that a more amply comparative approach was
necessary, since the comparison entailed in totalitarianism, primarily that
between Nazi Germany and Communist Russia, was too narrow. He also
criticized the concept for suggesting a broad comparison between Communism and Nazism rather than between Stalinism and Hitlerism, which he
thought more appropriate. Tucker had noticed that scholars strongly committed to the totalitarian point of view (he mentioned Hannah Arendt and the
historian Bertram D. Wolfe) in practice distinguished between the Soviet
Union under Lenin and under Stalin, ascribing totalitarianism or sometimes
"full-blown" totalitarianism only to the latter stage. Their "totalitarian
model," however, made no such distinction, treating Communism or
Bolshevism generally as indistinguishable from Stalinism. But there had been
change in the first ten years of the Soviet Union, and now with Stalin dead, it
was clear there was going to be more. The totalitarian model, as set forth by
Friedrich and Brzezinski, was useless in trying to analyze such changes.[34]

Tucker also argued for a kind of comparative focus that would allow a
broader range of modern dictatorships to be studied together with the
Soviet Union: Turkey under Atatürk, China under Sun Yat-sen and Chiang
Kai-shek, Egypt under Nasser, and Ghana under Nkrumah. Here was an
obvious violation of that distinction that Friedrich and Brzezinski had
thought so important between "authoritarian" and "totalitarian" states. It
also had the subtle effect of breaking down the isolation of the Soviet
Union, in particular the sense of the uniqueness of the regime's violence and
oppressiveness. Tucker's new category for comparison, "*revolutionary mass-
movement regimes under single-party auspices*,"[35] was in some ways a throw-
back to the prestatist point of view of the 1920s. It was used some by
scholars over the next few years, but other new categories soon emerged as
well. This new category's principal impact was to stir dissatisfaction with the
category of totalitarianism.

———

THE DECADE of the 1960s in the United States provided a variety of challenges to the idea of the totalitarian model for studying the Soviet Union, by
no means all of them methodological in character. Let us touch on some that
were not, that were really about the broad cultural and political context in
which scholarly analyses took place. It is well known that in the 1960s, the
Cold War and the many ideas and attitudes that it had spawned were called
into question, more broadly and radically as the decade wore on. Until this
point, for example, it had not been seriously questioned since the time of
Henry Wallace that there really was a huge gulf between the Western democ-

racies, led by the United States, and "Soviet imperialism." But almost from the turn of the decade, the young radicals who were creating the New Left began to disagree. Within a few years their disagreement became more and more militant, and vague and fuzzy versions of their ideas began to affect much broader circles, largely of young people.

As younger American scholars—many of them self-styled revisionists (few of whom were in Russian or Soviet studies or knew much about the Soviet Union)—began to question America's role in the world, the prevailing Western conception of the Cold War came under attack.[36] The Cold War was regarded less as the wise and stalwart containment of Communism and more as a regrettable crusade against the Left. Responsibility, it came to be thought, should also be much more equally apportioned between the two principal powers, which should in many ways to be understood as mirror images. The United States, for instance, came to be regarded as having a sphere of influence, in Latin America and sometimes in Western Europe, not essentially different from the Soviet sphere in Eastern Europe. The United States, like the Soviet Union, was frozen into a conflictual posture that prevented all efforts to ensure a freer and fairer existence for the peoples under its aegis.

At roughly the same time, but for rather different reasons, a romance began to develop between young American radicals and peasant societies resisting both major power blocs, but especially those resisting American capitalism. The figure of Fidel Castro was crucial to some of the radicals. He and the Cuban government he had created remained anathema to Cold War liberals, but to the young radicals, he was not a Soviet client but a visionary trying to create a new world.

His comrade Che Guevara, who died fighting for the "revolution," was an even more romantic figure. Although the American government still largely saw the Viet Cong and the North Vietnamese as allies of or surrogates for the Soviet Union, and therefore implicitly totalitarian, an increasingly influential group of young American radicals saw the Viet Cong as indigenous peasant rebels who accepted the support of the Soviet Union only because the Soviet Union was the enemy of American "imperialism."[37]

Here was a complicated political struggle. Starting out truly determined to avoid any connection with either bloc in the Cold War, the New Left grew increasingly hostile to American imperialism, which gradually led it to become less and less concerned about connections between "Third World" radicalism and organized Communist groups. In addition, the increasing glorification of rebellion led to a gradual blurring of the lines between that rebellion and the institutionalized revolution of the Soviet world. After 1964, the May Second Movement and its parent "Progressive Labor" contributed an authentically Marxist-Leninist component to the New Left.

As we have seen, the idea of totalitarianism had been the special point of view of those who believed in the necessity of what became the Cold War: from the journalists of the *New Leader* through Harry Truman and Dean

Acheson to the academic founders of Soviet studies like Merle Fainsod and Zbigniew Brzezinski. Anti-Communism was central to the Cold War liberals' sense of self. Starting with the earliest (1961) meeting of the Students for a Democratic Society (SDS) in Port Huron, Michigan, there was strong opposition to "anti-Communism" among the most influential participants.[38] To them, it was clearly connected to a critical attitude toward any systematic leftism or generous-minded utopianism. Over the next few years, the word *totalitarianism* became a particularly provoking reminder of Cold War thinking in general, the mere mention of which could stir strong emotions. The word had appeared in the original SDS constitution in a cautionary context, but was removed in 1965 as "a relic of a bygone era."[39]

At a New York debate in 1963, one of the founders of SDS, Tom Hayden, had an illuminating exchange with Irving Howe, the social-democratic editor of *Dissent*. Hayden claimed "that you couldn't call the countries of Eastern Europe totalitarian. 'What would *you* call them, Tom?' asked Howe with great scorn and to great rhetorical effect, filling Hayden," according to Todd Gitlin, another member of SDS, "with rage and contempt."[40] Ultimately following the late work of Herbert Marcuse, it was America that many of the radicals decided was totalitarian.[41]

Opposition to the war in Vietnam often led broader groups of college-age Americans to oppose the American policy of containment, which seemed to have spawned it.[42] Criticism of the containment policy for having gotten the United States into Vietnam frequently led in turn to a global opposition to the Cold War, which inevitably entailed a denial of the validity of the totalitarian model. There were some clear policy linkages here, which were often discussed, but it was more than a matter of policy. Fundamental attitudes were changing as well.

Many younger scholars found the Manichaean division into good and evil, white hats and black hats, democrats and totalitarians implausible and, after a while, insufferable. As the 1960s wore on, American institutions came under attack at home as well as abroad. The term *free world,* so often used as an antonym to *totalitarianism,* seemed increasingly hollow. All sorts of reprehensible governments were supposed to be part of the free world merely because they were anti-Communist, prominent among them the successive governments of South Vietnam.

Furthermore, those young people who were active in or paid attention to the civil rights movement were conscious as never before of profound flaws in American society.[43] After one had been beaten up or shot at in Birmingham, Alabama, or Jackson, Mississippi, one could never again have quite the same attitude toward "us" and "them."

Among the critical activists were some historians, and many more historians were influenced by what was going on around them. As they became more critical of the United States at home, they almost inevitably became less critical of America's opponents abroad. The old argument that the Soviet Union had legitimate security needs in Central Europe, long eclipsed by the (often implicit) Cold War belief that Soviet totalitarianism drove the Soviet Union to expand in both Europe and Asia, was revived. Often now, American historians criticized American policy makers for being insufficiently "understanding" about the security needs of a nation that had been so often invaded.[44] Some truly radical scholars even came to believe that American policy makers had simply invented the Soviet threat as a way of scaring the public into accepting a military buildup, whose real purpose was to underpin a crusade to make the world safe for American capital and markets.[45] William Appleman Williams of the University of Wisconsin was responsible for a somewhat milder attack on American "corporate liberalism," and many of his students were prominent in the New Left.[46]

Another factor playing a role in the pervasive hostility to the concept of totalitarianism that developed during the 1960s was the revival of Marxism as the vocabulary of choice for dissent among young European and American intellectuals. The Marxism most generally revived was, to be sure, "early Marxism"—the Marxism of alienation, rather than the later Marxism of *Das Kapital,* which had evolved into the institutionalized Marxism of the Second and then the Third International. But for Marxists or the Marxist minded, the totalitarian model had always been hard to swallow, since it reversed base–superstructure arguments and, by comparing Communism and Fascism directly, could be extremely damaging to the Left. The revival of Marxism was also connected with the rebirth of utopian thinking among young Americans. That spirit of rebellious utopianism was bound to clash dramatically with the chastened and pragmatic liberalism of older scholars.

IT WAS NOT merely the changes in American culture during the 1960s that altered attitudes toward totalitarianism. Developments within the Soviet Union played an important role as well. After the death of Stalin and the revelations of Khrushchev, terror in the Soviet Union began to decrease or, at any rate, to become more subtle and implied. This set off whole chains of reflections and new attitudes toward the model. For Hannah Arendt, of course, terror had been absolutely central. By the publication of the third edition of *The Origins of Totalitarianism* in 1967, she was ready to admit that Stalin's death had been decisive, followed "not merely by a successor crisis and a temporary 'thaw' until a new leader had asserted himself, but by an authentic, though never unequivocal, process of detotalitarianization."[47]

With the establishment of academic exchanges in the 1960s, American professors and (even more important) graduate students were able to spend relatively long periods of time in the Soviet Union. They were able to meet ordinary Soviet citizens and understand their lives in ways that foreigners had found extremely difficult to do for decades. Impressionistic evidence suggests that although a year in the Soviet Union usually had a devastating effect on leftist, pro-Soviet opinions, it also undermined the totalitarian model. The state was surely intrusive, but the gap between that intrusiveness and the nightmare vision of *Nineteen Eighty-Four* seemed considerable and growing. Not only had the state not succeeded in atomizing all Soviet citizens or eliminating private life, but the hospitality of Soviet citizens and the store that they set on friendship often impressed Americans and on occasion made them wonder whether they themselves were not the people who had become atomized.

A later generation came to regard the Soviet Union as not having a "civil society"—that is, a social–political sphere dominated by the private activity of individuals and groups. Understanding the Soviet Union as lacking a civil society was quite compatible with a revival of the idea of Soviet totalitarianism, but there was no concerted interest in this idea as such in the 1960s. What engaged people then was almost the opposite: discovering ways in which the Soviet Union might be understood as "normal" or similar to Western nations.

In a slightly different vein, the totalitarian model suggested that the Communist Party, its leadership, and the bureaucracy enjoyed between them a total monopoly on power; it suggested that the most important decisions were made by top people in the Party, guided by ideology, and imposed on a largely passive population. From Fainsod on, of course, all serious students of Soviet affairs knew that matters were not so simple, but during the 1960s, scholars became more conscious that their paradigm was pointing them in a direction that conflicted with new kinds of research that interested them. Historians were beginning to contrast developments at the "center" of social or intellectual systems with what happened on the "periphery," or events in the capital with those in the provinces. The totalitarian model did not facilitate such research; indeed, it strongly suggested that it was pointless.

It is clear that the radicalism of the 1960s affected students of the Russian and Soviet field largely indirectly. Perhaps one reason for this was the kind of person who typically went into that field. The Cold War had suggested to young people choosing a career that it was important to "know your enemy," an attitude that surely helped persuade many to enter some branch of Soviet studies. For this and other reasons, the field was not generally attractive to young people with romantic, revolutionary inclinations. Yet even this relatively conservative cohort could not remain unaffected by the political and cultural changes of the period. These changes provide the indispensable background for methodological developments in Soviet studies and occasionally emerge into the foreground.

———

ON THE SURFACE, the more obvious catalyst for the changing views of the totalitarian model after 1960 was the growing influence of social scientific points of view, felt principally through political science research agendas.[48] An important part of moving from the totalitarian model to "comparative

Communism" to something close to "comparative political systems" was the new idea that the study of Communism ought to be as "value free" as possible. To quote from an influential article: "The study of communism has become so pervaded with the values prevalent in the United States that we have not an objective and accurate knowledge of communism but rather an ideologically distorted image. Not only our theories, but the concepts we employ—e.g. 'totalitarianism'—are value-laden."[49]

Some scholars limited themselves to saying that the totalitarian model had yielded up most of what it could deliver and that new models were needed to study Communist states and societies in the post-Stalin world.[50] "In my opinion there is no such thing as a right or wrong sociological model," wrote sociologist Alex Inkeles, one of the founders of Soviet studies who had often spoken of Soviet totalitarianism. "There are richer and poorer ones."[51]

Increasingly, during the decade, social scientists came to feel that in order to understand Soviet political life, one had to understand how society functioned, through clientelistic networks, patronage, and even, in a muted way, political and economic "issues." Almost no one would have gone on to finish the sentence ". . . just as in the West," but students of Soviet politics increasingly gravitated toward a reliance on the same analytical tools used to study other industrial and "developing" societies.[52] Attitudes of the 1960s had helped create this situation by eating away at the sense of moral superiority that had enabled Americans and West Europeans to understand themselves as belonging to an entirely different moral and political universe than did the inhabitants of totalitarian countries.

While conceding, for example, that the totalitarian model "had served a valuable purpose," an early critic, perhaps influenced by Robert Tucker, found that it had been "preoccupied with structural and outward uniformities . . . less sensitive to the differences. . . . A common theoretical framework of totalitarianism for the analysis of systems widely divergent in other respects (social, economic and cultural) is likely to be misleading if the uniformities are construed too broadly and their significance is overemphasized."

The problem was not unlike trying to create a political model for such diverse entities as Great Britain, Ceylon, the United States, India, and Venezuela on the basis of shared political traits: "absence of official ideologies, economies combining private enterprise with government controls; popularly elected legislatures and elective executives; freedom of the press, religion, petition and assembly; the existence of law courts . . . independent of the executive; multiplicity of political parties, trade unions and interest groups, etc."

While conceding that Fascist Italy, Nazi Germany, and the Soviet Union did have traits in common, Alexander Groth doubted that a scholar could "understand each through the traits common to all" or "predict the future course of these entities from the common model." The "underlying differences" needed greater attention.[53]

To some of the social scientists now turning their attention to the Soviet Union, interest groups and their interaction seemed vital to the dynamics of society, and the "group approach" became something of a rallying cry for revisionists toward the end of the decade. H. Gordon Skilling was an important spokesman for this view, and in a series of important articles he clearly dissociated himself from the totalitarian model:

> The concept of "totalitarianism" that dominated the analysis of communism in the West has seemed to preclude the possibility that interest groups could challenge or affect the single ruling party as the fount of all power. The uniqueness of a totalitarian system has been deemed to lie in the very totality of its political power, excluding, as it were by definition, any area of autonomous behavior by groups other than the state or party, and still more, preventing serious influence by them on the process of decision-making.[54]

Skilling then identified "at least" eight groups that had forwarded, at one time or another, specific interests: intellectuals, jurists, managers, educators, representatives of the nationalities, scientists, the military, and special groups within the party itself. As political scientist Jeffrey Hahn pointed out, Skilling's perspective rejected the premise of the totalitarian model that Communist systems were completely different from other social and political systems. Furthermore, if these interests in some sense competed for their agendas in some kind of Soviet political arena, should not the Soviet Union be considered, to some degree, pluralistic?[55] Jerry Hough later observed that the "interest group" approach "treated 'bureaucrats' not as a Marxist ruling class, but as the educated middle class with a variety of interests and internal conflicts."[56] This step brought the Soviet Union still closer to Western societies.

By the latter part of the 1960s, even the more conservative scholars in the field were tending to ignore or modify the totalitarian model, if not to criticize it explicitly. Writing for an important *Slavic Review* symposium in March 1967, the established political scientist John Armstrong of the University of Wisconsin, a former adherent of the totalitarian model, thought that "today a model which incorporates personal dictatorship and mass terror as essential features is grossly out of touch with the reality of several communist systems."[57]

Terminology became increasingly refined as the social scientists warmed to their work. When Brzezinski and Friedrich had formulated their "syndrome" and then made it into a "model," most readers thought they knew what a model was. No longer. One influential, if rather scientistic, critic complained that not only Brzezinski and Friedrich but even such important revisionists as Robert Tucker used "model," "theory," and "ideal type" interchangeably![58]

Did Friedrich and Brzezinski's six traits really define totalitarianism, inquired Frederic Fleron, or merely generalize about totalitarian systems (implicitly defined in some other way)?

> If the latter, then what are the defining characteristics of the concept? In some places, it appears that the six traits are treated as prerequisites or antecedent conditions for the establishment of a totalitarian system. If they are antecedent conditions, are they necessary conditions, sufficient conditions, or both. . . ? Until these and other basic questions are resolved, we shall be unable to decide which political systems are denoted by the concept "totalitarianism."[59]

By the turn of the decade, another stimulus to criticism of the totalitarian model was a general scholarly consensus that Communist regimes were not static but went through different phases, in the course of which different aspects of the systems demanded special scrutiny. A milestone in the social science study of Communist systems was a long-term project put together under the auspices of the American Council of Learned Societies in the late 1960s that resulted in the publication in 1970 of a collective volume called *Change in Communist Systems*.[60] According to the editor, Chalmers Johnson, scholarship "on the various Communist systems was not adequately exploiting new social science concepts of change, development and 'modernization.' " More specifically, the totalitarian model was incapable of guiding research on two important questions: How do Communist systems change, and why?[61]

A consensus on those questions, Johnson understood, had emerged among the participants in the project. *Totalitarianism* was the best name for a characteristic early phase of Communist rule that demanded social mobilization, most often for industrialization. With the successful conclusion of that phase of industrialization requiring drastic mobilization of the population, it turned out that the revolutionary elite had been bureaucratized and that Communist society was becoming much more complex and differentiated. As a result of these developments, "the party . . . no longer speaks with one voice. It has become, in effect, an arena of politics."[62]

Richard Lowenthal's analysis in Johnson's volume dealt with these issues by taking up some of the challenges provided by Tucker's work, specifically his argument that scholars should compare Communist regimes with other kinds of modern dictatorships. Lowenthal set out to discuss the similarities and differences among various types of "mobilization regimes" or "dictatorships of development," as he preferred to call them—dictatorial regimes, Communist and non-Communist, that had resulted primarily from the need to survive in the international arena by industrializing rapidly.[63] Lowenthal found that whereas non-Communist dictatorships devoted to development could proceed quite pragmatically, if brutally, toward their goals, Communist dictatorships faced a whole set of additional difficulties stemming from their ideological commitment to a utopian agenda: the classless society, the withering away of the state, and so forth. The attempt not merely to speed development by political means, Lowenthal wrote, but also to enforce the artificial development of a utopian type required both the removal of oppositional institutions and social forces and the repeated "revolutionary" intervention by a dictatorial state to prevent the growth of ideologically undesirable social phenomena:

> The effort to destroy not merely specific superstitions and anti-modern traditions, but traditional religion itself in the name of a "scientific" world view embodied in the official ideology, requires the monopolistic imposition of that ideology on all media of information and instruction. The decision to maintain for an indefinite time an attitude of basic, unremitting hostility to the non-Communist world implies the need for long-term economic sacrifices so great that no scope is left for a free expression of different interests and opinions. Communist regimes thus constitute both the extreme, totalitarian form of a dictatorship of development and the specific form whose ideology does not recognize any built-in limits on its own function short of the attainment of utopia on a world scale.[64]

For a time, Lowenthal concluded, the struggle between utopian goals and those of industrialization and political stability were bound to continue, taking the form of generational differences among the elite, policy differences about the value of officially instilled enthusiasm and coercion as opposed to material incentives, and revolutionary intervention from above versus stability. But sooner or later, the modernizers would win out over the utopians. In Lowenthal's words, "once a Communist party regime recognizes that permanent revolution has reached its limit, it becomes extinct as a movement regime and turns into an essentially conservative bureaucracy; and such a change of function and values is bound to affect its institutional structure as well."[65]

Of all the political scientists who criticized the totalitarian model in the late 1960s and 1970s, no one stirred up more controversy than Duke University political scientist Jerry Hough, in part because his attack on the totalitarian model was so frontal and insistent. In several books, Hough used the tools of social science theory to move from the comparative Communism and comparative dictatorship models favored by Tucker to a straightforward "comparative politics," functionalist analysis of Communist societies as simply one kind of modern society.[66]

Hough called his approach *institutional pluralism;* in important respects, it derived from Skilling's work.[67] He maintained that the Soviet Union was evolving toward a certain pluralism and dispersion of power, as well as toward less repression. Although he was cautious about whether Communist regimes might ultimately "converge" with non-Communist regimes of the Western type, this conclusion was frequently drawn by his critics.[68] He believed that the bureaucrats who ran the Soviet Union should be understood as "analogous" to Western bureaucrats and that there was a real politics in the Soviet Union, "even on the most important questions." Social-ist policy was evolving slowly as well, toward a greater egalitarianism and a greater "participation." Hough particularly outraged his antagonists by maintaining that there was only a minimal difference between "participa-tion" in politics in the West and in the Soviet Union.[69] The Soviet Union, he concluded, had achieved from its citizens "a very basic legitimacy."[70] This was one reason that he changed the title of Fainsod's book when he revised it, from *How Russia Is Ruled* to *How the Soviet Union Is Governed*. If Hough was correct, that legitimacy was rapidly lost in less than two decades after the late 1970s.

Hough further asserted that the totalitarian model was misleading be-cause it suggested that only ideology could explain why and how the totali-tarian leaders made the decisions they did; that was the only "input." The model indicated that there simply *was* no input from Soviet society into the "black box" of decision makers, a conclusion that Hough vigorously dis-puted. The model "focussed almost exclusively on the 'output' side of politics—the decisions that the Soviet leaders (or really leader) took and the controls used to maintain power."[71]

WHILE MUCH of this new work[72] was appearing in print during the 1970s, a neoconservative reaction against the détente policies of Nixon and Kissin-ger was gathering steam in the United States, with a parallel movement taking shape in France. Most of these conservatives—regular and "neo"—detested Hough's comparative politics as the most disgraceful academic attempt to show that the Soviet Union was "a state like any other state" and that one could "do business with" its leaders, as pragmatic Americans were wont to say.

Alain Besançon of the Ecole des Hautes Études was one of the earliest neoconservatives to restore the full primacy of ideology to the vital task of understanding what the Soviet Union was. Both the Western governments then pursuing détente and social scientists like Hough wanted, he wrote, "the U.S.S.R. to enter into the concert of powers. They are treating the U.S.S.R. as if it were just like any other state, in the hope that it will finally behave that way." But Besançon and other conservatives were convinced that the Soviet Union could never modify its drive for global domination, since that would mean giving up ideology and consequently giving up power. Besançon's critique of Hough recalls the view of James Burnham in the 1950s that the Soviet Union "was not a conventional state but the 'main base of a world communist movement, an unprecedented enterprise' that was at once a secular religion, a world conspiracy, and a new kind of army, irrevocably pledged to world domination."[73]

For historians, the problem of writing about Russia and the Soviet Union had been different from those faced by political scientists. With the lack of intellectual self-consciousness characteristic of working historians in the English-speaking world, they paid, until well into the 1970s, relatively little attention to models. The British scholar Leonard Schapiro, as influential among historians as Merle Fainsod was among political scientists, provided analyses of the Bolsheviks before and after 1917 that were commensurate with the totalitarian model, although Schapiro referred explicitly to totalitarianism quite sparingly.[74]

Schapiro placed great stress on Leninist doctrine, which he tended to treat as a kind of original sin of Bolshevism; once it had been formulated, it was all-controlling, and what the Bolsheviks did after they came to power was almost totally implicit in Lenin's key ideas, some expressed back at the turn of the century. Those ideas were a particular, deeply Russian version of Marxism. Schapiro regarded the October Revolution as a "seizure of power," a "coup," or an "armed insurrection," rather than a democratic revolution, as the February one had been. He did not suggest that either Trotsky or Nikolai Bukharin offered any serious alternative to what happened under Stalin. And he treated the history of the "Communist Party of the Soviet Union"—he wrote a book by that title—as the key to the history of the Soviet Union. His books were as far from local or regional history as possible; what happened at the center and at the top was the whole story.

Insofar as historians did use recognizable categories to explain Soviet behavior, they tended to be traditional ones: nationalism, epic insecurity, the attempt to overcome "backwardness," authoritarian political cultures long in the making.[75] Much that is in these "explanations" did not explicitly contradict the view that the Soviet Union was a totalitarian state in some vague sense, but all of them are historically quite specific and lack the static quality that many critics of the totalitarian model noticed in it.[76]

For most of this period, however, historians tended, for good reasons, to concentrate on imperial Russia and leave the study of the Soviet Union to their colleagues in political science. Most historians need archives, and they had little success in getting into them until the 1970s were drawing to a close.

In 1974, Stephen Cohen of Princeton, formally a professor of politics rather than a historian, published what he called a "political biography" of Nikolai Bukharin.[77] In it he argued that Bolshevism had far greater evolutionary possibility than had commonly been realized and suggested that Bukharin might have won in his power struggle with Stalin. Had that happened, Bolshevism might have evolved in a much more moderate direction. Forced collectivization and the extremes of rapid industrialization would have been avoided, and the terrible purges of the 1930s as well. Cohen cautiously did not spell out any such radical alternative, merely noting that the viability of Bukharin's gradualist economic policies was being debated in the Soviet Union. He did emphasize, however, that the progress of "reform Communism" in the Soviet Union was linked to the "reformers' search for an authentic non-Stalinist tradition in the Soviet past."[78]

Within a year or two, Cohen was prepared to go much further. In a 1975 conference paper, he argued that Bolshevism and Stalinism were quite different, and that it was the fault of the totalitarian model that they had become blurred.[79] Bolshevism, far from having been given a definitive form in Lenin's early writings, contained a range of possibilities. The intellectual alternatives in the 1920s had been Trotsky's "left" program of rapid industrialization and Bukharin's "right" program, which allowed the peasants to prosper and to be taxed to finance a slower but more stable development. But the differences between Bukharin and Trotsky were miniscule compared with the extravagant, fantastic rapid developmental schemes put into effect by Stalin after 1929.[80]

Thus Stalin, rather than being understood to have developed Lenin's policies in a more or less continual way, was now viewed by Cohen as having instituted a "radical departure" from previous Bolshevik politics and economics. Had Trotsky or especially Bukharin been in charge, a more moderate development of Bolshevism might have been expected. Thus Cohen sought to correct the damage inflicted on the study of Soviet politics by the totalitarian model, here taken in the narrow sense of deriving Stalin's totalitarianism smoothly from Lenin's "totalitarian embryo," to use Merle Fainsod's phrase.

In this project of at least partially rehabilitating pre-Stalinist Bolshevism, it was important to see the October Revolution not as a coup d'état, but as an authentic revolution created at least partly from below, with democratic support. This question was, in the abstract, quite separable from whether Bolshevism was totalitarian; the fact that Hitler came to power legally in Germany played no role in the debate about German totalitarianism.[81] But for Cohen, wishing to retain for the Bolsheviks the possibility of a more humane development until the last possible historical moment, the matter was vital. In support of the idea that the Bolshevik Party was far more "open" and even in some ways democratic than had been generally admitted, he could point to a new study making precisely that point, Alexander Rabinowitch's *The Bolsheviks Come to Power.*[82]

But if Bolshevism might have had this more or less democratic evolution, why did it go so far in the other direction? If Bukharin were what one might have expected, how did Stalin come to power? Cohen admitted that the "party's growing centralization, bureaucratization, and administrative intolerance after 1917 . . . abetted Stalin's rise."[83] To a considerable extent, he blamed Stalin personally, seeing him as having changed Bolshevik ideology essentially, by "instituting the revival of nationalism, statism, anti-Semitism, and conservative, or reactionary, cultural and behavioral norms; the repeal of ideas [*sic*] and legislation favoring workers, women, school children, minority culture, and egalitarianism."[84] Like others who have tried to separate Lenin's Russia sharply from Stalin's, Cohen left the outsider to wonder how any single mortal could have changed the probable course of history so dramatically and so single-handedly.

Cohen added another piece to his argument. Downplaying the shaping importance of Lenin's long-held ideas about the necessity of an elite party to guide the unreliable masses, Cohen asserted that the harsh experience of the Russian civil war (1918–1921) had fostered less humane and generous, more callous and authoritarian values within the Bolshevik Party, some revived from earlier decades, others new. The civil war had revived "the self-conscious theory of an embattled vanguard, which had been inoperative or inconsequential for at least a decade and implant[ed] in the once civilian-minded party what a leading Bolshevik called a 'military soviet culture.'"[85]

Cohen's criticism of the totalitarian model remained the last word for only a short time. A young historian named Sheila Fitzpatrick, then at the University of Texas, soon added a new dimension to the debate. She was not convinced by Cohen's apparent belief that the civil war had been a kind of unfortunate accident that had had very bad effects on Bolshevism. "The Civil War," she wrote in a conference paper,

> gave the new regime a baptism by fire. But it was a baptism the Bolsheviks and Lenin seemed to want. The Bolsheviks were a fighting party— even a street-fighting party—in 1917; that was one of the main reasons for their popularity with workers, soldiers and sailors. Their manner of taking power in October was almost a provocation to civil war. . . . The Bolsheviks . . . had the formative experience they were looking for in the Civil War. It was the formative experience for which their past and thoughts had prepared them.[86]

Fitzpatrick was not interested in saving Lenin from complicity in Stalin's crimes. She did not dispute the continuity of the early 1920s, but criticized the totalitarian model for inhibiting the understanding of how Russian society actually had functioned during the Stalinist period. Trying to direct the attention of scholars away from the political directives emanating from the center toward the provinces, where they had been received, she explicitly sought to shape her work and that of her students and younger colleagues in the image of French social history. She wanted not only to avoid the top–down, center–out approach of the totalitarian model, but also to combat "the perceived 'Cold War bias' of earlier Sovietology."[87] She wanted to understand how different groups of ordinary people had made sense of what was happening to them under Stalin and whether they had felt involved in what was going on, whether on certain issues, at least, he might have spoken or acted for them or even been influenced by them. She wanted to move away from the capital and out into the provinces to see how the 1930s looked from there.

Fitzpatrick also changed the center of gravity of the debate. Rather than maintaining that developments after Stalin's death demonstrated the present uselessness of the totalitarian model, Fitzpatrick contended that even the period of high Stalinism—the late 1920s and the 1930s—could not be well understood through the lens of the totalitarian point of view.[88] She did not really analyze the totalitarian model in great depth; what she did was in part suggest its methodological biases and in part attack it for its connection with the waging of the Cold War.[89]

On the positive side, Fitzpatrick suggested a reciprocity between Stalin's policies and groups within Soviet society that stood to benefit by them: iconoclastic and radicalized youth and, above all, workers moving up into the Soviet "intelligentsia." Fitzpatrick's contention that Stalin's forced collectivization and implementation of the First Five-Year Plan had a "genuine proletarian component" clearly contradicted an essential aspect of the totalitarian model—that Soviet society was wholly passive or, at the very least, unable to undertake any real initiative in defense of its interests and that the policies of the time were formulated and implemented by the dictator and a small segment of the Party elite. As she observed in the preface to her *Cultural Revolution in Russia, 1928–1931,*

> instead of concentrating exclusively on the theme of Party intervention in culture (the major theme of previous Western studies), we [the contributors] have looked at what was happening within the cultural professions and sought to relate this to contemporary social and political changes, including the movement for worker promotion into the intelligentsia.[90]

In *Education and Social Mobility in the Soviet Union,* Fitzpatrick demonstrated at the very least that Stalin's policies had social beneficiaries, that numerous people in the Soviet Union possessed powerful ambitions, fears, and resentments that created support of various kinds and degrees for Stalin's policies. To assert this is to say that "civil society"—the world of private interest—was never completely moribund, even under Stalin. One must understand both the nature of Stalin's support and its limitations if one is to understand what happened in this crucial moment in the history of the Soviet Union. Whether it took the form of initiative from below is harder to demonstrate, nor is the nature of that support yet well understood.

In describing the undeniable social mobility that accompanied the destruction of the old intelligentsia and the kulaks—a central theme of her work and an original one—Fitzpatrick was fond for a time of characterizing the process as "affirmative action" and comparing it with American social policy during the 1960s and 1970s. No doubt there are some similarities, but the gain in understanding is more than offset by what the phrase leaves out in its linking of quite disparate situations. Any such comparison must inevitably have an exculpatory ring.[91]

Many criticisms were leveled at the work of Fitzpatrick and her younger students and colleagues. The minimizing of Soviet terror was one of the most important. "In all of their publications to date," charged Stephen Cohen,

> the terror is ignored, obscured or minimized in one way or another—by emphasizing the transcendent importance of other developments; by

disdaining relevant sources; by citing very low estimates of its casualties; by defining it mainly as the purge of 1937–38; by treating it as a quirky form of bureaucratic "tensions and "administrative housekeeping"; or by using such euphemisms as "state coercion" and "involuntary mobility."[92]

To this Peter Kenez of the University of California at Santa Cruz added:

> Historians must write about the terror not in order to vent their indigna-
> tion but because that subject is essential to our understanding of abso-
> lutely every aspect of Soviet life in the 1930s. Terror was not an epiphe-
> nomenon. It is not a topic like the history of Soviet sports or Soviet
> opera. Because of the terror, parents talked differently to their children,
> writers wrote differently, workers and managers talked to one another
> differently. Because of the terror, social mobility increased. Because of the
> terror, millions perished.[93]

Fitzpatrick also drew criticism for trying to overcompensate for the domination of state-centered work in the past by doing history with the state "left out," with a notion of "sometime in the future bringing it back in." According to Geoff Eley, a historian primarily of Germany, "the state is not something that can be removed or restored by historians at will, least of all . . . in a context where the state–civil society relationship was so heavily weighted to the former term."[94] Having (properly, Eley believed) elimi-nated the totalitarian theory of the state, Fitzpatrick needed to replace it with a better theory rather than simply leaving a gaping hole.[95]

Following the exchange on the work of Fitzpatrick and her colleagues between the fall of 1985 and 1986, there was for a time much less political argument about the concept's applicability to Russia and the Soviet Union. There was not much more to say on the academic side, and the neoconser-vatives in the Reagan administration were also less polemically interested in the term. Within a year or two, moreover, the attention of nearly everyone turned to the riveting and complex process of reform and collapse that ended in the dissolution of the Soviet Union. Whether the Soviet Union had been totalitarian was of less interest for a while, until its final days, when the debate broadened again to include academic outsiders and both Ameri-can and Soviet participants.[96]

EIGHT

The Cold War in Postwar Europe

France, Italy, and Germany

> To keep hope alive one must, in spite of all mistakes, horrors
> and crimes, recognize the obvious superiority of the socialist
> camp.
>
> *Jean-Paul Sartre*

> You know, the intellectual as prophet, the intellectual
> announcing the course of history has done terrible damage: in
> his name, all the totalitarian systems of the twentieth century
> have been justified.
>
> *Bernard-Henri Lévy*

A T THE END of World War II, usage of the concept of totalitarianism
was confined largely, but not entirely, to the English-speaking world.
It had never been of major importance in France, although the apostate
French Communist Boris Souvarine used it in his 1935 biography of Stalin.[1]
As we have seen, Hitler and the remaining Nazi leadership disliked the term,
and the many enemies of Nazism who had employed it had done so in
emigration. It had been of greater significance in Italy, being used by both
sides in the ideological arguments about Fascism, and it began to be used
again by notable critics of Fascism inside Italy even before the war was over.

During the German occupation of Italy, Alcide de Gasperi, the future
leader of the Christian Democrats (DC) then working in the Vatican,
attacked

> the totalitarian agencies bent upon seizing the whole individual in order
> to discipline him in ethical and philosophical and economic matters.
> Their heads are social philosophers and prophets as well as economists
> and statesmen, and their party is a philosophical system, a faith, a body of
> doctrines, and a vehicle for social and economic reforms.[2]

After some small usage in the France of the late 1930s, the term was taken
up after the war by those who wished to dispute the hegemony of the Left

in French cultural and political life. There was a great intellectual debate in postwar France about whether the Soviet Union, with the warts and blemishes that even the most radical participants recognized privately, was nevertheless the best hope for the creation of a more just social order worldwide. Leading intellectuals such as Jean-Paul Sartre, Maurice Merleau-Ponty, and Emmanuel Mounnier thought so, and they were not likely to use a term that suggested a Nazi-Soviet comparison. But a few academics, intellectuals, and writers, preeminently Raymond Aron and Albert Camus, were willing to use either the term or other concepts that implied it unmistakably. They were, of course, the most significant French critics of the Soviet Union, and for all their achievement, they were in crucial ways outsiders.

The German and Italian cases were different. Both had experienced totalitarian regimes directly. Both were dominated by Christian Democratic governments in the postwar period, eager to use the term in regard to their left-wing opponents. Both Christian Democratic parties were closely allied to moderate and conservative opinion in the United States, which was worried about Soviet expansion.[3] And in both nations, postwar politics was inevitably affected by recriminations about who was chiefly responsible for the Fascist or Nazi past.[4] Inevitably, the Catholic conservatives and centrists, now organized as Christian Democrats, had more members whose relations with the former regimes invited criticism.[5] In both nations they found it plausible to encounter charges from the Left that they were not free from Fascist or Nazi taint, by attacking left-wing parties and groups for their (variously) close relationship with the Soviet Union.

The concept of totalitarianism was ideal for such attacks, because by using it, the conservatives could not only polarize the political spectrum, but also suggest that if their opponents were under the influence of Soviet Communism, they were also in favor of a state and system that had much in common with Fascism or Nazism. As a result, concluded two American students of Italian Christian Democracy, "many Italian voters continue to see the PCI as it was portrayed by the DC in 1948 . . . as a party with a totalitarian vocation."[6]

As early as the end of 1946, Palmiro Togliatti, leader of the Italian Communist Party, felt he had to address the issue of totalitarianism.[7] He did so by trying to link his enemies with the Fascists, comparing the Christian Democratic slogan "either with Christ or against Christ" with similar Fascist slogans ("for us or against us") and asserting that the DC was returning to the point of view of the religious wars.[8] When the issue resurfaced in the crucial 1948 elections, Togliatti claimed that the charge was

> essentially the method of falsehood and of provocation applied to the political struggle. It ignores the real positions of the opposing parties, repels every objective understanding of the debate, ends discussion, binds the life of the country to a general propaganda and atmosphere of hatred, scorn, defamation and calumny against the most open and conse-

quently democratic forces, and . . . introduces throughout the life of society a profound break, an insuperable laceration.⁹

The Italian government of the late 1940s, especially those headed by Alcide De Gasperi, who first came to power at the end of 1945, were "especially gifted practitioners of the anti-Communist argument."¹⁰ Italy needed economic assistance in the worst way, and in 1947 it became clear that having a reliable Italian government to fight the Communist threat would help untie American purse strings. The Christian Democratic leaders reinforced and internationalized their domestic anti-Communism by holding out prospects for economic assistance.¹¹

Under the influence of the crisis in Greece and Turkey, American concern about the progress of Communism grew, and with the proclamation of the Truman Doctrine on March 12, 1947, it intensified. James Dunn, the American ambassador in Rome, was eager to deal a blow to Italian Communism and draw De Gasperi's government even closer to the United States. On May 7, he advised Washington that President Truman should

> say that the U.S. has deep and friendly interest in the growth of real democracy in Italy . . . and will be happy to continue to lend our support to these elements here who have deep and abiding faith in the democratic processes and the preservation of freedom and liberty of the Italian people and who are opposed to governments in Italy by totalitarian regimes either of the extreme right or extreme left . . . and that we are confident that the Italian people will not desire a totalitarian regime which would inevitably break down the close ties that bind together the Italian and American people.¹²

One may disagree about whether De Gasperi exploited the American fear of the Italian Communist Party or whether the Americans exploited De Gasperi's need for American aid. By early June, however, the Communists had been expelled from the government. The Americans quickly committed to an additional $100 million in aid, after De Gasperi advised Washington that "a failure on the part of his government [to obtain such aid] would bring on in Italy, without any doubt, a government of the extreme left."¹³ This new alignment meant increased political polarization in Italy, further exacerbated by continued Soviet pressure in Eastern Europe and especially by the fall of Czechoslovakia in the winter of 1948.¹⁴

Nor was the usage confined to members of the DC. As a result of the impact of the Greek crisis on Italian politics in January 1947, the moderate wing of the Italian Socialist Party (PSI) demanded that the party break with the Communists. When the leadership refused, an important political figure, Giuseppi Saragat, separated from the PSI and formed the Italian Social Democratic Party (PSDI), proclaiming a much deeper divide between Socialism and Communism than he had hitherto acknowledged. "Under communism," he wrote, "bourgeois liberalism is replaced by bureaucratic totalitarianism."[15] Saragat's secession made it still easier for the DC to expel the Communists and the more radical Socialists from the government.

In the 1948 elections, De Gasperi justified the expulsions as 'the defense of a free system in which no party has any other master than the law and no national sovereignty exists other than that of the Italian people ... anti-communism was not our political slogan but rather anti-totalitarianism."[16]

In fighting against such slogans as "Christ versus communism," Togliatti warned (not altogether coherently) that the "shadow of petty Catholic totalitarian tyrants, of the Austrian and Portuguese type, begins to hang threateningly over our country."[17]

THE FRENCH equivalent of the Italian Christian Democrats was the Mouvement Républicain Populaire (MRP). Although it was never able to attain anything like the hegemonic position of its counterpart, its rhetoric also included condemnation of "totalitarian statism."[18] As he waged his struggle against the French Communists after his fall from power, Charles de Gaulle was also quite willing to use the term. In a speech in early July 1947, he made his contribution to the crisis atmosphere prevailing in the West that year. After describing a continent shaken to its foundations by the war's losses and all of the subsequent ramifications, de Gaulle added, according to the *New York Times,*

> Over two-thirds of this devastated field, Russian action and force extend—that is, those of a great people, greatly tried itself, but forming a powerful reservoir of men and resources, bent under an implacable discipline, officially led by a totalitarian ideology whose very animating principle is to expand and that finds everywhere else organized groups ready to serve it exclusively.
>
> If matters should continue as they are, this Europe, as by a physical law, must sooner or later be absorbed by a hegemony under which its genius and its light would disappear. As for the world, its only destiny would be an immense and unpardonable war.[19]

The intellectual arena in France at this time was far closer to the political than elsewhere in Europe.[20] The remarkable existentialist philosopher Jean-Paul Sartre and his allies dominated the intellectual scene until after the student revolt of 1968 and the appearance in France of Solzhenitsyn's *Gulag Archipelago* (1975), although that dominance gradually attenuated. In the 1950s, two of his most prominent original allies, the phenomenologist Maurice Merleau-Ponty and the socialist David Rousset, a former Nazi prisoner, moved away from Sartre's tortuously pro-Communist position. Rousset, the author of an exposé of Nazi camps,[21] could not accept the existence of Soviet labor camps and remain close to the Communists, whereas Merleau-Ponty's anti-Communism developed after the North Korean invasion of South Korea in June 1950.[22] As late as May 1949, however, Merleau-Ponty joined with Sartre in asserting that "whatever the nature of present-day Soviet society, the USSR is, broadly speaking, in the current balance of power, located on the side of those who are struggling against the forms of exploitation familiar to us."[23] The staying power of this point of view, rapidly losing ground in the United States, was far greater in France.[24]

Sartre's great conservative–liberal rival, the sociologist and political philosopher Raymond Aron, used the term *totalitarianism* repeatedly over his long academic, political, and journalistic career. His influence in the French- and English-speaking worlds, extending into the 1990s, amounts virtually to a countertradition.

Already in the late 1930s, the term had become a significant one for Aron. After returning in the fall of 1933 from his years of study in Germany, he was drawn into the circle of the liberal historian Elie Halévy, then holding a chair at the Ecole Libre des Sciences Politiques in Paris. After Halévy's death, a collection of his work was published that included a brief "communication," intended for discussion purposes, on the evident and disconcerting similarities between socialism and fascism.[25] Entitled "The Era of Tyrannies," Halévy's "communication" gave its name to the entire posthumous collection of his unpublished work and was the occasion for Aron's first effort at discussing the phenomenon of totalitarianism, a substantial essay.[26]

At the end of his life, Halévy rendered a very severe judgment on socialism: He regarded it as having failed in the extraordinarily important task of preventing war; its nationalist rival had proved stronger. He also regarded socialism's hierarchical and bureaucratic elements as deeply incompatible with its professed liberating mission.

Pondering Halévy's opinions, Aron wrote that

> in spite of their evident differences, fascist and communist regimes nontheless have analogous origins and converging lines of evolution. The former move from an exacerbated nationalism to a kind of socialism; the latter, starting out from revolt and in the name of freedom, have resulted in a regime of authoritarian government and patriotic exaltation. The two forces . . . thus end in a paradoxical and perhaps odious reconciliation, thanks to "the almost limitless powers which the modern structure of the state places at the disposal of revolutionaries and men of action."[27]

Taking up Halévy's "implicit assimilation of the Soviet tyranny to the Nazi tyrannies," Aron found that the "absolute" power of the state, bolstered by a single, unrepresentative party, supported Halévy's contention, as did the domination of a tyrant and a dogmatic ideology represented as the "official truth." He also discerned a number of differences. Fascism preserved the existing class structure, but Communism destroyed it. Soviet trade unions, Aron believed, arose out of the working masses and preserved some connections with them, even though they were run from above. There were obvious ideological differences: "[C]ommunism is the transposition and caricature of a religion of salvation, whereas the fascist regimes no longer recognise humanity." But the major argument against Halévy, according to Aron, was that Fascist regimes were inherently imperialistic and the Soviet Union had not yet proved to be so.

Aron's meditation on Halévy's questions was very much in the fearful and apocalyptic spirit of 1939 and 1940, which we earlier observed in the United States and England. Both Halévy and Aron were afraid that the "intellectual tyranny" of the single doctrine and the single party were part of Europe's future. In a related way, they supposed that if the democracies were to prevail in the struggle against the tyrannies, they would have to adopt censorship and the sort of war economy that Halévy believed played the dominant role in the birth of the "era of tyrannies."[28]

The same agonized spirit is evident in a paper that Aron presented just two months before the signing of the Nazi-Soviet Pact on August 21, 1939, to the Société Française de Philosophie.[29] In both paper and discussion, controversy swirled around how far and in what ways the democracies should emulate the totalitarian states. According to Aron, "the democracies must show themselves capable of the same virtues as the totalitarian states." By this he meant that

> in the face of regimes which declared that might alone was right and that they were heroic while the democracies were cowardly, it was "laughable" to be continually talking of pacifism, because this served to confirm the fascist leaders in their view that the democracies were in fact decadent. When speaking to people who professed to despise peace, one had to say that it was not out of cowardice that one loved peace. It was "ridiculous" to oppose regimes that were founded on work by regimes that were founded on leisure, and "grotesque" to believe that guns could be resisted by butter and effort by repose.

A more succinct answer was that the democracies must prove themselves capable of heroism and hard work and must "willingly consent to necessities which, elsewhere, were imposed."[30] Aron was also intrigued by what the totalitarians were achieving through state-sponsored public works and similar economic measures and thought that something might be learned from them here, too. As we have seen with respect to the United States, the economic policies by which Germany especially emerged from the Great Depression were of widespread interest even in those nations hostile to Germany.

Another major theme of Aron's presentation was the nature of the totalitarian elites, which he understood through the theories of Vilfredo Pareto, the Italian sociologist best known for his studies of elites and their circulation. Following Pareto, Aron concluded that the totalitarian elite's attitude toward the masses was inevitably one of cynical exploitation rather than embodying any serious belief. By the latter 1950s, when he wrote the lectures that were published in English as *Democracy and Totalitarianism,* Aron had modified his views, coming to think that it would be a "mistake" to believe that the Soviet leaders do not believe in their own doctrine.[31]

Aron's secondary political affiliations changed over the next forty years, but never the strong anti-Communism that made him one of the most intelligent and implacable cold warriors in Europe. Sometimes his analyses seemed cold and dry, but his essays, read after the end of the Cold War, seem remarkably sensible, a positively heroic virtue in postwar France. He was also by temperament and by conviction a skeptic, not only about what he called totalitarianism, but also about any large and unifying point of view that might have "totalizing" implications.

In a series of books, beginning with *The Great Schism*,[32] Aron defended the Cold War as a political, economic, and moral necessity and portrayed the menace of totalitarianism as the principal challenge of his time. He analyzed the Soviet economy, its political system, Soviet and Western Marxism, and Marx's falsified historical predictions with an eye to unmasking what he regarded as their imposture. In the process he broke with Sartre, Simone de Beauvoir, and other of his former friends and allies.[33]

The Great Schism was a Tocquevillian analysis of the immediate postwar situation in Europe, concentrating on the two great powers that dominated Europe from the periphery. The smaller states in between were now caught up in a new, global balance of power diplomacy, in which the United States would play the role formerly played in the smaller European arena by England. The Soviet universal empire was oppressive and probably irreversibly driven to seek domination. Aron had by now changed his prewar position: The Soviet Union *was* imperialistic, although he still thought it was a more patient imperialism than Hitler's. And—intolerable assertion in Sartre's France—no one could be neutral in the face of Soviet totalitarianism. Joining with the United States was the only way for Europe to save itself.[34]

Aron followed *The Great Schism* with another ambitious piece of high journalism about the world situation: *The Century of Total War*. In this collection of essays, Aron examined how deep and direct the connection was between both "total wars" of the twentieth century and the totalitarian regimes of Germany and the Soviet Union. He concluded that despite the obvious historical connections (administrative centralization, economic planning, and ideological propaganda), "the essential characteristics of the totalitarian regimes derive from a quasi-religious doctrine and a will to power." Their objective is "a permanent unanimity expanded into a system of values and of thought."[35] He stressed that Stalinist totalitarianism was not merely the twentieth-century form of bureaucratic despotism, but a revolutionary impatience to remake the world in the service of an idea, or as he put it, a "phantom." He thus struck notes common to both Talmon and Arendt in a book published in 1951, the same year as theirs.[36]

In June 1950, Aron attended the founding meeting of the Congress for Cultural Freedom, at which he became a member of the executive committee. He also became the most important contributor to *Preuves,* the monthly analogue of the English *Encounter* and the German *Der Monat,* like them supported by the congress and ultimately the CIA.[37]

In the third of Aron's ambitious polemics, *The Opium of the Intellectuals,* published in France in 1955, he mounted a more philosophical challenge to the pro-Soviet positions of the French Left:

> The fashionable philosophies in France are Marxism and existentialism. The intellectuals of the Left who give their reserved and uneasy support to the Moscow cause without being members of the Communist Party use concepts taken from Hegel, Husserl or Kierkegaard to justify their semi-acceptance of it. To answer them effectively I have used the language that they use themselves. They would have rejected in advance the arguments of logical positivism, but they cannot dismiss criticisms derived from doctrines which they themselves invoke.[38]

Aron's courageous book—for he was almost totally isolated among French intellectuals—was to demystify such key Marxist terms as *revolution,* to discuss the actual situation of the European proletariat in the 1950s, to understand how the "Left" understood and defined itself, and to analyze the cult of history and why European intellectuals appeared alienated from their societies. At the outset, he again used the vocabulary of totalitarianism:

> In its identification of the Party with the State, in its *Gleichschaltung* of independent bodies, in its transformation of minority doctrine into a national orthodoxy, in the violence of its methods and the unlimited power of the police, the Hitlerite régime surely has more in common with Bolshevik Russia than with the daydreams of counterrevolutionaries. Right and Left, or Fascist pseudo-Right and Communist pseudo-Left can be said to meet one another in totalitarianism.[39]

As Talmon had, Aron invoked Tocqueville, understanding that one might envisage totalitarianism as resulting from "what the irresistible impulse of democracy would lead to if representative institutions were swept away by the impatience of the masses, if the sense of liberty, aristocratic in origin, fell into decay."[40] Aron, however, refused to see such a result as necessary, arguing that the transformation, even the expansion, of the modern state would not result inevitably in either liberation or enslavement.

Aron was widely denounced by the French Left as a traitor who had sold out his ideals for a mess of pottage. Annie Besse, a young critic and Communist Party member writing for *Nouvelle Critique,* accused him of going back on the generous ideals of his youth and then "drugging his shame with opium." But later, under the name of Annie Kriegel, she became a well-known and highly critical student of French Communism and "a fervent Aronian."[41]

It may be that during the 1950s the idea of totalitarianism subtly lessened in importance for Aron as the specific challenge of Marxism's attraction for radical intellectuals became a major focus of his interest. Still, he understood the Hungarian uprising in 1956 as "an antitotalitarian revolution," and he devoted an important sequence of his Sorbonne lectures on the sociology of industrial societies in 1957 and 1958 to the problem of totalitarianism.[42] Aron already saw that a movement to a more stable, less dynamic sort of bureaucratic absolutism—what the great sociologist Max Weber called the routinization (*Veralltäglichung*) of the revolution—was taking place in the Soviet Union, a development that he believed would play a profound role in the Soviet future.[43]

Even after resigning his professorship at the Sorbonne at the beginning of 1968, Aron, as director of studies at the Ecole Pratique des Hautes Etudes, ran a weekly "open seminar" that devoted much time to Russian and Soviet affairs. Several of the most passionate defenders of the idea of "totalitarianism," such as the American historian of Russia, Martin Malia, and the French scholars Alain Besançon and Annie Kriegel, were frequent participants.[44] Besançon took a particularly extreme view of the Soviet Union as an entity determined entirely by its visionary and universalist ideology.[45] Even the concept of totalitarianism was for him not an entirely satisfactory tool for analysis, since totalitarianism was really only "the political consequence, the embodiment on a social scale" of Marxism-Leninism.[46] Through Besançon and particularly through Malia, Aron's influence was projected back into the passionately partisan debates on the other side of the Atlantic as to whether the Soviet Union should be understood as totalitarian and what it meant to do so.[47]

The Romanian-born international relations specialist Pierre Hassner was also close to Aron for many years; Hassner's influence on the European and American debates about "totalitarianism," détente, and the Soviet future, more judicious and cautious than that of Besançon, was considerable.[48] Hassner refused to understand totalitarianism as a social science concept, finding the methodology of Brzezinski and Friedrich too narrowly empirical and ideological, as opposed to the "totalizing vision" of Arendt. Rather than totalitarianism per se, Hassner preferred to see "totalitarian behaviours, tendencies, logics, objectives and residues."[49]

Apart from Raymond Aron, the great opponent of the French Left's sympathy for the Soviet Union in the immediate postwar period was the writer and philosopher Albert Camus.[50] Although his opposition sprang from certain basic values that he shared with Aron—a deep mistrust of "totalizing" ideological systems was perhaps the deepest—it expressed itself in a very different way.[51] Aron was a profoundly academic person and a highly rational one. Camus, by contrast, was lyrical, personal, sensual, expressing himself most profoundly in subjective essays or works of fiction like *The Stranger*.[52] He had a deep respect for the individual's private sphere and for ordinary life. "For Camus," wrote Eric Werner, "the proper horizon for human beings is not *history* but *nature*. Camus did not concern himself with *transforming* the world, but with *contemplating* it. What he privileged was faithfulness to the earth, attachment to the concretely living."[53]

Camus was also not without an occasional tendency toward sententious-ness, ostentatious high-mindedness, and moralism. His writings, especially on historical–political themes, could be arbitrary and prolix. But he had plenty of intellectual courage and enormous personal magnetism; Hannah Arendt, visiting Paris to try to arrange for the publication of *The Origins of Totalitarianism* in French, even preferred him to Aron as an opponent of Sartrean hegemony.[54]

Like Aron, Camus had been a comrade of Sartre, and he too broke directly with Sartre over his refusal to criticize the Soviet Union during the early years of the Cold War. Camus's attitude toward politics at that time was exactly the opposite of Sartre's and Merleau-Ponty's: to reduce political questions to the ethical and the concrete, as one can see in his series of articles "Neither Victims nor Executioners," published in *Combat,* his news-paper, in the fall of 1946.[55] He was critical of utopias, pessimistic about the Communist one.

As issues of the Cold War began to replace those of the Resistance among French intellectuals, Camus agonized increasingly over the morality of revolutionary terrorism, whether one might legitimately condemn an-other human being to death and whether the end could justify the means. For Camus, these were new versions of old questions; he had at first sup-ported, and then come to loathe, the purge of collaborators that took place in France at the end of the war.[56] At the tail end of a party in the fall of 1946, Camus accused Merleau-Ponty and Sartre of justifying the Moscow purge trials, and afterward the friends had no contact for several months.[57] By the fall of 1947, Camus was working on the book that became *The Rebel.*[58]

Camus had long been privately critical of the Soviet Union and of the behavior of the French Communists, whom he believed had tried to appro-priate the heroic legends of the Resistance for their own ends.[59] When Merleau-Ponty argued in his famous book *Humanism and Terror* that Soviet violence and dissimulation, although they were to be deplored, were prefera-ble to American policies because of the great liberationist cause to which Soviet politics was connected, Camus took umbrage. He admitted that violence in contemporary politics was "inevitable" but added, "All I say is that we must refuse to make violence legitimate, whether as an absolute necessity of state or in the interests of a totalitarian ideology. Violence is both inevitable and unjustifiable."[60]

Starting from this dilemma, Camus went on to adumbrate one of the principal themes of his anti-Communist polemic, *The Rebel.* One cannot eliminate violence in politics altogether, nor should one, since to do so would ratify the already accomplished violence of the existing order. The task was somehow to set limits to violence so that it did not become institu-tionalized, so that there were not people on whom the exercise of violence was automatically justified by either the established order or the revolution.

Aspects of this problem surfaced in Camus's novel *The Plague* and his play *The Just Assassins,* but it was in *The Rebel* that Camus directly attacked the question of whether social progress justified revolutionary violence.[61] As he was embarking on it, he became embroiled in a public controversy with the pro-Communist journalist Emmanuel d'Astier de la Vigerie, whom he accused of the "justification of violence by totalitarians." Their quarrel about whether Soviet camps could be justified by historical necessity was premonitory of the later split with Sartre.[62] Also in 1948, Camus began to make common cause with such British and American anti-Stalinist writers and critics as George Orwell, Dwight Macdonald, Mary McCarthy, and Alfred Kazin. The liaison was the work of the Italian journalist Nicola Chiaromonte, who, like many others, subsequently associated himself with the Congress for Cultural Freedom.[63]

For Camus, the creation of the institutionalized violence of what he considered Soviet totalitarianism was encapsulated in his parable of how Prometheus, who rebelled against the gods for the sake of human beings, ultimately became Caesar.[64] This dramatic and striking story bears an unmistakable resemblance to the parable of the Grand Inquisitor from Dostoevsky's *The Brothers Karamozov*.

Prometheus, the revolutionary, is driven by compassion for the people. He steals fire and bestows it on them, leading them in revolt against Zeus. But the people are weak, cowardly, and hedonistic. They must be taught their own interests and made to fight for them. So Prometheus becomes Caesar, a new master who at first teaches and then commands. His minions, the "totalitarian theocrats of the twentieth century," become state terrorists.[65] This central anti-Jacobin and anti-Leninist point of view is elaborated and commented on by a kaleidoscopic set of chapters discussing how eighteenth-century rebellion turned into twentieth-century totalitarianism. In a general way, the extreme individualism of some forms of revolt led, by way of the marquis de Sade and Nietzsche, to Fascist totalitarianism. But Camus depicted the central drama as having begun with Rousseau and the Jacobins and moving to the Soviet purge trials of the 1930s.

As did Talmon in *The Origins of Totalitarian Democracy*, Camus took Rousseau's separation of the general will from the will of all as a device to force people to be free, and he depicted the Jacobins as the practicioners of protototalitarian politics.[66] Camus's "rebel," however, espousing classical and Mediterranean measure, started always from concrete injustice and aspired only to "unity," rather than to the "totality" of a rational history, which Camus identified with totalitarianism.[67]

The impressionistic, sometimes melodramatic and obscure writing of *L'Homme révolté* has not, over the long haul, been universally admired by philosophers, although the explication of Hegel's master–slave relationship with which he began his argument has been regarded as brilliant. Philosophical issues, however, were not the reason for the assault on *The Rebel* in Jean-Paul Sartre's journal *Les Temps modernes* by Sartre's surrogate, Francis Jeanson. His attack appeared in the wake of admiring reviews, ranging from the left-center (*Le Monde*) to the far right (*Aspects de la France,* the organ of the Action Française). These paeans of praise left an undercurrent of unease, even among some admirers, that the book had rendered a service to conservatives.[68] Jeanson's hostile review appeared in May 1952 under the title "Albert Camus, or the Revolted Soul." After ironically summarizing the praise from the Right, Jeanson attacked Camus for his inadequate understanding of Hegel and Marx, his sterile anti-Communism, and his "static" view of political struggle.[69]

Camus, of course, replied to Jeanson. Who is the shallow idealist, he asked, the person who pays attention to the actual suffering of millions of real people, or he who puts his faith in a vague, prophetic ideology and makes abstractions of them?[70] Both Jeanson and Sartre replied to Camus. Sartre told Camus that he could not stand outside history; the two power blocs, East and West, "reflected" each other. The development of McCarthyism in the United States, Sartre claimed, created additional forced labor in the Soviet Union.[71] He spoke witheringly of Camus's "portable pedestal." The subject of Jeanson's and Sartre's "silence" about Soviet labor camps was broached again, and Camus and Sartre's friendship was never restored.[72]

In the immediate aftermath of the dispute, most of intellectual Paris felt that Camus had been hurt most, although the anti-Communist Left in the United States was wholeheartedly for Camus. "The crudity of the arguments used by Sartre against Camus," wrote Nicola Chiaramonte in the *Partisan Review,* "cannot be explained if one does not assume that having established an intellectual connection with the Marxist-Leninist-Stalinist mentality, he is intellectually dominated by it."[73]

Both Sartre and Camus maintained their positions. In 1960, Camus died in an automobile accident. Despite his continuing popularity as a writer, his political influence was more obvious in the United States and in Eastern Europe[74] than in France until the days of the "new philosophers" of the late 1970s and 1980s, who embraced enthusiastically what they saw as his legacy.[75]

After 1968, the Left in France went into a steeper decline than it did in the United States, despite the 1972 electoral agreement between the Socialists and the Communists brokering an uneasy unity of the Left. In 1974, Valéry Giscard D'Estaing defeated the union of the Left by a narrow margin and became president of France. The emergence of Eurocommunism was a reflection of the increasing desire of many on the Left to avoid Soviet contamination as best they could. The Soviet invasion of Czechoslovakia, partly overshadowed by the other events during the remarkable year of 1968, played an important role in changing public opinion.

So did the emergence of the "new philosophers," almost all apostates from the Left. "I will soon be thirty," wrote the one of their leaders, Bernard-Henri Lévy, "and I have betrayed the dream of my youth a hundred times." Was he a *moraliste* like Camus? "Why not?"[76]

The impact of Alexander Solzhenitsyn's revelations, in *The Gulag Archipelago,* of Soviet repression and brutality also played an important role in this complex shift in French political attitudes and culture, building on the impression left by the destruction of the Prague Spring. Solzhenitsyn's anti-Communism was harder for a French intellectual to attack than Albert Camus's. No comfortable Parisian intellectual could accuse Solzhenitsyn of having a portable pedestal. Two former radicals, Lévy and André Glucksmann, were pleased to accept the idea that the Soviet Union was totalitarian, and soon they had followers.[77]

Even before Solzhenitsyn's writings appeared, however, French public opinion began to shift away from the old radical pieties. "Not long ago," wrote the editor of the journal *L'Express,* Jean-François Revel, "an anonymous hand wrote a striking phrase on the wall of the Sorbonne: 'Imagination has come to power.' And what has happened since then? Nothing. There is only the past and nothing but the past."[78] The success of Revel's irreverent journalism in the 1970s both suggested and increased the weariness of the educated French public with the old and its interest in a different agenda.[79]

In his first book, Revel criticized the frozen authoritarianism of the Communist world and the self-destructive utopianism of leftist intellectuals who had no interest in any practical movement toward socialism. France, and indeed Western Europe, had ceased to be a place where important things happened. The United States, with its revolutionary information technology and its creation of "dissidents" and nonviolent protest, was the real revolutionary power, a "laboratory society." Europeans were provincially ignorant of this, because anti-Americanism was the real ideology of the French Left.

In his second influential publications of the 1970s, *The Totalitarian Temptation,* Revel placed the concept at the center of his analysis. In a simpler and more journalistic way, his book recalls Aron's *The Opium of the Intellectuals.* "Does there lurk within us a wish for totalitarian rule?" he wrote early in the book.

> If so, it would explain a great deal about how people behave, about the speeches they make and the times they remain silent. Within what I shall call for the time being the "Left" in non-Communist nations, the faults of free societies are so magnified that freedom appears to mask an essentially totalitarian reality, while the faults of totalitarian societies are so minimized that these societies appear to be free, in essence if not in appearance.[80] Such societies are pictured as being fundamentally good, though for the time being they do not honor the rights of man, whereas free societies are evil in nature, even though their subjects live in greater freedom and less misery.[81]

Revel went on to explain this peculiar but frequently observed behavior by noting that part of the Left's criticism was its adherents' desire to improve their own societies and their ignorance of what Communist societies were really like. But there was another factor. How was it that serious anti-Communism was always regarded as a sinister product of the Right? His answer was that

having lost faith in itself as the only true leftist movement, social democracy fails to articulate a creative criticism of the communists, except on
those occasions when, having been kneed particularly hard in the groin
by the Stalinists, it bleats forth an appeal for human rights—to no avail,
of course. Thus the silence, the absence of effective response to Stalinism,
that we see in democratic societies.[82]

The Left, concluded Revel, continued to believe that Stalinism was at least a
move toward socialism, whatever its sins, and was thus better than even
liberal capitalism. It had not really evolved beyond Sartre's position.

It is hard to believe that Revel's rather simple and self-assured description of a left-of-center political spectrum divided solely between Stalinists
and social democrats would have convinced much of the French public
before Solzhenitsyn's revelations and the growing revulsion, beneath the
surface, against the political culture of the Sartre era. But despite a certain
crudity, Revel's attack on the non-Communist Left's sensitivity about annoy-
ing the Soviet Union had something tonic about it. Communism has been
awful, the subtext went; why not be honest and recognize that? This was a
point of view with a considerable future in the more conservative 1980s.

There was a great deal of criticism, in both English and French, of
Revel's lively and sometimes witty polemic, especially on the Left, but it was
significantly more qualified than the self-confident excommunications that
would have greeted such a pamphlet in the heyday of Sartrean hegemony.[83]
Discussion extended into 1978, by which time the opinion of the French
public toward leftist attitudes and the Soviet Union had changed dramatically from what it had been less than ten years earlier. If one may judge by
the declining appeal of the French Communist Party to French workers, the
trend was hardly confined to intellectuals.

IN ITALY, by contrast, as the Cold War drew on, the literature using the
term *totalitarian* became more academic, less political. In the 1950s, the
political usage declined, and there was not yet much academic study of
Fascism, although the former "Left" Fascist philosopher Ugo Spirito, a
pupil of Giovanni Gentile, used the term to discuss Hegel's statism, with a
special Italian emphasis on Gentile's version of it.[84] Another member of the
older generation, the Catholic philosopher Augusto del Noce, produced
some interesting, although not sustained, discussion of totalitarianism. He
treated it as the product of secularization, as a secular religion. He regarded
Lenin and Mussolini—both deriving from Marx—as the first totalitarians,
although Mussolini could produce in Italy only "truncated totalitarianism."
Both Bolshevism and, more obviously, Fascism were "failed revolutions."
National Socialism, though, was the totalitarian *answer* to Bolshevism, its
"irrationalist counterpart."[85]

By the 1960s, a few social scientists and a larger number of historians were studying Fascism, and many used the totalitarian rubric. The political scientist Alberto Aquarone produced an important study of the structure of the Fascist regime in 1965, which has long been in print. Aquarone strongly asserted Mussolini's totalitarian aspirations, but he refused to classify Fascist Italy as truly totalitarian because of the survival of the monarchy, the church, and the traditional elites, preferring to regard it as essentially Mussolini's own autocracy.[86]

The renowned student of Fascism and biographer of Mussolini, Renzo De Felice, developed more complex, indeed shifting, positions. Although he repeatedly described Mussolini's regime as "not much more than a mass-based authoritarian regime," he saw "totalizing processes" at work during the later years of Fascism. He also linked Fascism to "left totalitarianism" in a broad sense, regarding it as "in the political and cultural tradition of the Enlightenment and the French Revolution, with their ideas of progress and faith in the 'new man.' " German National Socialism, however, De Felice regarded as a rightist movement.[87]

The historian Emilio Gentile found it plausible to treat Italy during the entire Fascist period as totalitarian; he stressed the mythic dimension and aspects of state organization as particular Italian contributions to totalitarianism in the twentieth century.[88] Other scholars, such as S. Colarizi, came to regard the regime as having undergone a process of "totalitarianization" or as having "taken a totalitarian turn" in the last seven or eight years of its existence. Despite the absence of mass terror and concentration camps, Gentile suggested that the regime never lost sight of its goal of the total politicization of the population and the total transformation of the society.[89]

———

WEST GERMANY was, preeminently of all European states, a creation of the Cold War. This being the case, it is not surprising to find a German historian writing in the mid-1970s that "the theory of totalitarianism [is] the quasi-official ideology of the West German state."[90] This assertion was truer for the early stages of West German development, during which a deep opposition to both the Nazi state and the Soviet-dominated one to the east were indeed "official"; it was the easiest and most politically admirable thing in the world, therefore, to dwell on their similarities. In this sense, the British historian Ian Kershaw was right that the basic premise of the totalitarian point of view was clearly established in West Germany before the term itself had become important.[91]

Nevertheless, the use of the term in West Germany has been more or less controversial since the founding of the Federal Republic. During the latter 1960s and 1970s, when the Left was strong and strongly critical of the West German government, the term *totalitarian* was vigorously attacked. The term was far slower to gain a foothold in Germany than in Italy, and its initial employment clearly derived from abroad. Nevertheless, once it was established, "totalitarianism research" became a cottage industry.

In 1945, Wilhelm Röpke, a well-known political economist from Marburg who had spent the war in Turkey, published *The German Question* in Zurich.[92] The book suggested that there had been a kind of age of totalitarianism in Europe and that the particular evil of the German version resulted partly from a more universal sickness of the age.[93] Röpke emphasized the roots of totalitarianism in earlier "systems of domination" and the derivation of National Socialism from Fascism and Bolshevism. He also quoted Friedrich Hayek's *Road to Serfdom* to the effect that "there are totalitarians everywhere," and to prove the point he cited Lawrence Dennis's rather obscure *The Coming American Fascism*. Even "the radical madness" came to the Germans from "the Frenchman Gobineau."

Already we can see in Röpke's otherwise unexceptionable book a point of view that was developed later and more complexly in Germany: German totalitarianism may have been worse than other people's (although perhaps not worse than Russian?), but it was part of the age; therefore, the German experience under National Socialism was not essentially different from the totalitarian fate to which other parts of Europe fell victim.[94]

It took quite a while after the war for German historians to decide how they should understand the disasters, as they considered them, that had befallen their nation.[95] Initially, a few, following Anglo-American historians, adopted a continuity thesis that, carried to extremes, could find the roots of Hitler's Germany in that of Luther. The "Prussianism" and militarism that many Western historians had condemned reached far back into the German past.[96] Most historians, however, continued to develop the ideas that National Socialism was not specifically German and certainly not conservative. The conservative historian Hans Rothfels, who returned to Germany from the United States in 1950, had already produced a book in English, *The German Opposition to Hitler* (1948), attempting to demonstrate that conversely, it was precisely the conservatives who had opposed Hitler, that avatar of modernity and mass politics.[97]

Soon, however, German historians, jurists, and other scholars began to combine this sort of analysis with the use of the term *totalitarianism*, which was ideal for minimizing Germany's special responsibility for the sins of the Third Reich, as it was arguably Europe-wide. In the historiography of the succeeding period, the special, personal demonization of Adolf Hitler (as opposed to German elites or the German people in general) tended to fuse with the notion of totalitarianism.[98] This identification of Hitler with a monolithic totalitarianism also hindered any very intricate analysis of how the totalitarian system in Germany actually functioned.

In his 1948 book *The Demon of Power,* the historian Gerhard Ritter announced grandly that the totalitarian state "can be viewed as the culmination of a historical process that began with the Christian Middle Ages, with its bipolarity extending throughout the life of Western man, right up to modern paganism."[99] In *Europe and the German Question,* also published in 1948, Ritter set out to examine German history from Luther through the

Prussian experience to the "total people's state" of the Nazis. Ritter saw Italy as leading the way toward the totalitarian dictatorship that Germany later Prussianized and made its own. But he laid the ultimate blame for the totalitarian possibility in Europe on the appearance of the masses on the historical stage during the French Revolution: Their gullibility and lack of preparedness ultimately made totalitarian dictatorship possible in modern nations.[100] As in the work of Talmon, the Jacobins came in for special blame; the French democratic totalitarians were really responsible for German ones.

As German émigrés began to visit their country again after the war and, in a few cases, to resettle there and take up the threads of lives and careers, their vocabulary and methodology began to have an impact. A historian of political systems and structures, Ernst Fraenkel, returned from the United States to the University of Frankfurt. On a visit to Berlin, he met a young scholar whose interests, as did his, combined political science and history. His name was Karl Dietrich Bracher.[101]

Fraenkel's prewar study *The Dual State* had enjoyed some influence in the English-speaking world. It is likely that contact with Fraenkel pushed Bracher and his colleagues Gerhard Schulz and Wolfgang Sauer in the direction of the totalitarian paradigm, which played an important role in the major works they produced: *The Dissolution of the Weimar Republic* (1955), *The National Socialist Seizure of Power* (1960), and *The German Dictatorship* (1969).[102] They attempted to grasp the National Socialist regime as a specific, but historically derived, totality.

These three historical–political studies may be the most successful attempts ever made to integrate something like the Friedrich–Brzezinski model, with its structural focus, into a deeply researched and grounded historical narrative. Only Merle Fainsod's *How Russia Is Ruled* can compare with them on the Soviet side, and Fainsod, perforce, had nothing comparable to Bracher's database with which to deal.

Bracher appears to have understood the concept of totalitarianism as more and more central to his work over the course of the 1950s. In *The Dissolution of the Weimar Republic,* he applied this concept explicitly only to the Communist and Nazi *parties* (which grew out of the German revolution of 1918) and made no serious effort to define it. In *The National Socialist Seizure of Power,* however, Bracher reproduced Brzezinski and Friedrich's six-point "syndrome" in the introduction, which he combined with a historical essay on how the twentieth-century events made possible the rise of totalitarianism.[103] In so doing, he explicitly accepted Talmon's assertion that "the modern totalitarian dictatorship is a child of this democratic age [the Enlightenment]."[104] Despite his respect for Friedrich's six-point model, Bracher regarded Nazi totalitarianism as characterized by a revolutionary dynamism that found insufficient reflection in Friedrich's typology.

The decade of the 1950s saw a growing use of the term among German scholars, especially in the new discipline of political science rather than in

Soviet studies, as was happening in the United States. Much of this work centered on German National Socialism; some of it was devoted to careful comparisons with the Soviet Union, using the Friedrich–Brzezinski model or phenomenological comparisons from Arendt's *Origins of Totalitarianism*.[105] Some of it focused on the newly installed totalitarian system next door: East Germany.[106]

The totalitarian approach to studying both the Nazi past and the East European present spread rapidly during the 1950s in West Germany. It functioned simultaneously and complexly as an analytical tool and a weapon in the Cold War, and it became the basis for secondary-school curricula, finding its way into teacher's manuals, encyclopedias, and pamphlets, much as it did in the United States.[107] Despite these strong similarities, however, the background of these scholarly debates was subtly different from that prevailing in the United States at the same time.

Most significantly, the idea of totalitarianism in Germany was initially associated with either Americans or émigrés long Americanized. Those who used the term in the German context were open to the charge of being not only cold warriors but also junior officers on the Cold War general staff of the United States. Any growth of anti-Americanism and left-wing activism, therefore, was even more likely in West Germany than in the United States to lead to a struggle over the term's validity. But such radical changes were only beginning to emerge in the late 1950s.

Still, by the turn of the decade, Khrushchev's reforms suggested a continuing Soviet movement away from Stalinism. Carl Friedrich—whose intellectual authority was, if anything, greater in Germany than in the United States (he divided his time between Harvard and the University of Heidelberg)— suggested that totalitarian regimes might have greater evolutionary possibilities than had been believed.[108] If this were true, of course, it would prompt a further question: How should we understand the possibilities and limitations of "development" or change in totalitarian regimes? To what extent was it determined by highly specific historical circumstances, rather than following some general trajectory? What would be its consequences? Was the totalitarian model too static to analyze a series of developmental stages?[109]

An important conference in West Berlin in 1961 concluded that such questions could be answered only after doing more historical and empirical research.[110] Rather like Robert Tucker in the United States, German scholars were starting to seek a broader and at the same time a more precise way of framing comparisons.

Questions of objectivity and social science methodology were posed in Germany even earlier than in the United States. In both nations, 1961 saw the first significant criticism of the concept, but in Germany it was more far-reaching. In an influential article, the brilliant young political scientist Peter Christian Ludz argued that the geopolitical and ideological polarization of East and West complicated any Western effort to understand the other side.[111] The identity of each was intimately involved with antagonism to the other, especially for West German scholars who had experienced the violent hostility of the Nazis toward "world Bolshevism."[112] It therefore behooved German scholarship to use a variety of social science approaches rather than to rely exclusively on the automatically polarizing totalitarian model.[113] The same claim surfaced in English-language scholarship a short time later: that the existing version of the totalitarian model was too normative to be a really useful tool.

Furthermore, Ludz continued, the Friedrich model actually concealed far too many of the significant differences between Nazi Germany and the Soviet Union, obscuring, for example, the long and complex derivation of the Marxist conception of ideology behind a brief and mechanical formal definition and preventing us from seeing the complexity of its current functioning in the Eastern bloc. In another essay, published several years later, Ludz returned to the theme of what the totalitarian model had left out: the concrete social and economic conditions in which political systems function. He found the totalitarian model incapable of explaining social change or conflict in such a modern industrial society as East Germany was becoming.[114]

And might not ideological evolution facilitate a more general democratic evolution of Soviet society?[115] Certainly, the Soviet Union was evolving away from Stalinism, notably from Stalinist terror and "total politicization." Ludz's remark toward the end of his essay about "an industrialized society of the Bolshevik type" certainly pointed the way to the "comparative" discussions of the future.[116]

The decade of the 1960s in Germany was markedly similar to that in the United States, except that it began somewhat earlier. The process of radicalization had a common general pattern: Centered in the universities, it resulted in even more extreme polarization of Left and Right, both among students and more diffusely in the population at large.

In Germany, much of this was accomplished by the "Fischer controversy," which sharply divided German historians along political, methodological, and generational lines and led to a sharp increase in the willingness of West Germans to be self-critical.[117] It came in 1961, just as the first political demands from critics of the socially and pedagogically conservative German universities were beginning to be heard. Within a short period, radical historians and topics made their appearance.

Within a very few years, the political and cultural climate had changed substantially in Germany. As in the United States, young Germans also came to admire Third World radicals—Fidel Castro and Che Guevara—and to detest anti-Communist strictures as a threat to the freer and more democratic world of which they dreamed.[118]

Many young people found it impossible to believe in the founding myth of the Federal Republic, with its closeness to the totalitarian point of view: equal opposition to the Nazi past and the Soviet bloc to the East. Meanwhile, the Communist monolith continued to splinter, and it could no longer mobilize anti-Communism across the divide of generations and their politics. By the aftermath of 1968, the term *totalitarian* was criticized on the Left as excessively political.

At a minimum, scholars of the younger generation developed Ludz's critique of a concept drenched in values and of an utterly polarizing nature. Not only was such a contrast of dubious scholarly value, but it could lead to a dangerously self-righteous attitude toward one's own government, merely a weapon in the Cold War.[119] As one of the most active of the younger radical historians put it,

> There is no doubt that the fascist system of domination, from the standpoint of its intentions and the tendency toward total repression of the opposition, penetration of society, and the ideological guidance of the masses, should be called "totalitarian," if this concept did not call forth false associations. Unfortunately, the theory of totalitarianism laid its principal emphasis on the thesis that Communism and Fascism are in essence identical, because by doing so, it is hoped that Communism will be even more strongly discredited than Fascism. Thus a usable weapon for the Cold War is achieved.[120]

Proponents of the term counterattacked angrily, in an atmosphere exacerbated by student demonstrations and widespread criticism of the professoriat. For liberal professors, in Germany as in the United States, it was particularly galling to be treated as if they were no different from conservatives. Karl-Dietrich Bracher spoke for many of them when in 1976 he vehemently rejected the radicals' attack on the term as "part of a more general assault on liberal-democratic traditions and positions." These attacks, Bracher maintained, were carried out by an alliance of rightist intellectuals, of the Carl Schmitt type, and Marxists. He conceded that distinctions had to be drawn among totalitarianisms of the Left and the Right, but maintained that they did not negate the larger typological similarity. The conjunction of modern industrialization and "the democratic notion of popular sovereignty" had created a new kind of polity. At the same time, Bracher conceded, the term had suffered from an "almost dogmatic usage" and must be revivified. The age of the classic totalitarianisms may be over, he admitted, but there are a number of regimes with a "varying level of totalitarian content" that should be carefully analyzed. And—clearly with one eye on the chaos outside his study window—Bracher warned of the possibility of new totalitarianisms in the future.[121]

Two years later, he returned to the fray with an even more bitter attack on the contemporary German Left, entitled "Terrorism and Totalitarianism." At the outset, he resoundingly reaffirmed West Germany's founding myth:

> The Federal Republic of Germany continues to live under the impact of two experiences which were essential in giving it shape: the destruction of Weimar democracy by the National Socialists in 1932–33 and the estab-

lishment of a second dictatorship in Eastern Germany after 1945. In both cases one-party rule with totalitarian claims was implemented. Totalitarianism of the Right and of the Left were the fundamental experiences. The founders of the Second (West) German Republic, therefore, insisted on open democracy and a constitutional structure devised to protect the state from totalitarian tendencies.[122]

The debate had by this time become almost entirely politicized. Bracher was not concerned primarily with the academic plausibility of the totalitarian model, but with the rise of the New Left, the growing acceptability of Eurocommunism, and the powerful anti-Americanism fostered by the Vietnam War. Despite the nationalist "prefix" of the liberation movement (China, Cuba, Vietnam, Cambodia), Bracher wrote, they were "totalitarian in organization and ideology."[123] The terrorists of the so-called Red Army faction (the Baader–Meinhof Gang) were the product of the growing movement of the Left toward totalitarian modes of thinking. They and others like them were linking violence with "those democratic theories promising both total freedom and total social cohesion."[124] Their substitution of the Marxist paradigm of Fascism for the concept of totalitarianism was merely a sleight of hand to exculpate totalitarianism of the Left. The fundamental distinction between democracy and dictatorship had been blurred by the New Left. And in conclusion, Bracher reiterated seven characteristics common to totalitarian regimes of the Left and Right.[125]

There was another important distinction between the totalitarianism debate in the English- and German-speaking worlds, however. The question of whether Hitler's Germany should be understood as totalitarian has been of continuing significance to historians writing in German and, more recently, to those in the English-speaking world who share their interests. And there was much in that discussion that was not strikingly political, at least in the direct terms of the politics of the 1960s and 1970s.

The argument among German historians of Nazism, sometimes cast in terms of "intentionalists" versus "structuralists,"[126] emerged at the end of the 1960s, partly because the hegemony of the totalitarian model meant that

> the structure of the National Socialist system of domination was fundamentally monolithic, thus echoing the regime's own propagandistic self-interpretation. Later research, based primarily on documents impounded by the Allies and released after 1961, lent only partial support to the assumptions of the totalitarian model. This research revealed political fragmentation and instability in the institutions the Nazis created as well as those they had inherited. In doing so, it contradicted the image of a totalitarian system organized down to the last detail of power consideration.[127]

In the early stage of the discussions, the most important historians expounding the "structuralist" interpretation were Martin Broszat and Hans Mommsen. The former did not discard the idea of totalitarianism altogether. His interpretation of "the Hitler state," as he entitled his important book (completed around 1966 but not published until 1969) was different from that of Bracher, although indebted to Bracher's stress on structure, and not merely Hitler's ideology and political leadership.[128]

Broszat's interpretation of the Nazi state bore interesting resemblances to ideas prevailing among Italian historians writing about Fascism, in that he saw a conflict between what he referred to as the totalitarian character of the Nazi movement and the "old conservative forces in state and society" with which they were forced to interact.[129] The idea of the totalitarian here recovers something of its original Italian emphasis on ferocity, dynamism, and will, before the term received an altered impress from Italian statism. The balance of the forces in the Third Reich varied, depending on the period; as in Italy, it was not until the final seven years of the regime that the dynamic, totalitarian element prevailed.[130]

This struggle, according to Broszat, did not "strengthen . . . the hierarchical solidarity and uniformity of the state and Party as a whole, but implied a growing antagonism between the individual rival office holders, as well as an end to legal and administrative regularity, and in the last resort a 'denationalization' of the system."[131] Bracher had also noticed the overlapping of offices and the general chaos of Nazi institutions, but he attributed this to Hitler's conscious policies.[132] Broszat, by contrast, saw it as Hitler's unwillingness or inability to create a coherent system of authoritarian government. The result, in Ian Kershaw's apt paraphrase, was that

> the overall structure of government was reduced . . . to a shambles of constantly shifting power bases and warring factions—but a shambles which unleashed immense energy and contained its own inbuilt destructive momentum. In Broszat's interpretation, the Darwinian rivalry immanent to the system and the ill-coordinated attempts of the fractured government machinery to "interpret" the will of the Führer—to bureaucratize charismatic authority and channel vague ideological imperatives into coded law and practices of conduct—led inexorably to an accelerating decline into aggression, lawlessness, and criminal brutality.[133]

Hitler was seen as sanctioning pressures deriving "from different forces within the regime, rather than creating policy"; the symbolic "Führer authority" was the important thing, not "the direct governing will" of the actual Hitler. His charismatic personality and his ideas remained important, but "the fixed points of Hitler's personal Weltanschauung served . . . largely a functional role."[134]

More recently, the historian Hans Mommsen consolidated a number of earlier criticisms of the concept of totalitarianism and made a sustained assault on the term.[135] Some of his criticisms followed, or were suggested by, the work of Robert Tucker and other English-language critics; some followed from the tendency of Martin Broszat and other German historians to see the Third Reich as unstable, structurally incoherent, and fatally self-destructive; some went back to the earliest criticisms of a Fascist–Communist comparison. Nor was Mommsen entirely unsympathetic to those of his more radical colleagues who rejected the term as merely a weapon in the Cold War. He has, however, moderated their polemical tone and explicitly repudiated the simple Marxist notion of Fascism as an instrument of bourgeois domination in an age of crisis.

Mommsen focused above all on the static quality of the analysis that followed from the model propounded by Brzezinski and Friedrich. This model, according to Mommsen, simply could not grasp the "movement" phase of either Fascist or Bolshevik regimes. It also necessitated emphasizing the leader cult, the function of ideology, mass mobilization, and propaganda. Therefore, according to Mommsen, the totalitarianism paradigm can never explain illiberal right-wing regimes with some Fascist characteristics— boundary cases, one might say. Those who adhere to it always prefer to compare National Socialist Germany with the Soviet Union, rather than with Spain or Argentina. And in doing so, they always leave out of their account the role of the traditional elites in the inauguration of a Fascist regime. Although Mommsen specifically repudiated the Marxist concept that there is a straightforward class connection between Fascism and the upper bourgeoisie, he reiterated the point, made often and convincingly on the more moderate Left, that those circles in Germany undermined democracy's ability to resist extremist forces of the Right.

Mommsen added another argument that, although less often made in the past by critics, is a telling one. The concept of totalitarianism being primarily the result of a comparison of the Soviet Union under Stalinism and Germany under Hitler, the number of new insights it could yield in the study of those periods was limited; this he linked to criticisms going back to Peter Ludz of the concept's inability to grasp the evolution of Fascist regimes.

Another cluster of Mommsen's criticisms derived from the work of such "structuralist" historians of the Third Reich as Broszat and from Mommsen's own.[136] Mommsen has believed, from at least the mid-1970s, for example, that the concept of totalitarian dictatorship was a "mirror-image reverse" of the old Comintern theory of Fascism as the dictatorship of big capital in crisis, because both presuppose "a rationally structured government apparatus and an effective centre of political decision." Mommsen, like Broszat, denied that Hitler and the Nazis were able to provide that.[137] The Nazi Party was simply unable to establish the sort of hierarchy, organization, and political control characteristic of the Soviet Communist Party; Mommsen regarded it as engaged "almost exclusively in propaganda activities."[138]

Mommsen carried the contrast further, developing a key idea of Broszat's by contrasting Fascist and Communist institutions. Communists almost always felt that they must create new ones as soon as they could, but the National Socialists in Germany and the Fascists in Italy created a duality of the old and the new and then drove the old groups and organizations into the ground, undermining both their formal and their normative functions.

Their destruction meant the self-destruction of the regime. There was far less of this chaotic overlapping in Communist regimes.

The same was approximately true of bureaucracies. The totalitarian model specified a hierarchically organized bureaucracy, but Hitler's charismatic but indecisive leadership was a bureaucrat's nightmare. Things really got done in Nazi Germany by circumventing the bureaucracy.[139] The bureaucracy inherited by National Socialism, largely traditional in its procedures and (at first) its personnel, was seized as spoils by top Nazis and used for their clientelistic networks. As the pressures and secrecy of war developed, communication and the rational resolution of problems became even more difficult.

More recently, Mommsen added to his critique the very oldest objection to totalitarianism. From the 1930s until the present, some people on the Left have believed that, in Mommsen's words, whatever its sins, Communism "retains a rational core, serving positive political development and social justice." Then he attached the customary corollary: "[O]n the basis of experience up to now [1981] communist parties and systems do not necessarily preclude convergence with Western constitutional concepts. This can hardly be said of Fascist parties and systems."[140] The collapse of the Soviet Union and the evolution of Franco Spain into a democracy does not exactly prove Mommsen wrong on this point, but it surely does not support his claim.

As has largely been the case elsewhere since the mid-1980s, the arguments over totalitarianism in German history and politics have subsided, although they continued longer in East Germany. This is true in part because many of the participants were drawn into another debate, the so-called historians' quarrel or debate (*Streit*), which deals with some of the same issues: the responsibility of Germans—elites, political leaders, and ordinary people—for the past and the question of Germany's present national identity and its relationship to the troubled past.[141] Even some of the fiercest participants in the debate have begun to historicize the term somewhat more—to see the debate about the term, as well as the term itself, as part of the intellectual history of their time.[142] As in the United States and West European countries, popular usage of the term continues, but without much precision.

IN EXAMINING the usages—political, journalistic, and scholarly—of the term *totalitarianism* in the preceding chapters, we concentrated on analyzing the political struggle over the Cold War in the West. There the term was on the whole used by the more conservative segments of society, those most comfortable with society as it was. It tended to be opposed by some, or many, of those eager for change. But when we look at inhabitants of the Soviet Empire—at East or Central Europeans, for example—we find the situation almost totally reversed. Our analysis should suggest, among other things, why communication has been so difficult between what two scholars have described as "Eastern Left" and "Western Left."[143]

NINE

The Cold War in Eastern Europe

YES TO OPEN SOCIETY. NO TO TOTALITARIAN
MECHANISMS. PEOPLE OF THE WORLD UNITE AGAINST
THE RATS OF THE WORLD. MARX IS DEAD. LONG LIVE
MARX.

Ivan Sviták (1968)

The withholding of truth is a major strategy of power.

John and Bogdana Carpenter

Politics is not only the art of the possible, but as well the
search for, and even the *creation* of the possible.

Rudolf Battěk

IN WESTERN EUROPE and the United States, the struggle was over how
bad Communism was and therefore what fundamental attitude to take
toward it—in scholarly discussion, in domestic politics, or, ultimately, at
their point of intersection. Passions ran high; in the period of McCarthyism,
professional risks for left-wing Americans were quite real and could be very
serious for the relatively small minority with a Communist past. But most
people maintained their political positions, whatever they were, and went
on with their lives without feeling particularly at risk, even while exercising
a certain caution, conscious or unconscious, in their political expression.

In Eastern Europe, by contrast, the question of *precisely what attitude to
take toward Communism* was anything but academic, and everyone became
highly conscious of it. Not only was it fraught with the gravest practical
risks, but the assertion of political opinion unpalatable to one's government,
even in what one imagined to be private, could easily draw one into active
opposition to the regime. There was so little space for nonactivist politics.[1]
As Václav Havel, then a Czech dissident playwright, put the matter in 1979,
the sort of prepolitical opposition that he called "living within the truth"
threw those who did it "into a game of chance where the stakes [were] all or
nothing."[2]

Poland and Czechoslovakia had very different histories until they fell under Soviet domination in the late 1940s. The Left, especially the Communists, had always been weak in Poland, associated as they had recently been with Russia, a traditional and bitter enemy for centuries. The Communist movement in more industrialized Czechoslovakia, by contrast, had been quite strong, well before the coup in 1948. In the free elections of 1945, the Czech Communist Party polled almost 50 percent of the vote. Democratic traditions there were stronger, too.[3] Due in part to a more hazardous cultural relationship between Russia and Czechoslovakia in the nineteenth century, traditional Russophobia was less strong and pervasive than in Poland.

Their respective Communist experiences differed as well. In Czechoslovakia, Stalinism was less mediated, less contested, and therefore worse. In Poland, the Roman Catholic church remained at least a potential political force virtually without interruption, and the collectivization of the peasantry did not get very far.

The historical importance of intellectuals in Poland had been far greater than in Czechoslovakia.[4] "Every Polish schoolboy knows," wrote Timothy Garton Ash, "that since the time of the partitions, the *inteligencja* has had a mission to uphold the spirit and culture of the nation against the political powers that be."[5] Czechoslovakia, on the other hand, did not formally become a nation until 1919, and its intelligentsia traditions were tenuous. One should be cautious in ascribing substantial significance to "national identities," but Poland's tradition of insurrectionary, some would say quixotic, politics contrasted with less ancient Czech traditions of caution and indirection in the face of *force majeure*. As one prominent and courageous Czechoslovak dissident remarked drily, "Central Europe is an extremely unpromising setting for national heroics."[6]

No doubt the decision by Great Britain and France to abandon the country to its fate during the Munich crisis in 1938 played an additional role in suggesting to Czechs and Slovaks that fiery rebelliousness would merely lead them to the slaughter. An unusually sympathetic Polish observer believed that what happened before World War II helped account for a certain "resignation" observable in Czechoslovakia after the coup of 1948 and even after the crushing of the Prague Spring in 1968.[7] At all events, the Czech leaders, particularly Edvard Beneš, drew from Munich the lesson that cooperation with the Soviet Union and Soviet protection would be essential in the future.

But in both nations, spurred by the events of 1968, intellectuals guided liberationist, anti-Soviet politics until the collapse of Communism at the end of the 1980s. "In a society based on ideas—or on ideology, which is not quite the same thing," Dwight Macdonald once wrote, "intellectuals are as important a resource as coal mines."[8] Or as Nikita Khrushchev is supposed to have said about the Hungarian Revolution of 1956: "[N]one of this would have happened if a couple of writers had been shot in time."[9]

Not only was the politics of these intellectuals much more important than that of their opposite numbers in the West, but the task with which they were faced differed as well. In Eastern Europe, the relationship between anti-Communism in domestic politics—understanding the nation's position internationally and analyzing the Soviet regime—was so close that they became virtually a single thing. In Poland and Czechoslovakia, the usage of and discussions about the concept of totalitarianism did not in any significant way involve the government. The engaged intellectuals were mostly outside academia; indeed, when one became an opponent of the regime (which is what using the term meant), one's academic position was quickly forfeited.

Hungary presents a rather different case. The trauma of the suppression of the "Hungarian Revolution" in 1956 was great, but the compromise that the Kádár regime subsequently achieved with the Soviet Union was the most successful and in a broad sense the most "liberal" in Eastern Europe. The combination militated against the desperate risk taking that we find in different forms in Czechoslovakia and Poland, for the Hungarian government developed some real legitimacy. In part because the intellectual prestige and influence of the Hungarian Marxist philosopher György Lukács was so great, Marxist influence was more long lasting in Hungary.

Problems that were worked out in Poland or Czechoslovakia without relation to Marxism were often discussed in residual Marxist categories among Hungarians. At the turn of the 1980s, philosophically minded intellectuals like Agnes Heller, Mihaly Vajda, Maria Markus, Ference Fehér, and Andras Hegedüs still considered "alienation under socialism the central issue of East European societies."[10] The category of the totalitarian was frequently used, but in a less analytical or innovative way than in Prague or Warsaw.

Intellectuals in Eastern Europe who led the crusade against totalitarianism, in particular Poles and Czechs, had little fellow feeling for intellectuals in the West, particularly declared leftists, although the German writer Heinrich Böll was a good friend to the Czechs. For much of the Western Left, as we have seen, any forthright anti-Communism was seen as providing aid and comfort to the Right. But in Eastern Europe, *all* intellectuals were anti-Communist. "The Western Left," complained the Czech Václav Benda,

> may be right a hundred times over in their critical assessment of politics in their own countries, but as long as they fail to understand the vast difference between totalitarianism and democracy (and the Left does *not* understand them, and clearly, for very basic reasons, does not even want to), I have no confidence either in what they do or in the solution they propose.[11]

So the argument about totalitarianism in East and West differed with the life situations of the actors.

In Poland between 1945 and 1976, the intellectual community moved steadily away from Communism. There were a few liberals and anti-

Communist leftists who at first supported the new regime, but disillusion was not long in coming. The small group of serious Marxists in Poland first repudiated Stalinism in the name of true Marxism and then moved from Marxism to a less political "Marxist humanism" and finally abandoned all forms of Marxism.

Fairly early in this process, however, well before the term *totalitarianism* began to become crucial to the struggle for liberation in Poland and Czechoslovakia, a Polish émigré poet produced what has generally been regarded as one of the classic discussions of the totalitarian control over the minds of its victims. The author was the poet Czesław Miłosz, and the book, published in 1953, was *The Captive Mind*.[12] Miłosz was of middle-class background (his father was an engineer) and was from Lithuania. He had been quite radical in his youth and published his first poems before he was twenty; after 1945, he had served the Polish Communists as a diplomat in New York and Paris before asking the French government for political asylum in February 1951.[13]

Miłosz used the term *totalitarianism* infrequently in *The Captive Mind*, but almost from the moment of its appearance, the book was regarded as "an enormously important contribution to the understanding of Communist totalitarianism."[14] The basic aim of the book was to make West Europeans and Americans understand Communism as a political religion, as a "New Faith" that sought to remake its adherents. In that sense, the book has some similarities to Raymond Aron's *The Opium of the Intellectuals,* although its brilliance lies in the psychological acuteness of the case studies of Polish writers who fell under the sway of Marxism and/or the Polish government, rather than in any analytical and political attack on Communist doctrines. *The Captive Mind,* to commandeer Jean-François Revel's title, is one of the greatest studies of "the totalitarian temptation."

Miłosz stressed the aspirations of the Communist regime for total control and dwelt on the conversion experiences of Polish intellectuals. Some of these were heavily tinged by opportunism and venality; others were marked by more subtle social and ideological pressures; and still others were motivated by attitudes significantly religious, stemming from a deep commitment to the alleviation of suffering and a sense that under the circumstances one had to work to that end within the framework provided by history.[15]

The Polish intellectual historian Andrzej Walicki explained Miłosz's own early attitude toward Polish Communism by suggesting that if the Communists were "the new Christians," Miłosz's relation to them was that of a "good pagan"—somebody attracted by the "New Faith" but not truly converted:

> Like other progressive Polish intellectuals, he was profoundly disgusted with "God and country" nationalism—the dominant ideology of prewar Poland—and aware of the need for deep social reform. Nevertheless, he refused to become "baptized." The pagan values were a part of himself, and he was unable and unwilling to renounce his identity.

The priests of the "New Faith" solved all problems for the writers—both moral and material. They offered them great prestige and carefree, privileged existence. But for this they demanded the renouncement of freedom and truth. Their dialectical method . . . proved that lies could serve the cause of truth, and that true freedom consisted in the scientific understanding of necessity.[16]

Miłosz was quite unsparing in his attitude toward his colleagues who capitulated, which contributed to the book's power but also led to bitter resentment among those about whom he wrote. His own inability to serve the New Faith seems to have been partly visceral, related, apparently, to a "love of good" that he found in the writings of the atheist-mystic Simone Weil.[17]

The writing in *The Captive Mind* was contained but extraordinarily vivid, and the impression it made in the West was enormous. It appeared almost simultaneously in Polish, French, and English and was soon translated into German, Italian, Spanish, and other languages. No one in the West had read anything like it. The point of view of people "behind the Iron Curtain" was of great interest in the United States during the Korean War, and so was the little understood mentality of those who had helped bring about such regimes or who had come to accept them.

The 1960s in Poland saw Polish Marxism increasingly on the defensive. The Hungarian Revolution of 1956 and the less tumultuous but still highly significant demonstrations in Poznań and Warsaw that resulted in the recall of Gomułka to power in October of the same year induced hopes of Marxist "revisionism" and "humanism," which were gradually disappointed. Marxist philosophers like Leszek Kołakowski and Adam Schaff (who started from a more official position) soon more or less explicitly repudiated Soviet Marxism in favor of the exciting studies of alienation by the young Karl Marx, then becoming of great interest to intellectuals and scholars all over Europe. Already in Kołakowski's revisionism there were Kantian suggestions of the primacy of ethics over politics; such interests were an important step toward the more daring post-1968 intellectual world.

In more activist or general terms, *revisionism* was generally identified with the struggle for democratic socialism. Its leading practitioners at first made it an article of faith that they should remain inside the Communist Party, the better to influence its evolution. Devotees of "Marxist humanism" hoped for a less political, more philosophically radical, or more concrete Marxism. As Imre Nagy, the leader of the Hungarian Revolution, put it back in 1953, he was for "communism which does not forget about man."[18] Nagy's fate—he was executed by the Soviets in 1958—did not encourage those hoping that a more humanistic point of view might come to prevail any time soon. But even if one accepts the idea that the interest in Marxist revisionism was quixotic at the political level, it had its importance, stimulating social "activism, and with it a revival of political interest; it was opposed to that passivity in public life that was both a result and a condition of the existence of Stalinist monopoly. Even the eventual defeat of revisionism served the cause of rebuilding civil society."[19]

Of at least comparable long-term significance was the fact that among ordinary Poles, Czechs, and Slovaks, attachment to the historical nation increased with the awakening from the deep passivity of early East European Stalinism. These developments in Poland were connected to the fact that after 1956, the Catholic church was able to come to an accommodation with the regime. In return for the abandonment of all-out opposition to the regime, the primate of Poland, Stepan Cardinal Wysziński, was freed from prison. Administrative harassment lessened. Some church property was restored, and some religious instruction was allowed.

Thanks to the increased influence and security of the church, several groups of Catholic intellectuals in Poland were able to organize themselves openly, with the toleration of the regime. The "Znak" (sign) movement had deputies in the Polish parliament and operated a monthly journal, *Znak,* and a publishing house. Even more important was their weekly journal, the Cracow-based *Tygodnik Powszechny*. The intellectuals of the Więź group, who included the journal's editor, Tadeusz Mazowiecki, later an important political figure in post-Communist Poland, were farther to the Left and formed a kind of bridge to former revisionists like Kołakowski. There were also clubs for Catholic intellectuals, with several thousand members in all, mostly in Warsaw.[20] The Catholic opposition, initially quite reserved, was often called *neopositivism,* after Catholic opposition to Russian rule before 1918.

"Much like the revisionists," according to Adam Michnik, "the Catholic politicians believed in having concessions and rights 'granted' from above rather than in organizing pressure from below. They sought harmony, not conflict; they cared for order, seeking agreement with the party, and sought to avoid imputations of oppositional attitudes."[21]

The term *totalitarianism* made its first appearances in the oppositional literature during and in the aftermath of 1968;[22] earlier East European usages are isolated and fragmentary.[23] By the mid-1970s, the term was regularly employed by Polish (and, to a lesser degree, Czechoslovak) intellectuals to describe the world to which the Soviet regime had subjected them. Because of their actual political situation, the Poles and Czechs developed the idea of totalitarianism in a far more practical and activist way than did the intellectuals of Western Europe and the United States. They were not so concerned with what totalitarianism was (they thought they knew) as with how to escape from it, step by step. However, they did need to know, practically speaking, what the opposite of totalitarianism was or, to put it another way, precisely what they had lost under Soviet domination and how to set about getting it back. One answer to that question was their national identity, since "Soviet totalitarianism" was inextricably bound up with foreign domination. Another answer was a nongovernmental sphere, or what came to be known as "civil society."

In the history of the Cold War, 1968 was a big year, not least because of the significant intersection between the struggle of the power blocs and the drama of the 1960s: the waxing and waning of the New Left. In Paris and Chicago, and on university campuses from Berlin to Berkeley, protest came to a climax. But nowhere was the year 1968 more important than in Eastern Europe—in Prague, where the hopes for "socialism with a human face" were crushed, but also in Warsaw and in Budapest.

The destruction of the Dubček regime dealt a tremendous blow to all East European Communism. The comparison between the Nazi and the Soviet invaders was widely made, by both intellectuals and ordinary people, a comparison, of course, that was a central point in the charge of totalitarianism.[24] In the aftermath, there continued to be people who believed in socialism, and there were even a few Marxists, especially in Hungary, but there was virtually no belief that "real socialism" or "really existing socialism" (a Soviet term for satellite regimes, often used sarcastically by East Europeans) could evolve into anything tolerable. As Adam Michnik put it: "[R]evisionism was terminated by the events of March, 1968."[25] A student of the philosopher György Lukács gave a Hungarian and philosophical version of what happened after 1968:

> [S]lowly I have become estranged from Hegel, sometimes misjudging him in a very unjust way. I do not try to find out any more where the World Spirit has gone, where the given conditions are for the creation of a "true" freedom, of socialism. The World Spirit exists only for those who believe. Socialism as the true history succeeding prehistory, or the epoch of total sinfulness—this religious doctrine of redemption—is not for me any more.[26]

Perhaps, too, the governing authorities gave up trying to persuade their subjects to believe and prepared to settle for something less. If that is so, the potential usefulness to the government of intellectuals declined. They were now largely a danger. In addition, impressionistic evidence suggests that this loss of faith in any livable reality sponsored by the Soviet Union further stimulated Poles and Czechs to cherish their nationality.[27]

The Soviet invasion was followed by two years of intellectual revolt in Hungary. Prominent thinkers—Ferenc Fehér, György and Maria Markus, Agnes Heller—signed a petition against the invasion of Czechoslovakia, and unorthodox and unreliable intellectuals were removed from their university posts and from the Party.[28] In Warsaw, there was an even stronger reaction. *Forefather's Eve*, a famous (and highly anti-Russian) play by Adam Mickiewicz, was banned by the government. Mickiewicz was Poland's national bard, as central to the Polish psyche as Pushkin was to the Russian. The ensuing protests and demonstrations of Polish students and intellectuals in February and March 1968 were brutally crushed. Intellectuals who came to the students' defense were severely punished; professors were fired and students expelled from their institutions of higher learning. The first two to be dismissed were Adam Michnik and Henryk Szlajfer, both of whom later played important roles in the dissidence that followed. "At Warsaw University the departments of economics, philosophy, sociology and psychology were administratively dissolved."[29] An openly anti-Semitic campaign followed, which attempted to blame the unrest on Poland's small remnant of Jews, almost all of whom left the country.

There was no alliance with the workers, who remained aloof from the struggles of 1968. At his trial, Karol Modzelewski, once a pampered member of Poland's Communist elite, equated the Polish regime with the Nazis.[30] Previously, secular-minded leftists in Poland had tended to see the church as the milieu from which some kind of nationalist pseudo-Fascism might emerge. But these horrors had actually arisen within the Communist Party![31]

In 1970, it was the workers' turn. Things began when Gomułka's government embarked on an ambitious effort to discipline and rationalize Polish heavy industry within the framework of the entire socialist bloc (which would have meant the drastic downsizing of Polish shipbuilding, among other industries). Benefits were to be cut back; workers were excoriated by representatives of the government for their laziness. Then, about ten days before Christmas, came dramatic increases in food prices. Demonstrations, first in the shipyards of Gdańsk, led to confrontation, then riots, the destruction of Party buildings, the looting of stores. There were pitched battles with police and soldiers in Gdańsk and Szczecin and a massacre of workers in Gdynia. Somewhere between forty-five (the official figure) and several hundred people were killed.[32] When it was all over, Gomułka had been replaced by Eduard Gierek, but it was not clear that much else had been gained.

What had not happened may have been even more important. The students had not responded to the workers' appeals in Gdańsk and elsewhere and had gone home for an early Christmas vacation, as they had been told to do by the authorities. Nor had the Catholic church played any active role. One legacy of 1968 and 1970 was a realization that the workers, students, and the church had to stand together if anything were to change in Poland.[33]

Of all the Polish intellectuals who moved from leftist, especially Marxist, positions to sustained criticism of communism, none was more important than the philosopher Leszek Kołakowski. Kołakowski had joined the Communist Party as an eighteen-year-old in 1945 and remained a member until 1966, when he was expelled for giving a lecture on the tenth anniversary of the Polish and Hungarian revolts. By that time, his "Marxist humanism" was far removed from Party orthodoxy. In 1968, Kołakowski, the head of the modern philosophy section at the University of Warsaw, was expelled from his university position in March, after participating in the demonstrations. He left Poland the following year to teach at several Canadian and American universities before settling at All Souls College, Oxford.

In the summer of 1971, Kołakowski published an important article,

"Theses on Hope and Hopelessness," which foreshadowed the use of the term *totalitarian* in Polish (and Czech) political discussions and suggested the direction in which domestic opposition might go.[34] One Western scholar called it "the fundamental theoretical text of the Polish democratic opposition of the 1970s."[35]

Kołakowski began by giving his version of a commonly asserted pessimistic case about the possibilities of reform in Eastern Europe. The Soviet autocratic system could not be reformed and could not achieve either greater efficiency or moral acceptability because even though the terror had attenuated, society had no control over the "ruling apparatus," behind which stood Soviet military power. Freedom of information was "unthinkable." After the suppression of the Warsaw demonstrations of March 1968, Poles had endured "the massive promotion of ignoramuses, informers, or simple louts ('the invasion of the lice' as it was called in Warsaw)."[36] Like other despotisms, the Warsaw government aimed to create a "siege mentality" by inciting hostility against the outside world. Kołakowski stressed its "need to 'nationalize' all forms of social life" and its "continuous pressure aimed at destroying all spontaneous social ties in favour of compulsory pseudo-associations, whose only functions are negative and destructive." The ruling apparatus could not broaden citizens' rights even if it wanted to, because of the "huge reserves of hidden hostility and suppressed demands." The system, in sum, was "the characteristically socialist form of slavery."[37]

Having made this pessimistic case, Kołakowski turned around and tried to suggest its weaknesses. To begin with, he believed, the system was partly dependent on people's being convinced that the situation was truly hopeless, that no reform was possible. Therefore, people in the grip of the system had an obligation to overcome their pessimism and try to limit and weaken it as best they could.

Kołakowski went on to make another important point. Stalinist power simply could not be reestablished in the post-Stalin era because the post-Stalinist leadership was unwilling to accept the terrifying insecurity it brought to the elite. But once the apparatus "no longer fears its leader or its police so much," it pays by having to fear elements of the society over which it rules: inside competitors for power, workers, and intellectuals.

Kołakowski then took up a point that would be endlessly discussed over the next two decades: the fact that virtually no one any longer believed that Marxist-Leninist ideology could be used to mobilize the population. "Certain irreversible changes" have taken place: The ideological sphere has shrunk to the degree that "bureaucratic socialism has lost its ideological base." Kołakowski concluded with a quotation from a book by the Trotskyist writer Victor Serge on the old Tsarist secret police: "[A] system which nobody serves disinterestedly is doomed."[38] But in concrete terms, what did the atrophy of ideology mean? How could it contribute to the possibilities for resistance?

In the Soviet Union itself, Kołakowski believed, there was an unarticulated ideology conveyed to people between the lines, a "subtext" calculated to assuage the Russian sense of inferiority: that the current regime had at least brought Russians the glories of superpower status. And, Kołakowski predicted, this semisublimated Russian–Soviet nationalism would increase in the future as people lost all faith in Marxism-Leninism. At the same time, he believed, the Soviet regime could not achieve real prosperity without sharply modifying "despotic socialism." Its stagnation (an early use of the term) was therefore bound to continue until there was at some point an explosion.

In Soviet satellites like Poland, however, the situation was significantly different. Steady pressure by working people and intellectuals there might have some political effect because the government was torn between the security conferred by its dependence on the Soviet Union and its desire for greater independence.

Kołakowski also stressed the importance of the national cultures of Eastern Europe, specifically those of Poland and Czechoslovakia. Their preservation was essential in the face of a tyranny that sought to obliterate them, and it was the intelligentsia that had to take the lead in this vital cause.

What Poland had to have, therefore, was "a reformist orientation in the sense of a belief in the possibility of effective gradual and partial pressures, exercised in a long-term perspective, a perspective of social and national liberation." Further, "all the old-fashioned words—'freedom,' 'independence,' 'law,' 'justice,' 'truth'—can turn against the bureaucratic tyranny." And let us not, he exhorted, cooperate with evil!"[39]

Most of the ideas and opinions that would play such a major role in the Polish and Czech dissident movements are here, at least in embryo, starting with the knowledge that Soviet ideology no longer had real power over people's minds or hearts ("the idea of communism in its Soviet version has . . . ceased to exist"). There was the emphasis on national identity, on the cultural sphere and the leadership of the intelligentsia, on gradual pressure over a long period of time, and on the refusal to cooperate with "evil."

Several of Kołakowski's most important themes were soon taken up by another influential Polish intellectual, Jacek Kuroń. Born in 1934, Kuroń had been a Party activist early on, then in and out of the Party, then in and out of jail. Along with another young Communist, Karol Modzelewski, he wrote a critical "Open Letter to the Party" in 1965, charging it with betraying the working class by becoming itself a new exploiting class.[40]

Kuroń published an important essay, "Political Opposition in Poland," toward the end of 1974 in the Paris-based Polish-language journal *Kultura*[41]), read with attention by all Polish intellectuals, however widely dispersed.[42] He believed that under the conditions then existing in Poland, it was impossible to bring about democracy in the political institutions of the state, but that it might be done within Polish society. His conception of democracy was "the continual expansion of the scope for autonomous, non-coerced, social activity," much of which he understood as the creation of an independent culture. "The movement for independent culture," he wrote, "is not a *prelude* to political opposition; it is itself political opposition." Like any "state socialism," he believed, the Polish system necessarily aspired to be totalitarian. It could never succeed, but it could never stop trying. Any independent social activity or organization, therefore, had to be antitotalitarian.[43]

On June 24, 1976, the Polish government finally carried out drastic price increases on food and agricultural products, even larger than those of 1970. Overnight it was much harder for working families to put food on the table.[44] There were demonstrations in many factories, leading again to physical confrontation. Several days of rioting ensued, mostly in the city of Radom and in Ursus, a small factory settlement on the outskirts of Warsaw. At that point, the government backed down and agreed to take a harder look at the increases. Out of the disturbances of 1976, although somewhat less serious than those of 1970, came the first real organized opposition to the Polish government—the Workers Defense Committee, known as KOR.[45]

From the start, KOR operated within the circle of ideas propounded and developed over the previous several years by Kołakowski, Kuroń, and others. Adam Michnik, another important member, was determined that this time the intellectuals would not leave the workers in the lurch. Above all, these intellectuals accepted the idea that asserting moral values and acting openly and within the law were necessary to begin hollowing out within Soviet totalitarianism a sphere for independent activity.[46]

Jacek Kuroń's diagnosis of the situation in Poland in 1976 was simple and straightforward. In "an enormously influential article," he defined Poland's current situation and the sources and genesis of the existing opposition and then offered a prescription for the future.[47] Poland had lost its sovereignty, for the armed forces of the Soviet Union had forced totalitarianism on it, with the acquiescence of the Western powers ("in particular the United States and Great Britain"). Poland's stability was guaranteed, like that of other Warsaw Pact nations, by the willingness of the Soviet Union to rule by force.[48] What could be done?

Kuroń first turned to the sources of such opposition against the Soviet-sponsored government as had existed in the past: mostly "social movements," against some new development (peasants against threatened collectivization, workers organizing first to address specific grievances and then moving on to fight for broader issues); Catholics who fought for the independence of the church; and "writers, scholars and artists who create the national culture and stand for independence of thought and research." The limited nature of their success in 1956, 1968, and 1970, Kuroń thought, was due to the limited degree of their cooperation: "[O]nly well organized, conscious mass resistance movements can save our national existence and culture from totalitarian destruction."[49]

Kuroń then announced that in September 1976,

> the Workers' Defense Committee (KOR) was formed in Warsaw. This committee organizes aid for the victims of reprisals following the 25th of June 1976. It grew out of a nucleus of student and intelligentsia groups and in a short while acquired the support of thousands. Helpers collect money and information; they copy and distribute the communiques of the Committee. The activities of the committee brought the scale and brutality of the government campaign against the strikers into the open.

KOR's only specific demand was "full reinstatement of the workers fired after the 25th of July and . . . an amnesty for those sentenced as a result of the June events."[50] Announcing that an independent publishing movement had already begun, Kuroń called for a coalition of all the social forces in Polish society to force Soviet acceptance of a "Finlandized" Poland.[51] Such pressure could work, Kuroń assumed, because neither the Soviet nor the Polish government leaders any longer believed in their own ideology—which meant that, within limits, their behavior would be in accord with *raison d'état,* rather than with the dynamic imperatives of totalitarianism. In their own, more immediate way, Polish intellectuals also understood the loss of dynamism that scholars in the West were analyzing.

Even more influential in nascent Polish dissident circles was another article published in 1976 by Adam Michnik. This extraordinary activist was born in Warsaw in 1946 to parents whom he described as "Polish communists of Jewish origin."[52] Early on a zealous Marxist, like his father before him, he became involved with revisionism, became an outspoken critic of the Communist Party, was expelled from the University of Warsaw in 1968, served time in jail, and had recently acquired a master's degree in history at the extension division of the University of Poznań—all this before his thirty-second birthday. Within two years, he also helped found the so-called Flying University, one of the new, independent organizations for which intellectuals like Kuroń were calling. Its faculty gave lectures and seminars on political economy, Polish history, and other subjects from a highly unofficial point of view.

Michnik's essay was entitled "A New Evolutionism," and the title was often used subsequently to characterize the emergent dissident strategy generally.[53] He too noted that 1968 had indicated the futility of revisionism and the bankruptcy of Catholic neopositivism. In situations of open and violent conflict, such as those of 1968 and 1970, it was clear that both movements "accepted the government as the basic point of reference." In Michnik's opinion, however, the government should be ignored; it could not be influenced very far because of its anchor to the Soviet oppressor. That being the case, "an unceasing struggle for reform and evolution that seeks an expansion of civil liberties and human rights is the only course East European dissidents can take."[54]

Michnik then turned to an analysis of why he believed the opposition had a real chance of success. Their interests, he pointed out, coincided in one important respect with those of both the Soviet and the Polish leadership. For all of them, a full-scale Soviet invasion of Poland would be a disaster. Poles would be massacred, but the Polish Communist leadership would be utterly discredited, and the Soviet Union would suffer a major diplomatic defeat. So workers' organizations like KOR, student and intelligentsia groups, and those of the church together should be able to put considerable pressure on the government before the risks of Soviet intervention became too great. In this sense, Poland was in a postideological situation, and oppositional politics should reflect everybody's loss of faith.

Michnik's conclusion was very close to Kuroń's. Both of them also drew attention to a remarkable fact: the growing willingness of the church and its supporters, intellectual and otherwise, to work with former radicals, and vice versa. (Both Michnik and Kuroń were received in a private audience by Cardinal Wyszyński during the 1970s.)[55] Thus the long and developed hostility between the church and the Left was markedly lessening, and a kind of "popular front" was coming into existence."[56]

In closing his brief, thirteen-page essay, Michnik spoke of the students and intellectuals—his own people—and how the future of Poland would depend on their relationship with the workers and the church:

> When a free press and independent organizations do not exist, the moral and political responsibility of these groups is much greater than at any other time. The people of the opposition should renounce material profit and official esteem in order to fulfill this exceptional responsibility, so that we can expect the truth from them.
>
> In searching for truth, or, to quote Leszek Kołakowski, "by living in dignity," opposition intellectuals are striving not so much for a better tomorrow as for a better today. Every act of defiance helps us build the framework of democratic socialism, which should not be merely or primarily a legal institutional structure but a real, day-to-day community of free people.[57]

But if Kuroń and Michnik were right, if neither rulers nor ruled believed in Soviet ideology or were prepared to enforce its claims except under the most desperate circumstances, how could Poland be said to be in the grip of totalitarianism? According to the Polish historian and sociologist Andrzej Walicki, "the . . . emergence of an 'extrasystemic' opposition would not have been possible without a long process of internal detotalitarianization."[58]

Such would appear to be the case. Bribery, corruption, and what were to become known as "second economies" flourished in Poland, Hungary, Czechoslavakia, and the Soviet Union itself. Most scholars in the West had recognized that the belief of the Soviet rulers in their own ideology had long been in decline and that the rise of détente made them increasingly reluctant, after 1968, to intervene physically in Eastern Europe. Their interest in anything so ambitious as actively molding their subjects into "new Soviet people" had also been attenuating since Stalin's time. As one prominent Polish writer subsequently put the matter:

> From October 1956 Poland found itself . . . under a semitotalitarian government that allowed one to think but not to speak, allowed one to hum but forbade singing, allowed one to rest but did not allow one to work, allowed one to enter a church but would not consent to have one leave it.[59]

The emergence of organized dissident communities in both the Soviet Union and Eastern Europe testified to the changes that had taken place since Stalin's death. There was a growing (although by no means complete) consensus among Western observers that—whatever the Soviet Union had been under Stalin—it was by this time merely "authoritarian" and was in important respects highly conservative under Brezhnev.

The idea that they faced a totalitarian enemy was intellectually and emotionally appealing to East European intellectuals, and their emerging strategy was based on it. There was no consensus on how weakened Soviet or local "totalitarianisms" might actually be. There was to be a good deal of debate about this question, out of which would emerge a new category: posttotalitarianism. This concept allowed the East Europeans to recognize that their enemy—both the Soviet one and its national epigone—was not so formidable nowadays, and yet it allowed them to keep their vocabulary largely intact. And there was agreement that Soviet-type regimes still aspired to be totalitarian.

———

AS CZECHOSLOVAKIA emerged from the debacle of 1968, its situation was clearly worse than that of Poland or Hungary. After the 1956 Hungarian uprising had been crushed, János Kádár had concentrated on economic issues and over time improved Hungary's situation considerably. Polish intellectuals, as we have seen, were forging an alliance among traditional loci of opposition to Soviet domination. In Czechoslovakia, though, the Party had made a conscious decision not to compromise with reform elements. At the orthodox rerun of the Fourteenth Party Congress in May 1971, those forces supporting some political compromise and the continuation of economic development were defeated, and broad political repression followed.[60] Arrests of Party moderates, trials, and relatively severe sentences continued into 1972. Well over 100,000 people appear to have emigrated between 1968 and 1971.[61] Hard-liners were in control. Vasil Bilák was on hand to make sure that the conservative Gustav Husák (a Slovak, who had himself been a political prisoner for almost ten years) did not drift toward the center.

"The first half of the 1970s here in Czechoslovakia lives in my memory as a period of darkness," wrote Václav Havel a decade later.[62] In addition to the discrediting of the Party's moderate wing, students were expelled from the universities; professors were fired; literary, media, and cultural figures were blackballed. "Scholars and professional people were working as stokers or window-cleaners. Ordinary people were without rights and sought only a half-decent material life. . . . Few had much hope for change in the near future, or even in their lifetime."[63]

And yet the repression was not severe enough to prevent the emergence, in 1973, of Czechoslovak dissidence. Much of it took the form of circulating books—or *feuilletons,* as they were known in Czechoslovakia—essays of varying length on current themes, generally (but not always) elliptical.

Czech *samizdat* differed from the Russian variant, especially in its greater openness. Czech writers had a regular "publisher": Padlock Editions (Edice Petlice); works were often signed by their authors; and in many cases it was clearly typed on the cover that further reproduction and distribution was forbidden. The intent was to make them legally circulating first drafts that would some day be properly published, not "self-published" material, which was what *samizdat* means in Russian.[64]

The Czech "publishers" of *feuilletons* thus took risks still impossible for their Soviet oppositional or dissident counterparts; they also refused to accept that their activities were illegal. Like their Polish colleagues, they were harassed, arrested, and jailed, but their activities continued. Milan Simečka, a reform Communist until 1968, published a *samizdat* account of Czech "normalization" after he lost his university position in 1977. He agreed with his Polish colleagues that "existing socialism no longer has any ideological content." Toward the end of his book, he wrote that the Czechoslavak state "did not require [its subjects] to believe wholeheartedly the arguments put out by the daily propaganda. It would happily make do with passive loyalty." In "normalised" or "adapted" Czechoslovakia,

the unsupervised private sphere is quite extensive. The state allows adapted citizens to do what they like with the money they more or less honestly acquire. They may build houses, chalets and cabins, and fit them out as they wish . . . They may enjoy themselves as they like. They may travel abroad, so long as they can afford the shocking tax on the purchase of hard currency. [Of course very few could.] They may use their garden to grow fruit and vegetables such as you will never find in the market. They may not actually be able to read what they would like, but the State erects communal aerials to receive TV programmes from Vienna. . . . In the privacy of their own homes, adaptees may spread gossip about political leaders, laugh at political jokes, slander and insult the Republic, relate stories about West Germany, Sweden and Can-ada. . . . Adapted citizens may curse, revile and rail against the allies, and profane all the Soviet sacraments. So long as they keep this for their private life and display their adapted faces in public, and so long as no spiteful person reports them, the State makes no attempt to save their adapted souls. . . . The main thing is that the adapted citizen should turn out to vote for the Party candidates and take part in the May Day rally.[65]

To which the playwright Václav Havel added, in an "open letter" to Gustav Husák, that such behavior was "an escape from the public sphere" and even a "desperate substitute for living." The state, continued Havel, "by fixing a person's whole attention on his mere consumer interests . . . hoped to render him incapable of realizing the increasing extent to which he has been spiritually, politically and morally violated."[66] The émigré Czech journalist Jacques Rupnik, like other students of Eastern Europe, believed that in Czechoslovakia there was a kind of "social contract": The government allowed private consumerism in exchange for its citizens' renunciation of politics.[67]

This world is akin to the one in which Polish intellectuals were living before the founding of KOR. In Poland, too, it was widely believed that the regime was trying to buy off society: We will raise standards of living and allow you to enjoy life a bit more, and in turn you will stay out of politics. A Polish historian recently referred to this tacit agreement as a "quasi consensus," inaugurated by Gierek in 1970 and holding the opposition in check until 1976.[68] In both Czechoslovakia and Poland, the opposition to "consumerism" was an important part of the struggle against the regimes that gathered momentum in the mid-1970s.

But—fewer in numbers, without the support of the church, and with a tougher government in charge—Czech and Slovak intellectuals were weaker and more isolated than their Polish counterparts. They had been greatly demoralized by 1968, and they lacked the Polish insurrectionary spirit. Their apathy and discouragement were ultimately interrupted by a most unlikely series of events, beginning with the arrest, trial, and condemnation of a rock band with the improbable name Plastic People of the Universe.

The Plastic People was "one of hundreds of rock groups which had come into existence in Czechoslovakia in the mid- and late 1960s." Initially inspired by English and American groups, they had developed a certain lyric and intellectual connection with Czech national literature, as well as with the usual alcohol- and drug-prone bohemia of rock musicians.[69] Since the early 1970s they, and especially their leader, Ivan Jirous, had been under pressure from the authorities. Jirous had in fact served ten months in jail for having joked in a bar about "a friendly nation."[70]

Despite the apparent incongruity, there were a number of ways in which the protest over the fate of the fourteen Plastic People was an appropriate preamble to the creation of Charter 77. The issue of cultural autonomy was central among dissidents in Eastern Europe, and several of the musicians had been active in what had been called the "musical underground" since 1968. Long hair, outlandish costumes, lack of a settled life, and aversion to consumerism were even more threatening to the Czech authorities than to those in the capitalist world. But an important reason for the success of their protest was that they seemed innocent and not political in any obvious way.[71] Václav Havel, covering the trial, found them touching and appropriate symbols of artistic integrity: people who just wanted to compose their own songs and play them as they pleased. Havel also found his hostility toward guile suddenly increased, his revulsion to "emergency exits" from vital dilemmas.[72]

Letters of protest were written to figures in the West, such as the German novelist Heinrich Böll, and soon a committee of writers and intellectuals had formed to defend the musicians.[73] So despite its intent to defend artists rather than workers, Charter 77 had much in common with KOR in Poland, which came into existence at about the same time.

The charter was dated January 1, 1977. Only some two thousand words long, the document (to the drafting of which Václav Havel was central) stated that it was the work of

> a free informal, open community of people of different convictions, different faiths and different professions united by the will to strive, individually and collectively, for the respect of civic and human rights in our own country and throughout the world—rights accorded to all men by the . . . Final Act of the Helsinki Conference and by numerous other international documents opposing war, violence and social or spiritual oppression, and which are comprehensively laid down in the United Nations Universal Declaration of Human Rights.[74]

These covenants were the basic term of reference. The rights they guaranteed had been systematically violated, according to the charter. Initially there were 239 signatories; by June 1977, 751 people had signed; by June of the following year, there were more than 1,000.[75]

Like KOR in Poland, Charter 77 represented a coalition. There were former reform Communists disillusioned by 1968, a few non-Communist radicals, people of a vaguely (and sometimes specifically) Christian persuasion,[76] eminent intellectuals and professionals who had never been party members, and young people from the "musical underground."[77]

Although Havel was probably the most active in the events leading to the creation of Charter 77, the philosopher and historian of philosophy Jan Patočka was initially the best known and most respected.[78] But he was a septuagenarian under heavy pressure from the government, and he died of a cerebral hemorrhage in the middle of March, which left Havel as the charter's center of gravity, despite his several arrests and periods of incarceration.

Because of Havel's bourgeois origins, he had been forced to quit school in 1948 at age fourteen, when the Communists took power, and was not allowed to attend the university. He worked as a carpenter and a laboratory assistant; his first literary works were poetry. He had become involved with the theater while he was in the army, and his first important play, *The Garden Party*, was produced in 1963.[79]

In 1978, Havel wrote an essay entitled "The Power of the Powerless," which was published in *samizdat* the following year. This essay of some hundred pages was one of those arresting works that seem to embody the thinking of an era. It defined Czechoslovak reality as "posttotalitarian" and suggested how to struggle against it. Havel, who allowed that he wrote the essay very quickly, was still groping for what he meant by the term. He added rather confusingly that his vocabulary was "not the most precise" and that he did not mean by calling Czechoslovakia "posttotalitarian" to imply that it was no longer totalitarian, but that it was totalitarian "in a new way."[80]

When Havel demonstrated what he meant, however, he was brilliantly successful:

> The manager of a fruit and vegetable shop places in his window, among the onions and the carrots the slogan "Workers of the World, Unite!" Why does he do it? What is he trying to communicate to the world? Is he genuinely enthusiastic about the idea of unity among the workers of the world? Is his enthusiasm so great that he feels an irrepressible impulse to acquaint the public with his ideals? Has he really given more than a moment's thought to how such a unification might occur and what it would mean?[81]

The answer to these questions was obvious. The poster came to the grocer from the authorities, "along with the onions and carrots." He put them in the window

> because it has been done that way for years, because everyone does it, and because that is the way it has to be. If he were to refuse, there could be trouble. He could be reproached for not having the proper "decoration" in his window; someone might even accuse him of disloyalty. He does it because these things must be done if one is to get along in life. It is one of the thousands of details that guarantee him a relatively tranquil life "in harmony with society," as they say.[82]

Havel, of course, was far from arguing that the sign had no meaning. Its subliminal message was "I, greengrocer XY live here and I know what I must do. I behave in the manner expected of me. I can be depended upon and am beyond reproach. I am obedient and therefore I have the right to be left in peace."

If the grocer, Havel went on, had been asked by the regime to put a sign in the window saying that he was afraid and therefore obedient (which was the precise state of affairs), he would have been humiliated and embarrassed. By putting his expression of loyalty in the form of a text that could actually be defended if necessary, he could conceal from himself "the low foundations of his obedience." And the regime's reliance on force could be concealed behind an ideology in which no one any longer believed but that still maintained a remote and theoretical plausibility.

Confronted with his own degradation and trivialization, the grocer needed the ideology as much in his way as the regime did. In a posttotalitarian society, ideology

> acts as a kind of bridge between the regime and the people, across which the regime approaches the people and the people approach the regime. This explains why ideology plays such an important role in the post-totalitarian system: that complex machinery of units, hierarchies, trans-mission belts, and indirect instruments of manipulation which insure in countless ways the integrity of the regime, leaving nothing to chance, would be quite simply unthinkable without ideology acting as its all-embracing excuse and as the excuse for each of its parts.[83]

Havel argued that the system had enslaved even those who seemed to profit from it; that its purposes were not the mere preservation of power in the hands of a clique, as it seemed at first; and that the destinies even of the leadership had become subordinated to a kind of "blind *automatism* which drives the system." Even the most important individual's lust for power "is admissible only insofar as its direction coincides with the direction of the automatism of the system."[84]

Havel later added that "reality does not shape theory, but rather the reverse." Power derives its strength from theory, not from reality, and inevitably power begins to serve the ideology rather than the other way around. Not only does this ideology guarantee power in the present, but it increasingly becomes the guarantor of its continuity."[85]

This extraordinary situation, although bad enough in its own way, was quite different from the realities of Stalin's time. In posttotalitarian Eastern Europe, wrote Havel,

> ideology, in creating a bridge of excuses between the system and the individual, spans the abyss between the aims of the system and the aims of life. It pretends that the requirements of the system derive from the require-ments of life. It is a world of appearances trying to pass for reality. . . . That is why life in the system is so permeated with hypocrisy and lies: govern-ment by bureaucracy is called popular government; the working class is enslaved in the name of the working class; the complete degradation of the individual is presented as his or her ultimate liberation; depriving people of information is called making it available; the use of power to manipulate is called the public control of power, and the arbitrary abuse of power is called observing the legal code; the repression of culture is called its devel-opment; the expansion of imperial influence is presented as support for the oppressed; the lack of free expression becomes the highest form of free-dom; farcical elections become the highest form of democracy; banning independent thought becomes the most scientific of worldviews; military occupation becomes fraternal assistance. Because the regime is captive to its own lies, it must falsify everything.[86]

So despite the lessening of terror and the loss of ideological élan, it was at least possible to argue that the system in its decadence was still totalitarian, even a truer form of totalitarianism than Stalinism, if less obvious.

Havel reiterated that the grocer need not believe all this; indeed, no one does. But he must act as though he did. He must "live within a lie."[87] The victims of posttotalitarianism are totally implicated in it. Individuals not only make and confirm the system, but are the system—both the prime minister and the grocer.

It is important to notice that in "The Power of the Powerless," Havel did not make a fundamental distinction between the world dominated by totalitarianism and the modern "bourgeois" world of the West. Like Hannah Arendt, Havel connected mass society, the loss of coherent social identities and structures, and the emergence of totalitarianism, contending that the posttotalitarian society "is only an inflated caricature of modern life in general."[88]

Christianity served as a "point of departure" for Havel's critique; he aligned himself enthusiastically with the ecological movement; he criticized "technological civilization" in a general way; and he linked the privatism, careerism, and consumerism of East and West.[89] After 1990, Havel came increasingly to believe that the "modern age" or "modernity" was coming to an end, that in both East and West a new, more modest, ecologically sound, nonrationalist civilization was desperately needed.

Havel's remedy for the situation in which he and his friends found themselves at the turn of the 1980s was simple: to stop "living within a lie" and begin "living within the truth." Truth, he thought, had a force in posttotalitarian society akin to the child in the Hans Christian Andersen fairytale crying, "The Emperor is naked." Again like Hannah Arendt, Havel saw the contrast between real and fictitious worlds as central to totalitarianism. When even a single person breaks through the fabric of life as it is in theory, "everything appears in another light." The truth teller can be restored to his or her true identity, and the whole false world of ideology is put at risk.

"When I speak of living within the truth," Havel concluded,

> I naturally do not have in mind only products of conceptual thought, such as a protest or a letter written by a group of intellectuals. It can be any means by which a person or a group revolts against manipulation: anything from a letter by intellectuals to a workers' strike, from a rock concert to a student demonstration, from refusing to vote in the farcical elections, to making an open speech at some official congress, or even a hunger strike, for instance . . . every free expression of life indirectly threatens the post-totalitarian system politically.[90]

The implications of "living within the truth" went beyond individual revolt, despite the importance that Havel ascribed to how refusing the lie would restore the integrity of the individual. For if a critical mass of truth tellers were created, "parallel structures" would begin to emerge, and even an entire "second culture" might ultimately be created: The aggregate of *samizdat* publications, lectures and seminars, and private concerts amounted to what Václav Benda, Havel, and others were already calling a "parallel polis."[91] Ultimately, he hoped, the official one would just wither away and die.

The "parallel structures" about which Havel wrote were much farther along in Poland than in Czechoslovakia. In Poland, something approaching Havel's "second culture" appeared during the late 1970s and 1980s, whereas in Czechoslovakia Charter 77's supporters were limited to a few thousand. But in both societies, and even in the Soviet Union, it was becoming clear that the increasing visibility of people known as *dissidents* (although some did not care for the term) represented some ebbing of the power of the totalitarian state and therefore could be represented as in some way posttotalitarian. It was not clear, however, how much "space" they could recapture for what they soon learned to call "civil society" or that they had anything like the hopeful future Havel foresaw.[92]

Not all the chartists were prepared to accept Havel's analysis in its entirety, and well before the second year of Charter 77's existence had passed, a not entirely focused debate had begun. Jiří Hájek, a former cabinet minister before and during 1968, remained close to a revisionist Marxist point of view and did not speak of totalitarianism.[93] Peter Uhl, a Trotskyist, made a criticism of the chartists' activities that was more disturbing because it was made by others too and was unconnected to any particular program for the future: He accused the chartists of a certain moral exclusivity.[94] The best-known formulation of this criticism was by the longtime dissident writer Ludvík Vaculík, who in a *feuilleton* entitled "On Heroism" worried that Charter 77 might evolve into a small band of exalted heroes, cut off from the goodwill and honesty of ordinary people, so essential to the future.[95]

The debate about whether heroic elitism and the modest achievements of broader segments of the population were mutually exclusive and, if so, which was to be preferred remained rather theoretical, as the year 1979 saw Charter 77 decimated by arrests, including those of Havel, Benda, Uhl, and the former journalist Jiří Dienstbier. For the moment, there was no possibility of a larger movement.

In the late 1970s, "The Power of the Powerless" may have been more significant in Poland than in Czechoslovakia. Zbigniew Bujak, a worker and a Solidarity activist, later remembered how

> this essay reached us in the Ursus factory in 1979 at a point when we felt we were at the end of the road. Inspired by KOR, we had been speaking on the shop floor, talking to people, participating in public meetings, trying to speak the truth about the factory, the country and politics. There came a moment when people thought we were crazy. Why were we doing this? Why were we taking such risks? Not seeing any immediate

and tangible results, we began to doubt the purposefulness of what we were doing. Shouldn't we be coming up with other methods, other ways?

Then came the essay by Havel. Reading it gave us the theoretical underpinnings for our activity. It mainained our spirits; we did not give up, and a year later, in August 1980—it became clear that the party apparatus and the factory management were afraid of us. We mattered. And the rank and file saw us as leaders of the movement.

Bujak saw in the ultimate victories of Solidarity and of Charter 77, "an astonishing fulfillment of the prophecies and knowledge contained in Havel's essay."[96]

THE FOUNDERS OF KOR also continued to define their enemy as "totalitarian." According to one member who later wrote the organization's history,

from the very beginning, KOR acted consciously on the assumption that it would unite people in the struggle against totalitarianism, and in an area that left no doubt that what was at stake was the defense of ethical values; above all, by bringing organized help to people persecuted by the totalitarian authorities.[97]

Similar concerns led the founders to ensure that the organization's activities were overt and legal, in accord with Michnik's and Kuroń's ideas, and that the organization did not lie or engage in violence under any circumstances. A Christian ethos was strong, even among nonbelievers like Michnik and Kuroń, as was a defense of the nation. Aid was found for the workers of Radom and Ursus (and smaller numbers from elsewhere); underground newspapers and journals (*The Worker* [*Robotnik*], *KOR Communiqué*) were founded, along with a publishing house (NOWa) and underground lectures and seminars. George Orwell's *Nineteen Eighty-Four* and *Animal Farm,* among other subversive volumes, appeared in Polish translations.[98] In the late 1970s and 1980s, the Polish government often entrusted the physical attacks on dissidents to gangs of thugs rather than to uniformed police, thus making even more plausible the idea that Polish Communism had become indistinguishable from Fascism.[99]

The creation of the Solidarity trade union has been seen as a development of Kuroń's "new evolutionism" and has been understood as a consequent and careful effort to revive "civil society,"[100] a project not possible in Czechoslovakia or Hungary, where the leadership's moderation and limited legitimacy had undermined the will of intellectuals to press harder.[101] According to a respected Polish authority, "The broadcasting of Mass on state radio, the relaxation of control over censorship, the release of political prisoners and the toleration of dissent are examples of the wide-ranging, essentially public interests of the creators of the Solidarity movement."[102]

Some students of Solidarity, however, have stressed historically derived worker tactics rather than innovative intelligentsia action, minimizing the relationship between the strategies of intellectuals as we have observed them evolving and the creation of mass movements involving workers.[103] Still, there is no doubt that Solidarity was culturally and politically connected to KOR and to the "space" increasingly occupied by Poland's civil society, and its achievements vastly increased the scope for civil action. General Wojciech Jaruzelski's 1981 proclamation of martial law was a major setback, but he was not able to revive the *ancien régime*.

Mikhail Gorbachev's ascent to the Soviet leadership of course increased the pace of political change. Interviewed in 1987, Jacek Kuroń reported that "Polish society is outside the totalitarian system. Now we have to bring ourselves to inject our independence into dependent state structures . . . to form self-management workers' councils in factories, to make state enterprise autonomous, to replace administrative control with the market."[104]

In Hungary, György Konrád expressed much the same thought:

> The image of a civil society, based on a social contract, has ceased to be a utopia in Central Europe. It has its roots in spontaneous solidarity, swelling up from below, valuing self-determination above everything else. . . .
> It is a lifelong venture, without end. Our societies have decided that they intend to replace, step by step, the closed culture of the state with their own open culture.[105]

Pessimism was measurably greater in Czechoslovakia, almost to the end of Communist rule. As late as January 1987, Havel still regarded his nation as under totalitarian domination; indeed, he refused any longer even to call it posttotalitarian. But he was constrained to add that in recent years "independent culture as a whole has mushroomed" and expressed the hope that even Czechoslovakia was "rejoining history."[106] Three years later, on January 1, 1990, he gave his first major address as president of Czechoslovakia.[107]

TEN

The "Evil Empire"

In totalitarian governments there is much murder, but in
authoritarian governments they leave that to the private sector.

Jestingly attributed to Jeane Kirkpatrick by a
Washington newspaper cartoonist

Let me recapitulate the causes for this change in the "clerks":
The imposition of political interests on all men without any
exception; the growth of consistency in matters apt to feed
realist passions; the desire and the possibility for men of letters
to play a political part; the need in the interest of their own
fame to play the game of a class which is daily becoming more
anxious; the increasing tendency of the "clerks" to become
bourgeois and to take on the vanities of that class.

Julian Benda

I N THE United States, as in Europe, 1968 marked the high tide of the
radical 1960s. The increasing power of more moderate and conservative
points of view would not be visible, however, for some years, especially if
one were observing the world from a university campus. Oversimplifying a
bit, we may say that in France and Germany, the 1970s and 1980s were
decades of political conflict between intellectuals who defended leftist points
of view and their increasingly successful opponents. Attitudes toward the
Soviet Union were often central to these debates. In Communist Poland and
Czechoslovakia, the conflict was different but had similar elements. There,
after 1968, views of the world related to the traditional Western Left were
routed by oppositional points of view that, with their stress on "civil society" and their sympathy for religious and traditional ideas, were easily assimilated to conservatism. Serious Marxism disappeared there and, more slowly,
in Hungary too. In East Germany, it hung on longer.

In the United States during the 1970s and 1980s, a significant conservative movement—"movements" might be a better term, for goals differed
and motives varied—began to contest New Left and even liberal ideas, and

the American intellectual community developed major splits.[1] A reaction against the revolutionary romanticism of the 1960s was a powerful part of these developments; so was criticism of the détente policies of the 1970s that had been supported by influential elements among both Republicans and Democrats.

Many of the leaders of these new movements had been young during the heyday of the Cold War and saw everything that had happened since as a falling away from that heroic period, especially the decline in both the American government's and the academic community's hostility to Soviet Communism. For the purposes of our discussion, I will refer generally to former radicals and liberals who moved to the political right in the 1970s and 1980s as *neoconservatives,* although not all of them have accepted the term enthusiastically.[2]

It was mostly these highly political men and women who reintroduced the term *totalitarianism* into the broader reaches of American political discourse. Their enemies were both the Soviet leaders and the American political elite whom, they believed, had lost the will to confront them, in part because during the 1960s the American liberal establishment had at least tacitly accepted some Communist points of view, if in a more moderate form. These neoconservatives showed great sympathy for the dissident intellectuals of Eastern Europe—Havel, Kołakowski, Alexander Solzhenitsyn—and had significant ties to anti-Communist European intellectuals: Karl Dietrich Bracher, Jacob Talmon, and Raymond Aron above all.

These profound cultural and political changes were slow to affect professional students of the Soviet Union. As the English-speaking political and intellectual universe became more polarized, the political scientists and historians who dominated Sovietology continued to abandon "totalitarian" points of view for comparative and social science approaches to the Soviet Union, which stressed how "like" other states and societies it was, not how uniquely dreadful.

It was possible for this community of scholars to ignore the neoconservative intellectual challenge in the 1970s in part because they were for a long time still preoccupied with the campus challenge from the Left. But it was also the case that the détente policy, which most of them accepted, was forged not by liberals, but by moderate conservatives in the Republican administration of Richard Nixon—above all, Henry Kissinger. Kissinger occasionally spoke of the Soviet Union as totalitarian, but in the words of a recent scholar, he regarded it "not [as] a nation with a daily, functioning ideology. . . . It was far more a traditional state, confident in the flow of history but merely 'ruthlessly opportunistic,' in practice, playing a familiar game of power politics."[3] Kissinger respected and disliked the Soviet Union, but during his time as secretary of state he saw Soviet policies unfolding within a worldwide arena, whose contours and dynamics could best be understood in terms of the traditional "realism" of political scientists.

But despite the sponsorship of détente by the Republicans, many neoconservatives saw Kissinger as, in the words of Norman Podhoretz, the longtime editor of *Commentary*, "weak and uncertain" in his actions in the Arab world during the oil embargo in 1973 and toward the Soviet Union's steady military buildup during the 1970s. To Podhoretz, Kissinger's détente amounted to "appeasement."[4]

The succeeding Carter administration turned out to be a battleground between those, like Secretary of State Cyrus Vance, who supported a straightforward continuation of détente, and those who would try harder to modify Soviet behavior. The chief of these was Zbigniew Brzezinski who, as a young professor of government at Harvard, had cosponsored the by now widely criticized "totalitarian model." His view of the Soviet Union continued to be darker than that of Vance or Marshall Shulman, the former director of Columbia University's Russian Institute and an influential advocate of détente in the Carter State Department. But Brzezinski's views, like those of Kissinger, were understood by academics, even if they were regarded as too "hard-line."

Both the Vance–Shulman party and Brzezinski supported the Carter administration's stress on human rights. An astute student of the foreign policies of the 1970s summed up the differences between Kissinger's foreign policy and that of his successors by noting that Kissinger's world

> was one dominated by the "old politics" with its parochial interests, its hierarchical ordering and marked inequalities, its obsession with equilibrium and the careful balancing of power, and its reliance on forcible methods. By contrast, the world of the Carter administration was characterized by truly global interests, by growing mutual dependencies, by far less hierarchy, by less concern with equilibrium, and by the recognition that much less reliance could be placed on the forcible methods of the past.[5]

But outside the walls of academe, the voices of those proclaiming a far more demonic view of the Soviet Union continued to grow louder. Some of them objected simply to Carter's emphasis on human rights and his administration's criticisms of right-wing military regimes in Latin America.[6] Although Soviet leaders disliked Carter's increased stress on human rights, which they noted was frequently directed against them, Carter continued and even accelerated the existing détente policy at the same time.[7]

Far more irritating to neoconservatives was Carter's suggestion that in fighting the Cold War and particularly the Vietnam War, the United States had renounced its own values. In the grip of what Carter in 1977 described as an "inordinate fear of Communism," American policy makers had too often abandoned core American values for those of the Soviet adversary.[8] Now, under his stewardship, Carter asserted confidently, we were making our own commitment to human rights the basis of our policy. And the United States would invite the Soviet Union to join it in solving the problems of hunger and poverty in the Third World.[9]

One of Carter's critics was Daniel Patrick Moynihan, diplomat, professor of education and urban policies at Harvard, and subsequently a Democratic senator from New York. Moynihan did not object to a greater concentration on the problems of the "Third World" per se. But to him, the "central political struggle of our time [was] that between liberal democracy and totalitarian Communism," and he did not want the Carter administration to lose sight of that fact. The lengthy military buildup in the Soviet Union under Brezhnev was now quite apparent. Whereas Carter stressed the triumphs of democratic values, to Moynihan "the history of our time is the history of totalitarian advance."[10]

Henry Kissinger—to increasing numbers of neoconservatives the villain who had invented détente—now agreed. In the fall of 1977 at New York University, he told his audience that "the difference between freedom and totalitarianism is not transient or incidental; it is a moral conflict, of fundamental historical proportions, which gives the modern age its special meaning and peril." He went on to reassert Friedrich and Brzezinski's distinction between "totalitarian" regimes and "authoritarian" ones, which Jeane Kirkpatrick later made famous again:

> In the contemporary world it is the totalitarian systems which have managed the most systematic and massive repression of the rights of men. In recent decades, no totalitarian regime has ever evolved into a democracy. Several authoritarian regimes—such as Spain, Greece, and Portugal—have done so. We must therefore maintain the moral distinction between aggressive totalitarianism and other governments which, with all their imperfections, are trying to resist foreign pressures or subversion and which thereby help preserve the balance of power in behalf of all free peoples.[11]

The ultimate irony, Kissinger concluded piously, would be for the United States to assume a "posture of resignation toward totalitarian states and harassment of those who would be our friends and who have *every prospect* of evolving in a more humane direction."[12] Before the Carter administration's foreign policy was fairly launched, then, the use of the term *totalitarian* by an influential and critical public was on the rise.[13] Carter himself later conceded that he did not "fully grasp" how far-reaching his focus on human rights would be, how it would "cut clear across our relation with the Soviet Union and other totalitarian states, the emerging stable regimes, and even some of our long-time Western allies."[14]

While in their specialized journals, American academics were denigrating or ignoring totalitarianism, neoconservatives began again to speculate about its origins, often to a much larger public. Irving Kristol, whom we encountered in his twenties writing for the *New Leader* at the end of World War II, was a central figure. His energy and effectiveness as an anti-Communist journalist were evident in his deep involvement with such Cold War liberal journals as *Commentary* (in its early days), *The Reporter,* and the Congress of Cultural Freedom's *Encounter.*[15]

In a collection of articles eventually published during the first Reagan administration, Kristol produced a typology even more grandiose than Jacob Talmon's. He aimed to explain the difference between Anglo-American pragmatic liberalism and what he claimed was the continental tendency toward a fanatic hostility toward the world as it was, toward *what actually existed*.[16] One pole of his comparison was the "French-Continental Enlightenment" and the French Revolution, whose ideologues promised humanity "not only liberty, fraternity, equality, but 'happiness' itself." The "germs of twentieth-century totalitarianism, whether self-declared Left or Right, were activated by that grandiose, indeed utopian, commitment."

The Anglo-Scottish Enlightenment, by contrast, produced Adam Smith, Edmund Burke, and (in the United States) James Madison, who accepted "self-interest as a goad to economic and political activity" and tried to channel it "into the disciplinary context of the marketplace for goods, and into that simulacrum of a 'marketplace' for influence and ideas known as representative government."[17]

Kristol's diagnosis was that American liberalism during and after the 1960s had fallen under the influence of the insidious French-continental tradition, through Marxism and romantic leftism more generally. These influences had pushed American liberalism toward totalitarianism via a "clerisy" of unelected intellectuals—hostile toward economic competition and soft on the totalitarian powers of Russia and China—that had been brought into positions of influence by the Democratic administrations that followed the New Deal.

Kristol combined his antiutopian view of the French Revolution, intellectually undeveloped but similar to that of Talmon or Camus, with a positive defense of capitalism that may have owed something to Hayek. His attack on the "new class" of utopian-minded intellectuals and bureaucrats subsequently became a staple of neoconservative commentary.[18] As late as 1968, however, Kristol espoused a rather "realist" view of American foreign policy, not unlike that of Henry Kissinger, but soon thereafter he fell in line with the neoconservative diagnosis of the Soviet Union as a far more serious menace.[19]

Kristol's fears of the "new class" were echoed by the sociologist Robert Nisbet, another influential neoconservative. Nisbet believed that this clerisy's egalitarianism was its most dangerous objective and that "in its extreme form" its despotism became totalitarian.[20] "The greatest single revolution of the last century," he wrote, "has been the transfer of effective power in human lives from the constitutionally visible offices of government, the nominally sovereign offices, to the vast network of power that has been brought into being in the name of protection of the people from their exploiters." He noted that the "peculiar effectiveness" of this "new despotism" was its "liaison with humanitarianism."[21] Like Kristol, Nisbet found this new class thoroughly committed to untried and utopian schemes, to cleverness cut off from experience—to "political rationalism."[22]

Suspicion of socially unattached intellectuals committed to visionary schemes has been a staple of the intellectual Right since Edmund Burke, but it is striking how strongly it was echoed among American conservatives in the 1970s and 1980s.[23] Some East European dissidents also came to believe during these years that intellectuals constituted a new class that hoped to replace capitalism with a planned economy in which their technical skills would be vital.[24] The idea has been repeatedly formulated by leftists over the past 150 years, most of them "former." It can be found in James Burnham's *Managerial Revolution* and Milovan Djilas's *The New Class,* and earlier in Waclaw Machajski's *Mental Worker,* earlier still in Mikhail Bakunin's *Statism and Anarchy.* These leftist intellectuals are, remarked Kristol drily, " 'idealistic'—that is, far less interested in individual financial rewards than in the corporate power of their class." Such a conclusion is, of course, a matter of perspective. If one were favorably disposed toward the reforming point of view of the "new class," one might call them "intellectuals" or even "the intelligentsia"—terminology meaning much the same thing, but lacking the pejorative "class" and suggesting idealism rather than Kristol's "corporate power of their class."[25]

No one could have been more interested in power and influence than the editor of *Commentary,* Norman Podhoretz, but he too suddenly discovered the "new class" of power-hungry intellectuals as he moved toward neoconservatism in the 1970s.[26] He also alleged that the "new class" was not only hostile to Zionism, but, as a group, increasingly anti-Semitic in its attitudes toward both Israel and successful individual American Jews like himself.[27] A crucial aspect of such an analysis was the belief that the so-called new politics of the Democratic Party in the early 1970s, the elimination of some hierarchical elements, and the "opening up" of the party to underrepresented social groups were the direct results of the radical egalitarianism of the New Left. This development, in turn, threatened to create "quotas" for previously underrepresented groups, anathema to most American Jews. Although the politics of the American Jewish community did not change greatly during this period, the emergence of the quota issue and the New Left hostility toward Israel as (like the United States) an imperialist power ensured that former Jewish liberals would be well represented in the ranks of the neoconservative leadership.

The 1970s thus saw the beginnings of a serious reaction against détente and a marked growth in the influence of intellectuals who regarded the Soviet Union as an extremely sinister polity.[28] These intellectuals by and large saw themselves as "breaking ranks"[29] and leaving the "new class," but a more plausible reading was that the new class was splitting into liberal and conservative wings.[30] Some of the neoconservatives were American Jews who had been radicalized by Soviet support for the enemies of Israel in the Middle East and by the plight of the Soviet Jews, subject to discrimination in many forms, including rigid quotas in government and the universities and the refusal of permission to emigrate. Many American Jews also evinced a growing sensitivity to criticism of Israel, especially from people on the Left, who seemed to them insufficiently critical of more serious humanitarian lapses by Israel's opponents. Podhoretz denied that his new hostility toward the Soviet Union had arisen "primarily" because of its threat to Israel or because the Soviet Union "had become the single most powerful source of anti-Semitism since the fall of the Nazi regime in Germany." He preferred to state that "I loathed the Soviet Union because I loathed the system of Communist totalitarianism by which it was ruled, and the fact that this system included a hatred of Jews among its many sins and crimes only intensified the obligation I felt to take a stand against it."[31] One result was that *Commentary* not only took up the cudgels against the Soviet Union generally, but also began urging a major American military buildup to stave off a Finlandization of Western Europe and the United States and to ensure the survival of Israel through American military power.

These developments became clearer and clearer during the latter 1970s. But it was really with the election of President Ronald Reagan in 1980 that the neoconservatives, both inside and outside government, began a sustained drive for hands-on political influence. One of the prominent features of this campaign was a pugnacious revival of the idea that the Soviet Union had to be understood as "totalitarian"—the evil half of a revived comparison between Western democracy, led by the United States, and Soviet totalitarianism.

As is well known, Ronald Reagan had become a passionate anti-Communist during the latter 1940s. Key was his encounter with the strong Communist Party influence in the American Screen Actors Guild, of which he was a member and eventually president, and in a liberal organization, the Hollywood Independent Citizens Committee of the Arts, Sciences and Professions, known for obvious reasons simply as HICCASP.[32] So the first step in Ronald Reagan's political evolution away from Franklin Roosevelt and the Democratic Party was a personal experience that brought home to him the secrecy, mendacity, and manipulativeness of the American Communist Party.

At the beginning of the 1950s, Reagan's political orientation was that of a Cold War liberal. In his speeches and occasional journalistic efforts, he would sometimes accuse the Soviet Union of being totalitarian. His frequent comparison of the Soviet Union with Nazi Germany suggests the standard carryover from World War II. Communists, Reagan thought, mask their aggressive plans to conquer the world in idealistic rhetoric; they believe that the end justifies the means and so will stop at nothing. In a brief article for the Los Angeles magazine *Fortnight,* Reagan wrote that

> the real fight with this new totalitarianism belongs properly to the forces of liberal democracy, just as did the battle with Hitler's totalitarianism. There really is no difference except in the cast of characters. On the one hand is our belief that the people can and will decide what is best for themselves, and on the other (Communist, Nazi or Fascist) side is the

belief that a "few" can best decide what is good for all the rest. Unfortunately most of us were "touted" away from the fight when "professional hate groups" masked their racial and religious bias behind an "anti-communist" crusade, when anti-labor forces used "red-baiting" to fight unions, when individual politicians found it a handy way to electioneer.[33]

During the next decade, Reagan abandoned his aversion to "anti-Communist crusades" and those who promoted them and became one of the foremost anti-Communist crusaders in American political life. Perhaps because of his entirely domestic experience with Communism, Reagan saw espionage and subversion in the United States as an integral and central part of the Communist threat; and his language became increasingly apocalyptic.[34] In 1962, for instance, he told a Republican audience in Stockton, California, that "the issue of our times [was] the contest between totalitarianism and freedom"; this rhetoric was by now habitual.[35]

Well before he became president of the United States, Reagan also accepted the term as it had been defined beginning back in the 1940s by Friedrich Hayek: that there was a connection between liberal statism and totalitarianism, the one being an only somewhat less baneful form of the other. He also subscribed to the notion, first coined by Republicans like John Foster Dulles (although not acted on in Eastern Europe) that the United States should not merely contain Soviet power, but also "roll it back" if possible. Reagan noted in January 1978, for example, that Michael Manley, the socialist prime minister of Jamaica, was "taking that lovely island nation into totalitarian socialism."[36] At that time, however, there was little consistency in Reagan's usage, since he referred to China as merely authoritarian and repressive rather than totalitarian.

Soviet Communism is "the focus of evil in the modern world," announced President Reagan in a speech to the National Association of Evangelicals on March 8, 1983, repeating themes he had touched on in a speech before the British Parliament the previous May.[37] He also said: "Let us pray for the salvation of all those who live in totalitarian darkness.[38] And in the same speech he coined a term that in essence was his particular version of totalitarianism: "the evil empire." The phrase was actually the work of speechwriter Terry Dolan, who later produced an interesting gloss on it. Asserting that the presidential office itself made it necessary for its incumbent to instruct a "confused world" as to why democracy was superior to "totalitarianism," Dolan explained:

> The secret is to give the world a cliché, a semantic infiltration. Now and forever, the Soviet Empire is an evil empire. . . . The Soviet Union itself can't let go of it. It torments them; so they say it themselves . . . the Soviet Union knows the importance of words. That's why they have coined phrases like "Wars of National Liberation" and "People's Republics." The "evil empire" is one of the few semantic victories the West has won.[39]

No one did more to make this comparison politically effective than Reagan's representative to the United Nations, Jeane J. Kirkpatrick. Born Jeane Jordan, the daughter of an Oklahoma oil-drilling contractor, she attended Stephens College in Missouri and got her bachelor's degree from Barnard in the late 1940s before embarking on an academic career. At Columbia University, she wrote a master's thesis on the British Fascist Oswald Mosely, and then took a job at the State Department, where she analyzed interviews with refugees from Eastern Europe. She also interviewed Chinese soldiers who had surrendered in Korea and refused repatriation; these two experiences, she later told a reporter, made a strong anti-Communist of her.[40]

In 1955 she married Evron Kirkpatrick, director of the American Political Science Association, a man long close to Hubert Humphrey, and while starting a family, was out of academia for several years. Early in the 1960s, when Kirkpatrick was teaching part time at Trinity College in Washington, D.C., she was entrusted with the task of completing a collection of essays, entitled *Strategy of Deception,* upon the death of its passionately anti-Communist compiler, S. M. Levitas, longtime editor of the *New Leader.* Kirkpatrick's strong anti-Communism, even then, was very much in the *New Leader* tradition.[41] She received her doctorate from Columbia University in 1968, having written her dissertation on Perónism in Argentina. Both her M.A. and Ph.D. theses suggest the direction of her interests.

Under Reagan, Kirkpatrick created a solid, polemically effective, if intellectually eclectic, case for how totalitarianism had come into existence and what it was and then made it the centerpiece of the administration's efforts to reverse the détente policies of Carter, Ford, and Nixon. She accepted a typology akin to Friedrich's, but added Jacob Talmon's stress on the idea that "totalitarianism is utopianism come to power."[42] She also emphasized an important goal allegedly shared by all totalitarians: to realize their ideology by "turning it into culture"—that is, the way people actually live— employing the coercive power of the state to do so. In her examples of what totalitarianism was, Kirkpatrick dwelt rather abstractly on the intent of leaders, as manifested in ideological statements, rather than analyzing in any detail how their regimes actually functioned. Her examples of ideological statements were largely drawn from Lenin and Hitler, although she sometimes mentioned the Jacobins and Puritans. Of roughly contemporary "totalitarian" ideologues, she mentioned (fleetingly) only Herbert Marcuse and Frantz Fanon, the semi-Marxist spokesman for Third World revolution and author of *The Wretched of the Earth* (1965).

If Kirkpatrick was rather abstract and political in defining totalitarianism and discussing its origins, she was definitely policy oriented in pointing to its dangers in the present. She focused her attack on Carter's Latin America policy in particular, since it was there that Carter's stress on human rights, globalism, and North–South relations had done, she thought, the greatest damage, by allowing Cuban and Soviet influence to expand and American strategic hegemony to decline dramatically.[43] "The central goal of our foreign policy," she stated, "should not be the moral elevation of other nations, but the preservation of a civilized conception of our own national interest."[44]

Kirkpatrick, whose early political loyalties had been to Cold War liberalism, came to share the neo-Burkean, neo-Tocquevillian preoccupation with the "new class" and its abstract political rationalism and utopianism. She also shared the neoconservative belief that the twentieth-century political Left was obsessed with an impossible attempt to realize a drastic egalitarianism, an attempt entailing the coercion of an unwilling populace if seriously undertaken.[45] A form of this leftist ideology had captured the Democratic Party during the McGovern era, alienating its more conservative constituencies and destroying its traditional anti-Communism.[46]

"If we do precisely what the rationalist declines to do," wrote Kirkpatrick in the introduction to a collection of her most influential essays—that is, to

> look at experience with politics and evil—it becomes clear that, at least in the modern period, when great political evil occurred, coercion was employed in the service of a particular kind of rationalist political theory. I am not suggesting that rationalism *causes* totalitarianism, but that the totalitarian impulse is grounded in the search—through power—for virtue, solidarity and perfect unity: the end of conflict, the end of exploitation of man by man.[47]

Because the Western Left now dominated liberalism, liberal opinion in Western Europe and the United States, she maintained, was intellectually, psychologically, and politically connected to totalitarianism.

Kirkpatrick's "Dictatorships and Double Standards," her most famous essay, appeared in the November 1979 issue of Norman Podhoretz's *Commentary*. In it, she criticized President Carter for failing to prevent the overthrow of the shah's government in Iran and Somoza's in Nicaragua, pointing out how unfavorable to American "interests" were the accession to power of the Ayatollah Khomeini and the Sandinistas. In making her case, Kirkpatrick did not dwell on the unpleasant particulars of Somoza's rule in Nicaragua, but on the fact that it was a "traditional" regime, which although not a democracy, was capable of evolving into one. It was not fanatically leftist or theocratic; it was unfriendly to the totalitarian Soviet bloc; and it was well disposed to the United States.

In effect, Kirkpatrick rejected the Left–Right axis in the developing world in the way that American liberalism had tended to understand it, according to a vague and often unstated modernization theory. This liberal point of view suggested that "modernization" included not only the liquidation of feudalism, a commitment to industrialization, the development of a middle class, and so on, but also the extension of political and ultimately some form of social democracy to the entire nation in question. No doubt this view was a kind of "Whig interpretation" implying that the favorable trajectory for all these poor, underdeveloped, undemocratic countries would lead to middle-class and social democracy of the American or (better) West European kind and that achievement of this goal could be helped along by pressure and incentives from Western nations.[48]

The underpinnings of Kirkpatrick's analysis were entirely different. She suggested that such "traditional" rightist regimes as those of Somoza in Nicaragua, the Pahlavis in Iran, South Africa, Argentina, and Brazil could well evolve in a democratic direction, something that American policy makers should bear constantly in mind. But to make such an evolution a central objective of American policy was folly. Outsiders could not do much to foster such an evolution; at best, one ran the risk of increasing instability, and at worst, one could abet the rise of a "totalitarian" elite and ideology, as in the Nicaraguan case, and the nation in question might become a permanent part of the totalitarian world.

The fundamental cleavage in the world was not then between Left and Right, with the Left being "good," except in extreme cases, and ultimately producing modernity and stability; it was between the totalitarian and nontotalitarian worlds. "Traditional" regimes might be more or less attractive, from the standpoint of American values, but that was not the business of American policy makers. The United States' mission was to prevent the expansion of the totalitarian world, from which nations never returned.

Kirkpatrick's attitude toward "traditional"[49] nondemocratic regimes was quite Burkean:

> Traditional autocrats leave in place existing allocations of wealth, power, status and other resources, which in most traditional societies favor an affluent few and maintain masses in poverty. But they worship traditional gods and observe traditional taboos. They do not disturb the habitual rhythms of work and leisure, habitual places of residence, habitual patterns of family and personal relations. Because the miseries of traditional life are familiar, they are bearable to ordinary people who . . . learn to cope, as children born to untouchables in India acquire the skills and attitudes necessary for survival in the miserable roles they are destined to fill. Such societies create no refugees.[50]

Kirkpatrick was to be much criticized for her assertion that the (rather vague) category of "traditional autocracies" created no refugees; examples to the contrary abound.[51]

But the political point of Kirkpatrick's analysis was quite clear. It cut against Jimmy Carter's emphasis on human rights ("utopian," likely to be destabilizing) and recalled American policy makers to the primary task of confronting the Soviet Union and its allies. At the end, Kirkpatrick stated in no uncertain terms that revolutionary groups defining themselves as enemies of the United States should be treated as such, and she challenged guilty American liberals to abandon their "continuous self-abasement and apology" toward the "third world."[52]

This aggressive rhetoric was the sort of thing that Ronald Reagan was looking for, as Richard Allen, soon to become Reagan's national security adviser, realized when he read the article. After a certain amount of persuasion, Kirkpatrick agreed to become Reagan's chief delegate to the United Nations and a major—perhaps *the* major—figure in the foreign policy of his first administration. Even Reagan's first secretary of state, Alexander Haig, who often clashed with Kirkpatrick,[53] used the revived distinction between totalitarian and authoritarian, although with less self-confidence than she did:

> The totalitarian model unfortunately draws upon the resources of modern technology to impose its will on all aspects of a citizen's behaviour. The totalitarian regimes tend to be intolerant at home and abroad, actively hostile to all we represent and ideologically resistent [*sic*] to political change. . . . The authoritarian regime usually stems from a lack of political or economic development and customarily reserves for itself absolute authority in only a few politically sensitive areas.[54]

In addition to earning her an important position in the Reagan administration, Kirkpatrick's article dramatically rekindled the debate in the United States over the theoretical and practical utility of the term *totalitarianism*. The November 1981 issue of *Commentary,* for example, featured a symposium entitled "Human Rights and American Foreign Policy," in which the following questions were asked of participants:

1. What role, if any, should a concern for human rights play in American foreign policy? Is there a conflict between this concern and the American national interest?

2. Does the distinction between authoritarianism and totalitarianism seem important to you? If so, what follows from this practice? If not, what distinctions would you make in judging and dealing with non-democratic regimes?

3. Does the approach of the Reagan administration, to the extent that it can be inferred from statements of the President and other high officials, compare favorably or unfavorably with the Carter administration's human rights policy?[55]

Jeane Kirkpatrick herself participated in the symposium, recapitulating her position briefly and adding only that the Carter administration, based on its operational distinctions, had actually preferred totalitarian regimes to authoritarian ones.

The key point for William Barrett, a longtime *Partisan Review* journalist and then a fellow of the National Humanities Center, was the dominance of ideology in the totalitarian regime, entailing the complete and systematic management of human life by the state. Like others who used the term in the 1980s, Barrett stressed the aspiration of these regimes toward total regimentation, admitting that there was considerable variety in the degree to which it had been achieved. He concluded by asserting that Americans failed to grasp this ideological aspect, that they needed to understand that pleas to totalitarians for individual rights and liberties simply fall on deaf ears.

Peter Berger, a sociology professor from Boston University often considered a neoconservative, took a view very close to that of Kirkpatrick, stressing the historical novelty of totalitarianism while observing that authoritarian regimes had been an issue since Aristotle. Totalitarian regimes necessarily constituted an attack on human rights, above and beyond the particular outrages they committed. Berger also echoed Kirkpatrick's qualified support for regimes that opposed Soviet imperialism, however odious their domestic policies might be.

The sociologist Robert Nisbet also supported Kirkpatrick strongly, although he conceded at the end of his lengthy statement that "authoritarian" and "totalitarian" were, after all, ideal types, and clearly Hungary, Poland, and Czechoslovakia were less faithful representations of the totalitarian type than were the Soviet Union, China and Cuba.

Zbigniew Brzezinski, a one-time devotee of the term, took what from that standpoint was a surprising view and one that surely reflected his recent experience in government. The answer to the questions posed by *Commentary,* he argued, would not be found in some theoretical distinction. Suppose an authoritarian regime like Uganda blatantly violated human rights, and a totalitarian regime like Romania did so more selectively. Should we not criticize Idi Amin? Suppose a totalitarian regime is more friendly to the United States than an authoritarian regime is. Should we ignore this fact?

Rather than trying to derive proper action from such a rigid and abstract distinction, it would be more meaningful to ask if a regime, whether authoritarian or totalitarian, that grossly violates human rights is also involved in relationships important to us. If so, American policy makers should not press the human rights issue beyond some reasonable point. China's disregard for human rights, for example, should not lead the United States to abandon relations with China, a step that could only benefit the Soviet Union. And should we, Brzezinski asked rhetorically, refuse to negotiate arms control agreements with the Soviet government because it violates the human rights of dissidents? Difficult judgments had to be made, but they should have nothing to do with these academic typologies. What was at stake was the necessity of balancing whatever good the United States could achieve for human rights with the negative impact that such efforts might have on important relationships with various governments.

Charles William Maynes, editor of *Foreign Policy* magazine, argued similarly. Surely authoritarian Guatemala was more repressive than the regimes of Eastern Europe. And Maynes echoed points earlier made by academic critics of the term: that "totalitarian" and "authoritarian" were categories too broad to be meaningful. Both Mexico and El Salvador should presumably be categorized as "authoritarian"; Yugoslavia and North Korea as "totalitarian." Are the categories of any use in understanding how these four different regimes actually work? Maynes also rejected as unproven the proposition that Communist regimes simply could not change, as did the civil rights leader Bayard Rustin of the A. Philip Randolph Institute. Former Senator Eugene McCarthy took a similar position, arguing that Communist states could become merely authoritarian when the rulers lost faith in their principles.

Noam Chomsky, a linguistic innovator and longtime academic radical, regarded the distinction as plausible, but rejected it as the basis for contemporary policy. He denounced Kirkpatrick's cool assurance that "because the miseries of traditional life are familiar, they are bearable to ordinary people." Chomsky regarded the regimes that Kirkpatrick wished to support as those that acquiesced in the American imperialist plundering of their own people. Speaking as a liberal critic, Richard Falk, a professor of international law at Princeton, allowed the distinction intellectually but felt that it was not "fully satisfactory," as it was too ideological in practice, tending to focus American attention only on abuses in "totalitarian" regimes.

Nathan Glazer, a sociologist at Harvard often identified as a neoconservative, put forward a fresh perspective. He recalled that he had used the distinction himself five years earlier (July 1976) in *Commentary*. But his conviction that Communist states could never turn to democracy had been shaken. Yugoslavia had allowed free emigration; then had come the Prague Spring; then the rise of Solidarity in Poland. Meanwhile, certain authoritarian regimes in Latin America had been guilty of torturing large numbers of political opponents, unmatched recently in Communist countries. Perhaps, he concluded, torture is to some extent indigenous in certain cultures, a problem transcending the distinction between totalitarian and authoritarian.

Seymour Martin Lipset, like Glazer often considered a neoconservative, also denied that the totalitarian–authoritarian distinction simply meant Communist–non-Communist. Poland, for example, was clearly authoritarian. Lipset did not actually use the term *posttotalitarian,* but he noted that present-day Poland, Hungary, and Yugoslavia tolerated "private dissent" as long as it did not turn into organized political opposition. Even the Soviet Union, Lipset thought, was no longer totalitarian. The Brezhnev Doctrine, however, indicated that no regime within the Soviet bloc would be allowed to change its form of government beyond a certain point, let alone leave the bloc. The United States, therefore, had no option but to continue resisting any expansion of the Soviet sphere.

The old radical Max Lerner, now a professor at the Graduate School of Human Behavior of the U.S. International University in San Diego, finally accepted the distinction that he had fought against since the 1930s. In totalitarian regimes, he now thought, there was no possibility of evolution.

The *Commentary* symposium thus produced no consensus, with only the most conservative (such as the Basic Books editor Midge Decter) fervently and straightforwardly supporting the practical as well as moral utility of the distinction.[56] In the pages of less conservative journals, opinion was even less favorable to locating and combating totalitarianism as a practical policy aim.

The political philosopher Michael Walzer accepted the basic distinction but little else in Kirkpatrick's article. According to Walzer, writing in the *New Republic,*

> [I]t remains, to my mind, a useful guide to twentieth-century politics. But it can't just be applied mechanically, dividing the world, for totalitarianism is an "ideal type," a picture of horrifying perfection never quite achieved in fact, while authoritarianism is a catchall category. . . . The concentration camp, Hannah Arendt wrote, is the model of totalitarian control. The Hitler and Stalin regimes came as close as regimes have ever come to realizing that model, but even they realized it for some, not for all, of their subjects. And if we set aside the Soviet Union, where Stalinism remains today a regime-in-reserve, it is clear that all the other examples of post–World War II Communist and fascist governments are failed totalitarianisms. They don't measure up to Arendt's standard, they fall short of Orwell's brilliant science fiction, their terror isn't total.

Walzer was less optimistic than Kirkpatrick about the slow advance of democracy in the "traditional" world of authoritarian states, and he was not convinced that Communist states could not become democratized:

> Hungary, Czechoslovakia and Poland would probably be democratic states today were it not for the Red Army. The Red Army is a threat to human freedom, but communism, in these states at least, is an ugly but not a powerful political system. There is nothing in its internal mechanics that rules out a democratic transformation . . . social structure and political culture are far more important than their current regime in shaping [their] long-term evolution.[57]

Other commentators criticized Kirkpatrick from another angle: her refusal in any way to consider the world from the standpoint of the oppressed:

> In order to maintain their manichaean vision former liberals like Kirkpatrick must practice a heroic indifference to detail. The revolutionary who haunts their hysterical prose never acquires a face. Neoconservatives ask no questions about the particulars of time and place and program, about why a man or woman has assumed the awful peril of rebellion; they never ask because, for their crabbed purposes, they have all the necessary answers. Having taken up arms—some of them Cuban or Russian or otherwise tainted—against an anticommunist government, the revolutionary is either a totalitarian communist or a foolish tool, not to mention a "terrorist."
>
> You find an equivalent coarseness of thought in the pages of *Pravda,* where the Soviet counterparts of our intellectual thugs ask not "Who is Lech Walesa?" but rather, "Whom does Walesa consciously or uncon-

sciously serve?" Since his opponent is a loyal communist government, for *Pravda* the only possible answer is "U.S. imperialism."[58]

Many of Kirkpatrick's critics, and indeed some of her supporters, were thus clearly unhappy with the Manichaean opposition she established between totalitarian and authoritarian. "Virtually all dictatorships today," wrote the journalist and historian Alan Tonelson,

> display both totalitarian and authoritarian features. Reagan's sketch of the archetypical authoritarian ruler, content to amass personal wealth and the trappings of power while leaving traditional patterns of life and limited freedoms intact[,] has simply been mocked by former Ugandan President Idi Amin, Latin American tyrants who nearly exterminated their Indian populations, and the Salvadoran officers who crushed a 1932 revolt by killing some 30,000 peasants.

At the same time, Tonelson contended, the *caudillo* (single leader) structure to which Kirkpatrick pointed in Nicaragua has been replaced in several Latin American countries by a "bureaucratic authoritarianism" that aims "to destroy permanently a perceived threat to the existing structure of socioeconomic privilege by eliminating the political participation of the numerical majority."[59]

No single episode did more to blur the distinction between totalitarian and authoritarian regimes than the so-called Timerman Affair. Jacobo Timerman was a successful Argentine Jewish journalist who for criticizing the regime in print—he had publicized the disappearance of thousands of Argentineans in the 1970s—was arrested and episodically tortured for two years by the Argentine military. He was finally freed, partly through pressure applied to Argentina by the Carter administration. He subsequently moved to Israel, of whose invasion of Lebanon he was to be scathingly critical. Throughout, he made much of both his leftism and his Zionism.

Early in 1981, in the midst of the "totalitarian" revival, Timerman's *Prisoner Without a Name, Cell Without a Number* was published in New York. It recounted his experiences in Argentine prisons, including torture.[60] Over and over again, Timerman referred to the Perónist government as totalitarian and Fascist. He maintained that he was arrested both because he was a Jew and because his newspaper opposed the regime's radical right point of view. He was never charged with any crime.

Prisoner Without a Name had many literary echoes. Following his arrest, Timerman was blindfolded and told that he was to be shot and then was reprieved at the last minute, as the novelist Fedor Dostoevsky had been in Tsarist Russia. But most of the book's echoes suggested more modern antitotalitarian classics—the prison scenes of *Darkness At Noon*, for example.[61] The interrogation scenes were reminiscent of the writings of Soviet dissidents. There was a reference to Alain Resnais's film about the Nazi death camps, *Night and Fog*.[62] Timerman compared the extreme Right and the extreme Left again and again.

In sum, Timerman's book profoundly assimilated political behavior in rightist Argentina to both Fascist and Communist experiences, which he labeled *totalitarian*. Furthermore, Timerman was a Jew and a Zionist who went to live in Israel after he was freed, just as refugees from the Soviet Union did—only he was coming from a merely "authoritarian" regime. But in "authoritarian" Argentina, the military hung pictures of Hitler in rooms where Jewish prisoners were tortured.[63] Timerman's experiences undermined the hypothesis that the Soviet Union was a unique threat to Jews:

> No questions are asked [during a torture session]. Merely a barrage of insults, which increase in intensity as the minutes pass. Suddenly a hysterical voice begins shouting a single word: "Jew . . . Jew . . . Jew!" . . . Now they're really amused and burst into laughter. Somebody tries a variation while still clapping hands: "Clipped prick . . . clipped prick. . . ." It seems they're no longer angry, merely having a good time.
>
> I keep bouncing in the chair and moaning as the electric shocks penetrate my clothes. During one of these tremors, I fall to the ground, dragging the chair. They get angry, like children whose game has been interrupted.[64]

The book, clearly unhelpful to the neoconservative cause, produced a minor sensation in the press.[65] Worse yet, it became a TV documentary.

Irving Kristol led the neoconservative reviewers in the *Wall Street Journal*. Timerman, he told his readers, has "cast himself in the role of a Solzhenitsyn-of-the-left," and he repeated Kirkpatrick's definition of the difference between totalitarian and authoritarian governments, emphasizing the policy relevance of this "key distinction":

> A major intellectual and propaganda campaign is now being mounted by the left and liberal-left against this distinction. Some of the active participants are simply human rights purists. But there can be little doubt that the driving force behind this campaign is supplied by those who have more sophisticated political intentions. They understand very well that once the distinction between totalitarian and authoritarian nations is eliminated, most of our attention and energy are bound to be directed toward the latter, since in fact our State Department has more influence, however limited, on the governments of Argentina or Guatemala than on Cuba or Vietnam.[66]

Kristol allowed that the acclaim that Timerman had received for his book was deserved, and in passing he professed "outrage" at the "bestiality and paranoid anti-Semitism" of "some sections of the Argentine military." Nevertheless, he went on to attack Timerman for his "inflated self-centeredness" and linked him with a left-wing swindler and moneyman for urban guerrillas, although he admitted that "there is no evidence that Mr. Timerman knew what [Mr. Graiver] was up to." In fact, Kristol concluded,

> Mr. Timerman is above all a political person, far more interested in indicting, in the name of "human rights," the present regime in Argentina, the present administration in Washington and even the present government in Israel—which, in conversation, he blandly labels "fascist"—than he is with giving a true report about the facts of life in Argentina.[67]

Kristol, "a political person" himself if ever there was one, admitted that the Argentine political scene was sufficiently uncertain that in fact the worst might be yet to come, as Timerman suggested. But to say, as Timerman had, that it was "on the verge of happening" was "irresponsible and dishonest demagogy." With an "authoritarian" regime, such as the one run by the Argentine military, quiet diplomacy was the answer. The Argentine Jewish community believed in quiet diplomacy; Timerman denounced them for cowardice. Timerman was guilty of

> the politics of polarization, in which the left crusades against the right under the banner of "human rights," while the threat from the totalitarian left is altogether ignored. [Such a politics] appeals to their ideological bias as well as to their self-righteous passions. One might almost say it is their secret agenda.[68]

Although the discussion ended inconclusively, it seemed clear that the Reagan administration had learned the need for a more nuanced attitude toward human rights than the outright repudiation of them that had led to the defeat of Lefever as Assistant Secretary of State for Human Rights and Humanitarian Affairs. Elliott Abrams, about to be confirmed in that position, wrote a memo for his boss, Judge William P. Clark, and Secretary Haig affirming that

> human rights is at the core of our foreign policy because it is central to what America is and stands for. . . . Congressional belief that we have no consistent human rights policy threatens to disrupt important policy initiatives. . . . Our human rights policy must be at the center of our response. . . . This policy must be applied even-handedly. If a nation, friendly or not, abridges freedom, we should acknowledge it.

Although Abrams certainly agreed with Kirkpatrick that human rights was not advanced by replacing "a corrupt dictator with a zealous communist politburo," he was at pains to point out that "a human rights policy means trouble, for it means hard choices which may adversely affect certain bilateral relations. At the very least, we will have to speak honestly about our friends' human rights violations and justify any decisions wherein other considerations (economic, military, etc.) are determinative." Nevertheless, he concluded that a human rights dimension to American foreign policy was essential. "We desire to demonstrate," he wrote, "by acting to defend liberty and identifying its enemies, that the difference between East and West is a crucial policy distinction of our times."[69]

An unmistakable shift in emphasis soon followed. When the White House submitted Abrams's name for Assistant Secretary of State for Human Rights, President Reagan proclaimed that "in my administration, human rights considerations are important in all aspects of our foreign policy." An important administration assessment, appearing less than three months later, reaffirmed its commitment to expose human rights abuses in the Soviet bloc, but denied that the administration would pursue "a policy of selective indignation."[70] The Reagan administration continued over the next several years to excoriate left-wing regimes and pursue "quiet diplomacy" with right-wing ones, but there were no more explicit attacks on human rights.

The rise of Mikhail Gorbachev, the development of his reforms, and the slide from reform into the collapse of the Soviet Union profoundly affected the American discussion of totalitarianism. By the mid-1980s, it had become rather academic and historical in its focus. The most important instance was the debate between Sheila Fitzpatrick and her opponents in the *Russian Review* in 1985 and 1986, focused on how to write the history of the Soviet Union under Stalin.[71] There was much less contemporary political urgency even before the full magnitude of the Gorbachev reforms became evident.[72]

Neither the proponents nor the opponents of the totalitarian point of view remotely expected the rapid delegitimation and collapse of the Soviet Union. In an essay published in 1985, Stephen Cohen of Princeton ridiculed George Kennan's statement that if "anything were to occur to disrupt the unity and efficacy of the party as a political instrument, Soviet Russia might be changed overnight from one of the strongest to one of the weakest and most pitiable of national societies."[73]

When Jeane Kirkpatrick published a collection of her late 1980s newspaper columns in 1990 under the title *The Withering Away of the Totalitarian State,* she observed that these developments were "a great surprise to us all," but did not attempt the task of reconciling her previous views on the durability of totalitarian systems with the ongoing collapse of the Soviet Empire.[74] By April 1987, she seemed to accept the view of a Czech émigré journalist that "totalitarian states are under heavy pressure to change." Like other analysts, she was now drawn to the view that the new technologies of the information age were extremely important in making totalitarian regimes obsolete: Jiri Pehe "believes their total control over economics, culture, and politics produces bureaucratization and stagnation that are incompatible with the requirements of computer and communications technology in this information age."[75]

By October 31, 1988, Kirkpatrick believed it possible that "*Gorbachev and his colleagues [might] be ready to abandon the efforts at total control, the distinguishing characteristic of the totalitarian state.*" She asked whether the world might be "watching the early stages of an evolution of totalitarian states into authoritarian regimes."[76] By November 20, 1989, Kirkpatrick concluded that "Mikhail Gorbachev and his collaborators in Eastern Europe have abandoned the totalitarian project."[77]

The closest she came to offering a systemic explanation of what had happened was to assert the responsibility of a single individual—Mikhail Gorbachev—for the dismantling of the totalitarian system. She regarded him as a "sport" in the Soviet system.[78] But, one might ask, if Gorbachev was willing and able to accomplish such an extraordinary transformation, did that not mean that the Soviet Union had already ceased to be totalitarian? Kirkpatrick's columns, like her earlier writings on the Soviet Union, seldom analyzed or even described how it functioned, save at the level of ideological pronouncement or high politics.

THE END of the Cold War will not mean the end of arguments about totalitarianism, but it will probably for the moment deprive them of "actuality," as Soviet commentators used to say, unhook them from the deepest political passions of the age. Perhaps what has been called totalitarianism will over the next few years come to be seen as only the most extreme example of a phase in human history in which the transforming powers of the state, of politics, were greatly exaggerated by political actors, at the expense of slower and more complex cultural and economic change likely to be far more durable.

Perhaps this growth in the power and prestige of the state will be traced back to the impressive results of imperial German mobilization during World War I and the impact of that effort on Russia, Italy, and, again, Germany itself.

Elie Halévy's "era of tyrannies" may be said to have come to an end if one defines "tyranny" in the rather narrow, historically specific sense that he intended. It is difficult to deny some version of the thesis, pioneered by Talmon and Camus and revived by the neoconservatives, that the states labeled *totalitarian* were fired by missions of utopian social transformation of diverse kinds. Whereas Nazi Germany was defeated militarily, the others abandoned the pretense or the actuality of such ambitions, at tempos still not agreed on. At what point in their life history "totalitarian" states lapsed into what amounts to more traditional statist ambitions will remain a point of contention among historians of various political points of view.[79] To stress the utopian and transformational ambitions of these states is not, however, to agree with the neoconservative assertion that they can never be compared with other kinds of states or that nothing can be learned from the perspective of comparative politics.

The 1970s and especially the 1980s saw the evolution of "authoritarian" states (many with residues, overtones, or echoes of Fascism) like Portugal, Spain, Greece, Argentina, and Brazil toward more politically open, market-oriented societies, even as a similar process could be discerned among states often described as totalitarian. Among Third World states, this meant a steady loss in prestige for the Soviet model and a sometimes reluctant return to Western-influenced or "indigenous" development strategies.

The discussions of the early and mid-1980s in Europe and especially in the United States suggest that it was largely those closest to the ideological heart of neoconservatism who still accepted a clear-cut, practical distinction between totalitarian states and more traditional kinds of bureaucratic despotisms, however clear the distinction remained at the level of ideal type. When this distinction lost its political importance for the Reagan administration, interest in current totalitarianism languished further, to undergo a brief, celebratory revival as the Soviet Union came to an end.

Surely part of the reason had been foreseen by Polish dissidents as far back as the early 1970s. In a world where economic interconnectedness counted for so much, the political risks of massive repression grew apace. This was particularly so for "imperial" states like the Soviet Union. Mikhail Gorbachev no doubt deserves enormous credit for refusing to maintain the Soviet empire by force, but one must remember what the costs of maintaining the Soviet sphere in Eastern Europe would have been over time and the indirect, as well as direct, pressures not to do so. At the same time, many academic students of the Soviet Union were vividly aware, also by the 1970s, of its loss of dynamism. Even many who were unwilling to give up altogether the term *totalitarian* recognized that the Soviet Union was losing its appetite for mobilizing its population or drastically reshaping their inherited individualities.

Along with the pervasive loss of faith in the statist Left has come, in recent years, a more subtle loss of faith in revolutions to accomplish major and lasting social change in the world, especially through the application of state power. This kind of disillusion is connected to the loss of faith in "modernist" eschatologies more broadly, especially among intellectuals, and their loss of faith in the historical European Enlightenment. There is presumably a connection between the collapse of political, especially leftist utopias and the recrudescence, around the world, of fundamentalisms of all kinds. If there is no "political" utopia in the future, there must be a golden age in the past that can redeem individual lives or revitalize the world. No one can yet say for certain, but the rekindling of traditional religious and ethnic exclusivities and hatreds may yet present us with horrors comparable to those wrought by the transformational fantasies of totalitarian leaders, elites, and regimes.

EPILOGUE

The Russians Call Themselves Totalitarian

Thus in the political lexicon this term [totalitarianism] has become like a tennis ball. Almost all existing political forces and movements are trying to hit it harder into their opponent's court. . . . Almost no one now doubts that the regime established in this huge country after 1917 was totalitarian, even those who would like to turn back from the existing situation.

Iu. I. Igritskii

New conceptions, pretending to the role of an historiographical "philosopher's stone?" . . . But our general methodological ignorance more often gives rise not to a pithy synthesis of national and western ideas, but to the practice of a direct and at times extremely vulgar borrowing.

G. A. Bordiugov and V. A. Kozlov

ON JUNE 18, 1946, Richard C. Hottelet, the newly arrived correspondent for CBS News in Moscow, had a remarkable interview with Maxim Litvinov in his office. Litvinov had not been an influential figure in the formulation of the Soviet foreign policy since at least 1943, when he had been recalled as Soviet ambassador in Washington. Two months after Hottelet spoke with him, he was dismissed from his second-echelon position (Assistant Commissar for Foreign Affairs) and pensioned off.

Litvinov was in a somber mood that early summer afternoon about the prospects for Soviet–American relations. A close relationship between the superpowers, perhaps something that would later be described as a "great power condominium," was the only thing that could ensure world peace. It would be extremely hard to achieve, Litvinov noted, for the Soviet Union had chosen to return to the "reactionary" conception that the more territory one had, the greater one's security would be. In the course of the ensuing conversation, Hottelet, surprised to hear Litvinov criticize Soviet policy so roundly, asked him what would happen if the United States were suddenly to yield to all the major Soviet demands—the city of Trieste, the future of Germany, and so forth. Litvinov replied that such a Western surrender would lead, after a time, to a new set of Soviet demands.

Litvinov then spoke of how Hitler had probably genuinely understood his aggressive actions to be "preventive," forced on him by external circumstances. He then commented on the advantages that accrued to any totalitarian government that did not have to pay attention to public opinion. There was nothing, Litvinov assured Hottelet, that one could do to change a totalitarian government from within. He mentioned Hitler, Mussolini, and Franco, but he was centrally concerned not with them, but with Stalin.

Hottelet was amazed at Litvinov's indiscretion. Although the day was boiling hot, there was a fire in the fireplace, and he wondered whether Litvinov were burning his papers. The day after the interview, he went to the American embassy and told John Davies, the first secretary, about it. Davies arranged to have a cable sent over the signature of Ambassador Bedell Smith to Secretary of State Byrnes, summarizing Hottelet's account. The embassy's view: The "extent of this statement to a newly arrived correspondent is simply amazing to us."[1]

As nearly as I can discern, this singular episode marks the first time that any Soviet citizen in an official position ever said or strongly implied that his nation was "totalitarian," although the usage was common enough among émigrés. The term *totalitarianism,* in fact, almost never appeared in print in the Soviet Union until the last few years of its existence. It was used occasionally in lexical contexts, to characterize both extreme forms of statism in the bourgeois world—authoritarianism, Fascism, Bonapartism, *étatisme*—and a certain kind of Western anti-Communist propaganda.[2]

There is also evidence that Soviet citizens writing "for the drawer"—that is, not for publication—used the term *totalitarian* from some time after Stalin's death in 1953. The writer Vasilii Grossman, for example, used the term on several important occasions in his epic novel of the Stalin period, *Life and Fate,* which he completed in 1960. After he attempted to have it published in the journal *Znamia,* the KGB tried to confiscate all existing copies. Vladimir Suslov, then the principal ideological spokesman for the Communist Party, told Grossman that the novel could not be published for two hundred years. But another novelist, Vladimir Voinovich, succeeded in smuggling a copy abroad, and it appeared in the West several years later.[3]

In an important passage, Grossman described how totalitarian regimes prepared populations for mass murder through frenzied campaigns "to stir up feelings of real hatred and revulsion." Grossman identified the German extermination of the Ukrainian and Belorussian Jews with Stalin's campaign "to liquidate the kulaks as a class" and his "extermination of Trotskyist–Bukharinite degenerates and saboteurs."[4] Agonizingly, he declared that the violence of a totalitarian state is so great as to be no longer a means to an end; it becomes an object of mystical worship and adoration. How else can one explain the way certain intelligent, thinking Jews declared the slaughter of the Jews to be necessary for the happiness of mankind. That in view of this they were ready to take their own children to be executed—ready to carry out the sacrifice once demanded of Abraham? How else can one explain the case of a gifted, intelligent poet, himself a peasant by birth, who with sincere conviction wrote a long poem celebrating the terrible years of suffering undergone by the peasantry, years that swallowed up his own father, an honest and simple-hearted laborer?

Toward the end of the chapter he returned to the theme, asking:

Does human nature undergo a true change in the cauldron of totalitarian violence? Does man lose his innate yearning for freedom? If human nature does change, then the eternal and worldwide triumph of the dictatorial state is assured; if his yearning for freedom remains constant, then the totalitarian state is doomed.[5]

It is a pity that Grossman did not live to see the "yearning for freedom" reassert itself in the Eastern Europe and Soviet Union of the 1970s and 1980s.

The first appearances of the term *totalitarian* in the public prints were far from such passionate and unambiguous usages. In 1985, Georgii Shakhnazarov, a reformist "futurologist" and Central Committee official close to Gorbachev, published a short study entitled *Where Is Humanity Going: Critical Essays on Non-Marxist Conceptions of the Future*.[6] The book consisted of six essays cautiously paraphrasing, analyzing, and criticizing English, French, and American "futures." It began with a comparison of Aldous Huxley's *Brave New World* and Orwell's *Nineteen Eighty-Four,* entitled "Nightmares of Totalitarianism."

Shakhnazarov's essay is not easy to interpret, for some of its fulsome praise of socialism may have been deliberately exaggerated, as a sort of wink to the Soviet reader. The comparison of the totalitarian societies in the two novels apparently suggested to Shakhnazarov that liberal English writers feared that *both* capitalism and socialism might lead to a "totally organized" future.

Shakhnazarov's presentation thus set up a comparison, unprecedented in print, of capitalist and socialist futures, even though Shakhnazarov was much harder on Orwell's book, branding it "anti-communist propaganda" based on a false derivation of social relations from power, rather than the other way around.[7] The appearance of this essay, despite its complexities and ambiguities, suggested that the possible totalitarianism of the socialist world could now at least be discussed.

In the second half of the 1980s, the term *totalitarianism* became increasingly well established, more as a term of abuse than as a means to analyze Soviet reality. As Gorbachev's *perestroika* (restructuring) careened ahead and the country slipped into chaos, increasing numbers of citizens took to using the term to describe their past. Writers began to ask whether Marxism itself might be at least partially responsible for Soviet totalitarianism.[8]

Scholars also began to take note of the term. The direct comparison of the Soviet Union with Nazi Germany, so recently total anathema, became possible even before the end of the Soviet Union and commonplace by 1992.[9] Sociologists, lamenting their inability to understand Stalinism in isolation, decided that the category of totalitarianism might add the necessary comparative dimension.[10] In an article written late in 1991, A. A. Korchak, of the Academy of Sciences (formerly Soviet, now Russian), saw the Soviet Union as the premier example of "contemporary totalitarianism." Korchak's idea of contemporary totalitarianism was close to the general Western notion of bureaucratic authoritarianism, with ideology being less significant than organization and playing a conserving and stabilizing role, rather than a dynamic and mobilizing one.[11]

Almost half a century after the American Philosophical Society sponsored the first Western conference on totalitarianism, the Soviet Philosophical Society (Filosofskoe obshchestvo SSSR) sponsored the first one on Russian soil.[12] After a somewhat undisciplined roundtable, a young scholar from the Institute of World Economy and International Relations (IMEMO) posed the fundamental question for these Soviet scholars: Why had it happened to them? "Why after all does totalitarianism develop in some countries but not in others?" The question, she thought, was "still open."[13] And resolving it, she said, was complicated by the absence of developed traditions of creative social analysis in the Soviet Union.

In the individual contributions that followed, a great deal of the discussion centered on the shocks and traumas of Russia's late and violent modernization, with market culture perceived as particularly oppressive and alien in Russia. According to one historian, "the rational democracy of the Enlightenment conceded its place to a tribal consciousness raised to the power of totalitarianism."[14] One of his colleagues, however, believed just as strongly that Soviet totalitarianism constituted a real "dictatorship of development." If Stalin had merely wanted power, he would have become just another Third World dictator. But he wanted to be the leader of a "great power."[15] This point of view is close to that of the noted historian of Peter the Great, E. V. Anisimov, who regarded Peter the Great as the real founder of Russian totalitarianism, with its statism, "cult of the strong personality," oppressive bureaucracy, and spying, all to bring Russia into a place of honor among European nations.[16]

Some scholars blamed the working class (or the working class and the lower-middle class together) in particular; others thought that all Russian social classes were too weakly developed, with strong and incoherent "lumpen" elements, prone to breakdown.[17]

At the end of 1990, Iu. I. Igritskii, a section head at Moscow's respected Institute of Scientific Information (INION), undertook to introduce the Russian reader to a survey of Western writing about totalitarianism.[18] At the outset, he observed mordantly that scholarly analysis of the term had hardly begun in the Soviet Union. As a consequence, both scholars and ordinary people tended to answer the question of whether the Soviet Union was totalitarian on the basis of their practical experience rather than theoretical investigation. He also pointed out that usage varied according to one's politics. Mainstream reforming Communists regarded the task as changing an "authoritarian–bureaucratic structure." But the more radical "Democratic Union" of the Communist Party was already speaking of a "totalitarian system of power," which they contrasted with "genuine modern democracy."[19]

Igritskii's survey was intelligent and well informed, although based entirely on English-language literature. But his conclusions were extremely cautious. Even in Western scholarship, he thought, it could not be said with certainty whether the Soviet Union had been totalitarian since 1917, or just under Stalin—or at all, for there were still grave doubts about the essential meaning and explanatory power of the term. To decide these questions was an important task for Western scholars. But for Soviet scholars it was infinitely more vital, closely linked as it was with the recovery of their own past.[20]

Some two and a half years later, Igritskii returned to the fray. His second article was a much more straightforward attempt to interpret the history of the Soviet Union in terms of the totalitarian paradigm.[21] This time he found that the "parallels" among Fascist Italy, Nazi Germany, and the Soviet Union under Stalin could be observed "even by the naked eye."[22] About the pre- and post-Stalin periods he was far more ambiguous, but Stalin's Russia he found to be the principal exemplar of totalitarian state and society.[23]

Meanwhile, eclectic and speculative use of the term was spreading.[24] On May 21, 1990, the *Scales* (*Vesy*) television program broadcast a discussion of Dmitrii Volkogonov's recently published biography of Stalin, involving Volkogonov himself and another historian, A. N. Sakharov. Both used the term *totalitarian* to describe Stalin's Russia. Volkogonov believed that it was "the traditions of Tsarism," by which he meant primarily "the monolithic obsession," "the monopoly of power and the monopoly of thought," that were chiefly responsible. Sakharov, on the contrary, tended to see the intellectual traditions of Jacobinism, with "their own laws of development," as responsible.[25]

As most students of Russian history would agree, Russian intellectuals have been much better at reviving or recycling old categories than at inventing new ones. And perhaps the most durable of all is the distinction between Slavophiles and Westernizers. The Slavophiles were those intellectuals who believed that Russian culture represented the most vital social development of European Christian civilization, despite its apparent "backwardness." The worst thing Russia could do would be to borrow uncritically from "the

West." The Westernizers were those who believed that Russia had been cut off from the main lines of European civilization by some important aspect of its history, whether it was membership in the Orthodox (rather than the Roman Catholic) church or its poverty, backwardness, and authoritarian political culture.[26] The two sides agreed on many of the questions to ask about the apparent singularity of Russian development, but disagreed almost totally about the correct answers.[27]

The historian Andronik Migranian, for instance, believed that a "Western" kind of social structure, based on some kind of a middle class, was necessary to undergird the sort of European democracy toward which the Soviet Union (then nearing its end) should be evolving. On this basis, he criticized Gorbachev's reforms because they did not create the requisite Western social and economic structures first, but plunged the country into the turmoil of unfettered *glasnost* (openness). The Soviet Union, he believed, had to move from totalitarianism to authoritarianism before finally evolving into democracy.[28]

———

As WE have seen, the debate about totalitarianism in Europe and the United States has often displayed regional and national colorings as well as generational ones. The current debate in Russia about its putative totalitarianism seems likely to become caught up in the older debate about whether Russia's difficulties were homegrown and can be cured by rejoining "the West" (the Westernizer position) or whether they were brought to Russia by evil modern, "Western" ideas and their bearers and can be cured by a return to something truly Russian (the Slavophile position).[29] The path to the "common European home" about which Mikhail Gorbachev spoke so poignantly will be long indeed.

NOTES

Introduction

1. I take the term *grand failure* from Zbigniew Brzezinski, *The Grand Failure: The Birth and Death of Communism in the Twentieth Century* (New York: Scribner, 1989).

2. Michael Walzer, "On 'Failed Totalitarianism,'" in *1984 Revisited: Totalitarianism in Our Century,* ed. Irving Howe (New York: Harper & Row, 1983), pp. 104, 108.

3. Martin Jay, *Marxism and Totality: The Adventures of a Concept from Lukács to Habermas* (Berkeley: University of California Press, 1984).

4. Andrzej Walicki, "Marx and Freedom," *New York Review of Books,* November 24, 1983, p. 50. Similar arguments, of a more elaborately philosophical type, are made by A. James Gregor in *The Ideology of Fascism: The Rationale of Totalitarianism* (New York: Free Press, 1969), pp. 329–383.

5. Many of Kirkpatrick's most influential essays were published in *Dictatorships and Double Standards: Rationalism and Reason in Politics* (Washington, D.C.: American Enterprise Institute and Simon and Schuster, 1982).

6. Most of the political scientists who have discussed totalitarianism have commented on this normative–descriptive duality. For example, see Martin Jänicke's important *Totalitäre Herrschaft,* Soziologische Abhandlungen, vol. 13 (Berlin: Duncker und Humblot, 1971), pp. 11–15.

Chapter One

1. Herman Finer, *Mussolini's Italy* (New York: Holt, 1936), pp. 232–233. See also Charles Delzell, *Mussolini's Enemies: The Italian Anti-Fascist Resistance* (Princeton, N.J.: Princeton University Press, 1961), p. 8.

2. Adrian Lyttleton, *The Seizure of Power: Fascism in Italy, 1919–1929,* 2nd ed. (Princeton, N.J.: Princeton University Press, 1987), p. 125.

3. Ibid., p. 126.

4. Jens Petersen has done an excellent job in tracking down references to the word *totalitarian* in the Italian press before 1925. I am indebted to his research on a number of points. See Jens Petersen, "Die Entstehung des Totalitarismusbegriffs in Italien," in *Totalitarismus,* ed. Manfred Funke (Düsseldorf: Droste Verlag, 1978), pp. 105–128. There is an earlier Italian version: "La nascita del concetto di 'stato totalitario' in Italia," *Annali dell'Instituto storico italo-germanico in Trento,* vol. 1 (1975), which I have not been able to see. See Domenico Fisichella, *Totalitarismo: Un regime del nostro tempo* (Rome: NIS, 1987). "Totalitarian," Lyttleton wrote about this first

usage, suggested "the determination not to win a bare majority, but an almost unanimous plebiscite" (*Seizure of Power,* p. 269, n. 1).

5. Petersen, "Entstehung," p. 117.

6. "Un anno dopo," *Il Mondo,* November 2, 1923, p. 1. The article is unsigned but is attributed by Petersen to Amendola in "Entstehung," p. 118. My thanks to Lynn Gunzberg and Anthony Molho for help with the translation. I should point out, however, that the relatively backward state of the Italian communications media in the early 1920s sharply limited the kind of control possible for even the most ruthless single-party dictatorship.

7. Luigi Sturzo, *Italy and Fascismo* (London: Faber & Gwyer, 1926), pp. 127–128. On p. 214, Sturzo referred not to *totalitaria* but to *totalitarismo,* defined as "increasing the centralization of political and economic life, suppressing every free manifestation, turning the powers of the State into a single governing power, the Executive, and reducing this to a genuine dictatorship." On p. 233, Sturzo spoke of "totalitarianism," the only time he used the term in English translation. See also Leonard Schapiro, *Totalitarianism* (London: Pall Mall Press, 1972), p. 14.

8. See, for example, the passaage on "structure and superstructure" from his prison notebooks, quoted in *An Antonio Gramsci Reader,* ed. David Forgacs (New York: Schocken Books, 1988), pp. 192–193; and the discussion in Martin Jay, *Marxism and Totality* (Berkeley: University of California Press, 1984), pp. 153, 169. For an extremely cautious defense of Gramsci from charges that the totalism in his thinking was potentially totalitarian, see Walter L. Adamson, *Hegemony and Revolution: A Study of Antonio Gramsci's Political and Cultural Theory* (Berkeley: University of California Press, 1980), pp. 240–242.

9. Petersen, "Entstehung," pp. 120–121.

10. Giovanni Amendola, *La nuova democrazia: Discorsi politici (1919–1925)* (Milan, 1976), p. 303, quoted in Meir Michaelis, "Anmerkungen zum italienischen Totalitarismusbegriff: Zur Kritik der Thesen Hannah Arendts und Renzo de Felices," *Quellen und Forschungen aus italienischen Archiven und Bibliotheken* 62 (1982): 293–294. On these pages, Michaelis also provides other examples of oppositional usage in the late 1920s and 1930s.

11. Petersen, "Entstehung," p. 121. It is also possible that since the word *totalitarian* had a negative aura in respectable circles, the Fascists may have taken particular pleasure in applying it to themselves as an indication of their "revolutionary" intentions.

12. *Opera omnia di Benito Mussolini* (Florence, 1956), vol. 21, p. 362, quoted in Petersen, "Entstehung," p. 109.

13. For a thorough comparison of the "statist" and "voluntarist" usages of the term in Italy between 1925 and 1932, see Martin Jänicke, "Der Begriff des Totalitären im italienischen Faschismus," in *Totalitäre Herrschaft,* Soziologische Abhandlungen, vol. 13 (Berlin: Duncker und Humblot, 1971), pp. 20–36. Jänicke's excellent book traces the concept of totalitarianism into the 1970s. Although inevitably dated by now, it was a great help to me at the outset of my research.

14. The standard English-language work is by H. S. Harris, *The Social Philosophy of Giovanni Gentile* (Urbana: University of Illinois Press, 1966). Two important new

studies are those by Vito Belleza, *La problematica gentiliana della storia* (Rome: Bulzoni Editore, 1983), and Sergio Romano, *Giovanni Gentile, la filosofia al potere* (Milan: Bompiani, 1984), a readable study with a useful biography.

15. Harris, *Gentile,* pp. 151–152.

16. Ibid., pp. 172, 182–183. Gentile used the term in several speeches. See his *Che cosa è il fascismo: Discorsi e polemiche* (Florence: Vallecchi, 1925).

17. A. James Gregor, *The Ideology of Fascism* (New York: Free Press, 1969), p. 221.

18. A. James Gregor, "Totalitarianism Revisited," in *Totalitarianism Reconsidered,* ed. Ernest A. Menze (Port Washington, N.Y.: Kennikat Press, 1981), p. 132. Gentile's usage is strikingly close to Gramsci's at about the same time. Gramsci distinguished between the "false totalitarianism" for which Gentile spoke, which had only self-realization for its purpose, and "true" totalitarianism, whose means were totalitarian but whose purpose was the creation of the "Kingdom of Freedom" (*La costruzione del partito communista, 1923–1926* [Turin: Einaudi, 1971], p. 486, quoted in Michaelis, "Anmerkungen zum Italienischen Totalitarismusbegriff," p. 295).

19. Harris, *Gentile,* p. 125.

20. In some formulations, Gentile came very close to identifying philosophical truth with the concept of fact or "what is," despite the primacy of "thinking" in his system. See his *The Mind as Pure Act* (London: Macmillan, 1922), p. 15. See also Herbert Marcuse, *Reason and Revolution* (Boston: Beacon Press, 1954), pp. 403–409.

21. Lyttleton, *Seizure of Power,* pp. 376–377. On Gentile's views of the individual and the state, see Bellezza, *Problematica gentiliana,* esp. pp. 21–50, 139–197; and Harris, *Gentile,* pp. 57–76, 111–130.

22. Richard Bellamy, *Modern Italian Social Theory: Ideology and Politics from Pareto to the Present* (Cambridge, Mass.: Policy Press, 1987), pp. 129–131, 138–140. See also T. R. Bates, "Antonio Gramsci and the Bolshevization of the P.C.I.," *Journal of Contemporary History* 11 (1976): 116.

23. Harris, *Gentile,* p. 175.

24. This famous phrase appeared in Gentile's *Che cosa è il fascismo.* English excerpts can be found in Herbert Schneider, *Making the Fascist State* (New York: Oxford University Press, 1928), esp. p. 347.

25. Harris, *Gentile,* p. 116. See also Adrian Lyttleton, *Italian Fascisms from Pareto to Gentile* (London: Jonathan Cape, 1973), pp. 35–36.

26. Lyttleton, *Seizure of Power,* p. 377. See also A. James Gregor, *Contemporary Radical Ideologies* (New York: Random House, 1968), pp. 137–148.

27. For the "Doctrine of Fascism" in English translation, see John Somerville and Ronald E. Santoni, eds., *Social and Political Philosophy* (Garden City, N.Y.: Doubleday, 1963), pp. 424–440, quotation from p. 426; and Lyttleton, *Italian Fascisms,* pp. 301–315.

28. For Mussolini's personal and national "will to power in a Nietzschean sense," see Michaelis, "Anmerkungen zum italienischen Totalitarismusbegriff," p. 296.

29. Michaelis has a suggestive series of quotations from Mussolini's speeches on this point (ibid., pp. 294–298).

30. The literature on Carl Schmitt is substantial and growing. For example, see

the special issue of *Telos* devoted to him (Summer 1987). Schmitt is considered with other conservative intellectuals in Günter Maschke, "Im Irrgarten Carl Schmitts," in *Intellektuelle im Bann des Nationalsozialismus,* ed. Karl Corino (Hamburg: Hoffmann und Campe, 1980), pp. 204ff. Joseph Bendersky's *Carl Schmitt: Theorist for the Reich* (Princeton, N.J.: Princeton University Press, 1983), is a serviceable study. See also George Schwab's introduction and notes to his translation of *Der Begriff des Politischen* (New Brunswick, N.J.: Rutgers University Press, 1976), as well as Schwab's *The Challenge of the Exception: An Introduction to the Political Ideas of Carl Schmitt between 1921 and 1936* (Westport, Conn.: Greenwood Press, 1989). Schmitt is extensively discussed in Christian Graf von Krockow, *Die Entscheidung* (Stuttgart: Enke Verlag, 1958), a work increasingly criticized by recent students of Schmitt for exaggerating and overgeneralizing his "decisionism" and for suggesting misleading filiations between Schmitt and *völkisch* thinkers (Moeller van den Brück) and especially Ernst Jünger and Martin Heidegger. For Schmitt's relations with the Left, see the *Telos* issue and Ellen Kennedy's "Carl Schmitt und die Frankfurter Schule," *Geschichte und Gesellschaft,* no. 3 (1986): 380–419, and ensuing issues.

31. For Schmitt's sketch of the evolution of the modern state and his first use of the term, see *Der Hüter der Verfassung* (Tübingen: Mohr, 1931), esp. pp. 71–91. He developed it in "Die Wendung zum totalen Staat," in *Positionen und Begriffe im Kampf mit Weimar—Genf—Versailles, 1923–1939* (Hamburg: Hanseatische Verlagsanstalt, 1940), pp. 146–157. See also Schwab, *Challenge of the Exception,* pp. 77–80. For the following discussion, I am much indebted to the trenchant analysis in Jänicke, *Totalitäre Herrschaft,* pp. 36–41. See also Ernst Fraenkel, *The Dual State* (New York: Oxford University Press, 1941), pp. 60–62, who points out that several of Schmitt's early discussions of the desirability of a "qualitatively total state" and his denigration of the welfare state as "quantitatively total" were with conservative business audiences who welcomed this message. See also Franz Neumann, *Behemoth* (New York: Oxford University Press, 1942), p. 49.

32. Schwab, *Challenge of the Exception,* p. 62. Schmitt's language about Rousseau's "general will" is very close to that later used by J. L. Talmon in his discussion of "totalitarian democracy," although Talmon does not seem to have discussed Schmitt's work directly. See his *The Origins of Totalitarian Democracy* (New York: Praeger, 1951), passim.

33. Elie Halévy, *The Era of Tyrannies: Essays on Socialism and War* (New York: Doubleday, 1965), p. 267.

34. Schmitt, *Der Hüter der Verfassung,* p. 79; see the treatment by Gerhard Schulz in *Die nationalsozialistische Machtergreifung,* ed. Karl-Dietrich Bracher, Wolfgang Sauer, and Gerhard Schulz, 2nd ed. (Cologne: Westdeutscher Verlag, 1962), pp. 376–378. Three studies of Jünger that I found helpful were those by J. P. Stern, *Ernst Jünger* (New Haven, Conn.: Yale University Press, 1953); Hans-Peter Schwarz, *Der konservative Anarchist, Politik und Zeitkritik Ernst Jüngers* (Freiburg: Rombach, 1962); and Gerhard Loose, *Ernst Jünger* (New York: Twayne, 1974). See also Klemens von Klemperer, *Germany's New Conservatism* (Princeton, N.J.: Princeton University Press, 1957). Armin Mohler, *Die Konservative Revolution in Deutschland,*

1918–1932 (Stuttgart: Friedrich Vorwerk Verlag, 1950), contains many striking quotations from Jünger's work and an interesting analysis of his impact. I also benefited greatly from reading Jonathan Wiesen's "The Militarization of Labor," an unpublished paper written for my seminar at Brown University.

35. Ernst Jünger, *The Storm of Steel* (London: Chatto & Windus, 1929).

36. Quoted in Otto Ernst Schüddekopf, *Linke Leute von Rechts: Nationalbolschewismus in Deutschland von 1918 bis 1933* (Stuttgart: Kohlhammer Verlag, 1960), p. 39.

37. Ernst Jünger, *Der Arbeiter: Herrschaft und Gestalt,* vol. 8 of *Sämtliche Werke* (Stuttgart: Klett-Cotta, 1981), pp. 11–317.

38. "Militarizing the economy signifies, in the concrete conditions of Soviet Russia, that economic questions . . . must be equated . . . with military questions" (Leon Trotsky, "On Mobilizing the Industrial Proletariat, on Labor Service, on Militarizing the Economy, and on the Utilization of Army Units for Economic Needs: Theses of the Central Committee," in *How the Revolution Armed: Trotsky's Military Writings* [London: New Park, 1969], vol. 3, p. 67).

39. "Every class society (serf, feudal, capitalist), having exhausted its vitality, does not simply leave the arena, but is violently swept off by an intense struggle," Trotsky wrote in late 1921, "which immediately brings to its participants even greater privations and sufferings than those against which they rose" ("Military Doctrine or Pseudo-Military Doctrinairism," *Military Writings* [New York: Merit, 1969], p. 32).

40. Ernst Jünger, "Unsere Landschaft als eine Ubergangslandschaft," in *Sämtliche Werke* (Stuttgart: Klett-Cotta, 1980), vol. 7, p. 176.

41. Thus Trotsky: "This school of war . . . through its terrible realism, formulates a new human type" (quoted in Philip Pomper, *Lenin, Trotsky, and Stalin: The Intelligentsia and Power* [New York: Columbia University Press, 1990], p. 243).

42. See Roger Pethybridge, *The Social Prelude to Stalinism* (London: Macmillan, 1974), pp. 104, 105, and passim.

43. Jünger, *Der Arbeiter,* p. 29.

44. Ernst Jünger, *Die Totale Mobilmachung,* in *Sämtliche Werke,* vol. 7, pp. 119–141.

45. Ibid., p. 126.

46. Hans Buchheim, "Ernst Niekischs Ideologie des Widerstands," *Vierteljahreshefte für Zeitgeschichte,* October 1957.

47. Franz Neumann, *Behemoth: The Structure and Practice of National Socialism, 1933–1944* (New York: Harper & Row, 1966), p. 49.

48. On the intellectual universe of the time and the arguments among the various parties, see von Klemperer, *Germany's New Conservatism;* Mohler, *Die Konservative Revolution;* Schüddekopf, *Linke Leute von Rechts;* and Kurt Sontheimer, *Antidemokratisches Denken in der Weimarer Republik: Die Politischen Ideen des deutschen Nationalismus zwischen 1918 u. 1933* (Munich: Nymphenburger Verlagshandlung, 1962, 1968). Old-fashioned conservatives like Heinz Ziegler saw Schmitt's idea of the identity of the ruler and the ruled as unpalatable derivations of Enlightenment ideas, specifically Rousseau's general will. Ziegler could not accept the extreme central-

ization that Schmitt welcomed, especially the idea that the political realm could absorb everything. See Ziegler, *Autoritärer oder totaler Staat* (Tubingen: Mohr, 1932), passim.

49. Ernst Forsthoff, *Der totale Staat* (Hamburg: Hanseatische Verlagsanstalt, 1933). Mohler describes Forsthoff as "practical," ideologically a "young conservative," and strongly Protestant in orientation (*Die Konservative Revolution*, p. 83). He survived the Nazi period and enjoyed a lengthy academic career extending far into the postwar period. He was one of the coeditors for the *Festgabe* for Carl Schmitt, which appeared in 1968. Other significant contributions to the 1930s discussion came from Schmitt's chronic opponent, Hans Kelsen, *Wer soll der Hüter der Verfassung sein?* (Berlin: Rotschild 1931); and Gerhard Röhrborn, *Der autoritäre Staat* (Weida: Thomas u. Hubert, 1935).

50. Forsthoff, *Totale Staat,* p. 40.

51. Ibid., pp. 30–34.

52. Jänicke, *Totalitäre Herrschaft,* p. 41.

53. For a succinct description of the relationship between the Nazi movement and the German state, see Norman Rich, *Hitler's War Aims* (New York: Norton, 1973), vol. 1, pp. 11–16. See also Neumann, *Behemoth* (1966), pp. 63–65.

54. For citations to the *Völkische Beobachter*'s reporting of Hitler's speeches, see Neumann, *Behemoth* (1966), p. 48.

55. On Goebbels's usage, see F. Poetzsch-Heffter, C. H. Ule, and C. Dernedde, "Vom Deutschen Staatsleben," *Jahrbuch des öffentlichen Rechts* (1935), vol. 22, p. 135, quoted in Neumann, *Behemoth* (1966), pp. 480–481.

56. Alfred Rosenberg, "Totaler Staat?" *Völkische Beobachter,* January 1, 1934, p. 1. He returned to the same theme in the same paper on May 18. See the accounts of the episode in Neumann, *Behemoth* (1966), pp. 62–65, and Jänicke, *Totalitäre Herrschaft,* pp. 41–42.

57. Carl Schmitt, "Weiterentwicklung des totalen Staats in Deutschland," *Europäische Revue,* February 1933, pp. 65–70, in *Positionen und Begriffe,* pp. 185–190.

58. Jänicke, *Totale Herrschaft,* p. 42.

59. Carl Schmitt, "Totaler Feind, totaler Krieg, totaler Staat," in *Positionen und Begriffe,* pp. 235–239.

60. Erich Ludendorff, *Der totale Krieg* (Munich: Ludendorff Verlag, 1936).

61. Louis Clair, "Ernst Juenger: From Nihilism to Tradition," *Partisan Review,* September–October 1947, p. 456.

62. On derivative usage in Spain, see Martin Jänicke, "Der 'estado totalitario' der spanischen Falange," in *Totalitäre Herrschaft,* pp. 48–59; Stanley Payne, *Falange* (Stanford, Calif.: Stanford University Press, 1961), passim; and Sheelagh M. Ellwood, *Spanish Fascism in the Franco Era: Falange Española de las Jons, 1936–76* (New York: St. Martin's Press, 1987), passim.

63. See *Discursos y escritos, obras completas de José Antonio Primo de Rivera (1922–1936),* edited and with a prologue by Agustín del Río Cisneros, 2 vols. (Madrid: Instituto de Estudios Políticos, 1976), passim. In English there is *Selected Writings,* ed. Hugh Thomas (New York: Harper & Row, 1972). See especially his rather incoherent address of December 19, 1933, to the Cortes, "On the Totalitarian State,"

pp. 68–69; his "Guidelines of the Falange: The 26 Points," p. 133; and his rambling and contradictory "Spain and Barbarism," pp. 144–145.

64. Francisco Franco Bahamonde, *Palabras del caudillo, 19 abril, 1937–19 abril, 1938* (Madrid: Ediciones Fe, 1938), p. 119.

CHAPTER TWO

1. For a beginning bibliography of Sorel, see Karl Dietrich Bracher, *The Age of Ideologies* (New York: St. Martin's Press, 1984), p. 53.

2. Georges Sorel, "Reflections on Violence," in *From Georges Sorel*, ed. J. Stanley (New York: Oxford University Press, 1976), p. 205.

3. Sorel and Mussolini admired each other greatly, and Sorel thought that Lenin and Mussolini were two of the most extraordinary men of the day. Lenin, however, thought that Sorel was a "muddle-head and a mischief maker." See J. L. Talmon, "The Legacy of Georges Sorel," *Encounter*, February 1970, p. 47.

4. For some suggestive points of comparison between Fascism and Bolshevism and the syndicalist elements in both, see Robert C. Williams, *The Other Bolsheviks: Lenin and His Critics, 1904–1914* (Bloomington: Indiana Universisty Press, 1986), esp. pp. 81–104, 175–187.

5. Adrian Lyttleton, *The Seizure of Power: Fascism in Italy 1919–1929*, 2nd ed. (Princeton, N.J.: Princeton University Press, 1987), p. 333.

6. On Stakhanovism, see Lewis Siegelbaum, *Stakhanovism and the Politics of Productivity in the USSR, 1935–1941* (Cambridge: Cambridge University Press, 1988).

7. Quoted in Domenico Settembrini, "Mussolini and the Legacy of Revolutionary Socialism," *Journal of Contemporary History*, October 1976, p. 241.

8. Ibid.

9. A. James Gregor, *Italian Fascism and Developmental Dictatorship* (Princeton, N.J.: Princeton University Press, 1979), p. 125.

10. An interesting early example on the Italian side was Francesco Nitti's *Bolshevism, Fascism and Democracy* (London: Allen & Unwin, 1927). The first Italian edition had appeared in the previous year, and a French edition came out at the same time as the English edition. Although Nitti was much less hostile to Bolshevism than to Fascism, he made it clear that they represented an important historical sea change and a linked assault on liberalism and democracy.

11. In 1925, Giovanni Amendola, the inventor of the term, had seen its contours as a product of the "gleam of the conflagration in faraway Moscow" (Meier Michaelis, "Anmerkungen zum italienischen Totalitarismusbegriff: Zur Kritik der Thesen Hannah Arendts und Renzo de Felices," *Quellen und Forschuingen aus italienishcen Archiven und Bibliotheken* 62 [1982]: 302).

12. An early example was Waldemar Gurian's *Bolshevism* (New York: Macmillan, 1932). Gurian, born in Russia but educated in Germany, believed that the Soviet Union had to be studied in a primarily Russian context, not in a comparative and contemporary framework. But as early as 1931, when the book was being written, Soviet statism, the uninhibited use of coercion and control of public opinion, led Gurian to call it a "totalitarian state, bringing the entire life of society under its

sway." And toward the end of the book he wrote: "Carl Schmitt, who made the Fascist conception of the totalitarian state familiar in Germany, regards as its fundamental characteristic the disappearance of the nineteenth-century distinction between state and society. . . . No doubt since the nature of the Bolshevik totalitarian state is wholly determined by economic considerations, it is intended to assume finally the shape of a totalitarian state whose economic functions will render any political machinery superfluous. The actual development, however, takes the form of steadily increasing encroachments and extensions of the state machinery. And since the Bolshevik totalitarian state is based on a particular historical and philosophic creed, it cannot, like the Fascist, leave particular spheres of life—for example, religion—outside its orbit, undetermined by its authority" (pp. 82, 378–379).

13. Of course, this change did not take place overnight. In England, France, and the United States, some academic publications and intellectual journals continued to use "totalitarian" and the "total state" to refer only to Germany and Italy. But such usage became increasingly rare after 1936. See Jean Huszar, "Du parti à l'état: Etude sur le fascisme," *Revue des sciences politiques* 49 (1934): 519; and Boris Ischboldin, "Le Régime économique du National–Socialisme allemand," *L'Année politique française et étrangère* 9 (1934): 202. The liberal émigré historian of Russia, Michael Florinsky, in his *Fascism and National Socialism: A Study of the Economic and Social Policies of the Totalitarian State* (New York, 1936), also regarded Italy and Germany as "the" totalitarian states, but used the Soviet Union as the principal comparison. In *The Dual State* (New York: Oxford University Press, 1941), Ernst Fraenkel defined "totalitarian" in a sense directly derived from Carl Schmitt, but did not make much analytical use of it in his book. See other examples of this usage in Martin Jänicke, *Totalitäre Herrschaft*, Soziologische Abhandlungen, vol. 13 (Berlin: Ducker und Humblot, 1971), p. 62, esp. n. 7.

14. In addition to Luigi Sturzo, *Italy and Fascismo* (London: Faber & Gwyer, 1926), the publication of Giovanni Gentile's popularization, "The Philosophical Basis of Fascism," *Foreign Affairs,* January 1928, pp. 290–304, should be mentioned. For a characteristic English-language production by an émigré critic of Fascism, see the use of "totalitarian" by Gaetano Salvemini in "Parliamentary Reform in Italy," *Contemporary Review,* April 1928, pp. 447–454, passim.

15. See the *Times,* November 2, 1929, cited in H. J. Spiro, "Totalitarianism," *International Encyclopedia of the Social Sciences* (New York: Macmillan, 1968), vol. 16, pp. 106–107. According to Jänicke, the term *totalitarianism* was first used by the Italian delegation to the Third Congress of the Socialist International in 1928 (*Totalitäre Herrschaft*, p. 63, n. 9).

16. See Sabine's entry under "State" in *International Encyclopedia of the Social Sciences* (New York: Macmillan, 1934), vol. 14, p. 330. See also Domenica Fisichella, *Totalitarismo: Un regime del nostro tempo* (Rome: NIS, 1987), p. 15.

17. A good general account of the Frankfurt School, including its resettlement in New York, is Martin Jay, *The Dialectical Imagination* (Boston: Little, Brown, 1973).

18. Herbert Marcuse, "Der Kampf gegen den Liberalismus in der totalitären Staatsauffassung," *Zeitschrift für Sozialforschung* 3 (1934), in Marcuse, *Aufsätze aus der*

Zeitschrift für Sozialforschung 1934–1941 (Frankfurt: Suhrkamp Verlag, 1979), pp. 7–44. My citations are from Marcuse, "The Struggle Against Liberalism in the Totalitarian View of the State," in *Negations* (Boston: Beacon Press, 1968), pp. 3–42. See also the analysis in Jay, *Dialectical Imagination,* pp. 121–124. For a critique of the Frankfurt School's theory of Fascism, see Douglas Kellner, *Herbert Marcuse and the Crisis of Marxism* (Berkeley: University of California Press, 1984), pp. 112–115.

19. Marcuse was able to quote to good effect Gentile's famous letter to Mussolini, claiming that Italian Fascism represented the true liberalism of the postwar world ("Struggle Against Liberalism," p. 11).

20. Ibid., p. 19.

21. Ibid., p. 39.

22. Herbert Marcuse, "Studien über Autorität und Familie" (1936), in *Aufsätze aus der Zeitschrift für Sozialforschung 1934–1941,* pp. 178–179.

23. Herbert Marcuse, *Soviet Marxism* (New York: Vintage Books, 1961), and *One-Dimensional Man* (Boston: Beacon Press, 1964).

24. Harold Bleich, *The Philosophy of Herbert Marcuse* (Washington, D.C.: University Press of America, 1977), pp. 129–130. In *Eros and Civilization* (Boston: Beacon Press, 1966), Marcuse wrote that "totalitarianism spreads over late industrial civilization wherever the interests of domination prevail upon productivity, arresting and diverting its potentialities" (p. 93).

25. Franz Neumann, *Behemoth: The Structure and Practice of National Socialism, 1933–1944* (1942; Harper & Row, 1966), pp. 62–82, passim. He has an excellent collection of quotations from *Mein Kampf* and others of Hitler's works (pp. 62–65), suggesting that Hitler usually wrote about the state as if it were merely a means to an end.

26. Ibid., p. 48.

27. Max Horkheimer and Theodor W. Adorno, *Dialectic of Enlightenment* (New York: Seabury Press, 1972), p. 6, translation of *Dialektik der Aufklärung* (New York: Social Studies Association, 1944).

28. It was also remarkably similar to Marcuse's later critique of bourgeois American society, *One-Dimensional Man.* See also David McLellan, *Marxism After Marx* (New York: Harper & Row, 1979), pp. 261–267; Jay, *Dialectical Imagination,* pp. 253–280; Susan Buck-Morss, *The Origin of Negative Dialectics* (New York: Free Press 1977), pp. 59–62; and Christian Lenhardt, "The Wandering Enlightenment," in *On Critical Theory,* ed. John O'Neill (New York: Seabury Press, 1976), pp. 34–57, esp. pp. 34–39.

29. Paul Tillich, "The Totalitarian State and the Claims of the Church," *Social Research,* November 1934, pp. 405–433. On the émigrés at the New School and the founding of *Social Research,* see Thomas E. Lifka, *The Concept "Totalitarianism" and American Foreign Policy, 1933–1949* (New York: Garland, 1988), vol. 1, pp. 16–20. I ran across Lifka's work rather late in my research, but it is most informative and I profited very much from reading it.

30. Tillich, "Totalitarian State," p. 409.

31. Ibid., p. 411.

32. Ibid., p. 410.

33. Christopher Dawson, "Religion and the Totalitarian State," *Criterion,* October 1934, pp. 1–16, quotation from pp. 1–2.

34. Ibid., pp. 3–4.

35. It is interesting to compare this new writing published in 1934 and 1935 with studies in comparative history, politics, and economics from a year or two earlier, in which Bolshevism and Fascism are treated entirely as antipodes.

36. Max Lerner, "The Pattern of Dictatorship," in *Dictatorship in the Modern World,* ed. Guy Stanton Ford (Minneapolis: University of Minnesota Press, 1935), p. 19.

37. Lerner was a reformist, not a revolutionary, however, who believed that capitalism did not have to lead to Fascism but could be saved by rational economic planning.

38. Lerner, "Pattern of Dictatorship," pp. 18–19.

39. Hans Kohn, "Between Democracy and Fascism," in *Dictatorship,* ed. Ford, pp. 143–160.

40. Hans Kohn, "Communist and Fascist Dictatorship: A Comparative Study," in *Revolutions and Dictatorships: Essays in Contemporary History,* ed. Kohn (Cambridge, Mass.: Harvard University Press, 1939), pp. 179–199, esp. p. 198.

41. On this literature, see Lifka, *Concept "Totalitarianism,"* vol. 1, pp. 28–55.

42. For details on Hoover's career, see ibid., pp. 23–28.

43. Calvin B. Hoover, in *Bolshevism, Fascism and Capitalism* (New Haven, Conn.: Yale University Press, 1932), pp. 227–256.

44. Calvin Hoover, *Germany Enters the Third Reich* (New York: Macmillan, 1933).

45. Ibid., pp. 109–110.

46. Calvin B. Hoover, *Dictatorships and Democracies* (New York: Macmillan, 1937), p. vii.

47. Calvin B. Hoover, "Dictatorships and Democracies," *Virginia Quarterly Review,* April 1934, pp. 161–176. One must not overlook the small number of American writers—most of them close to Fascism in one way or another—who agreed that liberal capitalism was going through a crisis and argued that the United States must abandon it and itself turn to a "totalitarian" solution. Such a publicist was the former diplomat and banker Lawrence Dennis. See, in particular, his *The Coming of American Fascism* (New York: Harper, 1936). Although Dennis was clearly extremely unsympathetic to Communism, he was quite capable of comparing Soviet totalitarianism explicitly and favorably with American liberalism.

48. William Henry Chamberlin, "Russia and Germany—Parallels and Contrasts," *Atlantic Monthly,* September 1935, pp. 359–368. See also his earlier, premonitory "Farewell to Russia," *Atlantic Monthly,* November 1934, pp. 564–573.

49. This was apparently the first use of this provocative term. For a spirited argument on whether it was justified and what it meant for U.S.–Soviet relations, see Les K. Adler and Thomas G. Patterson, "Red Fascism: The Merger of Nazi Germany and Soviet Russia in the American Image of Totalitarianism, 1930's–1950's," *American Historical Review,* April 1970, pp. 1046–1064, and the ensuing discussion in the letters column. For an effective critique of Adler and Patterson's highly critical account of how Germany and the Soviet Union came to be studied in

the 1930s, see Thomas R. Maddux, "Red Fascism, Brown Bolshevism: The American Image of Totalitarianism in the 1930s," *The Historian* 40 (1977): 85–103.

50. Chamberlin, "Russia and Germany," p. 368.

51. Maddux, "Red Fascism," pp. 85–103. The comparison may also be found in the movies—for instance, *Ninotchka*. The film is about three Soviet officials who are sent to Paris to sell tsarist jewels to raise money for the Soviet Union. When these agents are corrupted by the good life that capitalism offers in Paris, another Soviet agent is sent, Ninotchka (Greta Garbo), who is represented as the perfection of Soviet womanhood until she is seduced by Melvyn Douglas. When the three Soviet agents go to the railroad station to meet the fourth, they are not expecting a woman. So they spot a man who looks like "one of them," whom they take to be the new agent. When they introduce themselves to this shabby but severe-looking fellow, he pushes them aside and storms off the screen with a "Heil Hitler."

52. Maddux, "Red Fascism," p. 89.

53. Some period English-language studies that use the term include Walter Lippmann, *The Good Society* (Boston: Little, Brown, 1937); William E. Rappard, *The Crisis of Democracy* (Chicago: University of Chicago Press, 1938); Peter Drucker, *The End of Economic Man: A Study of the New Totalitarianism* (New York: John Day, 1939); Hans Kohn, *Revolutions and Dictatorships,* 2nd ed. (Cambridge, Mass.: Harvard University Press, 1939); Charles Merriam, *The New Democracy and the New Despotism* (New York: McGraw-Hill, 1939); Alfred Cobban, *Dictatorship: Its History and Theory* (New York: Scribner, 1939); M. W. Fodor, *The Revolution Is On* (Boston: Houghton Mifflin, 1940); and Hans Kohn, *Not by Arms Alone* (Cambridge, Mass.: Harvard University Press, 1940). Even more important (and focused) studies include those by Ernst Fraenkel, *The Dual State* (New York: Oxford University Press, 1941); Sigmund Neumann, *The Permanent Revolution: The Total State in a World at War* (New York: Harper, 1942), with its heavy stress on personal dictatorship; and Franz Neumann, *Behemoth.* For England, in addition to Bertrand Russell, *Power: A New Social Analysis* (New York: Norton, 1938), see Paul Dukes, *An Epic of the Gestapo* (London: Cassell, 1940), esp. pp. 277–284. Dukes's book made a considerable impression on George Orwell.

54. Maddux points out that "leading columnists, such as Raymond Clapper, Dorothy Thompson, Herbert Agar, and Walter Lippmann, referred to a similar ruthlessness in their tactics as well as the collectivist–totalitarian nature of their regimes" ("Red Fascism," p. 92). For a good example, see Dorothy Thompson's "Guide to Isms," in *Political Guide: A Study of American Liberalism and Its Relationship to Modern Totalitarian States* (New York: Stackpole Sons, 1938), pp. 11–32. "In the totalitarian state," she wrote, "every single human activity: religion, education, work, business, even the relations between individuals—love, marriage—are all geared into line with a single cultural policy. All private organizations, whether they are philanthropic, social or economic . . . must be geared into line with the state's program. The Rotary Club is banished in Germany because it is international. So are the Masonic orders. Russia, Italy and Germany are all totalitarian states" (p. 15).

55. See André Liebich, "Marxism and Totalitarianism: Rudolf Hilferding and the Mensheviks," Occasional Paper, no. 217 (Washington, D.C.: Kennan Institute for Advanced Russian Studies, 1987), pp. 25–28 and passim.

56. John Dewey, "The Moscow Trials," in *The Later Works, 1925–1953*, vol. 11: *1935–1937* (Carbondale: Southern Illinois University Press, 1981–1990), p. 328 (italics added).

57. John Dewey, *Freedom and Culture*, in *The Later Works, 1925–1953*, vol. 13: *1938–1939* (Carbondale: Southern Illinois University Press, 1981–1990), pp. 63–188. "Conditions in totalitarian countries have brought home the fact, not sufficiently realized by critics, myself included, that the forms which still exist [in democratic societies] encourage freedom of discussion, criticism and voluntary associations, and thereby set a gulf between a country having suffrage and popular representation and a country having dictatorships, whether of the right or left—the differences between the two latter growing continually less as they borrow each other's techniques" (pp. 129–130). Not surprisingly, Leon Trotsky was willing to see Stalin's bureaucratic dictatorship as "totalitarian." Although he did not use the term analytically, Trotsky wrote in the summer of 1936 that Stalin's "regime had become 'totalitarian' in character several years before this word arrived from Germany" (*The Revolution Betrayed* [New York: Doubleday, Doran, 1937], p. 100).

58. See the numerous references in the essays collected in John Dewey, *The Later Works, 1925–1953*, vol. 14: *1939–1941* (Carbondale: Southern Illinois University Press, 1981–1990), passim. "I Believe" is on pp. 91–97.

In England, another philosopher, Bertrand Russell, was struck, as Dewey was, by the growing hostility to liberalism in the world and the rise of totalitarian states. Russell, however, took a much less Manichaean position than Dewey did. Although Russell did not take seriously the leftist position that totalitarianism was merely another word for Fascism (and he certainly regarded the Soviet Union as totalitarian), he did recognize that there was a general, if complex, relationship between liberal parliamentary democracy and a worldwide increase in the power of the state. Although Russell emphasized the evolution of totalitarianism out of more traditional forms of statism, he was convinced of its novelty. Much of this he ascribed to the technological advances that had enabled a far more total control of public opinion (Russell, *Power,* pp. 136–144 and passim).

59. "Editorial Statement," *Partisan Review,* December 1937, p. 3. The editors then were F. W. Dupee, Dwight Macdonald, Mary McCarthy, George L. K. Morris, William Phillips, and Philip Rahv.

60. Leon Trotsky, "Art and Politics," *Partisan Review,* August–September 1938, p. 4.

61. Victor Serge, "Marxism in Our Time," *Partisan Review,* August–September 1938, p. 28; Dwight Macdonald, "The Soviet Cinema: 1930–1938, Part II," *Partisan Review,* August–September 1938, p. 36.

62. This, for example, was the position of the future historian Bertram D. Wolfe, who gradually moved to a much more conservative position. "The Soviet Union," he wrote early in 1940, "is still in transition, but it is still developing into a totalitarian, bureaucratic slave-state with a ruling group not exactly comparable to the class or caste of earlier societies, but something historically new, in which all traces of workers state and socialism have been eliminated or turned into their opposites, into instruments of oppression" ("Souvarine on Stalin," *Partisan Review* 7 [1940]: 75–76).

63. Dwight Macdonald, "War and the Intellectuals: Act Two," *Partisan Review,* Spring 1939, p. 4.

64. Philip Rahv, "Twilight of the Thirties," *Partisan Review,* Summer 1939, p. 5.

65. *The Nation,* May 27, 1939, p. 626. The manifesto was submitted for publication by Sidney Hook, who had been closely associated with Dewey.

66. The manifesto appeared in *Partisan Review,* Fall 1938, pp. 49–52. The "Statement of the L.C.F.S." appeared in *Partisan Review,* Summer 1939, pp. 125–127. Apart from those directly associated with the *Partisan Review,* signers included James T. Farrell, Melvin Lasky, Kenneth Patchen, Harold Rosenberg, Meyer Schapiro, Paul Rosenfeld, and William Carlos Williams.

67. Freda Kirchwey, "Red Totalitarianism," *The Nation,* May 27, 1939, pp. 605–606.

68. "To All Active Supporters of Democracy and Peace," *The Nation,* August 26, 1939, p. 228, quoted in William L. O'Neill, *A Better World: The Great Schism: Stalinism and the American Intellectuals* (New York: Simon and Schuster, 1982), p. 15.

69. Dwight Macdonald, "I Choose the West," in *Memoirs of a Revolutionist* (Cleveland: Meridian Books, 1958), pp. 197–201.

70. Maddux, "Red Fascism," p. 93.

71. Liebich, "Marxism and Totalitarianism," p. 31.

72. See Richard Kern [Rudolf Hilferding], "Die Weltwirtschaft in Kriegsgefahr," *Neuer Voorwärts,* January 1, 1939, reprinted as "The Modern Totalitarian State," *Modern Review,* October 1947, pp. 598ff.

73. Quoted in Liebich, "Marxism and Totalitarianism," p. 53.

74. The episode is recounted in Frank A. Warren, *Liberals and Communism: The "Red Decade Revisited"* (Bloomington: Indiana University Press, 1966), p. 213.

75. For Roger Baldwin's tangled thinking on how the unity of the Left was essential but Popular Front organizations must be officered by liberals, see his "Liberalism and the United Front," in *Whose Revolution?* ed. Irving De Witt Talmadge (New York, 1941). I owe this reference to O'Neill, *Better World,* p. 41.

76. Mary S. McAuliffe, "The American Civil Liberties Union During the McCarthy Years," in *The Specter: Original Essays on the Cold War and the Origins of McCarthyism,* ed. Robert Griffith and Athan Theoharis (New York: New Viewpoints, 1974), pp. 155–156.

77. Lucile Milner, *Education of an American Liberal* (New York: Horizon Press, 1954), pp. 261–294, gives the best account. The quotation is from p. 283. See also Corliss Lamont, *The Trial of Elizabeth Gurley Flynn* (New York: Monthly Review Press, 1968); and Mary S. McAuliffe, "The Politics of Civil Liberties," in *Specter,* ed. Griffith and Theoharis, esp. pp. 155–156.

78. Maddux, "Red Fascism," p. 99.

79. See, for example, Franz Borkenau, *The Totalitarian Enemy* (London: Faber & Faber, 1940), esp. chap. 2. The book appears to have been written during the fall and winter of 1939/1940, just after the signing of the Nazi-Soviet Pact and during the first months of the "phony war." "This European war," Borkenau began his text, "is an 'ideological war.' It is a fight of the liberal powers of Europe against the biggest 'totalitarian' power, Germany, and Germany, in this war, is cooperating, though in

an ambiguous manner, with Russia, the other big totalitarian power of the world . . . the division could not be more clear-cut; liberal powers here, totalitarian powers there" (p. 11). Jänicke properly associates some of Borkenau's "militancy" with his status as an ex-Communist (*Totalitäre Herrschaft,* p. 66). For his list of the most militant publications opposing "democracy" and "totalitarianism" in extreme fashion around the outbreak of World War II, see *Totalitäre Herrschaft,* p. 67, n. 26.

80. *Seminar on the Totalitarian State: From the Standpoints of History, Political Science, Economics and Sociology. Proceedings of the American Philosophical Society,* vol. 82 (Philadelphia: American Philosophical Society, 1940).

81. T. S. Eliot, as often in the past, stood rather apart. He condemned totalitarianism as "pagan," but at the same time believed that neither liberalism nor democracy had sufficient positive content to serve as serious counterideals. Liberalism was a nineteenth-century movement, already passing into history, and "democracy" was impossible to define. What he stood for, of course, was Christian traditionalism. See T. S. Eliot, *The Idea of a Christian Society* (London: Harcourt, Brace, 1940), esp. chap. 1. See also the interesting review by Lionel Trilling, "Elements that Are Wanted," *Partisan Review* 7 (1940): esp. 369–370.

82. Reinhold Niebuhr, *Christianity and Power Politics* (New York: Scribner, 1940), passim.

83. See, inter alia, "Dictator Set-ups Sure to Fall: Dr. Leiper Predicts Ultimate Defeat Because of Their Basic Philosophies," *New York Times,* April 3, 1939, p. 18; "Totalitarian Aims Scored by Bennett," *New York Times,* June 16, 1939, p. 21; and "Calls Education to Guard Liberty: Monsignor Haas Declares That It Should Organize Fight Against Totalitarianism," *New York Times,* July 10, 1939.

84. Lifka, *Concept "Totalitarianism,"* vol. 1, pp. 203–206.

85. "Rally Here Scores Reich and Soviet: Hoover, Landon, LaGuardia and Green Are Heard by 20,000," *New York Times,* December 14, 1939, p. 1.

86. "Synagogue Youth Pledge Aid Abroad: League Votes to Cooperate with United Jewish Appeal," *New York Times,* April 1, 1940, p. 20.

87. "Methodists Ready to Aid Peace Move: But Bishops Are 'Unalterably' Opposed to U.S.–Vatican Link: Totalitarianism Scored," *New York Times,* April 26, 1940; "Presbyterians See Education in Peril: Dr. W. L. Young, New Moderator of Church in U.S.A., Cites Totalitarian Inroads," *New York Times,* May 27, 1940, p. 21.

88. Some strongly secularist opponents of totalitarianism, like Sidney Hook and George Orwell, referred on occasion to the Catholic church as a totalitarian organization or at least (this seems to have been Orwell's most considered opinion) as a precursor of modern totalitarianism. See Sidney Hook, "On Ideas," *Partisan Review* 8 (1940): 152–160.

CHAPTER THREE

1. "The Year in Books," *Time,* December 14, 1941, p. 108.

2. For a good discussion of the term's use among American officials, see Thomas E. Lifka, *The Concept "Totalitarianism" and American Foreign Policy, 1938–1939* (New York: Garland, 1988), vol. 1, pp. 76–80.

3. See the discussion in Ellsworth Barnard, *Wendell Willkie . . . Fighter for Freedom* (Marquette: Northern Michigan University Press, 1966), p. 259.

4. Herbert Hoover, "It Needn't Happen Here," *American Mercury,* July 1940, p. 269.

5. Of course, the Left shortly began discovering "totalitarian liberals," too. For Dwight Macdonald, they were advocates of state capitalism. See his *Henry Wallace: The Man and the Myth* (New York: Vanguard Press, 1947), pp. 36–38.

6. "Hoover Challenge: Says New Deal Leads to Same Suicide Road Trod in Europe," *New York Times,* June 26, 1940, p. 1. The question about the relationship between socialism and totalitarianism was already being posed, and not just by the likes of Herbert Hoover. "Where in general lies the guarantee that government-owned or government-controlled industry does not as its natural form beget the totalitarian state?" asked Eugene Lyons in the *Saturday Review of Literature,* March 16, 1940, p. 7, in a review of Max Eastman's *Stalin's Russia.*

7. Quoted in Robert E. Burke, "The Election of 1940," in *History of the American Presidential Elections, 1789–1968,* ed. Arthur M. Schlesinger, Jr. (New York, McGraw-Hill, 1971), vol. 4, p. 2941. For a more restrained comparison, see *This Is Wendell Willkie: A Collection of Speeches and Writings on Present-Day Issues* (New York: Dodd, Mead, 1940), p. 195.

8. Quoted in *New York Times,* June 17, 1940, p. 8.

9. "La Guardia Hails Italian Loyalty," *New York Times,* June 18, 1940, p. 20.

10. Lawrence Dennis, *The Coming American Fascism* (New York: Harper, 1936), passim, esp. pp. 10, 63, 130, 208, 290. See also his *The Dynamics of War and Revolution* (N.p., 1940), cited in Lifka, *Concept "Totalitarianism,"* vol. 1, pp. 110–111.

11. "Trend to Totalitarianism Seen," *New York Times,* January 1, 1940, p. 22.

12. Frederick L. Schuman, Lawrence Dennis, and Max Lerner, "Who Owns the Future?" *The Nation,* January 11, 1941, p. 37, quoted in William L. O'Neill, *A Better World: The Great Schism: Stalinism and the American Intellectuals* (New York: Simon and Schuster, 1982), p. 29.

13. Geoffrey Crowther, "Can Democracy Survive the War?" *New York Times Magazine,* January 21, 1940, p. 4.

14. "Topics of the Times," *New York Times,* May 7, 1941, p. 24.

15. Arthur Vandenberg to Alton Roberts, September 19, 1939, Vandenberg Papers, quoted in Lifka, *Concept "Totalitarianism,"* vol. 1, p. 134.

16. Lifka, *Concept "Totalitarianism,"* vol. 1, pp. 109–110.

17. Ibid., p. 111.

18. See the speech of Senator Robert Taft, made on June 24, 1941, quoted in ibid., p. 202.

19. Lifka, *Concept "Totalitarianism,"* vol. 1, p. 124. See also Aaron Levenstein, with William Agar, *Freedom's Advocate* (New York: Viking, 1965). Levenstein's account of the "antitotalitarians" in the early 1940s centers on the creation of Freedom House in New York.

20. Lifka, *Concept "Totalitarianism,"* vol. 1, p. 155.

21. One of the major proponents of the term, Sidney Hook, wrote more often for the *New Leader* after 1940 than for the *Partisan Review.*

22. Carlton J. H. Hayes, *A Generation of Materialism* (New York: Harper, 1941).

23. Carlton J. H. Hayes, "The Novelty of Totalitarianism in the History of Western Civilization," in *Seminar on the Totalitarian State: From the Standpoints of History, Political Science, Economics and Sociology, Proceedings of the American Philosophical Society,* vol. 82 (Philadelphia: American Philosophical Society, 1940), pp. 91–102. This essay was more influential than most of the contributions to the symposium. It was reprinted in German after World War II, for instance, in Bruno Seidel and Siegfried Jenkner, *Wege der Totalitarismus-forschung* (Darmstadt: Wissenschaftliche Buchgesellschaft, 1968), pp. 86–100.

24. "New Ambassador Scores Dictators: Professor Hayes to Represent the U.S. in Spain, Criticizes 'Pagan Totalitarianism,'" *New York Times,* April 26, 1942, p. 8.

25. See Stanley Payne, *Franco's Spain* (New York: Crowell, 1967), pp. 22, 44, and passim. "Though in the early years of his regime Franco made frequent verbal references to the ideal of a totalitarian, fully mobilized society, in practice he had always made it clear that the Nationalist dictatorship was a pragmatic proposition, not a doctrinaire, ideologically circumscribed government" (p. 44). Still, as late as the final days of 1939, the American ambassador to Madrid reported that "Franco rejects the possibility of a 'liberal' regime bringing Spain out of its present difficulties and extols the efficiency of the 'totalitarian' regime which he believes can alone administer government in Spain efficiently" (quoted in Lifka, *Concept "Totalitarianism,"* vol. 1, pp. 166–167).

26. "New Ambassador Scores Dictators," p. 8.

27. Carlton J. H. Hayes, *Wartime Mission in Spain, 1942–1945* (New York: Macmillan, 1945), quoted in Lifka, *Concept "Totalitarianism,"* vol. 1, p. 235.

28. Francisco Franco Bahamonde, "Speech to Falangist Party Council Praising German, Italian and Spanish Fascism," in *Voices of History, 1942–1943: Speeches and Papers of Roosevelt, Churchill, Stalin, Chiang, Hitler and Other Leaders Delivered During 1942,* ed. Franklin Watts (New York: Gramercy, 1943), p. 728.

29. "What Faith?" *Time,* August 17, 1942, p. 46.

30. "Year in Books," p. 108

31. Arthur Koestler, *Darkness at Noon* (New York: Bantam, 1968), pp. 215–216.

32. On this fascinating phenomenon, see Kerry Whiteside, *Merleau-Ponty and the Foundation of an Existential Politics* (Princeton, N.J.: Princeton University Press, 1988), pp. 168–171.

33. Ernst Fraenkel, *The Dual State* (New York: Oxford University Press, 1941). Carl J. Friedrich, then a young professor of government at Harvard, was one of the readers of Fraenkel's manuscript before it was published; it no doubt added to his interest in totalitarianism.

34. Sigmund Neumann, *Permanent Revolution: The Total State in a World at War* (New York: Harper, 1942).

35. James Burnham, *The Managerial Revolution* (New York: John Day, 1941). A useful biographical sketch of Burnham, although written from a relentlessly hostile point of view, may be found in Alan M. Wald, *The New York Intellectuals* (Chapel Hill: University of North Carolina Press, 1987), pp. 176–182 and passim.

36. More than 100,000 copies were sold in hardcover during the war and many

more in paperback. See Brian Crozier, "The Political Thought of James Burnham," *National Review,* April 15, 1983, p. 435; and John Patrick Diggins, *Up from Communism* (New York: Harper & Row, 1975), pp. 191–192. After the war, *The Managerial Revolution* was translated into French, German, Italian, Spanish, Chinese, Japanese, Arabic, Hebrew, Russian, Polish, Ukrainian, Greek, Swedish, and Hindi.

37. C. H. Waddington, *The Scientific Attitude* (Harmondsworth: Penguin Books, 1941), pp. 18–19. There is a blistering critique of Waddington's book in Friedrich Hayek, *The Road to Serfdom,* 2nd ed. (Chicago: University of Chicago Press, 1976), pp. 192–193.

38. Waddington, *Scientific Attitude,* p. 124.

39. Ibid., p. 19. Waddington did not admit that there was such a thing as freedom, although he was willing to admit that there was such a thing as a "feeling of freedom" (p. 110).

40. See *The Collected Essays, Journalism and Letters of George Orwell* (New York: Harcourt, Brace & World, 1968), vol. 4, pp. 160–181 and passim.

41. William Steinhoff, *George Orwell and the Origins of 1984* (Ann Arbor: University of Michigan Press, 1975), pp. 43–54.

42. George Orwell, "Literature and Totalitarianism," in *The Collected Essays, Journalism and Letters of George Orwell* (New York: Harcourt, Brace & World, 1968), vol. 2, pp. 134–135.

43. Ibid., p. 137.

44. George Orwell to H. J. Wilmett, May 18, 1944, in *The Collected Essays, Journalism and Letters of George Orwell* (New York: Harcourt, Brace & World, 1968), vol. 3, pp. 148–149. Recently, Peter Novick called attention to how many critics, like Orwell, linked the rise of relativism and the loss of "objective truth" with totalitarianism. Oliver Wendell Holmes and the "Legal Realists" were subjected to such attacks, and so were relativists in the historical and anthropological professions. See Peter Novick, *That Noble Dream: The "Objectivity Question" and the American Historical Profession* (Cambridge: Cambridge University Press, 1988), pp. 288–292.

45. George Orwell, in *Collected Essays, Journalism and Letters,* vol. 4, pp. 448, 460.

46. George Orwell, "Arthur Koestler," in *Collected Essays, Journalism and Letters,* vol. 3, pp. 234–244. See also Steinhoff, *Orwell and the Origins of 1984,* pp. 32–35.

47. George Orwell, "Why I Write," in *The Collected Essays, Journalism and Letters of George Orwell* (New York: Harcourt, Brace & World, 1968), vol. 1, p. 5.

48. Orwell, "Arthur Koestler," p. 235. See also Samuel Hynes, "Introduction," in *Twentieth Century Interpretations of 1984,* ed. Samuel Hynes (Englewood Cliffs, N.J.: Prentice-Hall, 1971), p. 18.

49. As many students of Orwell have pointed out, several of the themes of *Nineteen Eighty-Four* are adumbrated in *Animal Farm,* published in 1945, among them the rewriting of history, as when "all animals are equal" becomes "all animals are equal, but some animals are more equal than others." See the relevant passage in John Strachey, "The Strangled Cry," reprinted in part in Hynes, "Introduction," pp. 54–55. A good general account of the intellectual influences on Orwell as he was writing *Nineteen Eighty-Four* can be found in Steinhoff, *Orwell and the Origins of 1984,* esp. chaps. 2 and 3.

50. Dwight Macdonald, "Kulturbolschewismus Is Here," *Partisan Review,* November–December 1941, pp. 442–451, esp. pp. 446, 451. The article was later reprinted as "Kulturbolschewismus and Mr. Van Wyck Brooks," in Dwight Macdonald, *Memoirs of a Revolutionist* (Cleveland: Meridian Books, 1958), pp. 203–214. Other antimodernist intellectuals took similar positions. See, for example, Lewis Mumford, "The Corruption of Liberalism, *New Republic,* April 29, 1940, pp. 568–573. Despite the hysteria of reactions like Brooks's and Mumford's, Macdonald's anxiety was itself rather overdone. There was no such "drift toward totalitarianism" in the wartime United States.

51. For a good account of Macdonald's polemics and those of others, see Terry A. Cooney, *The Rise of the New York Intellectuals: Partisan Review and Its Circle* (Madison: University of Wisconsin Press, 1986), pp. 200–206. See also Novick, *That Noble Dream,* pp. 282–284.

52. Tresca had been an influential member of a civil rights defense committee that had defended eighteen Trotskyists from prosecution under the Smith Act.

53. "5,000 Pay Tribute to Carlo Tresca: All Forms of Totalitarianism Denounced at Service for Slain Radical Editor," *New York Times,* January 17, 1943, p. 40. David Dubinsky, president of the ILGWU, also used the term in his speech, describing Tresca as a "hater of totalitarianism."

54. Norman Thomas and Bertram D. Wolfe, *Keep America out of War* (New York: Stokes, 1939), quoted in Lifka, *Concept "Totalitarianism,"* p. 117.

55. Norman Thomas to Ray F. Carter, April 18, 1944, Thomas Papers, Box 46, New York Public Library, quoted in Norman Markowitz, "From the Popular Front to Cold War Liberalism," in *The Specter: Original Essays on the Cold War and the Origins of McCarthyism,* ed. Robert Griffith and Athan Theoharis (New York: New Viewpoints, 1974), p. 101.

56. Max Nomad, a man of the extreme Left, was nevertheless passionately critical of what he regarded as fellow traveling. See, for example, his "American Pseudo-Liberalism," *New Leader,* December 22, 1945, p. 3, an attack on the attitude toward the Soviet Union at the *Nation* and the *New Republic.* In it he wrote that "there are paradoxes and paradoxes. Some of them are profound truths, defying old worn-out commonplaces. Others are merely impudent and provocative pleas for old or new injustices. Of all the paradoxes of the latter kind, perpetrated in our time, two stand out in their baffling hypocrisy: the glorification and defense of Russia's ever growing inequalities of income and of her totalitarian imperialism, as steps toward higher forms of socialism and democracy." In his sardonic *Skeptic's Political Dictionary* (New York: Bookman Associates, 1953), Nomad defined totalitarianism as "the total enslavement of the human race, distinguished, as its total emancipation, either through the establishment of a 'total' state (Fascism) or through the total abolition ('withering away') of the State by means of the total subjection of all countries to the Universal Police Department which will take charge of a totally stateless Communist world" (p. 119). Nomad always insisted that Fascism could be understood only as totalitarianism. See the interesting debate on that point in the *New Leader,* July 16, 1949, passim, which continued into September.

57. André Liebich, "Marxism and Totalitarianism: Rudolf Hilferding and the

Mensheviks," Occasional Paper, no. 217 (Washington, D.C.: Kennan Institute for Advanced Russian Studies, 1987).

58. The only important woman who was a frequent contributor was the columnist Dorothy Thompson.

59. In 1943, for example, the *New Leader* published as a pamphlet an elaborate exposé of Joseph E. Davies's fellow-traveling film *Mission to Moscow*. For an amusing account of the episode, see O'Neill, *Better World*, pp. 76–78. Dwight Macdonald was the secretary, and the original protest was signed by him, James T. Farrell, Sidney Hook, Alfred Kazin, Norman Thomas, Edmund Wilson, and others.

60. For early 1945, see, for example, "No Cat's-Paw Totalitarianism," *New Leader*, January 27, 1945, p. 1; and Morton Goodman, "World Labor and Russian Power Politics: Should Free American Labor Cooperate with Soviet Totalitarian Unions?" *New Leader*, January 27, 1945, p. 4.

61. See *New Leader*, June 26, 1946, p. 14.

62. See the memorandum by Zivko Topalovich, the head of the Socialist Party of Yugoslavia, printed under the *New Leader*'s own headline: "Democracy or Dictatorship in Yugoslavia? Civil Strife will Continue Until Tito's Totalitarianism Goes," *New Leader*, September 8, 1945, p. 3.

63. Lin Yutang, "Communist 'Democracy' in China: The Completely Totalitarian Dictatorship in China Is in Yenan, Not Chungking," *New Leader*, September 8, 1945, pp. 8–9.

64. Vanni B. Montana, "The Crucifixion of Italian Democracy: Liberated from Fascism, Italy Moves Toward New Totalitarianism," *New Leader*, March 24, 1945, p. 9. A few weeks later, Silone was restored to favor when it appeared that he had been quietly working against Nenni's policies from within.

65. But by 1945, even previously rather neutral or even pro-Soviet journalists were starting to change. Kenneth Crawford, formerly the *New Republic*'s TRB columnist, criticized the false ideas of the progressives about the possibility of "free elections" in Europe. "Most Americans," he charged, "seem to understand the prime consequence of this war—the simple fact that we have beaten down one expanding totalitarian power and raised up another in the process—much better than do the heavy thinkers" ("The Double Talk of the Liberals," *Common Sense*, May 1945, p. 8, quoted in O'Neill, *Better World*, p. 87). Shortly afterward, Crawford began to write for the *New Leader*.

66. See Jonathan Stout, "Totalitarians and Union Rights," *New Leader*, June 26, 1948, p. 3. Rarely was there much expressed interest in what might become of the United States if its antitotalitarian zeal got out of hand. See Robert J. Alexander, "How Not to Fight Totalitarianism," *New Leader*, August 14, 1948, p. 6.

67. See, for example, "Was Mihailovich a Collaborator?" *New Leader*, July 12, 1947, p. 10; T. C. Kirkpatrick, "Open Letter to Seven Fellow-Travellers," *New Leader*, September 13, 1947, pp. 4, 15; and Fulton Oursler, "The Witch-Hunt Smokescreen," *New Leader*, October 25, 1947, p. 4.

68. Eugene Lyons, "Two Worlds," *New Leader*, March 17, 1945, p. 4. Lyons had been editor of the *American Mercury* since January 1939 and had made the journal reflect his passionate anti-Communism. He had been devoted to terms like "Red

Fascism" and "Brown Bolshevism" and was one of the most influential anti-Communist journalists of the immediate prewar and postwar periods.

69. Reinhold Niebuhr noted the similarity in usage, finding *The Road to Serfdom* no "more profound or prudent than Herbert Hoover's book on Liberty written a decade ago" (C. Hartley Grattan, "Hayek's Hayride," *Harper's Magazine*, July 1945, p. 49).

70. Friedrich Hayek, *The Road to Serfdom* (London: Routledge & Kegan Paul, 1944; Chicago: University of Chicago Press, 1944). For a helpful, if uncritical, analysis of Hayek's thought, see Calvin M. Hoy, *A Philosophy of Individual Freedom: The Political Thought of F. A. Hayek* (Westport, Conn.: Greenwood Press, 1984).

71. Hayek's work was similarly controversial in postwar West Germany. For references, see Seidel and Jenkner, *Wege der Totalitarismus-Forschung*, pp. 7–8.

72. Hayek, *Road to Serfdom*, pp. 56–57.

73. Ibid., p. 3

74. Ibid., pp. 72ff.

75. Ibid., p. 19.

76. Alvin Hansen, "The New Crusade Against Planning," *New Republic*, January 1, 1945, pp. 9–12.

77. Henry Hazlitt, "An Economist's View of 'Planning,' " *New York Times*, September 24, 1944, sec. 7, p. 1. Hazlitt went fairly far off the deep end, suggesting that *The Road to Serfdom* was a contemporary counterpart of John Stuart Mill's *On Liberty*.

78. Hansen, "New Crusade Against Planning," p. 9.

79. See the references to some of these interviews in Herman Finer, *The Road to Reaction* (Boston: Little, Brown, 1946), pp. x–xi. The *New Leader* split over Hayek's book. Max Eastman, becoming more and more conservative, was quoted in the book and was strongly favorable toward it. Abba Lerner reviewed it critically in the *New Leader*, January 20, 1945, p. 7. He accepted Hayek's distinction between good and bad planning and defended "good planning" but regretted that the book would be exploited by the Right. Sidney Hook launched a major attack on Hayek's attitude toward planning a few weeks later ("Freedom and Socialism," *New Leader*, March 3, 1945, pp. 4–6).

80. Grattan, "Hayek's Hayride," p. 46.

81. Harold J. Laski, "Tomorrow's World: Is It Going Left?" *New York Times*, June 17, 1945, sec. 7, p. 8.

82 Friedrich A. Hayek, "Tomorrow's World: Is it Going Left?" *New York Times*, June 24, 1945, sec. 7, p. 12.

83. Karl Popper, *The Open Society and Its Enemies* (Princeton, N.J.: Princeton University Press, 1950).

84. Ibid., p. 3. Popper did not demonstrate a real "tradition" other than the persistence of what he defined as historicism in Western culture.

85. Quoted in Karl E. Meyer, " 'Socialized Medicine' Revisited: How Doctors Doomed Truman's Health Plan," *New York Times*, August 2, 1993, p. A-14.

86. Arthur A. Ballantine, "Economic Planning: Some Implications in Wallace Statement Are Discussed," in "Letters to the Times," *New York Times*, February 25,

1945, sec. 4, p. 8. See also the ensuing discussion, particularly the letter by Manya Gordon on March 2, in which she writes that "in much that is now being written on this subject one finds the tendency to fall back on Professor Hayek instead of arguing the merits of the case" (p. 18).

87. Finer, *Road to Reaction,* p. ix.

88. Ibid., p. 16.

89. Andrzej Walicki, "The Captive Mind Revisited: Intellectuals and Communist Totalitarianism in Poland," in *Totalitarianism at the Crossroads,* ed. Ellen Frankel Paul (New Brunswick, N.J.: Transaction Books, 1990), p. 84.

90. Quoted in Lifka, *Concept "Totalitarianism,"* vol. 1, p. 321.

91. For a number of examples of this usage, see ibid., pp. 367–387.

92. On the deterioration in relations over the final months of 1945 and 1946 as seen from the American side, see John Lewis Gaddis, "Getting Tough with Russia," in *The United States and the Origin of the Cold War, 1941–1947* (New York: Columbia University Press, 1972), pp. 282–315.

93. Alan D. Harper, *The Politics of Loyalty: The White House and the Communist Issue, 1946–1952* (Westport, Conn.: Greenwood Press, 1969), p. 23. The Gouzenko case was later (1947 and early 1948) made into a heavy-handed propaganda film entitled *The Iron Curtain.* Bosley Crowther, reviewing it in the *New York Times,* observed that "the Russian villains are the Nazi villains of ten years back" (quoted in Les K. Adler, "The Politics of Culture: Hollywood and the Cold War," in *Specter,* ed. Griffith and Theoharis, esp. pp. 252–254). Reviewing a later anti-Communist film, *My Son John,* Pauline Kael wrote, along the same lines: "[T]he bit players who once had steady employment as S.S. guards are right at home in their new Soviet milieu; the familiar psychopathic faces provide a kind of reassurance that the new world situation is not so different from the old one" (quoted in ibid., p. 258).

94. Full text in *Foreign Relations of the United States* [henceforth cited as *FRUS*], vol. 6, 1946: *Eastern Europe; the Soviet Union* (Washington, D.C.: Government Printing Office, 1969), pp. 696–709. Almost a year later, *New Leader* writers were still asking why the United States government did not make better use of people like Kennan and Loy Henderson who actually knew something about the Soviet Union and spoke the language. See Jonathan Stout, "U.S. Attitude Towards Russia Changing," *New Leader,* February 8, 1947, p. 2. Naturally, the *New Republic* felt otherwise. See William Walton, "Men Around Marshall," *New Republic,* September 22, 1947, pp. 15–19, especially the description of Kennan and Bohlen as "Russophobes" (p. 17).

95. See the letters in the *New Leader,* February 2, 1946, and March 2, 1946.

96. Churchill had used the term on public occasions in 1945, but not, as far as I can determine, in such a way as to suggest that he was referring to the Soviet Union. See, for example, his use of the term in his broadcast speech of May 13, 1945, in *Winston S. Churchill: His Complete Speeches, 1897–1963,* ed. Robert Rhodes James (New York: Chelsea House, 1974), vol. 7, p. 7162.

97. Winston Churchill, "Iron Curtain" speech, in ibid., pp. 7287–7288. There is a good analysis of the speech and its reception in Fraser Harbutt, *The Iron Curtain: Churchill, America, and the Origin of the Cold War* (New York: Oxford University Press, 1986), pp. 183–208.

98. Churchill, "Iron Curtain" speech, p. 7290.

99. On the American response, see Harbutt, *Iron Curtain,* pp. 197–208. Moderate to conservative newspapers like the *San Francisco Chronicle,* the *Los Angeles Times,* and the *Phoenix Republican* emphasized "the menace of Soviet totalitarianism" in their response, but other newspapers of the center were more reserved in their support. Opposition was dominant on the liberal end of the spectrum, with intellectual weeklies like the *Nation* and the *New Republic* particularly hostile. In the summer number of *Partisan Review,* the editors (Philip Rahv and William Phillips) launched a bitter attack on the *New Republic, PM,* and the *Nation* for criticizing the policy of "getting tough" on the Russians. These "liberals," they proclaimed, will "continue to think that Stalin's totalitarianism is somehow different from Franco's, different from Hitler's. Alas yes; the considerable difference is that the former is able to enlist 'liberal' support" ("The 'Liberal' Fifth Column," *Partisan Review,* summer 1946, p. 285).

100. "The problems of the United States can be captiously summed up in two words," announced Charles Wilson of General Motors: "Russia abroad and labor at home" (quoted in Roger Morris, *Richard Milhous Nixon: The Rise of an American Politician* [New York: Holt, 1990], p. 265).

101. "Braden Declares Fascism Lives On," *New York Times,* May 27, 1946, p. 10.

102. As early as May 22, 1945, Truman was referring to the Soviet Union as "a totalitarian state" in his diary, although it is not crystal clear exactly what he meant. "I've no faith in any totalitarian state," he wrote. "They all start with the wrong premise—that lies are justified and that the old disproven formula that the end justifies the means is right and necessary to maintain the power of government" (quoted in William Hillman, *Mr. President* [New York: Farrar, Strauss and Young, 1952], p. 116). In Truman's executive order establishing his Temporary Commission on Employee Loyalty in November 1946, the dangerous points of view against which the order was directed were enumerated as "totalitarian, Fascist, Communist or subversive."

103. "Tyrants Remain, Truman Asserts: He Warns Liberals Vestiges of Totalitarianism Must Be Put Down," *New York Times,* June 6, 1946, p. 19.

104. Ibid. Fischer, having resigned from the accommodationist *Nation,* had been writing for the aggressively anti-Soviet *New Leader* since September 1945. On Fischer's break with Communism, see Louis Fischer, in *The God That Failed,* ed. Richard Crossman (New York: Harper, 1949), pp. 196–228. The vice president of the ILGWU took much the same line. See Samuel Shore, "Totalitarianism or Democratic World? Democracy Endangered at Home and Abroad," *New Leader,* June 8, 1946, p. 14.

105. *FRUS,* vol. 6, 1946, pp. 770–771.

CHAPTER FOUR

1. Sidney Hook, "The Future of Socialism," *Partisan Review,* January–February 1947, pp. 23–36, and succeeding issues. Rahv's and Phillips's pessimistic "Editors Note" is on p. 23. One can see how severely American working people have disappointed the brilliant crowd at the *Partisan Review.* Over the next few years, Sidney Hook became one of the most passionate and single-minded opponents of

totalitarianism. Much of his journalism stretching from around 1947 into the late 1950s has been collected in his *Political Power and Personal Freedom: Critical Studies in Democracy, Communism and Civil Rights* (New York: Criterion Books, 1959). See especially "The Individual in a Totalitarian Society," pp. 145–155.

2. Mary Sperling McAuliffe, *Crisis on the Left: Cold War Politics and American Liberals, 1947–1954* (Amherst: University of Massachusetts Press, 1978), pp. 6–7. On the founding of the ADA, see Steven Gillon, *Politics and Vision* (New York: Oxford University Press, 1987).

3. Quoted in Norman Markowitz, "From the Popular Front to Cold War Liberalism," in *The Specter: Original Essays on the Cold War and the Origins of McCarthyism*, ed. Robert Griffith and Athan Theoharis (New York: New Viewpoints, 1974), p. 112. Despite his initial salvo, Bowles worried about the ADA's seeming excessively anti-Communist and so delayed becoming a member for a year. See Gillon, *Politics and Vision*, p. 23.

4. Quoted in Thomas E. Lifka, *The Concept "Totalitarianism" and American Foreign Policy, 1933–1949* (New York: Garland, 1988), vol. 2, p. 495.

5. The "totalitarian liberal" usage at the *New Leader* dated back well into the mid-1940s. See, for example, the June 9, 1945, issue, in which the editors ran an unsigned report about how Louis Fischer had resigned from the board of contributing editors of the *Nation*, which was described on p. 7 as a "totalitarian liberal" weekly. In the same issue, Kenneth Crawford attacked Max Lerner and *PM* on p. 8 under the lead "The Totalitarian Liberals."

6. "70 Americans Send a Cable to Bevin," *New Leader*, January 25, 1947, pp. 1, 19. See also the news story in *PM* on Thursday, January 23, p. 3, and the editorial on p. 2 ("Opinion") by Max Lerner.

7. Some scholars take the view that the American response to the crises in Greece and Turkey provided a "positive model of international behavior when confronted by a totalitarian adversary to contrast with American policy toward Eastern Europe." See Bruce Kuniholm, *The Origins of the Cold War in the Near East: Great Power Conflict and Diplomacy in Iran, Turkey, and Greece* (Princeton, N.J.: Princeton University Press, 1980), p. xx.

8. "Truman Doctrine," *New York Times*, March 16, 1947, sec. 4, p. 1. Truman's speech is quoted in its entirety in Joseph Marion Jones, *The Fifteen Weeks*, 2nd ed. (New York: Harcourt, Brace & World, 1964), pp. 269–274; and in the *Public Papers of the Presidents . . . Harry S Truman, 1947* (Washington, D.C.: Government Printing Office, 1963), pp. 176–180.

9. This point is stressed by Randall B. Woods and Howard Jones in their *Dawning of the Cold War: The United States' Quest for Order* (Athens: University of Georgia Press, 1991), p. 145.

10. Quoted in Jones, *Fifteen Weeks*, p. 156. Truman wrote these words himself and inserted them into the text. Jones, who wrote much of the president's text, describes its drafting on pp. 148–170. His famous account makes clear how important the vocabulary of totalitarianism was deemed to be by the president's staff and how conscious they were of the necessity of mobilizing public support.

11. *Department of State Bulletin*, April 22, 1945, p. 751, quoted in Lifka, *Concept "Totalitarianism,"* vol. 1, p. 352.

12. Arthur Vandenberg, *Private Papers,* p. 339, quoted in Lifka, *Concept "Totalitarianism,"* vol. 2, p. 505.

13. Kennan used the term neither in his "Long Telegram" nor in the elaboration of it, his famous Mr. "X" article, "The Sources of Soviet Conduct," *Foreign Affairs,* July 1947, pp. 566–582. He did use the term once in a while to suggest the full extent of the Soviet Communist Party's internal power over its subjects or (in a different frame of mind) to characterize human frailty in modern times. See, for example, his dispatch from Moscow to the secretary of state, February 8, 1946, in *FRUS, 1946,* vol. 6: *Eastern Europe; the Soviet Union* (Washington, D.C.: Government Printing Office, 1969), pp. 673, 694; and "America and the Russian Future," *Foreign Affairs,* April 1951, p. 365. Around the time of the Greek crisis, Kennan used the term several times in lectures at the National War College. See Lifka, *Concept "Totalitarianism,"* vol. 2, pp. 518–519. On the only occasion that Kennan took up the term directly, he confessed his bewilderment at the problem of definition, alleging his "lack of theoretical erudition." He concluded that "when I try to picture totalitarianism to myself as a general phenomenon, what comes into my mind most prominently is neither the Nazi picture nor the Soviet picture as I have known them in the flesh, but rather the fictional and symbolic images created by such people as Orwell or Kafka or Koestler or the early Soviet satirists . . . its deepest reality lies strangely enough in its manifestation as a dream." His "Totalitarianism in the Modern World" was fundamentally an interesting exercise in comparative history. See Carl J. Friedrich, ed., *Totalitarianism* (New York: Grosset & Dunlap, 1954), pp. 17–31, esp. pp. 17, 19. Kennan's friend and colleague Elbridge Durbrow also used the term on occasion, and so did Charles Bohlen. On March 13, 1946, Bohlen wrote in support of Kennan's "Long Telegram," asserting that the United States was confronted with "an expanding totalitarian state," although he held out the hope of eventual peaceful coexistence. See Fraser Harbutt, *The Iron Curtain: Churchill, America, and the Origins of the Cold War* (New York: Oxford University Press, 1986), p. 225.

14. John Lewis Gaddis, "The Insecurities of Victory: The United States and the Perception of the Soviet Threat After World War II," in *The Truman Presidency,* ed. Michael J. Lacey (Cambridge: Woodrow Wilson Center and Cambridge University Press, 1989), p. 257.

15. Felix Belair, Jr., "Truman Assumes Lead in Fight on Communism," *New York Times,* March 16, 1947, sec. 1, p. 3.

16. Ibid.

17. For an interesting characterization of Braden, see Lifka, *Concept "Totalitarianism,"* vol. 1, pp. 432–433. Perón sometimes used the rhetoric of totalitarianism, even though his control was never anything like "total," nor was his ability to insulate his regime from the outside world. For Perón's totalitarian rhetoric, see Arthur Whitaker, *Argentina* (Englewood Cliffs, N.J.: Prentice-Hall, 1964), p. 116. I also benefited from an unpublished seminar paper by Zachary Morgan of Brown University describing Braden's "antitotalitarian" activities as ambassador to Argentina.

18. "Braden Denounces Fascism in Any Hue: Black or Red: It Blocks March of Civilization and Should Be Exterminated, He Says," *New York Times,* March 20, 1947, p. 5.

19. Braden was not the only American ambassador who continued to be preoccupied with "black Fascism." According to Lifka, Norman Armour in Madrid persistently pressured influential Spanish circles in Madrid to erase the "totalitarian characteristics" of the regime as quickly as possible, which meant ending the influence of the Falange (*Concept "Totalitarianism,"* vol. 1, p. 431). The historian Carlton Hayes had spoken to Franco in almost exactly the same terms when he was ambassador in Madrid earlier in the decade.

20. "Russia Accused on Propaganda: Benton Says 'Psychological Warfare' Is Being Waged Against the United States," *New York Times,* March 20, 1947, p. 5.

21. "The President's Special Conference with the Association of Radio News Analysts. May 13, 1947," *Public Papers of the Presidents . . . Harry S Truman, 1947,* p. 238. The reference to Nazism and Fascism was considered. As Margaret Truman put it, "By placing the emphasis on the fight between totalitarianism and freedom, Dad was attempting to rally the same emotional commitment that had fired America in the war against Hitler" (*Truman* [New York: Morrow, 1973], p. 344, quoted in Lifka, *Concept: "Totalitarianism,"* vol. 2, p. 516).

22. McAuliffe, *Crisis on the Left,* p. 27.

23. Executive Order 9835, in Alan Harper, *The Politics of Loyalty: The White House and the Communist Issue, 1946–1952* (Westport, Conn.: Greenwood Press, 1969), p. 260.

24. Quoted in McAuliffe, *Crisis on the Left,* p. 27.

25. It is interesting that the *New Leader* had already drawn the conclusion early in 1946 that European poverty and misery would promote "Soviet totalitarianism." See, for example, Irving Brown, "Food and the Russians in Austria: Program to Rescue Austrians from Starvation and Totalitarianism," *New Leader,* November 9, 1946, p. 7. Brown was an official of the American Federation of Labor, working in Europe.

26. Jones, *Fifteen Weeks,* p. 279. Acheson's remarks are reprinted in their entirety on pp. 274–281. Acheson's rhetoric distinctly changed in this period. He had earlier been regarded by the ferocious anti-Communists of the *New Leader* as soft on the Soviet Union.

27. For this and other poll data, see Nancy Bernkopf Tucker, *Patterns in the Dust: Chinese–American Relations and the Recognition Controversy, 1949–1950* (New York: Columbia University Press, 1983), pp. 159–161, esp. n. 25, 26. The State Department made extensive use of public-opinion polls in planning its campaign of support for the president's new policy.

28. The feud between the *New Leader* and *PM* continued throughout 1946 and 1947. See, for example, Ferdinand Lundberg, "How PM Gives 'Totalitarianism' a Liberal Camouflage," *New Leader,* July 20, 1946, p. 5.

29. The administration phrased it somewhat differently: The choice in Greece was "between totalitarianism and an imperfect democracy" (quoted in Susan Hartman, *Truman and the Eightieth Congress* [Columbia: University of Missouri Press, 1971], p. 62).

30. Alonzo Hamby, *Beyond the New Deal: Harry Truman and American Liberalism* (New York: Columbia University Press, 1973), p. 178. For a general discussion of the response to the speech among American liberals, see pp. 169–186.

31. "ADA—Matrix of 'Third Force,' " *New Leader,* February 22, 1948, p. 1.

32. Arthur M. Schlesinger, Jr., *The Vital Center: The Politics of Freedom* (Boston: Houghton Mifflin, 1949), pp. 53–54, 57. Another book important to the ideological wars that appeared in 1949 was that by Richard Crossman, ed., *The God That Failed* (New York: Harper, 1949). Crossman collected powerful anti-Communist testimony from such former Party members as Louis Fischer, Arthur Koestler, Richard Wright, and Ignazio Silone, but the concept of totalitarianism did not figure much in the discussion.

33. Gus Tyler, "The New Radicalism," *New Leader,* October 29, 1949, p. 12.

34. "America's Free Speech Defense Causes Uproar in Berlin Meeting. Melvin J. Lasky, Journalist, in Convention Sponsored by Russians, Angers the Reds with Attack on Totalitarianism," *New York Times,* October 8, 1947, p. 16. Lasky's own triumphant account, "Inside the Soviet Cultural Front," is in the *New Leader,* October 25, 1947, pp. 8–9, 15. A recent account of the episode alleges that after Soviet complaints, the United States commander, General Lucius Clay, considered expelling Lasky from Berlin. See Peter Coleman, *The Liberal Conspiracy* (New York: Free Press, 1989), p. 19. No evidence for this assertion is given.

35. The long struggle between Communists and anti-Communists within the unions of the CIO produced a certain amount of rhetoric about totalitarianism, but not of any new, deep, or illuminating sort. For example, at its 1949 convention, the National Maritime Union condemned "communism for what it is, a vicious form of totalitarianism carrying with it religious and political persecution of the worst kind." Resolutions are quoted in Max Kampleman, *The Communist Party vs. the CIO: A Study in Power Politics* (New York: Praeger, 1957), p. 89. It may be that American working people preferred the straightforwardness of "Communism" to "totalitarianism," with its implied comparisons and typology. See also David Oshinsky, "The CIO and the Communists," in *Specter,* ed. Griffith and Theoharis, pp. 116–151.

36. At a closed-door meeting with the Senate Foreign Relations Committee, Secretary of State Marshall was quoted as saying, "By intimidation, fraud and terror, communist regimes have been imposed upon Hungary and Czechoslovakia. Totalitarian control has been tightened in other countries of Eastern Europe" (*Time,* March 22, 1948, p. 19).

37. *New Leader,* March 20, 1948, pp. 7, 16.

38. See Albion Ross, "Benes Is Opposing Totalitarian Rule in Czech Deadlock," *New York Times,* February 22, 1948, p. 1, "Czechs to Impose Totalitarian Rule by Edicts on Radio," *New York Times,* March 1, 1948, p. 1, and "Czech State Is Rapidly Pressed into Totalitarian Mold," *New York Times,* March 7, 1948, sec. E, p. 5. See also the May 31 editorial.

39. *New York Times,* February 24, 1948, p. 24.

40. Raymond Daniell, "Pattern for a Totalitarian State," *New York Times Magazine,* April 11, 1948, pp. 7ff.

41. The question of whether the Soviet Union was really prepared, under the right circumstances, to move into Western Europe in the late 1940s remains a subject of conjecture and rather ideological debate. The 1993 discovery of the enormously detailed preparations (including massed armaments) made by the So-

viet Union and East Germany for an invasion of the West beginning a decade or so later would seem to support those who feared a Soviet invasion. See Marc Fisher, "Soviet Bloc Had Detailed Plan to Invade W. Germany," *Washington Post*, March 16, 1993, pp. A11–A12.

42. *New York Times*, May 27, 1948, p. 8.

43. Lifka, *Concept "Totalitarianism,"* vol. 2, p. 715.

44. "Mr. Truman's Appeal," *New York Times*, July 20, 1949, p. 24. In a separate article published the same day, Truman was reported to have declared in another speech that "the totalitarian system—by which he no doubt meant the Kremlin—would either destroy itself or abandon its attempt to dominate the world by forcing other nations into its pattern" ("Truman Says Soviet Regime Will Either Destroy Itself or Abandon Its Aggression," p. 1).

45. "Truman Deplores Totalitarianism," *New York Times*, June 25, 1950, p. 2. Across the political spectrum, Americans "viewed the North Korean agression in terms of Hitler's early, unopposed aggressions." See Alexander George, "American Policy-Making and the North Korean Aggression," *World Politics*, January 1955, p. 213. Among them: Arthur Krock (*New York Times*, June 28, 1950); Alfred Friendly, Sr. (*Washington Post*, June 28, 1950); John Foster Dulles (speech of July 1, quoted in *New York Times*, July 2, 1950).

46. George Orwell, "The Prevention of Literature," in *The Collected Essays, Journalism and Letters of George Orwell* (New York: Harcourt, Brace & World, 1968), vol. 4, pp. 59–72. See also his "The Future of Socialism," *Partisan Review*, July–August 1947, pp. 346–351.

47. George Orwell, "*We* by E. I. Zamyatin," in *Collected Essays, Journalism and Letters*, vol. 4, p. 75.

48. George Orwell, "Politics and the English Language," in ibid., p. 136.

49. March Schorer, "An Indignant and Prophetic Novel," *New York Times Book Review*, June 12, 1949, p. 1.

50. William Soskin, "What Can Be," *Saturday Review of Literature*, June 11, 1949, p. 12.

51. James Hilton, "Mr. Orwell's Nightmare of Totalitarianism," *New York Herald Tribune Book Review*, June 12, 1949, p. 3.

52. George Orwell to Francis A. Henson, in *Collected Essays, Journalism and Letters*, vol. 4, p. 502.

53. Isaac Deutscher, "The Mysticism of Cruelty," in his *Heretics and Renegades* (London: Cape, 1955), p. 35.

54. William Lee Miller, "*1984* and All That," *The Reporter*, May 10, 1962, pp. 46–51.

55. On occasion, individuals and organizations might even implicitly contrast the Fascist "reaction" with Communist "totalitarianism." See the ADA's 1947 condemnation of the Wallace third-party bid in December 1947, quoted in Markowitz, "From Popular Front to Cold War Liberalism," p. 113.

56. Stephen J. Whitfield, *The Culture of the Cold War* (Baltimore: Johns Hopkins University Press, 1991), p. 18.

57. "A Communist breaks," Chambers wrote, "because he must choose at last

between irreconcilable opposites—God or man, Soul or Mind, Freedom or Communism" (*Witness* [New York: Random House, 1952], p. 16, quoted in Sidney Blumenthal, *The Rise of the Counter-Establishment* [New York: Times Books, 1986], p. 19).

58. John Strachey, "The Absolutists," *The Nation,* October 4, 1952, pp. 291–293.

59. Elmer Davis, "History in Doublethink," *Saturday Review of Literature,* June 28, 1952, pp. 8–9, 30–32. See also Hannah Arendt, "The Ex-Communists," *Commonweal,* March 20, 1953, pp. 595–599.

60. Marya Mannes, " 'Did or Not . . . ,' " *The Reporter,* June 8, 1954, pp. 40–42, quotation from p. 41. Dwight Macdonald took a similar view, arguing at a meeting of the Congress for Cultural Freedom that McCarthy was a totalitarian liar "in [the] sense [that] his lies are so big and wholly without foundation." See the account in William L. O'Neill, *A Better World: The Great Schism: Stalinism and the American Intellectuals* (New York: Simon and Schuster, 1982), p. 300.

61. A careful, indeed laborious, essay arguing that McCarthy was not a totalitarian, despite the presence of certain "tendencies," may be found in James Rorty and Moshe Decter, *McCarthy and the Communists* (Boston: Beacon Press, 1954), pp. 109–124.

62. Ben Ray Redman, "The Silence of Conscience," *Saturday Review of Literature,* July 17, 1954, p. 10.

63. See House Report 2980 on the Internal Security Act of 1950, *U.S. Code Congressional Service 81st Congress,* 2nd series, 1950 (St. Paul: West and Edward Thompson, 1950), vol. 2, pp. 3886, 3892.

64. See the text in *U.S. Code Congressional Service 81st Congress,* 2nd series, 1950, vol. 1, pp. 984–1024, esp. pp. 984, 987–988, 1002, 1008, 1015.

65. "U.S. Put Visa Ban on Totalitarians of All Descriptions—State Department Sends Order to Officials Abroad to Carry out Internal Security Law—Is Faced with Problems—Trouble Is Seen in Applying Act so as not to Alienate Argentina, Spain, Yugoslavia," *New York Times,* October 1, 1950, p. 1.

66. The question was not, of course, new. At the very end of 1943, the American ambassador cabled Washington about the Perón government, asking, "Is not the real basis for the indictment of the Argentine government that they are a totalitarian government attempting to extend their system of government to other American republics and that they have actually succeeded in the case of Bolivia? . . . All indications point to an increasing totalitarian dictatorship in Argentina, the ideals of which are contrary to those principles for which the United Nations are fighting" (quoted in Lifka, *Concept "Totalitarianism,"* vol. 1, pp. 236, 309). As we have seen, similar usages continued through 1944 and into 1945. On the other hand, almost no recent scholarship takes seriously the "totalitarianism" of the Perón regime. See, for example, David Rock, *Argentina, 1516–1982* (Berkeley: University of California Press, 1985), pp. 285, 317; and Frederick Turner and José Enrique Miguens, *Juan Perón and the Shaping of Argentina* (Pittsburgh: University of Pittsburgh Press, 1983), pp. 153–154.

67. As late as 1949, John Foster Dulles continued to think of Spain as an example of "Fascist totalitarianism" and urged extreme caution. But military men concerned with bases and Catholic congressmen of an extremely anti-Communist kind forced

an improvement in relations with Spain on the administration. See Lifka, *Concept "Totalitarianism,"* vol. 2, pp. 725–726.

68. Richard P. Stebbins, *The United States in World Affairs* (New York: Harper & Row, 1950), pp. 250, 286.

CHAPTER FIVE

1. Pierre Grémion, "Berlin 1950: Aux origines du congrès pour la Liberté de la Culture," *Commentaire,* Summer 1986, pp. 270–271.

2. William Phillips, *A Partisan View* (Briarcliff Manor, N.Y.: Stein and Day, 1983), pp. 147–168. It is referred to as "The Americans for Intellectual Freedom" in Peter Coleman, *The Liberal Conspiracy: The Congress for Cultural Freedom and the Struggle for the Mind of Postwar Europe* (New York: Free Press, 1989), pp. 5–7.

3. Coleman, *Liberal Conspiracy,* p. 16. Much other information is provided on pp. xi–xii, 10, 46–50, 219–234. See also Christopher Lasch, *The Agony of the American Left* (New York: Random House, 1969), pp. 98–110. The *New York Times* exposed the CIA funding in 1967.

4. James Burnham had come a long way from his radical origins toward his final resting place on the far political Right. In *The Struggle for the World* (New York: John Day, 1947), Burnham told his readers that World War III had already begun against "totalitarian movements, with their steel discipline, their monolithic structure, their cement of terror, their rigid and total ideology, their perversion of every aspect of the lives of their members" (p. 12).

5. For most of the papers and a summary of the discussions, see "Der Kongress für kulturelle Freiheit in Berlin," *Der Monat,* July–August 1950, pp. 339–483. The congress's antitotalitarian manifesto is printed on the last two pages. A brief account of the conference by Sidney Hook appeared a few months later in *Partisan Review,* September–October 1950, pp. 415–422. See also Grémion, "Berlin 1950," pp. 269–280. In sharp contrast with Lasch's account, Grémion's is frankly celebratory; accounts of disagreements are largely missing.

6. For a rhetorical and acid portrait of critics of totalitarianism with totalitarian sensibilities, see Lasch, *Agony,* pp. 63–78.

7. Hook, in *Partisan Review,* p. 415. Later, when the Chinese intervened in the war, such left-wing intellectuals as Albert Camus and even Simone de Beauvoir feared a Soviet invasion of Western Europe. See Herbert R. Lottman, *Albert Camus* (Garden City, N.Y.: Doubleday, 1979), pp. 488–489.

8. John Lewis Gaddis, "The Strategic Perspective: The Rise and Fall of the 'Defensive Perimeter' Concept, 1947–1951," in *Uncertain Years: Chinese–American Relations, 1947–1950,* ed. Dorothy Borg and Waldo Heinrichs (New York: Columbia University Press, 1980), p. 71. The study, SM-8388, was published on June 9, 1947, and subsequently appeared in *FRUS,* 1947 (Washington, D.C.: Government Printing Office, 1972), vol. 7, p. 840.

9. *New York Times,* June 20, 1947, p. 17, quoted in William Whitney Stueck, *The Wedemeyer Mission: American Politics and Foreign Policy During the Cold War* (Athens: University of Georgia Press, 1984), p. 38.

10. Ambassador Stuart to Secretary Marshall, *United States Relations with China, with Special Reference to the Period 1944–1949* (Washington, D.C.: Department of State Publication 3573, 1949), pp. 895, 897. This was the famous "China White Paper." See also *FRUS,* 1949, vol. 8: *The Far East: China* (Washington, D.C.: Government Printing Office, 1978), pp. 108, 175, 256, 406.

11. Senate Committee on Foreign Relations, *Hearings on the Nomination of Philip C. Jessup to Be U.S. Representative to the Sixth General Assembly of the United Nations,* 82nd Cong., 1st sess., 1951, p. 603, quoted in Russell D. Buhite, " 'Major Interests': American Policy Toward China, Taiwan, and Korea, 1945–1950," *Pacific Historical Review,* August 1978, p. 432.

12. See n. 10 for the China White Paper. See also Acheson's remarks about the Chinese Communist attempts "to establish a totalitarian domination over the Chinese people in the interests of a foreign power," in *State Department Bulletin,* August 15, 1949, pp. 236–237, quoted in Lewis McCarroll Purifoy, *Harry Truman's China Policy: McCarthyism and the Diplomacy of Hysteria, 1947–1951* (New York: New Viewpoints, 1976), pp. 135–136. Another example may be found in Acheson's memorandum to Secretary of Defense Louis Johnson, July 26, 1949, in *FRUS,* 1949, vol. 9: *The Far East: China* (Washington, D.C.: Government Printing Office, 1974), p. 1386.

13. On the debates and political controversies, see Nancy Bernkopf Tucker, *Patterns in the Dust: Chinese–American Relations and the Recognition Controversy, 1949–1950* (New York: Columbia University Press, 1983).

14. Ibid., pp. 30–31, 149–150.

15. Waldo Heinrichs, "American China Policy and the Cold War in Asia: A New Look," in *Uncertain Years,* ed. Borg and Heinrichs, p. 289.

16. For a general view, see David Caute, "The State Department and the China Experts," in his *The Great Fear: The Anti-Communist Purge Under Truman and Eisenhower* (New York: Simon and Schuster, 1978), pp. 303–324; and, more recently, William L. O'Neill, "China: Progressive Paradox," in his *A Better World: The Great Schism: Stalinism and the American Intellectuals* (New York: Simon and Schuster, 1982), pp. 252–283. A popular novel of 1951, Helen MacInnes's *Neither Five nor Three* (Greenwich, Conn.: Fawcett Crest), portrayed the United States as being endangered by Communist agents and therefore in need of policies such as McCarthy's. MacInnes also believed in a totalitarian point of view, strongly linking Communists to Nazis in a continuing, if not seamless campaign against the democracies, led by the United States.

17. Leonard A. Kusnitz, *Public Opinion and Foreign Policy: America's China Policy, 1949–1979* (Westport, Conn.: Greenwood Press, 1984), pp. 24–25.

18. Eugene Kinkead, *In Every War but One* (New York: Norton, 1959), p. 18. An earlier version appeared under the rubric of "A Reporter at Large," *New Yorker,* October 26, 1957.

19. Edward Hunter, *Brainwashing* (New York: Farrar, Straus & Cudahy, 1956), p. 10.

20. The English term might be originally derived from Orwell's *Nineteen Eighty-Four.* Toward the end of O'Brien's interrogation of Winston Smith, he states: "We

make the brain perfect before we blow it up. No one whom we bring to this place ever stands out against us. Everyone is washed clean. There is nothing left in them except sorrow for what they have done and love of the party. The beg to be shot quickly so that they can die while their minds are still clean" (quoted in the Group for the Advancement of Psychiatry, "Symposium no. 4, Methods of Forceful Indoctrination," *Reports and Symposiums* [New York: Publications Office, 1968], vol. 3, p. 233).

21. Edward Hunter, *Brainwashing in Red China* (New York: Vanguard Press, 1951). Hunter interviewed refugees from Communist China in Hong Kong and Southeast Asia in 1950 and early 1951.

22. Eleutherius Winance, *The Communist Persuasion* (New York: Kennedy and Sons, 1958), p. 18. The term is apparently best rendered in English as *hsueh-hsi*. Robert J. Lifton prefers a more general term, *szu hsiang kai tsao,* which he translates as "ideological remolding" ("Chinese Communist 'Thought Reform': Coercion and Reeducation of Western Civilians," *Bulletin of the New York Academy of Medicine,* September 1957, p. 626).

23. J. A. C. Brown, *Techniques of Persuasion from Propaganda to Brainwashing* (London: Penguin Books, 1963), p. 267.

24. As early as 1956, a Catholic bishop in Kansas was accusing the faculty in secular colleges of "brainwashing" their students; he used this alleged practice as a justification for forbidding Catholic students to attend these institutions. See Seth S. King, "Certain Classes Banned by Bishop; Kansas Prelate Hits Courses in Psychology, Philosophy at Non-Catholic Colleges," *New York Times,* September 3, 1956, p. 11.

25. Quoted in Brown, *Techniques of Persuasion,* p. 269.

26. The North Koreans, it appears, seldom used techniques more sophisticated than executions, beatings, exposure, and forced marches. Of course, there was a good deal of more or less random brutality toward North Korean prisoners in the south as well.

27. Kinkead, *In Every War but One,* pp. 22–23.

28. "2 Challenge Views on Brainwashing; Physicians Deny That Victim Is Permanently Changed—Call Technique Old; Effect Is Said To Vanish; Study of P.O.W.s Finds Some Reverse Stands and Now Hate Communism," *New York Times,* September 22, 1956, p. 19. Very careful and sophisticated studies of such "reversals" can be found in Robert J. Lifton, *Thought Reform and the Psychology of Totalism: A Study of Brainwashing in China* (London: Victor Gollanez, 1961). "Virtually all [released] prisoners," he writes, "showed a general tendency to revert to what they had been before prison, or at least to a modified version of their previous identity" (p. 150).

29. David G. Bromley and James T. Richardson, eds., *The Brainwashing/ Deprogramming Controversy: Sociological, Psychological, Legal and Historical Perspectives,* vol. 5 of *Studies in Religion and Society* (New York: Edwin Mellen Press, 1983), pp. 5–6.

30. Lifton, *Thought Reform.* The term *totalism* seems to have been suggested originally by Erik Erikson, who defined it as "total immersion in a synthetic identity (extreme nationalism, racism or class consciousness)" ("Wholeness and Totality—A Psychiatric Contribution," in *Totalitarianism,* 2nd ed., ed. Carl J. Friedrich [New York: Grosset & Dunlap, 1964], p. 159).

31. Lifton, *Thought Reform*, p. 5.

32. For descriptions of such marches, see Max Hastings, *The Korean War* (New York: Simon and Schuster, 1987), p. 291; and Philip Deane, "I Was a Captive in Korea," *Reader's Digest*, August 1953, pp. 65–70. Deane was a war correspondent for the *London Observer*, and his story was originally published by the *New York Herald Tribune*, April 30, May 1–7, 1953.

33. "Totalitarianism," observed Carl Friedrich and Zbigniew Brzezinski, "is a system of rules for realizing totalist intentions" (*Totalitarian Dictatorship and Autocracy* [Cambridge, Mass.: Harvard University Press, 1965], p. 17).

34. Hannah Arendt, *The Origins of Totalitarianism* (New York: Harvest Books, 1973), p. 438.

35. Waldemar Gurian, in *Totalitarianism*, ed. Carl J. Friedrich (New York: Universal Library, 1954), p. 126.

36. Else Frenkel-Brunswik, in *Totalitarianism*, ed. Friedrich, p. 173.

37. Arendt, *Origins of Totalitarianism*, p. 325.

38. Lifton, *Thought Reform*, p. 389. Lifton also attributes the stress on evil and guilt to Western influences, channeled through Soviet Communism, pointing out the absence of these in traditional Chinese culture.

39. Edgar H. Schein, with Inge Schneier and Curtis H. Barker, *Coercive Persuasion: A Socio-Psychological Analysis of the "Brainwashing" of American Civilian Prisoners by the Chinese Communists* (New York: Norton, 1961), p. 62.

40. Ibid., p. 23.

41. Ibid.

42. Liu Shao-ch'i, *How to Be a Good Communist* (Peking: Foreign Language Press, 1964). Excerpts may be found in Franz Schurman and Orville Schell, eds., *The China Reader* (New York: Random House, 1964), pp. 68–76.

43. Robert J. Lifton, "Thought Reform of Chinese Intellectuals: A Psychiatric Evaluation," *Journal of Social Issues* 13 (1957): 17. For additional evidence, see William C. Bradbury, Samuel M. Meyers, and Albert D. Biderman, *Mass Behavior in Battle and Captivity: The Communist Soldier in the Korean War* (Chicago: University of Chicago Press, 1968), passim.

44. Mao Zedong, "Correcting Unorthodox Tendencies in Learning, the Party and Literature and Art," in *A Documentary History of Chinese Communism*, ed. Conrad Brandt, Benjamin Schwartz, and John Fairbank, quoted in Group for the Advancement of Psychiatry, "Methods of Forceful Indoctrination," p. 238.

45. Benjamin Schwartz, "New Trends in Maoism," *Problems of Communism*, July–August 1957, p. 7.

46. Maurice Meisner, "Iconoclasm and Cultural Revolution in Russia and China," in *Bolshevik Culture*, ed. Abbott Gleason, Peter Kenez, and Richard Stites (Bloomington: Indiana University Press, 1985), p. 282.

47. "The Lenient Policy," in Schein, *Coercive Persuasion*, pp. 286–289. See also Edgar H. Schein, "Reaction Patterns to Severe Chronic Stress in American Army Prisoners of War of the Chinese," *Journal of Social Issues* 13 (1957): 22. Lifton discusses the Lenient Policy in "Chinese Communist 'Thought Reform,'" pp. 631–632, and calls it an "opportunity for rebirth" (p. 640).

48. Of course, there was no brainwashing under South Korean and United Nations auspices. But life in the South Korean camps could be extraordinarily vicious and degrading for the North Koreans, with South Korean brutality augmented by the worst sort of American racism. See, for example, Hastings, *Korean War,* pp. 305–313. (*Koje-do* is account of an uprising by North Korean and Chinese prisoners in a South Korean and American camp and the vicious fighting that ensued.)

49. Ibid., p. 289. According to a more recent student of the matter, "the Lenient Policy was a pale shadow of the brainwashing that went on in China itself. Nor did its practitioners expect to convert the mass of prisoners. A few would suffice; a nucleus, that is to say, who would argue the case with their companions and, if there was reason to, inform on them" (Richard Garrett, *P.O.W.* [Newton Abbot: David & Charles, 1981], p. 206).

50. Lifton, "Chinese Communist 'Thought Reform,'" p. 639. "Dr. Vincent" spoke of death and rebirth in his interview with Lifton (*Thought Reform,* p. 20).

51. Lifton, *Thought Reform,* pp. 25–30.

52. For interesting impressions of the "extraordinary vigor" with which the Chinese pursued campaigns, see Klaus Mehnert, *Peking and Moscow* (New York: NAL, 1964), pp. 204–207.

53. For an example, see Lifton, *Thought Reform,* pp. 20–23.

54. Brown, *Techniques of Persuasion,* pp. 261–62.

55. Lifton, *Thought Reform,* pp. 67–68.

56. Ibid.

57. An American intelligence officer related that "during indoctrination class one day, a prisoner pointed out that if, as the instructor had said, South Korea had started the war, and not North Korea, it was odd that by the end of the first day of combat the North Koreans had not only repelled the treacherous onslaught of the South Koreans all along the front, but were already knocking at the gates of Seoul, forty miles to the south. The instructor was furious. 'You are a stupid, ignorant fool,' he said. 'Everyone else in the class knows the south Koreans started the war. Why don't you?' But the prisoner was obdurate. He demanded an answer, whereupon the instructor ordered the entire class to stand, and remain on its feet until this one man abandoned his objection. After some hours of standing, the other prisoners began to mutter against the objector. Under this pressure the man capitulated. But the incident did not end there. The next day, the prisoner had to compose and read to the class a long criticism of his own conduct, ending with an apology to the class and to the instructor. On each of the following four or five days, he had to repeat his self-criticism and elaborate on it. His classmates were ordered to criticize him, which they did. Then he, in turn, was made to criticize his classmates" (Kinkead, *In Every War but One,* p. 108).

58. Ibid., p. 115.

59. A point impressed on me by Jerome Grieder of Brown University.

60. Albert D. Biderman, *March to Calumny: The Story of American POWs in the Korean War* (New York: Macmillan, 1963), p. 74.

61. Lifton, *Thought Reform,* p. 81. Lifton's analytical account of the evolution of the "confession" through stages is fascinating.

62. "Text of Report to Defense Secretary by Advisory Committee on Prisoners of War," *New York Times,* August 18, 1955, p. 10.

63. Lifton, "Chinese Communist 'Thought Reform,' " p. 643. Historian Arthur Wright agreed. See his "The Chinese Monolith, Past and Present," *Problems of Communism,* July–August 1955, pp. 1–8, passim.

64. Subsequently, some of the most careful and sophisticated students of brainwashing (Albert Biderman, Lawrence Hinkle, and Harold G. Wolff of the Cornell Medical Center, Robert Lifton, then of Massachusetts General Hospital) suggested that for the pure extractions of information, the old-fashioned brutality of the North Koreans could achieve its goals "more quickly and economically" than the Chinese methods could. See the account of the meetings of the New York Academy of Medicine in *New York Times,* November 14, 1956, p. 10.

65. William Dean, *General Dean's Story* (New York: Viking, 1954), p. 107.

66. Garrett, *P.O.W.,* p. 209.

67. Joseph C. Goulden, *Korea: The Untold Story of the War* (New York: Times Books, 1982), p. 600; Charles Stevendon, "The Truth About 'Germ Warfare' in Korea," *Reader's Digest,* April 1953, pp. 17–20.

68. David Rees, *Korea: The Limited War* (London: Macmillan, 1964), pp. 352–353; Edgar O'Ballance, *Korea: 1950–1953* (Hamden, Conn.: Archon Books, 1969), pp. 140–141. Neither account gives a primary source. William Lindsay White, *The Captives of Korea* (New York: Scribner, 1957), p. 147, alleges that in late December 1951, "a Moscow magazine" distributed among U.S. prisoners charged that typhus was being spread in North Korea by the U.S. Air Force, but he provides no further details.

69. Bevin Alexander, *Korea: The First War We Lost* (New York: Hippocrene Books, 1986), p. 456.

70. Richard Whelan, *Drawing the Line: The Korean War, 1950–1953* (Boston: Little, Brown, 1990), p. 334. A purported text of the Moscow Radio broadcast is in Rees, *Korea,* p. 353.

71. Louis J. West, in Group for the Advancement of Psychiatry, "Methods of Forceful Indoctrination," p. 270.

72. Alexander, *Korea,* p. 456; Rees, *Korea,* p. 353.

73. Morris Wills, *Turncoat: An American's Twelve Years in Communist China* (Englewood Cliffs, N.J.: Prentice-Hall, 1966).

74. A. M. Rosenthal, "Reds' Photographs on Germ Warfare Exposed as Fakes," *New York Times,* April 3, 1952, p. 1.

75. Anthony Leviero, "New Code Orders P.O.W.s to Resist in 'Brainwashing'; All Data Limited; Captive to Give Name, Rank, Number, Age—Mercy for Tortured," *New York Times,* August 18, 1955, pp. 1, 8. The confessions of Quinn, Enoch, and a number of others were published in the *Report of the International Scientific Commission for the Investigation of the Fact Concerning Bacterial Warfare in Korea and China* (Peking, 1952), which I have not been able to see.

76. West, in Group for the Advancement of Psychiatry, "Methods of Forceful Indoctrination," pp. 273–285.

77. So did Max Hastings. His anecdotal account stresses the cultural confusion that marked the encounter of the Chinese with their British and American prisoners.

The Chinese regarded the constant obscenities as a deliberate insult. "Why you always effing, effing, effing?" (*Korean War,* pp. 297–298).

78. Quoted in Goulden, *Korea,* p. 600.

79. David Rees discusses support for the charges in "Peking: Bacteria for Peace," in *Korea,* pp. 347–363.

80. Ibid., p. 360.

81. Burton Kaufman, *The Korean War* (New York: Knopf, 1986), p. 265. See also Biderman, *March to Calumny,* p. 77; and White, *Captives of Korea,* p. 149.

82. John Dollard, "Men Who Are Tortured by the Awful Fear of Torture," *New York Times Book Review,* July 29, 1956, p. 6.

83. For Jean-Paul Sartre's justification of the demonstration, see "Les Communistes et la paix," in *Situations VI* (Paris: Gallimard, 1964), pp. 342–343.

84. Kaufman, *Korean War,* p. 267. See also "Germs of Untruth," *Time,* April 7, 1952, p. 30. One of the arguments used by the North Koreans and Chinese to convince prisoners to sign these confessions was that if they did so they would cease to be war criminals and recover their rights as prisoners of war. The opposite was in fact the case, for any such confession really made them liable to prosecution under the Geneva Codes as war criminals.

85. For some instances, see "Our Own Reds Still Parrot the Germ-Warfare Lie," *Saturday Evening Post,* December 15, 1955, p. 10.

86. White, *Captives of Korea,* pp. 265–266. Many of the U.S. servicemen who fell into North Korean and Chinese hands were taken prisoner while in retreat at the Chosin Reservoir in midwinter. The horrific four-day march that generally followed capture was "the first . . . and often the worst" ordeal of the POW. On one such march, five hundred out of seven hundred prisoners died. See *POW: The Fight Continues After the Battle,* a Report by the Secretary of Defense's Advisory Committee on Prisoners of War (Washington, D.C.: Government Printing Office, August 1955), p. 8.

87. Secretary of Defense, *POW,* pp. vi, 79–82; Garrettt, *P.O.W.,* pp. 217–218. See also Whelan, *Drawing the Line,* p. 362; and Senate Subcommittee on Investigations, *Communist Interrogation, Indoctrination and Exploitation of American Civilian and Military Prisoners: Hearings Before the Permanent Subcommittee on Investigations of the Committee on Government Operations* (Washington, D.C.: Government Printing Office, June 1956), p. 1.

88. Kinkead, *In Every War but One,* p. 16. The estimate given by most students of the subject is that 10 to 15 percent of the prisoners engaged in some kind of collaborationist activity. See, for instance, Edgar Schein's testimony in Group for the Advancement of Psychiatry, "Methods of Forceful Indoctrination," p. 259. Julius Segal of George Washington University told a Senate subcommittee that "70 percent of all the repatriated army PW's made at least one contribution to the enemy's propaganda effort. By that I mean signed one petition or made one confession or made one recording" (Senate, *Communist Interrogation, Indoctrination and Exploitation,* p. 89).

89. Segal, in Senate, *Communist Interrogation, Indoctrination and Exploitation,* p. 89. "None would admit he had informed on the others," wrote White, "but a good

meal, secretly given in the Chinese mess, could be a terrible temptation" (*Captives of Korea*, p. 104).

90. *New York Times*, January 26, 1954, p. 1.

91. Hastings, *Korean War*, p. 304. The reference is to the novel of that name by Richard Condon (1959), subsequently made into a brilliant film by John Frankenheimer. The plot turns on a prisoner of war who was not only "brainwashed" by the Chinese, but also "programmed" to assassinate the president of the United States when the time is ripe. The elaborate plot makes his potential successor turn out to be a McCarthyesque figure—who turns out himself to be controlled by Communists, through his wife! The film inverts, brilliantly and outrageously, some of the deepest American fears of the 1950s. For example, some seventy-five Communist agents trying to return on the POW swaps were actually discovered by Western counterintelligence—true "Manchurian candidates" of a kind. See Kinkead, *In Every War but One*, pp. 78–80.

92. Kinkead, *In Every War but One*, pp. 36–62.

93. See Lieutenant Colonel Edwin L. Heller, as told to Hugh Morrow, "I Thought I'd Never Get Home," *Saturday Evening Post*, August 20, 1955, pp. 17–19, 58, 60; August 27, 1955, pp. 34–35, 46–47, 50, 52; and Captain Harold E. Fischer, Jr., as told to Clay Blair, Jr., "My Case as a Prisoner was 'Different,'" *Life*, June 27, 1955, pp. 146–160. Subsequent letters split on whether Fischer should be blamed for his confession. One reader wrote that "you can break anyone in 36 hours" ("Letters to the Editor," *Life*, July 18, 1955, p. 7). A precursor was *General Dean's Story*, as told to William L. Worden. See also H. Jordan, "You Too Would Confess," *Argosy*, February 1957, pp. 15–17, 57–63. When reading these narratives, one should remember how psychologically complicated any such effort to "tell one's own story" must be. For particularly propagandistic articles, see Frederic Sondern, Jr., "U.S. Negroes Make Reds See Red," *Reader's Digest*, January 1954, pp. 37–42, and "The Brainwashing of John Hayes," *Reader's Digest*, July 1955, pp. 27–33.

94. "Freed Flier Cites Red Persuasion; Col. Arnold Breaks Down at News Parley in Tokyo, Recalling Peiping 'Spy' Pressure," *New York Times*, August 7, 1955, p. 5.

95. *New York Times*, July 11, 1955, p. 22, and August 18, 1955, p. 8. Senator Estes Kefauver was among many who found the use of the word *turncoat* objectionable when it applied to men who had been tortured. See "Kefauver Scores New P.O.W. Code," *New York Times*, August 21, 1955. p. 30.

96. Anthony Leviero, "For the Brainwashed: Pity or Punishment?" *New York Times Magazine*, August 14, 1955, pp. 12, 16, 18, quotation from p. 12.

97. Senate, *Communist Interrogation, Indoctrination and Exploitation*, pp. 154–180.

98. For an American list of those camps considered the worst and descriptions of several, including "Pak's Palace," see Secretary of Defense, *POW*, pp. 8–11.

99. Major David MacGehee, U.S. Air Force, with Peter Kalischer, "Some of Us Didn't Crack," *Collier's*, January 22, 1954, pp. 82–88, and "Tortured in Pak's Palace," *Collier's*, February 5, 1954, pp. 68–75.

100. For personnel, see Kinkead, *In Every War but One,* pp. 191–192. In setting up the committee, the government appears to have been particularly influenced by the case of Colonel Frank Schwable of the U.S. Marines, who had confessed to germ-warfare charges, which he later repudiated. A Marine Corps court of inquiry subsequently ruled that he had resisted torture "to the limit of his ability" and recommended the drafting of a code of conduct that would spell out such things. But Schwable's career was over. See "Red Tactics Spur Code for POWs, U.S. Policy Would Combat Brainwashing and Torture to Force 'Confessions,' " *New York Times,* August 14, 1955, pp. 1, 21. See also Goulden, *Korea,* pp. 602–603.

101. Secretary of Defense, *POW.* See also Edgar Schein's "Epilogue" to "Brainwashing," *Journal of Social Issues* 13 (1957): 56–60.

102. Morris Wills, the "turncoat," later wrote that "I had never heard of Marxism. As far as I can remember, Marx had never been mentioned in our school. He should have been; we ought to have been given a basic idea of his theories. There is absolutely no way of combatting an argument in his favor unless you know something about him" (*Turncoat,* p. 55). For a typical journalistic response, see *The Reporter,* September 8, 1955, pp. 2, 4.

103. Biderman, *March to Calumny,* p. 261.

104. The text of the report was published in the *New York Times,* August 18, 1955, pp. 10–11. The text of the code appears in Garrett, *P.O.W.,* pp. 219–220; and in Senate, *Communist Interrogation, Indoctrination and Exploitation,* pp. 131–132. See also Leviero, "New Code," pp. 1, 8.

105. Garrett, *P.O.W.,* p. 220; *New York Times,* August 18, 1955, p. 11.

106. The purpose of the code, it was specifically stated, was to "indoctrinate servicemen in the principle that they must be prepared to die for their country and never surrender of their own free will" ("Red Tactics Spur Code," *New York Times,* August 14, 1955, pp. 1, 21).

107. "P.O.W. Code Upheld, Criticized in Debate," *New York Times,* August 22, 1955, p. 3. The critic in the televised debate was Albert Somit, associate professor of government at New York University, formerly with the Army Psychological Warfare Division.

108. Anthony Leviero, "Army's 'Toughest' Trained in Wilds, Special Force Faces Swamps and Mountains to Acquire Skills of Guerrillas," *New York Times,* August 31, 1955, p. 9.

109. "British to Instruct Troops on Capture," *New York Times,* February 16, 1956, p. 2.

110. Steven W. Mosher, *China Misperceived: American Illusions and Chinese Reality* (New York: HarperCollins, 1990), p. 88.

111. Henry R. Lieberman, "Mainland China Is New, Tight, Communist State. Control of All Phases of Life Has Been Imposed by Small Group at Top," *New York Times,* December 16, 1951, sec. 4, p. 5.

112. W. W. Rostow, *The Prospects for Communist China* (New York: MIT Press and Wiley, 1954), pp. 309, 313.

113. John King Fairbank, *The United States and China* (Cambridge, Mass.: Har-

vard University Press, 1958), p. 314. Significantly, Fairbank did not use the term in the first edition (1948) and omitted it in the third (1971). It is fair to deduce that the impact of the 1950s is responsible. See also Mosher, *China Misperceived,* p. 225. We should also note, however, that Fairbank returned to the term in his final work, *China: A New History* (Cambridge, Mass.: Harvard University Press, 1992), pp. 45, 257, 337, 397, 401, 420, 430.

114. Schwartz, "New Trends in Maoism," p. 7, quoted in Mosher, *China Misperceived,* p. 88.

115. Wright, "Chinese Monolith," quoted in Mosher, *China Misperceived,* p. 225.

116. Roderick MacFarquhar, "Totalitarianism via Industrialization? The Case of Communist China," *Problems of Communism,* September–October, 1958, p. 7.

117. Jost A. M. Meerlo, *The Rape of the Mind: The Psychology of Thought Control, Menticide and Brainwashing* (Cleveland: World, 1956). On the final page of *Rape of the Mind,* the reader learns that "under the Nazi occupation of the Netherlands," Meerlo, a Dutch psychiatrist who subsequently emigrated to the United States, "was able to observe at firsthand the methods of mental torture and forced interrogation described in this book." For a rather favorable review, see Dollard, "Men Who Are Tortured," p. 6.

118. Pat Frank, *Hold Back the Night* (New York: Bantam, 1951), p. 48.

119. LeSelle Gilman, *The Red Gate* (New York: Ballantine, 1952), p. 85.

120. Kinkead, "Reporter at Large," later expanded and published as *In Every War but One;* British edition, *Why They Collaborated* (London: Longmans Green, 1959). Irving Kristol judged that the book is really a "skillful, popularly written official army report" ("The Shadow of a War," *The Reporter,* February 5, 1959, p. 40). William Peters contradicted several of Kinkead's assertions in "More on Our POWs," *The Reporter,* March 5, 1959, pp. 40–42. A number of POWs did escape, although none managed to return to American lines safely. The use of violence, including many instances of torture, was widespread, contrary to Kinkead's account ("Reporter at Large," p. 38).

121. Schein, *Coercive Persuasion.*

122. Lifton, *Thought Reform,* p. 13.

123. Ibid., p. 397.

124. Robert J. Lifton, *Revolutionary Immortality. Mao Tse-tung and the Chinese Cultural Revolution* (New York: Random House, 1968).

125. Ibid., pp. 22–23.

126. Ibid.

127. See especially Simon Leys, *Chinese Shadows* (New York: Viking Penguin, 1977), published earlier in France as *Ombres chinoises* (Paris: Union Générale d'Editions, 1974).

128. Leys, *Chinese Shadows,* p. 10.

129. Simon Leys, "Human Rights in China," in his *The Burning Forest: Essays on Chinese Culture and Politics* (New York: Holt, 1987), p. 114. In 1971, Pierre Ryckmans published his first critical analysis of the Cultural Revolution, *Les Habits neufs de président Mao,* but did not mention Orwell or use the term *totalitarianism.* The term does, however, appear in the 1977 postscript to the English translation, *The Chair-*

man's New Clothes: Mao and the Cultural Revolution (New York: St. Martin's Press, 1977).

CHAPTER SIX

1. Elisabeth Young-Bruehl, *Hannah Arendt: For Love of the World* (New Haven, Conn.: Yale University Press, 1982), pp. 184 ff.

2. Ibid., pp. 158, 177–178, 199–200.

3. Hannah Arendt to her editor at Houghton Mifflin, Mary Underwood, September 24, 1946, quoted in ibid., pp. 200–201. Seven years later, Arendt wrote: "The book . . . does not really deal with the 'origins' of totalitarianism—as its title unfortunately claims—but gives a historical account of the elements which crystallized into totalitarianism, this account is followed by an analysis of the elemental structure of totalitarian movements and domination itself" ("A Reply," *Review of Politics,* January 1953, p. 78).

4. See Hannah Arendt to the German philosopher Karl Jaspers, September 1947, quoted in Young-Bruehl, *Hannah Arendt,* p. 204.

5. Young-Bruehl takes this quotation from a December 1948 memo in Arendt's papers (*Hannah Arendt,* pp. 204–206). Arendt said essentially the same thing in print somewhat earlier: "An insight into the nature of totalitarian rule, directed by our fear of the concentration camp, might serve to devaluate all outmoded political shadings from right to left and . . . introduce the most essential political criterion for judging the events of our time: will it lead to totalitarian rule or will it not?" ("The Concentration Camps," *Partisan Review,* July 1948, p. 747). Stephen J. Whitfield noted that the appearance of the book seemed almost an answer to Orwell's 1948 appeal "for someone to write a scholarly work on concentration and forced-labour camps" (*Into the Dark: Hannah Arendt and Totalitarianism* [Philadelphia: Temple University Press, 1980], p. 8).

6. For a good description of Arendt's position on Italy and a summary of the debate in Italy itself, see Meir Michaelis, "Anmerkungen zum italienischen Totalitarismusbegriff: Zur Kritik der Thesen Hannah Arendts und Renzo de Felices," *Quellen und Forschungen aus italienischen Archiven und Bibliotheken* 62 (1982): 270–302, esp. pp. 270–278. Michaelis opposes Arendt's view, arguing that neither Germany nor the Soviet Union ever came close to being "fully totalitarian" and that it is more useful to discuss Fascist Italy together with these two regimes than to analyze it as a nationalist, authoritarian dictatorship with a few totalitarian excrescences.

7. Some reviewers seemed almost to assert that the book's principal merit was that it broke new ground. Although Arendt's analysis "left many questions unanswered," wrote August Heckscher, it is "brilliantly creative," illuminated by "little-known facts and unfamiliar relationships" (*New York Herald Tribune Book Review,* April 8, 1951, p. 6). The historian Oscar Handlin's review in the *Partisan Review,* November–December 1951, pp. 722–723, struck a similar note. I owe these and other references to C. Michelle Murphy's unpublished paper on the reception of *The Origins of Totalitarianism* in the United States.

8. The only other book with comparable ambitions was Adorno and Hork-

heimer's *Dialektik der Aufklärung,* which appeared seven years earlier. But because of its intellectual complexity, German idiom, and radicalism, Adorno and Horkheimer's work was not published in English until 1972.

9. David Riesman, with Nathan Glazer and Reuel Denney, *The Lonely Crowd: A Study of Changing American Character* (New York: Doubleday, 1950).

10. Margaret Canovan's account encouraged me to take this final interpretive leap. See her *Hannah Arendt: A Reinterpretation of Her Political Thought* (Cambridge: Cambridge University Press, 1992), p. 20.

11. This is not to say that her analysis did not in all probability have an impact on some Amerian historians of Germany, such as Georg Mosse (*The Crisis of German Ideology*), Fritz Stern (*The Politics of Cultural Despair*), and perhaps even Hans Rosenberg, whose analysis of Prussian bureaucracy (*Bureaucracy, Aristocracy and Autocracy*) may have owed something to Arendt.

12. The "mob" seems close to Karl Marx's idea of a *Lumpenproletariat,* a group of people from many classes who, in the wake of the triumph of the bourgeoisie, have lost any connection with any class and who therefore are prepared for any adventure. This concept, in turn, was derived from Hegel. For a criticism of the vagueness of Arendt's idea of the mob, see David Spitz, "Brutal Trinity," *New Republic,* September 3, 1951, p. 19. Margaret Canovan explains Arendt's terminology as well as anyone. According to her, Arendt "distinguishes between the 'masses' and the 'mob.' By the latter she means the socially disreputable, the outcasts and criminal elements, and she notes that the leaders of the Nazi and Bolshevik movements were drawn from the band of adventurers accustomed to war against established society." But neither Lenin nor Trotsky was from this sort of milieu. "By the masses, on the other hand, she means people who would in any stable society be perfectly content to fill the role to which they were born, but who found themselves cut off, isolated from their fellows, convinced of their own helplessness and unimportance, and prepared to devote themselves to any organization that gave them a place in the world and a reason for living" (Margaret Canovan, *The Political Thought of Hannah Arendt* [London: Dent, 1974], pp. 19–20).

13. Canovan, *Hannah Arendt: A Reinterpretation,* p. 53

14. Arendt, "A Reply," p. 81.

15. Philip Rieff, "The Theology of Politics: Reflections on Totalitarianism as the Burden of Our Time," *Journal of Religion,* April 1952, p. 120.

16. Hannah Arendt, *The Origins of Totalitarianism* (1951; New York: Harcourt Brace Jovanovich, 1973), p. 474.

17. Canovan, *Hannah Arendt: A Reinterpretation,* p. 23.

18. Quoted in George Kateb, *Hannah Arendt: Politics, Conscience, Evil* (Totowa, N.J.: Rowman & Allenheld, 1983), p. 66.

19. Canovan, *Political Thought of Hannah Arendt,* p. 42.

20. Young-Bruehl, *Hannah Arendt,* p. 219.

21. Kateb made the interesting suggestion that "the real continuity between the earlier movements and totalitarianism is found in the readiness of European peoples to think in racist and imperialist categories, to accept the normality of, sympathize

with, or embrace ardently such modes of response and half-thought" (*Hannah Arendt*, p. 56).

22. Arendt, *Origins*, pp. 189–191 and passim.

23. Canovan, *Political Thought of Hannah Arendt*, pp. 26–27.

24. Ibid., p. 220.

25. Ibid., p. 31.

26. Arendt, *Origins*, pp. 392, 458–459. See also Robert Burrowes, "Totalitarianism: The Revised Standard Version," *World Politics*, January 1969, p. 275.

27. Quoted in Kateb, *Hannah Arendt*, p. 79

28. Canovan, *Hannah Arendt: A Reinterpretation*, p. 25.

29. Arendt ultimately changed her mind about whether evil was "radical." In her correspondence with her critic, Gershom Scholem, about her Eichmann book, Arendt wrote that "it is indeed my opinion now that evil is never 'radical,' that it is only extreme, and that it possesses neither depth nor any demonic dimension. It can overgrow and lay waste the whole world precisely because it spreads like a fungus on the surface. . . . Only the good has depth and can be radical" (quoted in Kateb, *Hannah Arendt*, p. 79).

30. See the remarks of E. H. Carr in *New York Times Book Review*, March 25, 1951, p. 24. "Miss Arendt," he wrote, "has all too clearly set out to generalize the overwhelming experience of Hitler's Germany." Arendt recognized this difficulty herself and spent much of the mid-1950s working on a study tentatively entitled "Totalitarian Elements of Marxism." It was never completed, but elements of it found their way into a number of her other publications. See Young-Bruehl, *Hannah Arendt*, pp. 276–278.

31. Arendt, *Origins*, p. 224.

32. In an otherwise admiring review, Hughes found the book "open to serious objections" on those grounds. See H. Stuart Hughes, "Historical Sources of Totalitarianism," *The Nation*, March 24, 1951, p. 281.

33. Whitfield, *Into the Dark*, pp. 87–89.

34. David Riesman, review in *Commentary*, April 1951, p. 397. Riesman knew Arendt quite well and had read the book in manuscript. Arendt was originally to have contributed a chapter to the book that became *The Lonely Crowd*. See Young-Bruehl, *Hannah Arendt*, pp. 252–253. "You assume that the Nazis knew at the beginning what they wanted at the end," Riesman wrote to Arendt in a letter dated June 8, 1949 (quoted in ibid., p. 252).

35. Rieff, "Theology of Politics," pp. 119–126.

36. Canovan, *Political Thought of Hannah Arendt*, p. 43.

37. Eric Voegelin, "A Review of the Origins of Totalitarianism," *Review of Politics*, January 1953, pp. 68–76.

38. Hannah Arendt, *The Human Condition* (Chicago: University of Chicago Press, 1958). The best and fullest account of Hannah Arendt's struggle to find the connection between Marxism and totalitarianism is in Canovan, *Hannah Arendt: A Reinterpretation*, pp. 63–98.

39. Canovan, *Hannah Arendt: A Reinterpretation*, p. 75.

40. Ibid., pp. 83, 85.

41. Ibid., pp. 89–90, 97.

42. J. L. Talmon, *The Origins of Totalitarian Democracy* (London: Secker and Warburg, 1952).

43. J. L. Talmon, *The Myth of the Nation and the Vision of Revolution* (London: Secker and Warburg, 1981), p. 535, quoted in Yehoshua Arieli, "Jacob Talmon—An Intellectual Portrait," in *Totalitarian Democracy and After: International Colloquium in Memory of Jacob L. Talmon, Jerusalem, 21–24 June, 1982* (Jerusalem: Magnes Press, Hebrew University, 1984), pp. 5–6.

44. On Tocqueville and Talmon, see Arieli, "Jacob Talmon," pp. 7–9; and Talmon, *Origins of Totalitarian Democracy,* p. 257.

45. Quoted in Arieli, "Jacob Talmon," p. 8.

46. Talmon, *Origins of Totalitarian Democracy,* pp. 6–8.

47. Ibid., p. 249.

48. Ibid., pp. 1–2.

49. Ibid., p. 11.

50. Ibid., pp. 38–40.

51. Ibid., p. 43.

52. An exception was Irving Kristol. He thought the book important, but objected to Talmon's belief in the absolute centrality of ideology. He also suggested that such profound differences as those between "democracy" and "totalitarianism" could not have entirely originated in differences of emphasis among such similar thinkers as the *philosophes*. See Irving Kristol, "Two Varieties of Democracy," *Commentary*, September 1952, pp. 287–289.

53. Crane Brinton, "Idealists in a Hurry," *New York Times Book Review*, August 10, 1952, p. 9.

54. F. C. Green, *Jean-Jacques Rousseau: A Critical Study of His Life and Writings* (Cambridge: Cambridge University Press, 1955), quoted in J. Salwyn Shapiro, "Rousseau: Totalitarian?" *Saturday Review of Literature*, February 11, 1956, p. 45. See also Shapiro's review of the second volume of Talmon's work, *Political Messianism: The Romantic Phase*, in *American Historical Review*, July 1961, p. 1014.

55. John W. Chapman, *Rousseau—Totalitarian or Liberal?* (New York: Columbia University Press, 1956), pp. vii, 78–80.

56. J. L. Talmon, *Political Messianism: The Romantic Phase* (London: Secker and Warburg, 1960).

57. J. L. Talmon, "Utopianism and Politics: A Conservative View," *Commentary*, August, 1959, pp. 149–154.

58. Ibid., pp. 149–151.

59. Ibid., pp. 153–154. Rather prophetically, Talmon thought already in 1959 that de-Stalinization and the emergence of "national communism" had destroyed Communist universality, thereby marking "the beginning of the end."

60. Talmon, *Political Messianism*, p. viii.

61. Ibid., p. 514.

62. Ibid., pp. 514–515.

63. The anonymous reviewer in the *Times Literary Supplement*, November 11,

1960, p. 724, in a generally favorable review, observed that *Political Messianism* contained "few surprises." He also referred to "some of the few adverse criticisms made of the first volume [among them that] Dr. Talmon was then accused of having represented history as a conflict of abstract ideas, and of having grossly underrated the effect of economic circumstances and pure chance on the course of events."

64. Charles Taylor, "The Quest for the Millenium," *New Statesman and Nation*, December 24, 1960, pp. 1013–1014.

65. Alfred Cobban, *In Search of Humanity: The Role of the Enlightenment in Modern History* (London: Jonathan Cape, 1960), p. 183. Several years earlier, Carl J. Friedrich had compared *Totalitarian Democracy* with W. M. McGovern's *From Luther to Hitler* (1941), observing that "it seems basically unsound to pick out of past intellectual history some one or several exponents or supposed exponents of some aspects of totalitarian views, for instance, of an authoritarian society, be it Plato or Thomas Aquinas, Hobbes or Rousseau, Hegel or Carlyle—and hold him 'responsible' for the totalitarian movements or societies by claiming that he was a totalitarian. . . . The road of Western thought runs from Luther to Lincoln, as it does from Luther to Hitler; the seamless web of history is woven of many intertwined strands, and totalitarianism, for all its uniqueness, does not spring from the head of any ideologue or demagogue without antecedents. But those antecedents did not 'cause' the phenomenon and there was nothing inevitable about Hitler or Stalin" (*Totalitarianism* [Cambridge, Mass.: Harvard University Press, 1954], pp. 58–60).

66. Peter Gay, *The Party of Humanity: Essays in the French Enlightenment* (New York: Knopf, 1964), p. x. Like Taylor, Gay believed that Talmon overestimated the power of ideas: "Neither the Terror in the French Revolution, nor the totalitarian regimes of our time are merely the product of certain ideas, the 'ultimate result' of speculations by eighteenth-century writers who were thinking of something else and hoping for a far different future" (p. 282).

67. Ibid., p. 280.

68. Ibid., p. 281.

69. Richard Hunt, *The Political Ideas of Marx and Engels,* vol. 1: *Marxism and Totalitarian Democracy, 1818–1850* (Pittsburgh: University of Pittsburgh Press, 1974), pp. 12–13.

70. Bernard Yack, *The Longing for Total Revolution: Philosophic Sources of Social Discontent from Rousseau to Marx and Nietzsche* (Princeton, N.J.: Princeton University Press, 1986), pp. 4–5, 13–14. Martin Jay described Talmon as "ungenerous" for discussing Rousseau as the progenitor of "totalitarian democracy." Jay claimed, without citing evidence, that Rousseau "realized that the social contract made sense only in small communities where public life between equals was a real possibility. . . . He thus held out no hope for the realization of his political solution to personal fragmentation in the modern world of giant nation-states, and recognized the dangers in trying to achieve it. . . . Like his other answers, the social contract remained only a thought-experiment which lacked any means of implementation" (*The Idea of Totality: The Adventures of a Concept from Lukács to Habermas* [Berkeley: University of California Press, 1984]), p. 42).

71. In 1984 Jan Marejko quoted a colleague approvingly that the last thing that

was needed was "the n-th interpretation of the *Social Contract* or the perpetuation of the debate over Rousseau the totalitarian vs. Rousseau the liberal." Still, Marejko's book was an investigation of closely related questions, and it owed a certain debt to Talmon's earlier work. See Raymond Trousson, "Quinze années d'études rousseauistes," *Dix-huitième siècle*, no. 9 (1977): 342–386, quoted in Jan Marejko, *Jean-Jacques Rousseau et la dérive totalitaire* (Lausanne: L'Age d'homme, 1984), pp. 25–26. For an early 1980s appreciation of Talmon's work, see Karl Dietrich Bracher, *The Age of Ideologies: A History of Political Thought in the Twentieth Century* (New York: St. Martin's Press, 1984), pp. 83, 112, 114, and passim.

72. Robert Wistrich, "The Myth of the Nation and the Vision of Revolution," *Times Literary Supplement*, September 17, 1982, p. 1016. Wistrich repeated earlier criticisms: that Talmon had employed "too disembodied an approach to the history of ideas, which disconnects them from their roots in European social and economic history; at times, too, it is difficult to resist the feeling that rhetorical exaggeration and straining for effect have overcome the requirement of careful analysis and the critical examination of the author's unspoken assumptions."

73. Bracher, *Age of Ideologies,* p. 112. Bracher frequently refers to Talmon's work (see pp. 83, 112, 114).

74. Charles Taylor, *The Ethics of Authenticity* (Cambridge, Mass.: Harvard University Press, 1992), p. 28.

75. They were much more likely to be familiar with Karl Wittfogel's *Oriental Despotism: A Comparative Study of Total Power* (New Haven, Conn.: Yale University Press, 1957). Wittfogel attempted to derive modern "bureaucratic totalitarianism" from what he called the "hydraulic societies" of the ancient world, via societies analyzable in terms of an "Asiatic mode of production." Wittfogel's thesis was arrresting, but very few scholars believed that he had successfully demonstrated the link between ancient despotisms and modern ones.

CHAPTER SEVEN

1. For a brief introduction to these developments, see Abbott Gleason, "Russian and Soviet Studies in the United States," in *Modern Encyclopedia of Russian and Soviet History* (Gulf Breeze, Fla.: Academic International Press, 1983), vol. 32, pp. 45–52. A more searching account that strongly emphasizes the politicization of Soviet studies is that by Stephen Cohen, "Sovietology as a Vocation," in *Rethinking the Soviet Experience* (New York: Oxford University Press, 1985).

2. See the acknowledgments in Raymond A. Bauer, Alex Inkeles, and Clyde Kluckhohn, *How the Soviet System Works* (Cambridge, Mass.: Harvard University Press, 1956). Columbia was involved in a related, subsidiary project. See Sigmund Diamond, *Compromised Campus: The Collaboration of Universities with the Intelligence Community, 1945–1955* (New York: Oxford University Press, 1992), pp. 84–88.

3. See the rather jaundiced account in Diamond, *Compromised Campus,* pp. 50–110, esp. pp. 68–70, 108–110.

4. That there was some pressure and intimidation is demonstrated by Diamond in *Compromised Campus* and by Cohen in "Sovietology as a Vocation," esp. pp. 8–19.

5. Barrington Moore, Jr., *Soviet Politics—The Dilemmas of Power: The Role of Ideas in Social Change* (Cambridge, Mass.: Harvard University Press, 1950).

6. Merle Fainsod, *How Russia Is Ruled* (Cambridge, Mass.: Harvard University Presss, 1953), p. ix.

7. For example, see ibid., p. 477.

8. Jerry Hough, who revised Fainsod's book for republication, wrote that "Fainsod did not define totalitarianism as a movement to transform society, but rather as the leader's drive for political control" (*How the Soviet Union Is Governed* [Cambridge, Mass.: Harvard University Press, 1979], p. vi.

9. Fainsod, *How Russia Is Ruled*, pp. 31–59.

10. Ibid., p. 59.

11. Carl J. Friedrich, ed., *Totalitarianism* (Cambridge, Mass.: Harvard University Press, 1954).

12. Erik Erikson's interesting paper discussed ego development, juxtaposing "wholeness" with "totality." By the former he meant "an assembly of parts, even quite diversified parts, that enter into fruitful association and organization," and by the latter, "a *Gestalt* in which an absolute boundary is emphasized: given a certain arbitrary delineation, nothing that belongs inside must be left outside; nothing that must be outside can be tolerated inside. A totality is as absolutely inclusive as it is utterly exclusive . . . whether or not the parts really have, so to speak, a yearning for one another" ("Wholeness and Totality—A Psychiatric Contribution," in *Totalitarianism*, ed. Friedrich, pp. 161–162).

13. Else Frenkel-Brunswik was one of Theodor Adorno's collaborators on an influential political–psychological study, *The Authoritarian Personality* (New York: Harper, 1950).

14. George Kennan, "Totalitarianism and Freedom," in *Totalitarianism*, ed. Friedrich, pp. 25–27. In his paper, Carl J. Friedrich modestly declared that the totalitarian societies were "basically alike" and "historically unique," but "why they are what they are we do not know" (ibid., p. 60).

15. Point 1 seems close to Talmon's definition of "political messianism."

16. Friedrich, in *Totalitarianism*, pp. 52–53.

17. Ibid., p. 274. The political scientist Karl Deutsch used a joke to illustrate Friedrich's point: "In a democracy . . . everything that is not forbidden is permitted; under an authoritarian regime, everything that is not permitted is forbidden; under totalitarianism, everything that is not forbidden is compulsory" (in *Totalitarianism*, ed. Friedrich, p. 309). Deutsch believed that the Soviet Union would be able to stave off disintegration for only fifty years at most (ibid., pp. 331–333).

18. Carl J. Friedrich and Zbigniew Brzezinski, *Totalitarian Dictatorship and Autocracy* (1956; New York: Praeger, 1966).

19. Ibid., pp. 4, 15.

20. Ibid., p. 21.

21. Zbigniew K. Brzezinski, *The Permanent Purge: Politics in Soviet Totalitarianism* (Cambridge, Mass.: Harvard University Press, 1956), pp. 12–24, passim. See also his "Totalitarianism and Reality," *American Political Science Review* 50 (1956): 751ff.

22. Barrington Moore, Jr., *Terror and Progress USSR: Some Sources of Change and*

Stability in the Soviet Dictatorship (Cambridge, Mass.: Harvard University Press, 1954), passim.

23. Isaac Deutscher, *Stalin: A Political Biography,* 2nd ed. (New York: Oxford University Press, 1966), p. 568.

24. "Fascism is here construed as a developmental dictatorship," A. James Gregor wrote in the preface to one of his books, "appropriate to partially developed or under developed, and consequently status deprived national communities in a period of intense international competition for place and status" (*The Ideology of Fascism: The Rationale of Totalitarianism* [New York: Free Press, 1969], p. xiii). Gregor proceeded to relate Italian Fascism to other, variously totalitarian states like Spain, Portugal, Romania, and Hungary during (roughly) the 1940s. See, above all, Gregor's *Italian Fascism and Developmental Dictatorship* (Princeton, N.J.: Princeton University Press, 1979). Cf. Karl Dietrich Bracher, "Totalitarianism," in *Dictionary of the History of Ideas,* ed. Philip P. Wiener (New York: Scribner, 1974), vol. 4, p. 410. Totalitarianism "is part of the modernizing process of nations and societies in the age of mass democracy, bureaucracy, and pseudo-religious ideologies."

25. See, for example, William Ebenstein,*Totalitarianism: New Perspectives* (New York: Holt, Rinehart and Winston, 1962), sponsored by the American Jewish Committee and the National Council for Social Studies; and Betty B. Burch, ed., *Dictatorship and Totalitarianism: Selected Readings* (Princeton, N.J.: D. Van Nostrand, 1964).

26. See R. R. Palmer, *History of the Modern World* (New York: Knopf, 1950), pp. 781ff. In the fourth edition (1971), the communization of Eastern Europe and the Chinese Revolution were also described under the rubric of totalitarianism. See R. R. Palmer and Joel Colton, *History of the Modern World* (New York: Knopf, 1971), pp. 804, 862–877, 940–946, 949.

27. Werner Haftmann, *Painting in the Twentieth Century* (New York: Praeger, 1960), vol. 1, p. 303. The first German edition was published by Prestel Verlag in Munich and appeared in 1954/1955, and the principal passage on "totalitarian art" appears on pp. 420–426 in vol. 1. The concept of totalitarian art enjoys considerable popularity among art critics from the former Soviet Union. See Igor Golomstock, *Totalitarian Art* (New York: HarperCollins, 1990).

28. In discussions of "totalitarian art," the essay by Clement Greenberg, "The Avant-Garde and Kitsch," *Partisan Review,* Fall 1939, pp. 34–49, was fundamental.

29. Haftmann, *Painting,* vol. 1, p. 303.

30. Ibid., p. 305.

31. Bauer, Inkeles, and Kluckhohn, *How the Soviet System Works,* p. 20. See also Raymond A. Bauer, with Edward Wasiolek, *Nine Soviet Portraits* (Cambridge, Mass.: MIT Press, 1955).

32. *How the Soviet System Works* was a revised version of a report, *Strategic Psychological Strengths and Vulnerabilities of the Soviet Social System,* originally prepared for the U.S. Air Force. According to a later analyst, the air force project "drew data from 329 extended life-history interviews, including detailed personality tests; 435 supplementary interviews; almost 10,000 questionnaires on special topics; 2,700 general questionnaires, and 100 interviews and psychological tests, administered, for

control purposes, to a matched group of Americans" (Daniel Bell, "Ten Theories in Search of Reality," *World Politics,* April 1958, p. 348).

33. Tucker's paper, "Towards a Comparative Politics of Movement Regimes," was published in *American Political Science Review,* June 1961, pp. 281–289, and subsequently anthologized with minor changes in *The Soviet Political Mind: Studies in Stalinism and Post-Stalin Change* (New York: Praeger, 1963), pp. 3–20. I quote from the journal article version, p. 281.

34. Tucker, "Towards a Comparative Politics," pp. 282, 288–289.

35. Ibid., p. 283.

36. An older generation of scholars, critical of American policies in one way or another, suddenly moved from the margins to the center of debate. C. Wright Mills was one, *The Causes of World War III* (New York: Simon and Schuster, 1958); and William Appleman Williams, *The Tragedy of American Diplomacy* (Cleveland: World, 1959), was another.

37. Nigel Young, *An Infantile Disorder? The Crisis and Decline of the New Left* (Boulder, Colo.: Westview Press, 1977), p. 16.

38. An impressionistic history of SDS and a number of important documents (some, unfortunately, edited) can be found in G. Louis Heath, *Vandals in the Bomb Factory: The History and Literature of the Students for a Democratic Society* (Metuchen, N.J.: Scarecrow Press, 1976). Jim Miller's study, *Democracy Is in the Streets* (New York: Simon and Schuster, 1987), is more recent and authoratative.

39. The relevant part of the constitution originally read: "SDS is an organization of democrats. It is civil libertarian in its treatment of those with whom it disagrees, but clear in its opposition to any totalitarian principle as a basis for government or social organization." In June 1965, "totalitarian" was changed to "antidemocratic." See Todd Gitlin, *The Sixties: Years of Hope, Days of Rage* (New York: Bantam, 1987), p. 190; Young, *Infantile Disorder?* p. 174; and Irwin Unger, *The Movement: A History of the American New Left, 1959–1972* (New York: Harper & Row, 1974), pp. 88–89.

40. Gitlin, *Sixties,* p. 175. Sidney Hook was sometimes used as a particularly pathological personification of liberal anti-Communism, whose fanaticism made him laughable (p. 176). At the same time, conservatives were quite won over by the same quality, so that whereas Hook considered himself a liberal or even a socialist, most of his admirers were conservative.

41. Young, *Infantile Disorder?* p. 343.

42. For a careful discussion of the connection between containment policy and American military action in East Asia, see John Lewis Gaddis, "The Defensive Perimeter Strategy in East Asia," in *The Origins of the Cold War,* ed. Thomas G. Patterson and Robert J. McMahon (Lexington, Mass.: Heath, 1991), pp. 257–274. See also John Lewis Gaddis, *Strategies of Containment* (Oxford: Oxford University Press, 1982).

43. "Look at all the hate there is in Red China / Then take a look around at Selma, Alabama" (P. F. Sloan, "Eve of Destruction," quoted in Gitlin, *Sixties,* p. 196).

44. This, for example, is the general view of a late revisionist work by Daniel Yergin, *Shattered Peace: The Origins of the Cold War and the National Security State* (Boston: Houghton Mifflin, 1977).

45. See, in particular, Joyce Kolko and Gabriel Kolko, *The Limits of Power: The World and United States Foreign Policy, 1945–1954* (New York: Harper & Row, 1972), passim.

46. Unger, *Movement*, p. 19.

47. Hannah Arendt, *Origins of Totalitarianism* (1951; New York: Harcourt Brace Jovanovich, 1973), p. xxv.

48. As noted by Martin Malia, "From Under the Rubble, What?" *Problems of Communism*, January–April 1992, esp. pp. 94–99. See Alex Inkeles, "Models and Issues in the Analysis of Soviet Society," *Survey*, July 1966, pp. 3–17; and Robert Tucker, "On the Comparative Study of Communism," *World Politics*, January 1967, p. 242, in which the author stresses the necessity of employing "contemporary social sciences" in understanding Communism.

49. Frederic Fleron, "Soviet Area Studies and the Social Sciences: Some Methodological Problems in Communist Studies," *Soviet Studies*, January 1968, p. 339.

50. "As the social sciences develop more discriminating concepts of comparison," wrote Herbert J. Spiro in an influential formulation, "as the developing political systems discover that the invention of new methods of modernization may obviate their need for slavishly copying more coercive methods from models whose experience is no longer relevant, and as, hopefully, the more glaring differences between the major parties parties to the cold war begin to wither away, use of the term 'totalitarianism' may also become less frequent. If these expectations are borne out, then a third encyclopedia of the social sciences, like the first one, will not list 'totalitarianism' " ("Totalitarianism," *International Encyclopedia of the Social Sciences* [New York: Macmillan and Free Press, 1968–1976], vol. 16, p. 112).

51. Inkeles, "Models and Issues," p. 3, quoted in Chalmers Johnson, ed., *Change in Communist Systems* (Stanford, Calif.: Stanford University Press, 1970), p. 2.

52. An early proponent of using "systematic political science" to study Communist regimes, Robert Sharlet opined that to do so successfully would be an "uphill struggle," but "not a Sisyphean task" ("Systematic Political Science and Communist Systems," *Slavic Review*, March 1967, p. 26). In setting out the problem of how to define a Communist system, Sharlet provided six points of his own, which may be interestingly compared with those of Brzezinski and Friedrich, formulated more than a decade earlier: "(1) a Communist political system is set within a 'closed society,' a society relatively inaccessible to the Western social scientist; (2) a Communist system has no autonomous subsystems; (3) the major political resources, that is, strategic political positions, are concentrated in the hands of a narrow elite stratum that enjoys hegemony over the policy-making process; (4) the policy-making process is not directly observable or accessible to reliable methods of investigation; (5) the structures, functions, and roles in a Communist system tend to be relatively undifferentiated; (6) boundaries between a Communist political and social system tend to be weak or nonexistent" (pp. 22–23). Whether this is a brilliant capsule definition or maddeningly abstract, I will leave to the social scientists. There is no question, however, about its value-free quality. Coercion is never mentioned.

53. Alexander Groth, "The 'Isms in Totalitarianism," *American Political Science Review*, December 1964, p. 888.

54. H. Gordon Skilling, "Interest Groups and Communist Politics," *World Politics,* April 1966, p. 435. It appeared, in slightly revised form, in an influential collection edited by Skilling and Franklyn Griffiths, *Interest Groups in Soviet Politics* (Princeton, N.J.: Princeton University Press, 1971). For a sense of the debate, a valuable bibliography, and an effective statement of the opposing view, see William E. Odom, "A Dissenting View on the Group Approach to Soviet Politics," *World Politics,* July 1976, pp. 542–567, and the same author's "Choice and Change in Soviet Politics," *Problems of Communism,* May–June 1983, pp. 1–21.

55. See the discussion in Jeffrey W. Hahn, "Conceptualizing Political Participation in the USSR: Two Decades of Debate," Occasional Paper of the Kennan Institute, no. 190 (Washington, D.C.: Kennan Institute for Advanced Russian Studies, 1984), pp. 2ff.

56. Jerry F. Hough, "The 'Dark Forces,' the Totalitarian Model, and Soviet History," *Russian Review,* October 1987, p. 399.

57. John Armstrong's concluding remarks from an important *Slavic Review* symposium, March 1967, p. 27.

58. Fleron, "Soviet Area Studies," p. 334.

59. Ibid., p. 329.

60. Johnson, ed., *Change in Communist Systems.*

61. Ibid., pp. 1–2.

62. Ibid., pp. 25–26.

63. He also used Robert Tucker's term, "movement regimes." See Richard Lowenthal, "Development vs. Utopia in Communist Policy," in *Change in Communist Systems,* ed. Johnson, p. 35.

64. Ibid., pp. 49–50.

65. Ibid., p. 54. Thirteen years later, Lowenthal's views had not changed markedly. He still saw the same exhaustion of the transforming element of regimes that had been called totalitarian. By this time, however, a new term had been coined to describe them: *posttotalitarian.* See Richard Lowenthal, "Beyond Totalitarianism," in *1984 Revisited: Totalitarianism in Our Century,* ed. Irving Howe (New York: Harper & Row, 1983), pp. 209–267.

66. See Jerry F. Hough, *The Soviet Prefects: The Local Party Organs in Industrial Decision-Making* (Cambridge, Mass.: Harvard University Press, 1969); and, in particular, his *The Soviet Union and Social Science Theory* (Cambridge, Mass.: Harvard University Press, 1977), and *How the Soviet Union Is Governed,* a revision of Merle Fainsod's *How Russia Is Ruled* that attracted the ire of many defenders of the totalitarian model.

67. See H. Gordon Skilling, "Interest Groups and Communist Politics Revisited," *World Politics,* October 1983, pp. 1–27; and Susan Gross Solomon, *Pluralism in the Soviet Union: Essays in Honour of H. Gordon Skilling* (London: Macmillan, 1983).

68. Malia, "From Under the Rubble, What?" p. 98.

69. For a nuanced discussion of the difference between participation in Western democracies and participation in the Soviet Union, see Juan Linz, "Totalitarian and Authoritarian Systems," *Macropolitical Theory,* vol. 3 of *Handbook of Political Science,*

ed. Fred I. Greenstein and Nelson Polsby (Reading, Mass.: Addison-Wesley, 1975), pp. 191–194.

70. Hough, *Soviet Union and Social Science Theory,* pp. vii–xi, 1–5, 19–215, 109–124, 222–239.

71. Hough, "The 'Dark Forces,' " pp. 397–398.

72. Some scholars tried to combine new social science points of view with the older literature. A particularly successful example is Linz, "Totalitarian and Authoritarian Systems," pp. 175–411.

73. James Burnham, *Containment or Liberation?* (New York: Day, 1953), quoted in Jerome L. Himmelstein, *To the Right* (Berkeley: University of California Press, 1990), p. 39.

74. Leonard Schapiro, *The Communist Party of the Soviet Union* (New York: Random House, 1960), and *The Origin of the Communist Autocracy: Political Opposition in the Soviet State: First Phase, 1917–1922* (New York: Praeger, 1965). In the former, Schapiro wrote that "the 'atomization of society,' which some have seen as the most characteristic feature of totalitarian rule, was completed in the years of the terror" (p. 431). In the latter, Schapiro expressed his hope that the Russians would not have to live under "totalitarian rule" forever (p. ix). In 1972 Schapiro wrote a book about the concept, which suggested his continuing belief in its utility but also that the debates about it over the previous decade had suggested to him that there were other ways to discuss Communist regimes. See *Totalitarianism* (New York: Praeger, 1972), esp. pp. 118–125.

75. An ambitious earlier effort to stress the continuity of Soviet Russia with the Tsarist past was Ernest J. Simmons, *Continuity and Change in Russian and Soviet Thought* (Cambridge, Mass.: Harvard University Press, 1955). One of the best statements that historical Russian insecurity has played an important role in Soviet expansionism remains Louis J. Halle, *The Cold War as History* (New York: Harper & Row, 1967). Theodore Von Laue made a persuasive case for the argument from "backwardness" in a global struggle with "the West" in *Why Lenin? Why Stalin? A Reappraisal of the Russian Revolution 1900–1930* (Philadelphia: Lippincott, 1964).

76. "Within the confines of the so-called 'totalitarian model' it is hard enough to conceptualize 'development' and its consequences—that is, to say at what rate a communist regime is moving toward achieving some or all of its self-proclaimed, ideologically circumscribed socioeconomic investment goals. It is even harder to conceptualize the resulting unintended changes in the social structure and the consequences of those changes" (Johnson, ed., *Change in Communist Systems,* p. 2).

77. Stephen E. Cohen, *Bukharin and the Bolshevik Revolution: A Political Biography, 1888–1938* (New York: Knopf, 1974).

78. Ibid., pp. 386–387.

79. Stephen F. Cohen, "Bolshevism and Stalinism," in *Stalinism: Essays in Historical Interpretation,* ed. Robert C. Tucker (New York: Norton, 1977), pp. 3–29.

80. This assertion differed from the usual perspective, in which both Stalin and Trotsky were understood to be "left," rapid industrializers, with Bukharin on the other side. No one, of course, knew what Trotsky would have done confronted with the economic dilemmas of 1929, but scholars have generally assumed he would have been less extreme than Stalin. A similar position is taken by Robert Tucker in

"Stalinism Versus Bolshevism? A Reconsideration," Colloquium Paper (Washington, D.C.: Kennan Institute for Advanced Russian Studies, 1984).

81. This point was recently conceded by Martin Malia. "The old debate," he wrote, "about whether October was a proletarian revolution or a *coup d'état* . . . was really a debate about the legitimacy of the Soviet regime" ("Why Amalrik Was Right," *Times Literary Supplement,* November 6, 1992, p. 9). Richard Pipes now agrees. See his "1917 and Revisionists," *National Interest,* Spring 1993, p. 69.

82. Alexander Rabinowitch, *The Bolsheviks Come to Power: The Revolution of 1917 in Petrograd* (New York: Norton, 1976).

83. Cohen, "Bolshevism and Stalinism," p. 17.

84. Ibid., p. 16.

85. Ibid., pp. 15–16.

86. Sheila Fitzgerald, "The Civil War as a Formative Experience" (Paper delivered at the Kennan Institute for Advanced Russian Studies, May 1981). It appears in Abbott Gleason, Peter Kenez, and Richard Stites, eds., *Bolshevik Culture: Experiment and Order in the Russian Revolution* (Bloomington: Indiana University Press, 1985), pp. 57–74, quote from p. 74.

87. Sheila Fitzpatrick, "New Perspectives on Stalinism," *Russian Review,* October 1986, p. 358.

88. See, in particular, Sheila Fitzpatrick, *Cultural Revolution in Russia, 1928–1931* (Bloomington: Indiana University Press, 1978); *Education and Social Mobility in the Soviet Union, 1921–1934* (Cambridge: Cambridge University Press, 1979); and *Russian Revolution* (New York: Oxford University Press, 1982). See also J. Arch Getty, *Origins of the Great Purges: The Soviet Communist Party Reconsidered, 1933–1938* (Cambridge: Cambridge University Press, 1985); Roberta Manning, "Government in the Soviet Countryside in the Stalinist Thirties: The Case of Belyi Raion in 1937," *Carl Beck Papers in Russian and East European Studies,* no. 301 (Pittsburgh, n.d.); and Lynn Viola, *The Best Sons of the Fatherland: Workers in the Vanguard of Soviet Collectivization* (New York: Oxford University Press, 1987).

89. Fitzpatrick and some of her colleagues, prominently Roberta Manning of Boston College, are—or were—distinctly people of the Left. Involved in the criticism of their work—almost always beneath the surface—has been a certain amount of animus left over from the wars of the 1960s. They have also been notably at odds with political émigrés.

90. Fitzpatrick, *Cultural Revolution in Russia,* p. 4.

91. Although it seems to me most unfair to characterize such a view as "soft Stalinism," as Malia did ("From Under the Rubble, What?" p. 100).

92. Stephen Cohen, "Stalin's Terror as Social History," *Russian Review,* October 1986, p. 378.

93. Peter Kenez, "Stalinism as Humdrum Politics," *Russian Review,* October 1986, p. 399.

94. Geoff Eley, "History with the Politics Left Out—Again?" *Russian Review,* October 1986, p. 392.

95. Ibid., p. 394.

96. Spearheading the academic revival was Martin Malia. See his pseudonymous

"To the Stalin Mausoleum," *Daedalus,* Winter 1990, pp. 295–340 (the author is disguised as "Z," perhaps to suggest George Kennan's earlier "X"), as well as "From Under the Rubble, What?" pp. 89–106.

CHAPTER EIGHT

1. The new word *totalitarian* was perfectly suited to describe both Bolshevism and Fascism, Boris Souvarine wrote, because "these movements show so many similarities, and are open to so many mutual plagiarisms, they borrow and exchange so many things from one another" (*Staline: Aperçu historique du bolchévisme,* rev. ed.[Paris: Plon, 1935], vol. 2, p. 611). The brilliant religious and social thinker Simone Weil picked up the term from Souvarine's biography. See Simone Weil, "Reflections Concerning the Causes of Liberty and Social Oppression," in *Oppression and Liberty* (London: Routledge and Paul, 1958), p. 83; and David McClellan, *Utopian Pessimist: The Life and Thought of Simone Weil* (New York: Simon and Schuster, 1990), pp. 81–87, 90, 125, 132, 142, 146, 156, 228, 239–241, 252, 258, 275.

2. "Demofilo" [Alcide De Gasperi], *Tradizione e "ideologia" della Democrazia Cristiani* (Rome, 1944), pp. 17–18, quoted in Mario Einaudi and François Goguel, *Christian Democracy in Italy and France* (South Bend, Ind.: Notre Dame University Press, 1952), p. 33.

3. "After April 1944, the image of the PCI [Italian Communist Party] as an insidious force opposing the Allies and Democracy, and as a tool of Soviet policy in Italy, became America's *ideé fixe* in Italy" (Ennio di Nolfo, "The United States and the PCI: The Years of Policy Formation, 1942–1946," in *The Italian Communist Party: Yesterday, Today, and Tomorrow,* ed. Simon Serfaty and Lawrence Gray [Westport, Conn.: Greenwood Press, 1980], p. 48).

4. A Communist version of the argument was Lelio Basso, *Due totalitarismi: Fascismo e Democrazia Cristiani* (Milan: Garzanti, 1951).

5. A number of future Christian Democratic leaders, notably Amintore Fanfani, had strongly sympathized with various Fascist doctrines: corporativism, imperialism, and racism. See Richard Webster, *The Cross and the Fasces* (Stanford, Calif.: Stanford University Press, 1960), esp. chap. 12.

6. Robert Leonardi and Douglas Wertman, *Italian Christian Democracy: The Politics of Dominance* (New York: St. Martin's Press, 1989), p. 7.

7. Palmiro Togliatti, "Totalitarismo?" *Rinascita,* November–December 1946, reprinted in Togliatti, *Linea d'una politica* (Milan: Sera Editrice, 1948), pp. 87–94.

8. Ibid., pp. 88–89, 93.

9. Palmiro Togliatti, "Considerazioni Sul 18 Aprile," *Rinascita,* April–May 1948, p. 137.

10. Simon Serfaty, "The United States and the PCI: The Year of Decision, 1947," in *Italian Communist Party,* ed. Serfaty and Gray, p. 60.

11. Economic incentives alone did not bring about such close Italian–American cooperation on the issue of Italian Communism. The role of the Catholic Church was essential. According to two American political scientists, "the assumption by Italy of a subordinate, cue-taking role in foreign affairs was the mechanism by which

Italy recognised the military and political outcome of the Second World War and effectively ended its international isolation" (Leonardi and Wertman, *Italian Christian Democracy,* pp. 6, 246–247).

12. Quoted in ibid., p. 66.

13. Ibid., p. 70.

14. For the Christian Democratic point of view on the 1948 elections of the socialist split into "democratic" and "totalitarian" factions, see Francesco Campagna, *La lotta politica italiana nel secondo dopoguerra e il Mezzogiorno* (Bari: Latedrza i Figli, 1950), pp. 114–128, esp. p. 118. In his introduction to Piero Malvestiti's *La lotta politica in Italia* (Milan: Casa Editrice Bernabò, n.d. [1948]), Pio Bondoli wrote that "the peril of tyranny yesterday was from the right; today it is from the left. Fascism and communism, 'lineal' descendants of Hegel's ethical state, meet again and fuse into the totalitarian and police state, to oppress the individual and negate personal dignity" (p. xi). See also Piero Fossi, "Due antifascismi," *Il Momento,* February 1948, reprinted in Fossi, *La lotta per la liberta* (Florence: Uniedit, 1980), pp. 102–103.

15. Quoted in Giuseppi Maranini, *Socialismo non Stalinismo* (Florence: All'-insegna di alvernia, 1949), p. vi.

16. Alcide De Gasperi, *Discorsi parlamentari (1921–1949)* (Rome: Camera dei deputati, Segreterai generale, 1985), vol. 1, p. 413.

17. Togliatti, "Totalitarismo?" p. 93. Later on, Togliatti often used the term *totalitarianism* to refer to the statification of Italian Fascism after 1925. See his *Lezioni sul Fascismo* (Rome: Riuniti, 1970); and the discussion of this book in Renzo De Felice, *Interpretations of Fascism* (Cambridge, Mass.: Harvard University Press, 1977), pp. 149–151.

18. An August 1945 document of the MRP, quoted in Einaudi and Goguel, *Christian Democracy,* p. 129.

19. "Russian Menace Like German May Mean War, de Gaulle Says," *New York Times,* July 10, 1947, p. 3.

20. "English writers of the *avant-garde,*" wrote Raymond Aron a few years later, "whose names are probably unknown in the House of Commons, are overcome with rapture when they come to Paris and settle down in Saint-Germain-des-Prés. They at once develop a passionate interest in politics, a subject the dispiriting sobriety of which at home discourages their attention. And indeed the discussions they will hear in Paris are elaborated with a subtlety that cannot but enthrall those who live by the mind. The last article of Jean-Paul Sartre is a political event, or at least is greeted as such by a circle of people which, though narrow, is convinced of its own importance. The political ambitions of successful French novelists collide with the literary ambitions of French statesmen, who dream of writing novels just as the others dream of becoming Ministers" (*The Opium of the Intellectuals* [Garden City, N.Y.: Doubleday, 1957], p. 219).

21. David Rousset, *L'Univers concentrationnaire* (Paris: Edition du Pavois, 1946), published in English as *A World Apart* (London: Secker and Warburg, 1951).

22. Rousset's split with Sartre came in November 1949, when he publicly advocated a commission of inquiry to look into the existence of Soviet camps. The results were later disseminated in French, English, and Italian. See David Rousset, *Police-*

State Methods in the Soviet Union (Boston: Beacon Press, 1953), and *Coercion of the Worker in the Soviet Union* (Boston: Beacon Press, 1953). On Merleau-Ponty, see his *Les Aventures de la dialectique* (Paris: Gallimard, 1955). There is a good discussion of his break with Sartre in Barry Cooper, *Merleau-Ponty and Marxism: From Terror to Reform* (Toronto: University of Toronto Press, 1979), pp. 107–133.

23. Quoted in Raymond Aron, *Memoirs: Fifty Years of Political Reflection* (New York: Holmes & Meier, 1990), p. 246.

24. For an erudite and stimulating essay on why this should have been so, see Tony Judt, *Past Imperfect: French Intellectuals, 1944–1956* (Berkeley: University of California Press, 1992).

25. Elie Halévy, *The Era of Tyrannies* (Garden City, N.Y.: Doubleday, 1965), p. 266.

26. Raymond Aron, "L'Ere des tyrannies d'Elie Halévy," *Revue de métaphysique et de morale* 46: 283–307, reprinted in *Commentaire* 8 (1985): 28–40.

27. Ibid., pp. 283–284, quoted in Robert Colquhoun, *Raymond Aron*, vol. 1: *The Philosopher in History, 1905–1955* (London: Sage, 1986), p. 188.

28. Ibid., pp. 190–192.

29. Raymond Aron, "Etats démocratiques et états totalitaires," *Bulletin de la Société française de philosophie* 40 (1946): 41–92. An abridged edition was published in *Commentaire* 6 (1983–1984): 701–717. Because the original article did not appear in print until 1946, its impact was limited.

30. Colquhoun, *Raymond Aron*, vol. 1, p. 194.

31. Ibid., vol. 2, p. 149.

32. Raymond Aron, *Le Grand Schisme* (Paris: Gallimard, 1948).

33. Among the few French intellectuals expressing similar similar views was Jules Monnerot. See his *Sociologie du communisme* (Paris: Gallimard, 1949), published in English as *Sociology of Communism* (London: Allen & Unwin, 1953). On Monnerot's views, see Robert Desjardins, *The Soviet Union Through French Eyes, 1945–85* (New York: St. Martin's Press, 1988), pp. 67–68.

34. Aron, *Le Grand Schisme*, pp. 13–97; Colquhoun, *Raymond Aron*, vol. 1, pp. 65–72.

35. Raymond Aron, *Les Guerres en chaîne* (Paris: Gallimard, 1951), p. 104, published in English as *The Century of Total War* (Garden City, N.Y.: Doubleday, 1954), pp. 89–90.

36. Aron, *Les Guerres en chaîne*, pp. 466–485. (This section, "Le totalitarisme," is omitted in the English translation.)

37. On Aron's relations with the congress, see Peter Coleman, *The Liberal Conspiracy* (New York: Free Press, 1989), pp. 38–43, 49–51, and passim.

38. Aron, *Opium of the Intellectuals*, p. xiii.

39. Ibid., p. 14. Aron thought it possible to argue, as Talmon had, that one could distinguish between right-wing and left-wing totalitarianism, but without discussing the matter systematically, he tended to regard the Soviet regime as continuing to shed its Enlightenment inheritance.

40. Ibid., p. 21, quoted in Colquhoun, *Raymond Aron*, vol. 1, p. 460.

41. Colquhoun, *Raymond Aron*, vol. 1, pp. 479–480.

42. Raymond Aron, "Une Révolution antitotalitaire," *Preuves*, December 1957, pp. i–xiii, reprinted in Melvin J. Lasky and François Bondy, *La Révolution hongroise: Histoire du soulèvement d'octobre* (Paris: Plon, 1957), pp. i–xiv. For the publishing history of this important article, see Colquhoun, *Raymond Aron*, vol. 2, pp. 616–617. On the Sorbonne lectures, published in English as *Democracy and Totalitarianism* (Ann Arbor: University of Michigan Press, 1968), see Colquhoun, *Raymond Aron*, vol. 2, pp. 137–161.

43. Aron, *Democracy and Totalitarianism*, pp. xiii, 217–229.

44. Annie Kriegel has written extensively on the French Communist Party. Several of Martin Malia's works are referred to in Chapter 7. Alain Basançon, like Kriegel, was a former radical. Among his other works, see, in particular, *The Soviet Syndrome*, with a forward by Aron (New York: Harcourt Brace Jovanovich, 1978), and *The Rise of the Gulag* (New York: Continuum, 1981). The French title, *Les Origines intellectuelles du leninisme*, gives a better idea of the book's content. A Norwegian student of Aron's, Jon Elster, believed that "Aron never felt quite at home in his own seminar," due to the "shrillness" of the anti-Communism expressed especially by Kriegel and Besançon. Aron, Elster thought, was "more disposed to consider Marx and Marxism serious intellectual challenges" ("Rules of the Game," review of French edition of *Memoirs*, by Aron, *London Review of Books*, December 22, 1983, p. 6). I owe this reference to Colquhoun, *Raymond Aron*, vol. 2, p. 367.

45. See, for example, Besançon, *Soviet Syndrome*, pp. 91–93. In some of his later writings in particular, Aron bordered on such a characterization. For the strain in Aron's writings that particularly emphasizes ideology as fundamental to totalitarianism, see the discussion in Desjardins, *Soviet Union Through French Eyes*, pp. 69–70.

46. Desjardins, *Soviet Union Through French Eyes*, p. 80.

47. On the seminar, see Colquhoun, *Raymond Aron*, vol. 2, pp. 367–369.

48. Most of Pierre Hassner's work has been in the form of essays. See, for example, "Western European Perceptions of the USSR," *Daedalus*, Winter 1979, pp. 113–151; "American Foxes and French Hedgehogs," *Studies in Comparative Communism*, Winter 1982, pp. 365–373; and "Le Totalitarisme vu de l'ouest," in *Totalitarismes*, ed. Guy Hermet (Paris: Economica, 1984), pp. 15–41. On Aron's recollected impression of Hassner's early brilliance, shortly after he emigrated to France from Romania, see Aron, *Memoirs*, pp. 236–237.

49. Hassner, "Le Totalitarisme vu de l'ouest," esp. pp. 35–37; Desjardins, *Soviet Union Through French Eyes*, p. 78.

50. The most useful biography is by Herbert Lottman, *Albert Camus* (Garden City, N.Y.: Doubleday, 1979).

51. In 1948, Camus wrote scornfully to a pro-Soviet journalist of "a prodigious myth of the divinisation of man, of domination, of the unification of the universe by the powers of human reason alone. What has caused it is the *conquest of the totality*, and Russia believes itself to be the instrument of this messianism without God" (quoted in Eric Werner, *De la violence au totalitarismes* [Paris: Calmann-Lévy, 1972], p. 51 [italics added]).

52. Albert Camus, *L'Etranger* (Paris: Gallimard, 1942).

53. Werner, *De la violence au totalitarisme*, p. 31.

54. Elisabeth Young-Bruehl, *For Love of the World* (New Haven, Conn.: Yale

University Press, 1982), p. 281. The remark occurs in a letter and was not perhaps very considered.

55. Reprinted in Albert Camus, *Actuelles: Chroniques, 1944–1948* (Paris: Gallimard, 1950), pp. 141–179.

56. Initially he accepted Merleau-Ponty's argument that the end could justify the means; then he changed his mind. Arthur Koestler, then visiting Paris, was an active and influential participant in the circle that included Sartre, Camus, and Merleau-Ponty. Koestler was deeply, although still ambiguously, anti-Communist, and Camus began to incline toward his positions. See Lottman, *Albert Camus,* pp. 403–405. For the powerful impact of Koestler's *Darkness at Noon* even on people who came to disagree with it, see Kerry Whiteside, *Merleau-Ponty and the Foundations of an Existential Politics* (Princeton, N.J.: Princeton University Press, 1988), pp. 167–181.

57. Lottman, *Albert Camus,* p. 405.

58. Albert Camus, *L'Homme révolté* (Paris: Gallimard, 1951), published in English as *The Rebel* (New York: Knopf, 1956).

59. Germaine Brée, *Camus and Sartre: Crisis and Commitment* (New York: Delacorte Press, 1972), pp. 206–207.

60. Quoted in ibid., p. 211.

61. Albert Camus, *La Peste* (Paris: Gallimard, 1947), and *Les Justes* (Paris: Gallimard, 1950).

62. Lottman, *Albert Camus,* pp. 447–448; Camus, *Actuelles,* pp. 201–202. D'Astier de la Vigerie, like a surprising number of postwar French Communists and Communist sympathizers, had been a rightist. See Tony Judt, *Past Imperfect* (Berkeley: University of California Press, 1992), p. 64.

63. Lottman, *Albert Camus,* pp. 458–461. Camus and his friends drafted and signed a manifesto promoting their efforts to provide relief for the victims of totalitarianism.

64. Camus, *L'Homme révolté,* p. 301; *The Rebel,* pp. 244–245.

65. Camus, *The Rebel,* pp. 175–176.

66. Ibid., pp. 112–132. On Rousseau and the general will, see esp. p. 116.

67. Martin Jay, *Marxism and Totality: The Adventures of a Concept from Lukács to Habermas* (Berkeley: University of California Press, 1984), p. 21.

68. For a sample of reviewers' opinions, see Lottman, *Albert Camus,* pp. 496–500.

69. Francis Jeanson, "A. Camus, ou l'Ame révoltée," *Temps modernes,* May 1952, pp. 2077–2090. On the attack and the responses to it, see Werner, *De la violence au totalitarisme,* pp. 10–11, 32–33, 231–239; Brée, *Camus and Sartre,* pp. 207, 247; Germaine Brée, *Camus* (New Brunswick, N.J.: Rutgers University Press, 1959), pp. 192, 218; and Lottman, *Albert Camus,* pp. 501–503.

70. See the discussion in Werner, *De la violence au totalitarisme,* p. 33.

71. Jean-Paul Sartre, "Réponse à Albert Camus," *Temps modernes,* August 1952, pp. 334–353; David Caute, *Communism and the French Intellectuals, 1914–1918* (London: Andre Deutsch, 1964), p. 253.

72. Camus's reply to Jeanson, in *Temps modernes,* August 1952, pp. 317–333, re-

printed as Albert Camus, "Révolte et servitude," in *Actuelles II, Chroniques 1948–1953* (Paris: Gallimard, 1953), pp. 85–124.

73. Nicola Chiaramonte, "Paris Letter," *Partisan Review,* November–December 1952, p. 686.

74. On Camus's influence in Eastern Europe, see Robert Kostrzewa, *Between East and West: Writings from Kultura* (New York: Hill and Wang, 1990), p. x; Vladimir Tismaneanu, *The Crisis of Marxist Ideology in Eastern Europe* (London: Routledge & Kegan Paul, 1988), pp. 21, 73, 143; Adam Michnik, *The Church and the Left* (Chicago: University of Chicago Press, 1993), p. 212; and Leszek Kolakowski, *Main Currents of Marxism,* vol. 3: *The Breakdown* (Oxford: Clarendon Press, 1978), p. 463.

75. For an appreciation of Camus, Rousset, and the (late) Merleau-Ponty as opponents of "totalitarianism," see Bernard-Henri Lévy, *Barbarism with a Human Face* (New York: Harper & Row, 1979), p. 153. The "new philosophers" do not seem to have cared much for Raymond Aron, nor he for them. "They do not represent an original way of philosophizing," Aron wrote dismissively, " . . . they write essays outside university guidelines. Their success has been fostered by the media and by the absence in Paris of a judicious and recognized political position" (*Memoirs,* p. 443).

76. Lévy, *Barbarism with a Human Face.* The French original was published in 1977, just two years after *The Gulag Archipelago* first appeared in Paris. Lévy and André Glucksmann, the two best known of the "new philosophers," were former Maoists, students of the structuralist-Marxist Louis Althusser, and veterans of 1968. After the May events, "they became leaders of a Maoist grouplet that fancied itself the beginning of a new 'Resistance' in a France 'occupied' by the bourgeoisie. They advocated guerrilla warfare and 'peasant' revolution to overthrow the 'fascist' Pompidou regime. Very few activists heeded their call to 'take to the countryside' to build guerrilla bases. Even fewer French 'peasants' joined their 'long march' " (Arthur Hirsh, *The French New Left: An Intellectual History from Sartre to Gorz* [Boston: South End Press, 1981], p. 194).

77. In addition to Lévy's *Barbarism with a Human Face,* see André Glucksmann, *Les Maîtres penseurs* (Paris: Bernard Grasset, 1977), pp. 287–310 and passim.

78. Jean-François Revel, *Ni Marx ni Jésus* (Paris: Editions Robert Laffont, 1970), published in English as *Without Marx or Jesus* (Garden City, N.Y.: Doubleday, 1971), p. 25.

79. And that of Jean-Jacques Servan-Schreiber, *The American Challenge* (1968) and *The Radical Manifesto* (1970).

80. For the West German radical Petra Kelly, West German society in the 1970s and 1980s was "bankrupt"; there was no difference between East and West: "The system is the same" (quoted in Timothy Garton Ash, "The German Question," in his *The Uses of Adversity* (New York: Random House, 1989), p. 96.

81. Jean-François Revel, *La Tentation totalitaire* (Paris: Editions Robert Laffont, 1976). I quote from the English translation, *The Totalitarian Temptation* (Garden City, N.Y.: Doubleday, 1977), p. 23.

82. Revel, *Totalitarian Temptation*, p. 37.

83. See, for example, Jacques Fauvet, "Suicide socialiste?" *Le Monde*, January 13, 1976, p. 1; André Fontaine, "Les Paradoxes de Jean-François Revel: Brejnev maurassien," *Le Monde*, January 17, 1976, pp. 1, 6; and John Taylor, "The Wit and Wisdom of the Bull-Frog," *The Nation*, September 10, 1977, pp. 252–254. See also Revel's *La Nouvelle Censure: Exemple de mise en place d'une mentalité totalitaire* (Paris: Editions Robert Laffont, 1977).

84. Ugo Spirito, *Il Communismo* (Florence: Sansoni, 1965), pp. 31–57. Back in the 1930s, Spirito had written that "one does a disservice to Fascism in conceiving it antithetical to Bolshevism, as one might oppose good and evil or truth and error. . . . If today the energies of the political orientation [of our time] find expression in Fascism and Bolshevism, it is clear that the future belongs not to that regime which negates the other, but that which, of the two, has shown itself capable of incorporating and transcending the other in a more advanced form" (quoted in A. James Gregor, *The Ideology of Fascism* [New York: Free Press, 1969], p. 298).

85. See the essays of Augusto del Noce in Constanzo Castucci, *Il Fascismo: Antologia di scritti critici* (Bologna: Il Mulino, 1961); and the discussion in De Felice, *Interpretations of Fascism*, pp. 58–60, 71–75.

86. Alberto Aquarone, *L'organizzazione dello stato totalitario* (Turin: Einaudi, 1965). There was a second edition in 1974. An abridged English-language version of the conclusion may be found in Ernest A. Menze, ed., *Totalitarianism Reconsidered* (Port Washington, N.Y.: Kennikat Press, 1981), pp. 81–93. See also Meir Michaelis, "Anmerkungen zum italienischen Totalitarismusbegriff: Zur Kritik der Thesen Hannah Arendts and Renzo De Felices," *Quellen und Forschungen aus italienischen Archiven und Bibliotheken* 62 (1982): 279–280. See also Domenico Fisichella, *Analisi del Totalitarismo* (Messina–Florence: D'Anna, 1976). Fisichella defended the term against some of its earlier critics.

87. The quotation is from the introduction to De Felice, *Interpretations of Fascism*, p. ix. See also Renzo De Felice, *Mussolini il fascista*, vol. 2: *L'organizzazione dello stato fascista, 1925–1929* (Turin: Einaudi, 1968), pp. 9, 176–200, 297–304, 352–353, and *Mussolini il duce*, vol. 2: *Lo stato totalitario, 1936–1940* (Turin: Einaudi, 1981), in which the Fascist system is characterized as "imperfect totalitarianism" on pp. 3ff. The discussion in Michaelis, "Anmerkungen," pp. 280–292, is extremely helpful in guiding the reader through the maze of De Felice's various analyses.

88. Emilio Gentile, "Italian Right-Wing Radicalism: Myth and Organisation," in *Altro Polo: Intellectuals and Their Ideas in Contemporary Italy*, ed. Richard Bosworth and Gianfranco Cresciani (Sydney: University of Sydney Press, 1983), pp. 17–30. See also his *Le origini dell' ideologia fascista* (Rome: Laterza, 1975), and *Il mito dello stato nuovo dall'antigiolittismo al fascismo* (Bari: Laterza, 1982).

89. Emilio Gentile, "Fascism in Italian Historiography," *Journal of Contemporary History*, April 1986, p. 188. This viewpoint echoes the earlier conclusion of Dante Germino, a student of Carl Friedrich. "If correctly viewed," he wrote, arguing with Arendt's assertion that Fascist Italy had not been totalitarian, "totalitarianism is a process of becoming. Fascist Italy did not come as close to achieving its totalitarian *telos* as did Nazi Germany or the Soviet Union. But the strange men who ruled Italy

never took their eyes off the totalitarian target. Only the hand of time prevented the maturation of yet more monstrous projects, already conceived in the fertile minds of the Fascist leaders (*The Italian Fascist Party in Power* [Minneapolis: University of Minnesota Press, 1959], p. 144).

90. Wolfgang Wippermann, "The Post-War German Left and Fascism," *Journal of Contemporary History* 11 (1976): 193. For a similar quotation from Wippermann's article, see Ian Kershaw, *The Nazi Dictatorship: Problems and Perspectives of Interpretation* (London: Arnold, 1985), p. 12.

91. Kershaw, *Nazi Dictatorship*, p. 12. For a good, brief statement of the relationship between the political and nonpolitical usage of the term in Germany, see Günter Plum's introduction to *Totalitarismus und Faschismus* (Munich: Oldenbourg Verlag, 1980), pp. 7–9.

92. Wilhelm Röpke, *Die deutsche Frage* (Zurich: Rentsch Verlag, 1945). See also his *Civitas humana: Grundfragen der Gesellschafts- und Wirtschaftsreform* (Zurich: Rentsch Verlag, 1946).

93. Röpke, *Deutsche Frage*, pp. 31–32.

94. A much more forthright condemnation of the Nazi version of totalitarianism came from the liberal constitutional lawyer Gerhard Leibholz, who broadcast a lecture on the BBC from London in November 1946, calling it "the political phenomenon of the twentieth century." Leibholz's lecture was reprinted several times as "Das Phänomen des totalen Staates"; it is accessible in *Strukturprobleme der modernen Demokratie* (Karlsruhe: Verlag C. F. Müller, 1967), pp. 225–231, quotation from p. 225. It can also be found in an excellent anthology of writings on totalitarianism, Bruno Seidel and Siegfried Jenkner, eds., *Wege der Totalitarismus-Forschung* (Darmstadt: Wissenschaftliche Buchgesellschaft, 1968), pp. 123–132.

95. For a good, recent survey of postwar West German historiography on the Nazi period, see Konrad Kwiet, "Die NS-Zeit in der westdeutschen Forschung 1945–1961," in *Deutsche Geschichtswissenschaft nach dem Zweiten Weltkrieg (1945–1965)*, ed. Ernst Schulin (Munich: Oldenbourg Verlag, 1989), pp. 181–198.

96. Wippermann, "Post-War German Left and Fascism," pp. 186–187.

97. Hans Rothfels, *The German Opposition to Hitler* (Hinsdale, Ill.: Regnery, 1948). There is a later and enlarged German edition, *Die deutsche Opposition gegen Hitler* (Frankfurt: Fischer, 1958). In Italy, intellectuals like Benedetto Croce took the same line. See De Felice, *Interpretations of Fascism*, pp. 14–30.

98. Kwiet, "Die N-S Zeit," p. 191.

99. Quoted in De Felice, *Interpretations of Fascism*, p. 18.

100. Gerhard Ritter, *Europa und die deutsche Frage* (Munich: Münchner Verlag, 1948), pp. 53–195, passim. Ritter's view of Jacobin democracy as the forerunner of totalitarianism was close to that later made famous by Jacob Talmon. See Klaus Hildebrand, "Stufen der Totalitarismus-Forschung," *Politische Vierteljahresschrift*, September 1968, p. 398.

101. Hartmut Lehman and James Sheehan, *An Interrupted Past: German-Speaking Refugee Historians in the United States After 1933* (Washington, D.C.: German Historical Institute, and Cambridge: Cambridge University Press, 1991), pp. 211, 213; conversation with Volker Berghahn.

102. Karl Dietrich Bracher, with Wolfgang Sauer, *Die Auflösung der Weimarer Republik: Ein Studie zum Problem des Machtverfalls in der Demokratie* (Stuttgart: Ring Verlag, 1955); Karl Bracher, Wolfgang Sauer, and Gerhard Schulz, *Die national-sozialistische Machtergreifung: Studien zur Einrichtung des totalitären Herrschaftssystems in Deutschland 1933/34* (Cologne: Westdeutscher Verlag, 1960); Karl Bracher, *Die deutsche Diktatur: Entstehung, Struktur, Folgen des Nationalsozialismus* (Cologne: Verlag Kiepenheuer & Witsch, 1969), published in English as *The German Dictatorship* (New York: Praeger, 1970).

103. In addition to Friedrich and Brzezinski's *Totalitarian Dictatorship and Autocracy,* Bracher and co-authors refer approvingly to Sigmund Neumann's *Permanent Revolution: The Total State in a World at War* (New York: Harper and Bros., 1942). See Bracher, Sauer, and Schulz, *Die national-sozialistische Machtergreifung,* pp. 9–15.

104. Bracher et al., *Die national-sozialistische Machtergreifung,* pp. 6–7.

105. There are numerous surveys of the literature in German. See Seidel and Jenkner, eds., *Wege,* pp. 197 ff.; Hildebrand, "Stufen der Totalitarismus-Forschung," pp. 397–427.

106. Max Gustav Lange, *Totalitäre Erziehung: Das Erziehungssystem der Sowjetzone Deutschlands* (Frankfurt: Verlag der Frankfurter Nefte, 1954). See also Ernst Richert, *Macht ohne Mandat: Der Staatsapparat in der SBZ Deutschlands* (Cologne: Westdeutscher Verlag, 1958). See especially the introduction by Martin Drath, "Totalitarismus in der Volksdemokratie," pp. ix–xxxiv.

107. For some citations to this literature, see Martin Greiffenhagen, Reinhard Kühnl, and Johann Baptist Müller, *Totalitarismus: Zur Problematik eines politischen Begriffs* (Munich: List Verlag, 1972), p. 23, nn. 2 and 3. For a sociological study of German youth between 1945 and 1955 that uses the term extensively, see Helmut Schelsky, *Die skeptische Generation: Eine Soziologie der deutschen Jugend* (Düsseldorf: E. Diederich, 1957, pp. 438–440, 458–459, and passim.

108. Carl J. Friedrich, "Freiheit und Verantwortung: Zum Problem des demokratischen Totalitarismus," *Hamburger Jahrbuch für Wirtschafts- und Gesellschaftspolitik* 4(1959): 124ff., cited in Hildebrand, "Stufen der Totalitarismus-Forschung," p. 415. See also Richard Lowenthal's plea that the category be made to encompass the dynamism of totalitarian regimes: "Totalitäre und demokratische Revolution," *Der Monat,* November 1960, pp. 29ff.

109. By the early 1970s, even a determined defender of the category wondered. "Evidently," wrote Karl Dietrich Bracher, "a modern dictatorship cannot be reduced to a few variables" ("Totalitarianism," in *Dictionary of the History of Ideas,* ed. Philip. P. Wiener [New York: Scribner, 1973], vol. 4, p. 409).

110. Hildebrand, "Stufen der Totalitarismus-Forschung," p. 416.

111. Ludz was a man of many interests, including political science, sociology, philosophy, and intellectual history. He was quite at home among American scholars as well as German ones. He took his own life in 1979. See *Kölner Zeitschrift für Soziologie und Sozialpsychologie* 31 (1979): 822–824, 33 (1981): 207–208; and G. L. Ulmen, "Peter Christian Ludz (1931–1979): Foreward and Farewell," *Telos,* Fall 1979, pp. 172–175.

112. Peter Christian Ludz, "Offene Fragen in der Totalitarismus-Forschung,"

Politische Vierteljahresschrift, December 1961, pp. 319–348, esp. p. 321. His article was later reprinted in Seidel and Jenkner, eds., *Wege,* pp. 466–512.

113. Ludz stressed this in another article, published the same year. See his "Totalitarismus oder Totalität? (Zur Erforschung bolschewistischer Gesellschafts- und Herrschaftssysteme)," *Soziale Welt* 12 (1961): 129–145. He suggested at the end that the concept of the "totalitarian" might be supplemented analytically by the concept of the "total" to produce a deeper, more specific and more integrated analysis of the social as well as the political system of the East bloc countries.

114. Peter Christian Ludz, "Entwurf einer soziologischen Theorie totalitär verfasster Gesellschaft," in *Wege,* ed. Seidel and Jenkner.

115. Ludz, "Offene Fragen," pp. 330–334. He made this point also in "Totalitarismus oder Totalität."

116. Ludz, "Offene Fragen," p. 341.

117. In 1961, the Hamburg historian Fritz Fischer published a highly controversial (but archivally well grounded) book entitled *Germany's Grab for World Power (Deutschlands Griff nach der Weltmacht),* which demonstrated that Germany had entertained far-reaching plans for European hegemony during World War I and argued convincingly that the lion's share of blame for the outbreak of the war belonged to Germany. His book thus was highly damaging to the pretensions of German scholars of his own generation that Nazism was an "aberration" in German history. As with Denna Fleming and William Appleman Williams in the United States, the radicalization process in Germany moved previously marginalized scholars to the center of contemporary intellectual debate.

118. Seidel and Jenkner, eds., *Wege,* pp. 4–6.

119. Martin Jänicke, "Untersuchung zum Begriff totalitärer Herrschaft" (Ph.D. diss., Free University of Berlin, 1969), pp. 79–81.

120. Reinhard Kühnl, *Formen bürgerlicher Herrschaft* (Hamburg: Rowohlt, 1971), pp. 155–156. For a fuller exposition of the Marxist position of the early 1970s, see also Greiffenhagen, Kühnl, and Müller, *Totalitarismus.* Especially significant in the polemics of the time was Greiffenhagen's essay, "Der Totalitärismusbegriff in der Regimenlehre," pp. 23–59. Not everyone on the Left agreed. The Heidelberg philosopher Andreas Wildt continued to regard Stalinism as close to Fascism. See his "Totalitarian State Capitalism: On the Structure and Historical Function of Soviet-Type Societies," *Telos,* Fall 1979, pp. 33–57.

121. Karl Dietrich Bracher, "The Disputed Concept of Totalitarianism," translated from *Zeitgeschichtliche Kontroversen um Faschismus, Totalitarismus und Demokratie* (Munich, 1976), in *Totalitarianism Reconsidered,* ed. Menze, pp. 11–33. The article is similar to Bracher's essay "Totalitarianism."

122. Karl Dietrich Bracher, "Terrorism and Totalitarianism," from *Der Weg in die Gewalt* (Munich, 1978), in *Totalitarianism Reconsidered,* ed. Menze, p. 108.

123. Ibid., pp. 112–113.

124. In making this point, Bracher invoked Jean-François Revel's *The Totalitarian Temptation,* which had just been published in France. See Bracher, "Terrorism and Totalitarianism," pp. 112, 116.

125. According to Bracher, (1) their methods of political fighting employ violence

whether open or cloaked in pseudolegality; (2) their exclusive claim on truth and the right to govern; (3) the monolithic character of their ideologies; (4) their promise of total solution of all problems; (5) their destruction of the individual as person and their fiction of a new man who, fully coordinated, fuses with community and society; (6) their chimera of total liberation brought about by the coerced total identity of the governed and the government, citizen and party, people and leadership; and (7) their fundamental denial of free criticism and opposition ("Terrorism and Totalitarianism," pp. 118–119). See also his remarks in *Totalitarismus und Faschismus,* in which he directly compares the German New Left with the enemies of democracy in the final years of the Weimar Republic (pp. 11–12).

126. The opposition was apparently coined by the British historian of Germany Tim Mason. See his "Intention and Explanation: A Current Controversy About the Interpretation of National Socialism," in *Der "Führerstaat": Mythos und Realität,* ed. Gerhard Hirschfeld and Lothar Kettenacker (Stuttgart: Klett-Cotta, 1981).

127. Hans Mommsen, "Reappraisal and Repression: The Third Reich in West German Historical Consciousness," in *Reworking the Past: Hitler, the Holocaust and the Historians' Debate,* ed. Peter Baldwin (Boston: Beacon Press, 1990), pp. 174–175.

128. Martin Broszat, *Der Staat Hitlers: Grundlegung und Entwicklung seiner Inneren Verfassung* (Munich: Deutscher Taschenbuchverlag, 1969), published in English as *The Hitler State: The Foundation and Development of the Internal Structure of the Third Reich* (London: Longman, 1981).

129. It was important to Broszat that whereas Stalin depended for his power on his control of the party apparatus, Hitler relied ultimately on his charisma. See Broszat, *Hitler State,* p. x.

130. Ibid., pp. x, 352. The reader will also recall from Chapter 7 how in English-language studies of the Soviet Union there was also some tendency to reduce the "totalitarian" from an ideal type of a new kind of society, or a "model," to a phase in the life of states, much of whose development was understood in more traditional ways. Cf. Chalmers Johnson, *Change in Communist Systems* (Stanford, Calif.: Stanford University Press, 1970). This case was also made by German historians like Bracher's colleague Wolfgang Sauer, then teaching in the United States at the University of California at Berkeley. See his "National Socialism: Totalitarianism or Fascism?" *American Historical Review,* December 1967, p. 407.

131. Broszat, *Hitler State,* p. xi.

132. Bracher mentioned "the typical coexistence of extremely arbitrary acts with administrative and legal continuity, in the sense of a 'dual state' (E. Fraenkel) in which order and chaos, stability and revolution, form a pair. In reality, such a dualism was only tolerated to provide pseudolegal cover for arbitrary actions, with no legal security or predictability available outside the will of the leader" ("Totalitarianism," p. 410). His account suggests how historiographically important Ernst Fraenkel's *The Dual State* (New York: Oxford University Press, 1941) has turned out to be.

133. Kershaw, *Nazi Dictatorship,* p. 67.

134. Ibid.

135. My discussion of Hans Mommsen's critique of the concept of totalitarianism is derived from "National Socialism—Continuity and Change," in *Fascism: A Reader's Guide,* ed. Walter Laqueur (Berkeley: University of California Press, 1976), pp. 179–210; from his contribution to *Totalitarismus und Faschismus,* pp. 18–27; from "The Concept of Totalitarian Dictatorship Versus the Comparative Theory of Fascism," in *Totalitarianism Reconsidered,* ed. Menze, pp. 146–166; and from "Reappraisal and Repression: The Third Reich in West German Historical Consciousness," in *Reworking the Past,* ed. Baldwin, pp. 173–184.

136. Hans Mommsen, *Beamtentum im dritten Reich* (Stuttgart: Deutsche Verlagsanstalt, 1966).

137. Mommsen, "National Socialism—Continuity and Change," p. 179.

138. Ibid., pp. 181–182.

139. One might point out that Communist regimes also had their campaigns, their mobilization of labor resources for "storming," and their tendency to avoid regular organization and rational procedures when things had to get done quickly.

140. Mommsen, "Concept of Totalitarian Dictatorship," pp. 164–165.

141. Two useful English-language introductions to the *Historikerstreit* are Richard J. Evans, *In Hitler's Shadow: West German Historians and the Attempt to Escape from the Nazi Past* (New York: Pantheon, 1989); and Baldwin, ed., *Reworking the Past.*

142. Karl Dietrich Bracher, *The Age of Ideologies: A History of Political Thought in the Twentieth Century* (New York: St. Martin's Press, 1984). The German original appeared in 1982.

143. Ferenc Fehér and Agnes Heller, *Eastern Left, Western Left: Totalitarianism, Freedom and Democracy* (Atlantic Highlands, N.J.: Humanities Press International, 1987).

CHAPTER NINE

1. The Czech writer Milan Kundera's novel, *The Joke* (New York: Harper & Row, 1982), describes such a case. Alexander Solzhenitsyn's biography provides another example: his 1944 arrest for disparaging remarks about Stalin (referred to by a pseudonym) in private correspondence. For a characteristic example that took place in 1975, see also Peter Raina, *Political Opposition in Poland, 1954–1977* (London: Poets and Painters Press, 1977), pp. 208–209.

2. Václav Havel, "The Power of the Powerless," in *The Power of the Powerless: Citizens Against the State in Central-Eastern Europe,* ed. John Keane (Armonk, N.Y.: Sharpe, 1985), p. 44.

3. "In contrast to the 'gentry nations,' namely Poland and Hungary, whose political style was characterized by defiance and a romantic or libertarian commitment to independence, the Czech political style was bourgeois, democratic, fairly egalitarian, rational and pragmatic" (Jacques Rupnik, *The Other Europe* [New York: Pantheon, 1989], p. 16).

4. For an introduction to the traditions of the Polish intelligentsia, see Jan Tomasz Gross, "In Search of History," in *Poland: Genesis of a Revolution,* ed. Abra-

ham Brumberg (New York: Random House, 1983), pp. 3–9; and Leszek Kołakowski, "The Intelligentsia," in *Poland*, ed. Brumberg, pp. 54–67.

5. Timothy Garton Ash, "The Uses of Adversity," in *The Uses of Adversity* (New York: Random House, 1989), p. 105.

6. Milan Šimečka, *The Restoration of Order: The Normalisation of Czechoslovakia* (London: Verso, 1984), p. 162.

7. Bronisław Geremek, "Between Hope and Despair," in *Eastern Europe . . . Central Europe . . . Europe*, ed. Stephen Graubard, *Daedalus*, Winter 1990, p. 95. "At the end of the war," wrote the Czech critic Antonin Liehm, "the Soviet solution seemed to many of us to be the only one, because the Western solution had crashed so badly at Munich in 1938 and after" (quoted in Rupnik, *Other Europe*, p. 214).

8. Dwight Macdonald, "In the Land of Diamat," *New Yorker*, November 7, 1953, p. 161.

9. Quoted in Rupnik, *Other Europe*, p. 212.

10. Rudolf Tökés, ed., *Opposition in Eastern Europe* (Baltimore: Johns Hopkins University Press, 1979), p. 20.

11. Václav Benda, "Catholicism and Politics," in *Power of the Powerless*, ed. Keane, p. 111. See also the discerning and careful essay by Václav Havel, "An Anatomy of Reticence," *Cross Currents* 3 (1984): 29–47. There were exceptions. For a long time, Adam Michnik regarded himself as a "sixties person," as a kindred spirit of Western peace activists. From early in his evolution, however, he was more "liberal" than the Western New Left. See David Ost's introduction to Adam Michnik's *The Church and the Left* (Chicago: University of Chicago Press, 1993), pp. 5–6. For a nuanced discussion of the issues, see Ferenc Fehér and Agnes Heller, *Eastern Left, Western Left: Totalitarianism, Freedom and Democracy* (Atlantic Highlands, N.J.: Humanities Press International, 1987).

12. Czesław Miłosz, *The Captive Mind* (New York: Knopf, 1953). He apparently took the title from the writings of the remarkable Simone Weil, the unclassifiable atheist Catholic mystic of Jewish origin, who had a powerful influence not only on Miłosz, but also on other opponents of totalitarianism, like Albert Camus, Adam Michnik, and Hannah Arendt. On Weil, see David McClellan's *Utopian Pessimist* (New York: Simon and Schuster, 1990).

13. For biographical information, see Ewa Czarnecka and Aleksander Fiut, *Conversations with Czeslaw Milosz* (New York: Harcourt Brace Jovanovich, 1987), pp. 7–12.

14. Andrzej Walicki, "The 'Captive Mind' Revisited: Intellectuals and Communist Totalitarianism in Poland," in *Totalitarianism at the Crossroads*, ed. Ellen Frankel Paul (New Brunswick, N.J.: Transaction Books, 1990), p. 51. Dwight Macdonald wrote that except for Arendt's *The Origins of Totalitarianism*, "I know of no study of the totalitarian mentality as subtle and imaginative as this one" ("In the Land of Diamat," p. 157).

15. Walicki, " 'Captive Mind' Revisited," pp. 60–62.

16. Ibid., pp. 58–59. Walicki based his account on an article that Miłosz had published in the Paris-based journal *Kultura* in 1951, the year that *The Captive Mind* appeared.

17. Leonard Nathan and Arthur Quinn, *The Poet's Work: An Introduction to Czeslaw Milosz* (Cambridge, Mass.: Harvard University Press, 1991), pp. 36–40, 52–53.

18. Geremek, "Between Hope and Despair," p. 100.

19. Ibid., p. 101. Adam Michnik had earlier expressed similar ideas. See his "A New Evolutionism," in *Letters from Prison* (Berkeley: University of California Press, 1985), pp. 135–137.

20. On these Catholic individuals, groups and journals, see Andrzej Micewski, *Współrządzić czy nie kłamać? PAX i Znak w Polsce, 1945–1976* (Paris: Libella, 1978), esp. pp. 179–190. I have used the summary in Mark Szorc, "The Flight from Utopia: Opposition in Poland and Czechoslovakia in the 1970's" (senior thesis, Brown University, 1992), pp. 16–19. See also Michnik, *Church and the Left,* passim.

21. Michnik, "New Evolutionism," p. 140.

22. Ivan Sviták, "Heads Against the Wall" (Lecture given to the philosophy faculty of Charles University, Prague, March 20, 1968). Sviták analyzes the Czechoslovak government in terms of a general model roughly congruent with the version provided in Brzezinski and Friedrich's *Totalitarian Dictatorship and Autocracy.* "Totalitarian dictatorship," Sviták wrote, "is the new form of absolutism, the modern shape of despotism. The essence of a totalitarian dictatorship is the reduction of the human being to a tool of the power apparatus. Thus, every totalitarian dictatorship must destroy personality and individuality—not because the leaders are sadists (they are that too) but because this trend results from the character of absolute, centralized and unlimited power. Propaganda and terror, the control of mass information and the secret police are the most important means used for the functionalization of man" (*The Czechoslavak Experiment, 1968–69* [New York: Columbia University Press, 1971], p. 27).

23. See, for example, Jacek Kuroń and Karol Modzelewski's "Open Letter to the Party" of early 1965, in which they refer to the Stalinist system of "total police dictatorship." See the letter reprinted under the authors' names in Colin Barker, ed., *Solidarność: The Missing Link* (London: Bookmarks, 1982). The term is used on p. 55.

24. Zdenek Mlynar, *Nightfrost in Prague* (New York: Karz, 1980), pp. 198–200.

25. Michnik, "New Evolutionism," p. 138. "The Russian occupation means an end to the revisionist communist movement in Czechoslovakia," wrote the philosophy professor Ivan Sviták, "a movement designed as an alternative to the totalitarian ideology and monopoly of power inherent in neo-Stalinist Communism" (*Czechoslovak Experiment,* pp. 159–160).

26. Mihaly Vajda, *The State and Socialism* (New York: St. Martin's Press, 1981), p. 2.

27. One might infer this from Zbigniew Herbert's influential poem "Mr. Cogito—The Return." For the "Mr. Cogito" poems, see his *Pan Cogito* (Warsaw: Czytelnik, 1974). An excellent English version of "Mr. Cogito—The Return" is in Zbigniew Herbert, *Report from the Besieged City,* ed. and trans. John Carpenter and Bogdana Carpenter (New York: Ecco Press, 1985), pp. 14–16.

28. George Schöpflin, "Opposition and Para-Opposition: Critical Currents in Hungary, 1968–1978," in *Opposition in Eastern Europe,* ed. Tökés, pp. 170–178.

29. David Ost, *Solidarity and the Politics of Anti-Politics* (Philadelphia: Temple University Press, 1990), p. 50.

30. See the excerpts from Modzelewski's statement in Raina, *Political Opposition in Poland*, pp. 171–172.

31. David Ost, Introduction to Michnik, *Church and the Left*, p. 4.

32. Discussion of the figures in Jadwiga Staniszkis, *Poland's Self-Limiting Revolution* (Princeton, N.J.: Princeton University Press, 1984), p. 41. In 1980, Solidarity erected monuments to the fallen workers in both Gdańsk and Gdynia.

33. For an excellent general account of the events of 1970, including the nonparticipation of students and the church, see Roman Laba, *The Roots of Solidarity: A Political Sociology of Poland's Working-Class Democratization* (Princeton, N.J.: Princeton University Press, 1991), pp. 15–82.

34. Leszek Kołakowski, "Tezy o nadziei i beznadiejności," *Kultura*, June 1971, pp. 3–21. It also appeared as "Hope and Hopelessness, *Survey*, Summer 1971, pp. 37–52.

35. Ost, *Solidarity*, p. 58.

36. Kołakowski, "Hope and Hopelessness," pp. 38–40.

37. Ibid., pp. 41–42.

38. Ibid., pp. 46–50.

39. Ibid., pp. 49–51.

40. In addition to the edition cited in note 23, see the translation published in *New Politics*, Spring 1966, pp. 5–46, and Summer 1966, pp. 72–99, republished as Jacek Kuroń and Karol Modzelewski, *A Revolutionary Socialist Manifesto, London* (London: Pluto Press, n.d.). Kuroń's autobiography is entitled *Wiara i Wina: Droga do i od Komunizmu* (Warsaw: NOWa, 1989).

41. For a suggestion of *Kultura*'s importance in Polish culture in the 1970s and 1980s, see Robert Kostrzewa, *Between East and West: Writings from Kultura* (New York: Hill and Wang, 1990), pp. ix–iv, 3–21.

42. Jacek Kuroń, "Political Opposition in Poland," *Kultura*, November 1974; see also Ost, *Solidarity*, pp. 64–66.

43. Kuroń, "Political Opposition in Poland."

44. One source estimated that food prices increased by 46 percent. See Jan Jozef Lipski, *KOR: A History of the Workers' Defense Committee in Poland, 1976–1981* (Berkeley: University of California Press, 1985), p. 32.

45. For translations of many of the most important documents surrounding the demonstrations, trials, and the founding of KOR, see Raina, *Political Opposition*, pp. 286–344. For letters of protest and unofficial accounts, see pp. 500–530.

46. Lipski, *KOR*, pp. 44–45.

47. Ost, *Solidarity*, p. 67.

48. Jacek Kuroń, "Reflections on a Program of Action," *Polish Review*, September 1977, pp. 51–69. The text here published is a reconstruction of one seized from Kuroń when his house was searched in November 1976.

49. Ibid., pp. 60–64.

50. Ibid., p. 67. After a year of activity, KOR added the phrase "Committee for the Self-Defense of Society" (KSS) to its official designation.

51. Ibid., pp. 68–69. "Finlandization" referred to the situauation in which, from the end of World War II until the end of the Soviet Union, Finland retained its independence but remained neutral in the realm of foreign policy and avoided any active steps that could be understood as actively anti-Soviet.

52. Michnik, *Letters from Prison,* p. xix.

53. Michnik, "New Evolutionism," pp. 135–148.

54. Ibid., p. 142.

55. Michnik's *Kościół, Lewica, Dialog,* published illegally in 1977, is an extremely important document of the antitotalitarian coalition between secular intellectuals and the church. See the English version, *Church and the Left.* See also Anna Chmielewska, "Lettre aux amis," in *La Pologne: Une société en dissidence,* ed. Z. Erard and G. M. Zygier (Paris: François Maspero, 1978), pp. 137–194.

56. A few years later, Timothy Garton Ash looked back on this "deliberate, difficult and fruitful coming together of intellectuals from traditions that just twenty years before had been bitterly opposed: Jewish socialists sat down with Christian Democrats, former Stalinists with Home Army veterans, hardened ex-revisionists with inspissated Thomists" (*Uses of Adversity,* p. 149).

57. Michnik, "New Evolutionism," p. 148. For a touching memoir of Michnik and the founding of KOR, see Stanislaw Baranczak, "On Adam Michnik," in *Breathing Under Water and Other East European Essays* (Cambridge, Mass.: Harvard University Press, 1990), pp. 43–47.

58. Andrzej Walicki, "From Stalinism to Post-Communist Pluralism: The Case of Poland," *New Left Review,* January–February 1991, p. 101. For Walicki's opinion of the continued presentation of the Polish and Soviet governments as "totalitarian," see pp. 95–103; and Walicki, "Totalitarianism and Liberalism: Rejoinder to Mizgala," *Critical Review,* Spring 1989, esp. pp. 356–360. For another view of "detotalization" in Poland, see Staniszkis, *Poland's Self-Limiting Revolution,* pp. 150–188, esp. p. 150. Staniszkis's view of Polish evolution after 1968 also stresses its movement from totalitarianism to bureaucratic authoritarianism. She described the Polish system in the late 1970s as "lame pluralism." Juan Linz described it as "irresponsible pluralism" (ibid., p. 164).

59. Adam Zagaewski, *Solidarity, Solitude* (New York: Ecco Press, 1990), p. 26.

60. Vladimir V. Kusin, *From Dubcek to Charter 77: A Study of "Normalization" in Czechoslovakia, 1968–1978* (New York: St. Martin's Press, 1978), pp. 141–147.

61. Ibid., pp. 171–178.

62. Václav Havel, Introduction to Ludvík Vaculík, *A Cup of Coffee with My Interrogator* (London: Readers International, 1987), p. i. For a significant expression of the doldrums of 1973 and 1974, see Pavel Kohout, "An Open Letter to the Minister of Culture," in *A Beseiged Culture: Czeckoslovakia Ten Years After Helsinki* (Stockholm: Charter 77 Foundation, 1985), pp. 265–271.

63. H. Gordon Skilling, *Charter 77 and Human Rights in Czechoslovakia* (London: Allen & Unwin, 1981), p. xiii.

64. See the description in Kusin, *From Dubcek to Charter 77,* pp. 214–215.

65. Šimečka, *Restoration of Order,* pp. 140, 144, 156.

66. Václav Havel, "Dear Dr. Husak," in his *Open Letters: Selected Writings, 1965–*

1990 (New York: Knopf, 1991), p. 59. This long, brilliant tirade, centrally about the destruction of the humanity of Czechs and their culture, was first published in *Listy* in July 1975 and in that same month in the British journal *Survey,* in translation. It was then published in the September 1975 issue of *Encounter.* Many of the signers of Charter 77 spoke in similar ways about Czechoslovak "consumerism." See the essays in Keane, ed., *Power of the Powerless.*

67. Jacques Rupnik, "Totalitarianism Revisited," in *Civil Society and the State,* ed. John Keane (London: Verso, 1988), pp. 276. Rupnik had earlier made a similar case for Poland. See his "Dissent in Poland, 1968–1978," in *Opposition in Eastern Europe,* ed. Tökés, p. 82. The similar if more agreeable Kádár compromise in Hungary meant that "the basic structure was not called into question by the intellectuals, while . . . the party leadership did its utmost to ensure that within these limitations life was as tolerable as possible." But there, too, "people settled down into apathy" (Vajda, *State and Socialism,* p. 126).

68. Jerzy Mackow, *Die Krise des Totalitarismus in Polen,* Osteuropa: Geschichte, Wirtschaft, Politik, vol. 2 (Munster, 1992), pp. 154–155.

69. One of their albums was entitled *Egon Bundy's Happy Hearts Club Banned,* a wry Central European refraction of the Beatles.

70. Skilling, *Charter 77,* pp. 7–8. Jirous subsequently became an art historian and remained a significant figure in Czechoslovakia's opposition.

71. "What else is youth but a guest, arriving from the unknown to begin life anew?" wrote the distinguished philosopher Jan Patočka, one of the influential founders of Charter 77 ("On the Matter of the Plastic People of the Universe and DG307," December 1976, p. 206, quoted in Skilling, *Charter 77,* p. 206).

72. Havel, "The Trial," in *Open Letters,* pp. 106–107. Two years later, in "The Power of the Powerless," Havel wrote that "the freedom to play rock music was understood as a human freedom and thus essentially the same as the freedom to engage in philosophical and political reflection, the freedom to write, the freedom to express and defend the various social and political interests of society" (p. 46).

73. For documents, including the letter to Böll, see Skilling, *Charter 77,* pp. 199ff. The letter was signed by Jaroslav Seifert, a major Czech poet; Václav Czerny, a literary historian; the philosopher Jan Patočka; the revisionist Marxist philosopher Karel Kosík; and three important writers, Havel, Ivan Klíma, and Pavel Kohout. There are later documents in *A Besieged Culture.*

74. Reprinted in Skilling, *Charter 77,* pp. 209–212; and in Keane, ed., *Power of the Powerless,* pp. 217–221. The three spokesmen for the signatories were Václav Havel, Jan Patočka, and Jiří Hájek, a former minister of foreign affairs.

75. Skilling, *Charter 77,* p. 40; cited in Szorc, "Flight from Utopia," p. 34.

76. See, for example, Josef Zverina, "On Not Living in Hatred," in *Power of the Powerless,* ed. Keane, pp. 207–216.

77. A number of the founders were also active in a second organization, the Committee for the Defense of the Unjustly Persecuted (VONS), founded in April 1978.

78. For Havel's *feuilleton,* see "The Trial," pp. 102–108. For a brief biography of Jan Patočka, see Skilling, *Charter 77,* pp. 20–23. His legacy may be summed up in

these words from his "exposition" of the Charter: "The whole concept of *human rights* is nothing but the conviction that states and society as a whole consider themselves to be subject to the sovereignty of moral sentiment, that they recognise something unqualified above them, something that is bindingly sacred and inviolable even for them, and that they intend to contribute to this end with the power by which they create and ensure *legal* norms" (Skilling, *Charter 77*, p. 218). For a good introduction to Patočka's thought, including his intellectual relationship to philosophers Heidegger, Husserl, Arendt, and Jünger, see Patočka, *Essais Hérétiques* (Paris: Verdier, 1981). The *samizdat* original was published in Prague in 1975.

79. See Havel's conversational autobiography, *Disturbing the Peace* (New York: Knopf, 1990).

80. Havel, "Power of the Powerless," p. 27.

81. Ibid.

82. Ibid, p. 28.

83. Ibid., p. 29.

84. Similar ideas were common in French academic circles in the 1980s regarding Soviet "political discourse," sometimes referred to as the "wooden tongue" (*langue de bois*). The radical Charles Bettleheim, for instance, saw the wooden and ritualized Soviet political vocabulary as a "code of allegiance" whose role was that of an "instrument of social submission." See Robert Desjardins, *The Soviet Union Through French Eyes, 1945–1980* (New York, St. Martin's Press, 1988), pp. 86–88.

85. Havel, "Power of the Powerless," pp. 32–33.

86. Ibid., pp. 30–31.

87. What Havel meant by "living in the truth" seems close to what Kołakowski had earlier intended when he wrote of "living in dignity."

88. In *Between Past and Future* (New York: Viking, 1968), Hannah Arendt wrote that "a mass society is nothing more than that kind of living which automatically establishes itself among human beings who are still related to one another but have lost the world once common to all of them" (p. 90).

89. Havel, "Power of the Powerless," pp. 43, 70, 89–91. In Havel's critique of technology, he declared himself indebted to Martin Heidegger (p. 90) and aligned himself with Alexander Solzhenitsyn's attack on consumerism in his Harvard speech (p. 91). In his sympathy for ecological points of view, Havel also resembles Solzhenitsyn; like Solzhenitsyn, he blames "the European West" for "natural science, rationalism, scientism, the industrial revolution, and also revolution as such, as a fanatical abstraction, through the displacement of the natural world to the bathroom down to the cult of consumption, the atomic bomb and Marxism" ("Politics and Conscience" [1984], in *Open Letters,* p. 258).

90. Havel, "Power of the Powerless," p. 43.

91. Benda wrote an influential essay of that title in May 1978, which circulated in *samizdat*.

92. The term *civil society* had been used by philosophers from John Locke to Karl Marx to speak of social space between the private world of the family and the world of the state. Marx gave the world of civil society great importance in his dialectics of development, but since it was a realm of bourgeois egoism, he thought it destined to

be replaced by a higher, more fruitful, and harmonious "total" development of society. During the 1980s, the term *civil society* began to be used increasingly to describe something of central importance taken away by totalitarianism. For an excellent study, broader than its title suggests, see Z. A. Pełczyński, *The State and Civil Society: Studies in Hegel's Political Philosophy* (Cambridge: Cambridge University Press, 1984).

93. Jiří Hájek, "The Human Rights Movement and Social Progress," in *Power of the Powerless,* ed. Keane, pp. 134–140.

94. This criticism was made even more emphatically in a *feuilleton* by Peter Pithart, "On the Shoulders of Some," which analyzed the first two years of Charter 77's activities. See Skilling, *Charter 77,* p. 78; and Szorc, "Flight from Utopia," p. 42.

95. Vaculík, "On Heroism," in *Cup of Coffee,* pp. 47–51.

96. Conversation with Paul Wilson, quoted in Havel, *Open Letters,* pp. 125–126. ("The Power of the Powerless" seems to have first appeared in Polish in *Krytyka,* Spring 1980.) The Polish writer Stanislaw Baranczak regards "The Power of the Powerless" as "arguably the best work ever written on the intricacies of consent and dissent in Eastern European societies" (*Breathing Under Water,* p. 54). But Jan Walc, a member of KOR, concurred with Uhl and Pithart regarding Havel's strategy as "dangerous" because it "concentrat[ed] exclusively on the individual's personal aspect, thinking only about his psychology, rejecting all that concerns the community or group, that to be a dissident is merely 'to live in truth,' founding all action purely on moral imperatives" ("Słabość Wszechmocnych," *Krytyka,* Summer 1980, p. 1, quoted in Szorc, "Flight from Utopia," p. 44).

97. Lipski, *KOR,* p. 44.

98. There is an enormous amount on Orwell's reception in Eastern Europe. See, for example, Thomas Stalinski, "One Kind of Magic," *Survey,* Summer 1971, pp. 95–97; Rupnik, *Other Europe,* pp. 225, 228–233, and "Le Totalitarisme vu de l'Est," in *Totalitarismes,* ed. Guy Hermet (Paris: Economica, 1984), pp. 53–54; Ash, *Uses of Adversity,* pp. 171–172, 175, 213; and H. Gordon Skilling, "The Muse of History— 1984: History, Historians and Politics in Communist Czechoslovakia," *Cross Currents* 3 (1984): 30, 43–44. A French translation of a significant Czech document is by Milan Šimečka, "Mon camarade Winston Smith," *Lettre internationale,* no. 1, Summer 1984, pp. 12–20.

99. Peter Raina, *Independent Social Movements in Poland* (London: Orbis Books, 1981), pp. 82–92 and passim; Lipski, *KOR,* esp. pp. 371–383, 484–485.

100. For example, see Zbigniew Pełczyński, "Solidarity and the Rebirth of Civil Society in Poland," in *Civil Society and the State,* ed. Keane, p. 363.

101. Even so, Mihaly Vajda, at the end of the late 1970s, defined the task for Hungarian intellectuals too as "creat[ing] a public sphere in Eastern Europe" ("Is Kadarism an Alternative?" in *State and Socialism,* p. 141).

102. Pełczyński, "Solidarity," p. 369.

103. See Laba, *Roots of Solidarity,* esp. pp. 169–182.

104. Quoted in Rupnik, "Totalitarianism Revisited," p. 285.

105. György Konrád, quoted in H. Gordon Skilling, "Independent Communications in Communist East Europe," *Cross Currents,* no. 5 (1986): 71. See also György

Konrád, *Antipolitics* (New York: Harcourt Brace Jovanovich, 1984); and Fehér and Heller, *Eastern Left, Western Left.*

106. Václav Havel, interview with Erica Blair, "Doing Without Utopias," *Times Literary Supplement,* January 23, 1987, pp. 81–83. In this interview, Havel's thought continued to show marked parallels with that of Alexander Solzhenitsyn, although without the latter's nationalism. He now put secularism as well as the growth of mechanical, impersonal ways of life in both East and West as the root of a crisis of modernity. See also Václav Benda, Milan Šimečka, Ivan Jirous, Jiří Dienstbier, Václav Havel, Ladislav Hejdánek, and Jan Šimsa, "Parallel Polis: An Inquiry," *Social Research,* Summer 1988, pp. 211–246; and Václav Havel, "The Post-Communist Nightmare," *New York Review of Books,* May 27, 1993, pp. 8–10.

107. Tony Judt wrote that the Czech "Velvet Revolution" took place "with no distinct sense, on anyone's part, of political strategy or policy. Overtaken by events and in many cases just emerging from prison . . . the members of the opposition . . . were as confused as the communists whom they defeated and replaced" ("Metamorphosis: The Democratic Revolution in Czechoslovakia," in *Eastern Europe in Revolution,* ed. Ivo Banac [Ithaca, N.Y.: Cornell University Press, 1992], p. 100).

CHAPTER TEN

1. The rise of the "New Right," neoconservatism, the so-called religious Right, and other related movements has by now generated a very substantial literature. For an intelligent, if hostile, introduction, see Jerome L. Himmelstein, *To the Right: The Transformation of American Conservatism* (Berkeley: University of California Press, 1990), esp. pp. 1–62. Also useful and more sympathetic is the book by Paul Gottfried and Thomas Fleming, *The Conservative Movement* (Boston: Twayne, 1988).

2. Irving Kristol, *Reflections of a Neoconservative* (New York: Basic Books, 1983), p. 74.

3. J. David Hoeveler, Jr., *Watch on the Right: Conservative Intellectuals in the Reagan Era* (Madison: University of Wisconsin Press, 1991), p. 149.

4. Norman Podhoretz, *Breaking Ranks* (New York: Harper Colophon, 1980), pp. 345–347.

5. Robert W. Tucker, "America in Decline: The Foreign Policy of 'Maturity,' " *Foreign Affairs* 58 (1979): 462, quoted in Hoeveler, *Watch on the Right,* p. 159.

6. For an assessment and bibliography, see E. Thomas Rowe, "Human Rights: Assessing the Impact on Nongovernmental Organizations," in *Evaluating U.S. Foreign Policy,* ed. John A. Vasquez (New York: Praeger, 1986), pp. 113–134; D. Kommers and G. Loescher, eds., *Human Rights and American Foreign Policy* (Notre Dame, Ind.: University of Notre Dame Press, 1979); and the American Association for the International Commission of Jurists, *Human Rights and U.S. Foreign Policy* (n.p., 1984).

7. International Commission of Jurists, *Human Rights and U.S. Foreign Policy,* p. 16.

8. Jimmy Carter's speech, in *Morality and Foreign Policy: A Symposium on President Carter's Stance,* ed. Ernest W. Lefever (Washington, D.C.: Ethics and Public

Policy Center, Georgetown University, 1977), pp. 3–10. Lefever, a professor at Georgetown University, was Reagan's candidate for Assistant Secretary of State for Human Rights in 1981. His candidacy was withdrawn, largely because of his opposition to making human rights a central focus of American foreign policy. Lefever told Senator Charles Percy of Illinois that groups opposed to his nomination were "communist-inspired." See Howard Stanislawski, "Lefeverish Activity," *New Republic,* May 30, 1981, p. 13.

9. The historian John Lewis Gaddis has given a soberly negative view of Carter's foreign policy: "At a time when defeat in Vietnam had severely shaken American self-confidence, when the energy crisis appeared to be demonstrating American impotence, when the military balance seemed to be shifting in the Russians' favor, and when the domestic consensus in favor of détente was rapidly dissolving, he had chosen to launch an unprecedented effort to shift the entire basis of foreign policy from power to principle. Carter's timing was terrible; his implementation was haphazard and inconsistent; only his intentions were praiseworthy, and in the climate of the late 1970s, that was not enough" (*The United States and the End of the Cold War* [New York: Oxford University Press, 1992], p. 120).

10. Daniel Patrick Moynihan, commencement speech (1977) at Baruch College, in *Morality and Foreign Policy,* ed. Lefever, pp. 32–37.

11. Kissinger's remarks in ibid., pp. 59–66, quotations from pp. 62, 63.

12. Ibid., p. 64 (italics added).

13. See also Ernest W. Lefever, "The Trivialization of Human Rights," *Policy Review,* Winter 1978, pp. 11–26. Lefever's piece was less polemically effective and appeared in a more obscure journal, but in many of its points it anticipated Jeane Kirkpatrick's "Dictatorships and Double Standards," the article that again made totalitarianism a major political issue.

14. Jimmy Carter, *Keeping Faith: Memoirs of a President* (New York: Bantam, 1982), quoted in International Commission of Jurists, *Human Rights and U.S. Foreign Policy,* p. 25.

15. For a careful and balanced sketch of Kristol's life and ideas, see Hoeveler, *Watch on the Right,* pp. 81–113.

16. For Kristol's critical observations on Talmon's *Rise of Totalitarian Democracy,* see Chapter 6, n. 52.

17. Kristol, *Reflections of a Neoconservative,* pp. x–xi, 139–147.

18. The term *new class* derived from the famous book by the Yugoslav critic of Marxism, Milovan Djilas, *The New Class* (New York: Praeger, 1957). For Djilas, the "new class" was made up of postrevolutionary, usually Marxist, bureaucrats with a modernization mission. Their core, was, in the paradigmatic Communist version, the Party.

19. For Kristol's earlier "realism," see his "Why We Can't Resign as Policeman of the World," *New York Times Magazine,* May 12, 1968, pp. 26ff.

20. See Robert Nisbet, *Twilight of Authority* (New York: Oxford University Press, 1975), pp. 222, 225, and, for the connection between "loss of community" and "totalitarianism," *Prejudices* (Cambridge, Mass.: Harvard University Press, 1982), p. 55.

21. Nisbet, *Twilight,* pp. 195–196. On Kristol, see also Hoeveler, *Watch on the Right,* pp. 177–206.

22. Jeane Kirkpatrick, *Dictatorships and Double Standards: Rationalism and Reason in Politics* (Washington, D.C.: American Enterprise Institute and Simon and Schuster, 1982), pp. 10–12.

23. B. Bruce-Briggs, ed., *The New Class?* (New Brunswick, N.J.: Transaction Books, 1979), is a representative collection of (largely) neoconservative views of the "new class."

24. George Konrad and Ivan Szelenyi, *The Intellectuals on the Road to Class Power: A Sociological Study of the Role of the Intelligentsia in Socialism* (New York: Harcourt Brace Jovanovich, 1979).

25. Taken together, the contributions to Bruce-Briggs's anthology *The New Class?* indicate that in 1979 at least there was little agreement even among devotees of the term as to precisely what groups it encompassed. "About as solid as jello" was how socialist Michael Harrington expressed it (p. 123); "a mentality, not a concept" wrote sociologist Daniel Bell, who was close to the neoconservatives (p. 186).

26. Podhoretz, *Breaking Ranks,* pp. 290–291. Jeane Kirkpatrick was more consistent. Although she found the new class of intellectuals "more liberal than conservative," she freely conceded that many right-wing intellectual activists also belonged to this "new class." And she associated ideological politics with the Republican Party as well as the Democrats. See "Politics and the 'New Class,' " in her *Dictatorships and Double Standards,* pp. 186–203, esp. pp. 194–195.

27. Podhoretz, *Breaking Ranks,* pp. 329–335. At the same time, Podhoretz urged the Jewish community to act on the basis of the "old question, 'Is it good for the Jews?' "

28. Not all the intellectuals aligned with neoconservatism made the totalitarianism of the Soviet Union the central focus of their attacks. The historian Richard Pipes of Harvard University, for example, took an extremely dark view of the Soviet Union, but his analysis grew largely out of Russian history and relied substantially on continuity. He sometimes called the Soviet Union "totalitarian"; indeed, he did so in his first major synthesis of Russian history: *Russia Under the Old Regime* (New York: Scribner, 1974), p. 312. The term, however, was not analytically central for him. See Pipes, *U.S.–Soviet Relations in the Era of Détente* (Boulder, Colo.: Westview Press, 1981). For an example of how Pipes used the term *totalitarian,* see p. 18. In his most recent book, however, *Russia Under the Bolshevik Regime* (New York: Knopf, 1994), the term has become more analytically and polemically central for him; see, especially, chap. 5.

29. The title of Podhoretz's characteristically self-serving version of his break with the Left. See n. 26.

30. After all, conservative ideologues have frequently also been unattached intellectuals who put their clerkly talents in the service of the powers that be, rather than joining the ranks of reformers or revolutionaries. Even Edmund Burke might be partially understood in this light. The author of a collection of largely neoconservative essays on the "new class" admitted that its public identification in the early

1970s "might be interpreted as one clique of literary intellectuals bad-mouthing another" (Bruce-Briggs, *New Class?* p. 6).

31. Podhoretz, *Breaking Ranks,* p. 350.

32. There is a balanced and concise account in Lou Cannon, *President Reagan: The Role of a Lifetime* (New York: Simon and Schuster, 1991), pp. 282–287. For Reagan's own account, see Ronald Reagan, *An American Life* (New York: Simon and Schuster, 1990), pp. 105–115.

33. Ronald Reagan, "How Do You Fight Communism?" *Fortnight,* January 22, 1951.

34. "Determining precisely when Reagan first began to present apocalyptic speeches is difficult," two students of Reagan's rhetoric have recently written, "because his anti-communist speeches of the early 1950s so clearly foreshadowed the form. The turning point came when Reagan began to speak of intrusive government regulations and programs not merely as misguided applications of taxation and censorship, but as a domestic threat to American liberty that paralleled the foreign threat of communism. Starting with his 1957 commencement address at Eureka College, Reagan's speeches became increasingly apocalyptic in tone" (Kurt Ritter and David Henry, *Ronald Reagan: The Great Communicator* [Westport, Conn.: Greenwood Press, 1992], p. 15). Many students of Reagan have noted his fascination with the theme of Armageddon. See, for example, Cannon, *President Reagan,* pp. 288–291.

35. Quoted in Ritter and Henry, *Ronald Reagan,* p. 17.

36. Quoted in Ronnie Dugger, *On Reagan: The Man & His Presidency* (New York: McGraw-Hill, 1983), p. 519.

37. Ronald Reagan, "Remarks at the Annual Convention of the National Association of Evangelicals in Orlando, Florida" (March 8, 1983), *Public Papers of the Presidents of the United States: Ronald Reagan 1983* (Washington, D.C.: Government Printing Office, 1984), vol. 1, pp. 359–364. See also Anthony Lewis, "Onward Christian Soldiers," *New York Times,* March 10, 1983, cited in Dugger, *On Reagan,* p. 469. For an excellent analysis of the "evil empire" speech and its sources, see William K. Muir, Jr., "Ronald Reagan: The Primacy of Rhetoric," in *Leadership in the Modern Presidency,* ed. Fred I. Greenstein (Cambridge, Mass.: Harvard University Press, 1988), esp. pp. 273–278.

38. Quoted in Dugger, *On Reagan,* p. 353.

39. Terry Dolan, interview with Muir, in "Ronald Reagan," pp. 276–278.

40. Mary Schwarz, "Jeane Kirkpatrick: Our Macho UN Ambassador," *National Review,* January 21, 1983, p. 50.

41. Kirkpatrick concluded her introduction by writing that "Communist leaders' determination to revolutionize society and culture leads them to attempt to control by regulation a very wide range of activities normally governed by custom and personal preference. Where the state regulates, it stands ready to coerce. Extension of regulation and coercion into all spheres of society is the meaning of totalitarianism. Since regulation in social and cultural areas is uniquely difficult to enforce, it requires more police, more surveillance, more terror. This is the reason that totalitarian

regimes are uniquely repressive" (Jeane J. Kirkpatrick, ed., *The Strategy of Deception* [New York: Farrar, Strauss, 1963], pp. xx–xxi).

42. Jeane Kirkpatrick, "Reflections on Totalitarianism. 1. The Counterculture of Totalitarianism," in *Dictatorships and Double Standards,* pp. 96–125, esp. p. 101. It may be sheer coincidence, but an influential text history of the Soviet Union, which also stressed its utopianism, was first published in 1982, in both Russian and French. Although the term *totalitarian* is not central to the book's analysis, the point of view is close to that of Alain Besançon in France. See Mikhail Heller and Aleksandr M. Nekrich, *Utopia in Power: The History of the Soviet Union from 1917 to the Present* (New York: Simon and Schuster, 1986).

43. See, in particular, Jeane Kirkpatrick, "U.S. Security in Latin America," *Commentary,* January 1981, revised version in *Dictatorships and Double Standards,* pp. 53–90. For a critique, see Tom J. Farer, "Reagan's Latin America," *New York Review of Books,* March 19, 1981, pp. 10–16.

44. Jeane Kirkpatrick, in *U.S. News & World Report,* March 2, 1981, quoted in International Commission of Jurists, *Human Rights and U.S. Foreign Policy,* p. 33.

45. Kirkpatrick, Introduction to *Dictatorships and Double Standards,* pp. 7, 17.

46. Jeane J. Kirkpatrick, *Dismantling the Parties: Reflections on Party Reform and Party Decomposition* (Washington, D.C.: American Enterprise Institute, 1978), reprinted in *Dictatorships and Double Standards,* pp. 141–171.

47. Kirkpatrick, *Dictatorships and Double Standards,* pp. 13–14.

48. I use the term *Whig history* in the customary general sense, to mean a teleological kind of history in which one's own historical situation is more or less consciously justified by the way in which one depicts historical development. The reference was originally to English historians of a Whig persuasion, from Thomas Babington Macaulay to George Trevelyan. See Herbert Butterfield, *The Whig Interpretation of History* (London: Bell & Sons, 1951).

49. The category of "traditional" seems to have been rather loose and catchall in Kirkpatrick's thinking.

50. Kirkpatrick, *Dictatorships and Double Standards,* pp. 49–50.

51. Ibid., pp. 50–51. For criticism, see Michael Walzer, "Totalitarianism vs. Authoritarianism," *New Republic,* July 4 and 11, 1981, p. 25. For some figures on refugee totals in the Carter and Reagan administrations and some criticism of the early Reagan policy on human rights, see America's Watch, "The Reagan Administration's Human Rights Policy: A Mid-Term Review," *Human Rights Internet Reporter* (Washington, D.C., 1983), pp. 616–619.

52. Kirkpatrick, *Dictatorships and Double Standards,* pp. 51–52.

53. See, for example, Jeane Kirkpatrick, interview with Ann Tremblay, *Working Woman,* May 1983, esp. p. 109.

54. Quotation alleged to be from a speech by Haig to the Trilateral Commission, quoted in Jenny Pearce, *Under the Eagle* (Boston: South End Press, 1982), p. 182. Unfortunately, the exact location of the primary source is not given in *Under the Eagle.* The speech may have been one entitled "Human Rights and American Interests," which Haig gave in Washington in June 1981.

55. The three questions and the responses are in *Commentary,* November 1981, passim.

56. Kirkpatrick's reply to her critics added little to the discussion. She expressed surprise that her usage of a term that was "purely analytical" could arouse such fury but allowed on the next page that the term had, after all, "ideological as well as analytic significance" ("Reflections on Totalitarianism. 1.," pp. 96–97).

57. Walzer, "Totalitarianism vs. Authoritarianism," pp. 21, 24.

58. Farer, "Reagan's Latin America," pp. 10–11. See also Charles Maechling, Jr., "The Argentine Pariah," *Foreign Policy,* Winter 1981/1982, p. 75.

59. Alan Tonelson, "Human Rights: The Bias We Need," *Foreign Policy,* Winter 1982/1983, pp. 59–60.

60. Jacobo Timerman, *Prisoner Without a Name, Cell Without a Number* (New York: Knopf, 1981).

61. Ibid., pp. 1–9.

62. Ibid., p. 51.

63. Ibid., p. 131.

64. Ibid., pp. 60–61.

65. Anthony Lewis, in the *New York Times Magazine,* May 10, 1981, pp. 1, 30–32, went so far as to entitle his review "The Final Solution in Argentina." If that notion bordered on hysteria, he was on stronger ground when in light of Timerman's book, he ironically recalled Kirkpatrick's contention that "authoritarian regimes" respect "habitual patterns of family and personal relations" (p. 1). Lewis pointed out that the silence of the Argentine Jewish community, among other constituencies, helped the world ignore what was going on in Argentina (p. 33).

66. Irving Kristol, "The Timerman Affair," *Wall Street Journal,* May 29, 1981, pp. 24–25. If neoconservatives tended to believe that Timerman was the instrument of a liberal conspiracy, liberals took exactly the opposite point of view. "Administration propagandists who happen to be Jews," wrote Alfred Kazin, "have been rallied to attack Timerman" ("The Solitude of Jacobo Timerman," *New Republic,* June 20, 1981, p. 32). For expressions of skepticism about Kristol's ideas of conspiracy, see John Lieber, "Kristol Unclear," *New Republic,* June 27, 1981, pp. 18–19.

67. Kristol, "Timerman Affair."

68. Ibid.

69. Quoted in International Commission of Jurists, *Human Rights and U.S. Foreign Policy,* p. 37.

70. Ibid.; "Country Reports on Human Rights Practices for 1981," February 1982, quoted in ibid., p. 38.

71. See Chapter 7. For a once-over-lightly on the state of the academic debate in 1985/1986 (just before the discussions in the *Russian Review*), see Walter Laqueur, "Is There Now, or Has There Ever Been, Such a Thing as Totalitarianism?" *Commentary,* October 1985, pp. 29–34. In this inconclusive survey, Laqueur, close to the American neoconservatives, took note of French and East European coinages: "posttotalitarianism" and "failed totalitarianism." His choice was "totalitarianism in decline."

72. A few days before Reagan's first summit with Gorbachev, however, he met with some conservatives eager to preserve the "Star Wars" antimissile program.

When a *Wall Street Journal* editorial writer gave Reagan a Darth Vader doll to prepare him to meet Gorbachev, Reagan opined that the Russians "really are an evil empire" (Michael Schaller, *Reckoning with Reagan: America and Its President in the 1980s* [New York: Oxford University Press, 1992], p. 119). Nevertheless, Reagan was quick to grasp the opportunities that Gorbachev presented to him.

73. Stephen Cohen indicted Kennan's remarkable "Mr. X" article, loftily pointing to the connection between Kennan's "poor historical and poor political analysis" (*Rethinking the Soviet Experience* [New York: Oxford University Press, 1985], p. 26).

74. Jeane J. Kirkpatrick, *The Withering Away of the Totalitarian State* (Washington, D.C.: American Enterprise Press, 1990), p. 2 and passim.

75. Jeane Kirkpatrick, "Communist Contradictions" (April 6, 1987), reprinted in *Withering Away,* pp. 26–28, quotation from p. 27.

76. Kirkpatrick, *Withering Away,* pp. 46, 48.

77. Ibid., p. 78.

78. Ibid., p. 17. Daniel Patrick Moynihan came to much the same conclusion. Although he referred to the fact that the Soviet Union was collapsing, he wrote that "change appeared in the person of Mikhail Gorbachev. He awakened one morning and found that he didn't believe any of those things [Communist dogmas] anymore" ("Totalitarianism R.I.P.," *Washington Post National Weekly Edition,* August 26–September 1, 1991, p. 29).

79. It seemed plausible, for example, to a veteran *New York Times* reporter, in the fall of 1993, to describe China as already having passed from "totalitarianism" to "authoritarianism" (Nicholas D. Kristof, "China Sees 'Market Leninism,' as Way to Future," *New York Times,* September 6, 1993, pp. 1, 5).

EPILOGUE

1. In order not to endanger Litvinov, Hottelot did not describe this interview until after Litvinov's death on January 31, 1951. See Hottelet's account in the *Washington Post,* January 21, 1952, p. 1, January 22, p. B-11, January 23, p. 13, January 24, p. 13, and January 25, p. 21. Ambassador Bedell Smith's summary cable to the State Department is in *FRUS,* 1946, vol. 6: *Eastern Europe; the Soviet Union* (Washington, D.C.: Government Printing Office, 1969), pp. 763–765.

2. See the entries for *totalitarzm* in *Filosofskii entsiklopedicheskii slovar'* (Moscow: Sovetskaia entsiklopediia, 1983), p. 690; *Filosofskii slovar'* (Moscow: Izdatel'stvo politicheskoi literatury, 1986), p. 486; and *Sovetskii entsiklopedicheskii slovar',* 3rd ed. (Moscow: Sovetskaia entsklopediia, 1984), p. 1338. The last volume appeared in a new edition in 1987 with its definition of *totalitarizm* unchanged.

3. Robert Chandler, Introduction to Vasily Grossman, *Life and Fate* (New York, Harper & Row, 1987), pp. 7–10.

4. Grossman, *Life and Fate,* p. 213. I owe this reference to Professor Nina Tumarkin of Wellesley College.

5. Ibid., pp. 215–216. In a much later chapter, Grossman mentioned *totalitarianism* again, in such a way that it is clear that he believed that under totalitarian regimes, "society" no longer existed. See p. 487.

6. G. Kh. Shakhnazarov, *Kuda idet chelovechestvo (Kriticheskie ocherki nemark-sistskikh kontsepsii budushchego* (Moscow: Mysl', 1985).

7. Ibid., pp. 19–20. Perhaps it is significant that Shakhnazarov shows consider-able knowledge of Orwell's Western critics from the Left, like the radical English socialist Raymond Williams. He suggests that despite his anti-Communism, Or-well's picture of the totalitarian world was really based on Fascist societies and even complexly reflected the blemishes of the Western "democracies."

8. V. V. Sogrin, "Vinovat li marksizm?" *Argumenty i fakty,* no. 2 (1990).

9. For a recent example, see K. S. Gadizhev, "Totalitarizm kak fenomen XX veka," *Voprosy filosofii,* no. 2 (1992): 3–25. By mid-1992, fascism and "corporatism," were being written about as if they might play a role in Russia's future. See, for example, Ivan Prostakov, "Korporativizm kak ideia i real'nost'," *Svobodnaia mysl',* no. 2 (1992): 54–63; and Alexander Galkin, "Fashizm: Ugroza mnimaia i deist-vitel'naia," *Svobodnaia mysl',* no. 4 (1993): 21–36.

10. "Priroda totalitarnoi vlasti (obsuzhdenie za 'kruglym stolom' redaktsii)," *Sotsiologicheskie issledovaniia,* no. 5 (1989): 41–52.

11. A. A. Korchak, "Contemporary Totalitarianism: A Systems Approach," *East European Quarterly,* March 1993, pp. 1–46.

12. *Totalitarizm kak istoricheskii fenomen* (Moscow: Filosofskoe obshchestvo SSSR, 1989).

13. O. Iu. Iartseva, "V poiskakh uterianogo razuma," in ibid., p. 52.

14. L. B. Volkov, "Diktatura razvtiia ili 'kvazimodernizatsiia'?" in ibid., p. 90.

15. I. A. Zevelev, "Magistrali i tupiki industrial'noi epokhi," in ibid., p. 121.

16. Evgenii V. Anisimov, *The Reforms of Peter the Great: Progress Through Coer-cion in Russia* (Armonk, N.Y.: Sharpe, 1993), p. 296. The Russian-language original was published in 1989.

17. Iartseva, "V poiskakh," pp. 55–57. This line of analysis, however convincing one might find it, was strikingly Arendtian.

18. Iu. I. Igritskii, "Kontseptsiia totalitarizma: Uroki mnogoletnykh diskusii na zapade," *Istoriia SSSR,* December 1990, pp. 172–190.

19. Ibid., p. 172. The Democratic Union's founding "platform" usage of "totali-tarianism" can be found in *The Glasnost Reader,* ed. Jonathan Eisen (New York: NAL, 1993), pp. 134–135. There Leninism is alleged to "constitute the foundation of totalitarianism." See also "Leader of Democratic Platform Interviewed," *Foreign Broadcast Information Service, The Soviet Union* [henceforth cited as *FBIS-SOV*], May 30, 1990, pp. 65–66.

20. Igritskii, "Konseptsiia," p. 187.

21. Iu. I. Igritskii, "Snova o totalitarizme," *Otechestvennaia istoriia,* no. 1 (1993): 3–17.

22. Ibid., p. 14.

23. Ibid., p. 15.

24. Some of them are truly strange, especially on the fringes of the political Right. See, for example, Viacheslav Kondrat'ev, "Khristos na krasnom flage?" *Li-teraturnaia gazeta,* May 19, 1993, p. 3. Kondrat'ev appears to speak for what might be called a "Christian–Communist imperial totalitarianism." Since the Mongol inva-

sion in the thirteenth century, he believes, Russia has "known no other direction than totalitarianism," except for the brief interlude between February and October 1917, whose anomalies were soon overcome.

25. See the account of the program, "Volkogonov Book on Stalin Discussed," in *FBIS-SOV*, May 24, 1990, pp. 51–54.

26. I was able to find only a summary of I. S. Kuznetsov, *Umstvennye istoki russkago totalitarizma* (Novosibirsk: Gumanitarnyi tsentr, 1993), which appears to make some of these points.

27. For a brief historical characterization of the categories of Slavophilism and Westernism, see my definitions in *Handbook of Russian Literature*, ed. Victor Terras (New Haven, Conn.: Yale University Press, 1985), pp. 423–425, 517–518.

28. Andranik Migranyan, "Dolgyi put' k evropeiskomu doomu," *Novyi Mir,* no. 7 (1989): 166–184. See also Ed A. Hewett and Victor H. Winston, eds, *Milestones in Glasnost and Perestroika: Politics and People* (Washington, D.C.: Brookings Institution, 1991), passim. This volume contains considerable discussion of Migranian's views, although not from the standpoint of his use of *totalitarianism*.

29. This is the view, for example, of I. A. Il'in, an émigré philosopher now being revived in post-Soviet Russia. See his " 'Nashi zadachi,' *Izbrannye stat'i (1948–1954 gg.*)," *Iunost'*, no. 8 (1990): 60–71. The scholars in the roundtable that begins *Totalitarizm kak istoricheskii fenomen* are divided in their sympathies. See pp. 1–39. Sometimes the suggestion that Russian peasant backwardness was a major precondition for Soviet totalitarianism gives the work of contemporary Russian historians a certain kinship with the work of earlier generations of English-language historians (and even with political scientists of a historical bent, like Merle Fainsod). See, for example, B. N. Mironov's unpublished paper, "Krest'ianskaia narodnaia kul'tura i proiskhozhdenie sovetskogo totalitarizma." His position, needless to say, is, by implication, very much a Westernizer one.

INDEX